Drugs in Perspective

Fourth Edition

Drugs in Perspective

A Personalized Look at Substance Use and Abuse

Richard Fields, Ph.D.

Director, FACES, Family and Addiction Conferences and Educational Seminars

Redmond, WA
Tucson, AZ

Boston   Burr Ridge, IL   Dubuque, IA   Madison, WI   New York   San Francisco   St. Louis
Bangkok   Bogotá   Caracas   Lisbon   London   Madrid
Mexico City   Milan   New Delhi   Seoul   Singapore   Sydney   Taipei   Toronto

McGraw-Hill Higher Education

A Division of The **McGraw-Hill** *Companies*

DRUGS IN PERSPECTIVE: A PERSONALIZED LOOK AT SUBSTANCE USE AND ABUSE
FOURTH EDITION

3 4 5 6 7 8 9 0 QPF/QPF 0 9 8 7 6 5 4 3 2

ISBN 0–697–29426–9

Vice president and editor-in-chief: *Kevin T. Kane*
Executive editor: *Vicki Malinee*
Senior developmental editor: *Melissa Martin*
Senior marketing manager: *Pamela S. Cooper*
Project manager: *Mary Lee Harms*
Media technology associate producer: *Judi David*
Production supervisor: *Kara Kudronowicz*
Coordinator of freelance design: *Michelle D. Whitaker*
Freelance cover designer: *Jamie A. O'Neal*
Cover images: top: © *Bruce Ayres/Stone Images;* bottom: *PhotoDisc, Vol. 25 and Background Series, Vol. 9*
Senior photo research coordinator: *Lori Hancock*
Compositor: *Shepherd, Inc.*
Typeface: *10/12 Times Roman*
Printer: *Quebecor Printing Book Group/Fairfield, PA*

The credits section for this book begins on page 337 and is considered an extension of the copyright page.

Library of Congress Cataloging-in-Publication Data

Fields, Richard.
    Drugs in perspective : a personalized look at substance use and abuse / Richard Fields. —
    4th ed.
        p.   cm.
    Includes bibliographical references and index.
    ISBN 0–697–29426–9 (acid-free paper)
    1. Drug abuse. 2. Alcoholism. 3. Drug abuse—Prevention. 4. Alcoholism—Prevention.
    5. Drug abuse—Treatment. 6. Alcoholism—Treatment. I. Title.

HV5801 .F48   2001
362.29'17—dc21   00–058728
                                                                          CIP

www.mhhe.com

I dedicate this book to my family and friends

Contents

Preface

The major emphasis of the fourth edition of *Drugs in Perspective* is on a multidimensional approach that emphasizes confounding variables—biological, psychological, social, and family systems. Within the past decade and at the beginning of the new millennium we have seen an emerging awareness of the impact of alcohol/drugs on the individual, the family, and the community.

The 11 chapters are designed to give readers as full an understanding of the dynamics of chemical dependency as possible. Each chapter is developed to integrate concepts that build on each other.

The goal of the book is to help readers develop an effective perspective on the multifaceted aspects and problems associated with alcohol/drug use, abuse, and addiction.

❋ Acknowledgments

Thanks to you, the readers, who have on occasion come up to me at conferences to let me know how much you appreciate the book and how you use it in your learning and clinical setting. Thanks to the numerous teachers and counselors who have adopted the book for students and clients.

A special thanks to all my private clients, who have taught me about having compassion, humility, strength, courage, spirituality, connectedness, and vision. Thanks for enjoying my sense of humor.

Thanks to the staff at McGraw-Hill: Melissa Martin, Vicki Malinee, and Mary Lee Harms.

Introduction

⚔ The Myth of the Simple, Magical Solution

Drug use, abuse, and dependence are not easily understood. Too often, people search for that simple solution to an epidemic problem or for a simple explanation. Philosopher H.L. Mencken remarked that "any solution to a big problem that is simple, is usually wrong."

Having spent more than twenty-five years working with individuals and their families, I still struggle case by case to try to find some common patterns and new insights into what works in treatment. I am constantly questioning what may have caused alcohol/drug problems and how best to engage, motivate, and approach clients with drug abuse and dependence. For some, the solution is abstinence and strong involvement in self-help groups; for others, it is a different path. For many, it is the acceptance of the "disease," while others label their alcohol/drug use as an "allergy" or a problem with tolerance. Some individuals can stay sober for a month or two and then experience a "binge relapse," while others can abstain for several years. Many, through the help of Alcoholics Anonymous, Narcotics Anonymous, a sponsor, and a recovery support group, can maintain sobriety as a life choice.

This book attempts to give a relatively unbiased view or reporting of the literature on alcohol/drug prevention, intervention and treatment. It is biased in that it is influenced by my clinical work with substance abusers, addicts/alcoholics, and their families over the past 25 years. I have to admit that the fourth edition of the book is different from previous editions. The material has been updated, the design and order changed, and new material added and older material deleted, but it also reflects changes in my own understanding and thinking about substance abuse and addiction.

This book can help you better understand the confounding variables of substance abuse and dependence and develop prevention, intervention, and treatment techniques and skills. I hope it will help you explore your own personal perspective about drugs, and it won't give you a "simple solution."

I Approaches to Alcohol/Drug Abuse

Historically, we have failed dramatically in our responses to the alcohol/drug problem in the United States. From the 1930s to the 1960s, public and private responses to alcohol/drug abuse caused tremendous damage, which we are still trying to overcome. These approaches were riddled with emotional and political biases, which denied the real dimensions of the problem. Scare tactics—a politically biased approach that alienated young people—began in 1937 and continued for the next 30 years in a variety of forms. For example, the following marijuana scare story appeared in the July 1937 issue of *American* magazine:

> An entire family was murdered by a youthful marijuana addict in Florida. When officers arrived at the home, they found the youth staggering about in a human slaughterhouse. He had ax murdered his father, mother, two brothers, and a sister. He seemed to be in a daze. He had no recollections of having committed the multiple murders. The officers knew him ordinarily as a sane, rather quiet young man; now he was pitifully crazed. They sought the reason. The boy said he had been in the habit of smoking something with youthful friends called "muggles," a childish name for marijuana.

The co-author of this article was Henry J. Anslinger, then commissioner of the Federal Bureau of Narcotics and Dangerous Drugs. After reviewing this single case and a study of the paranoid schizophrenic reactions of heavy hashish smokers in India, Anslinger expounded on the evils of marijuana. He described marijuana as a drug that would consistently result in violent, aggressive, paranoid behavior, as evidenced in the Florida case.

Another scare tactic example is the 1936 movie *Reefer Madness*. This movie's serious intent to discourage marijuana use backfired because the situations were so absurd that audiences viewed it as a humorous farce.

Those using scare tactics assumed that, if young people were frightened by adverse reactions to drug use, they would be too frightened to use the drug. For the young people who perceived drug use as incongruent with their values, goals, and lifestyle, scare tactics were effective. For most young people, however, scare tactics proved to be an ineffective approach because much of the information was exaggerated, overgeneralized, or sensationalized. As a result, young people did not perceive the source of such information as credible. What young people heard did not bear any resemblance to what most users experienced. All in all, scare tactics alienated young people, heightened their curiosity, and increased rather than decreased their experimentation with drugs.

In the late 1960s and early 1970s, President Richard Nixon declared his famous war on drugs. Even though an all-out warlike effort was needed and money was readily available to fight drug addiction, no one knew how to tactically fight this war on drugs. Drug use had spread to epidemic proportions. Also, President Nixon was not the ideal general for this war, having already alienated young people during another war, in Vietnam.

During this same time period, the government was also duped by treatment programs, which mismanaged funds for treatment. At that time, there were few experts and little, if any, clear direction to the battle. The failure of Nixon's war on drugs left a bitter taste in the mouths of government funding sources. Money for treatment programs was cut each year thereafter, and the focus shifted to prevention. Realizing that the war was being lost, the government developed a new, more positive approach: if we can reach the kids before they become dependent on drugs, we will prevent a future generation of drug casualties.

These early prevention efforts emphasized drug-specific information. The assumption was that, if young people were to receive credible drug-specific information, they would then wisely decide not to use drugs. Unfortunately, the reverse held true. Drug-specific approaches heightened curiosity and alleviated the fears associated with drug use, resulting in increases of drug use by young people.

Throughout the ensuing years, U.S. administrations continued to fail in developing a comprehensive and cohesive drug policy. Most of the administrations put a major emphasis on the supply side of the drug problem and significantly neglected the demand side. Emotional and political biases of these administrations caused them to be blind to the many causes of drug dependence and resulted in an adherence to "a simple, magical solution" that was politically advantageous. Administration after administration adhered to a strong supply-side approach, without addressing the reasons for the demand that perpetuated the problem. The Clinton administration repeated this cycle, focusing on the politically expediate supply-side approach of trying to stop drug trafficking, with little effort toward the "demand side" of the problem.

❧ What Is the Trend of Drug Use by Secondary School Students?

It is interesting that the use of drugs by adolescents stabilized in 1999. Personally, I hope that this stabilization will follow with a decrease in drug use by young people. I have the faith that our young people are smarter, more intuitive, more aware, and even more mature than previous generations. I suspect this "**.com generation**" is more hopeful for their future than previous generations. More important, I believe that young people are recognizing that drug abuse and addiction are, indeed, harmful, with significant negative consequences to the individual and their family.

According to the Monitoring the Future Study, conducted by the University of Michigan Institute for Social Research (ISR), drug use by adolescents has stabilized after several years of increases. Most drug use reached peak levels in the mid-1990s:

- Inhalant use peaked in 1995; use has continued a long-term, very gradual decline since 1995.
- Hallucinogens, including LSD and PCP, peaked in 1996.
- Marijuana peaked in 1996.
- Amphetamines peaked in 1997.

The 25th national survey of high school seniors, and the ninth national survey of eighth- and tenth-graders, had a sample size of 17,300 eighth-graders, 13,900 tenth-graders, and 14,100 twelfth-graders (Table 1). The results indicated that drug use among American adolescents held steady in 1999, except for MDMA (Ecstasy) and anabolic steroids. Unfortunately, MDMA, a so-called club drug, rose in use among the older teenagers (tenth- and twelfth-graders) in 1999. Anabolic steroid use among eighth-grade boys increased from 1.6 percent in 1998 to 2.5 percent in 1999, and tenth grade boys showed an increase from 1.9 percent to 2.8 percent. Crack cocaine use showed a significant decline among eighth- and tenth-graders in 1999, following several years of gradual increase. Heroin use remained stable for eighth-, tenth- and twelfth-graders for the past three years, while the rate doubled from 1991 to 1995. Alcohol use also remained stable in adolescents for 1999. Principal investigator Lloyd D. Johnston, states: "We do not have any ready explanation of why the use of marijuana and a number of other drugs seemed to level off in 1999, but we think there is a fair chance that it simply reflects a pause in a longer term decline."

TABLE 1

Trends in Lifetime Prevalence of Use of Various Drugs for Eighth-, Tenth-, and Twelfth-Graders (Entries are Percentages)

	1991	1992	1993	1994	1995	1996	1997	1998	1999	'98–'99 Change
Any illicit drug[a]										
8th grade	18.7	20.6	22.5	25.7	28.5	31.2	29.4	29.0	28.3	–0.7
10th grade	30.6	29.8	32.8	37.4	40.9	45.4	47.3	44.9	46.2	+1.3
12th grade	44.1	40.7	42.9	45.6	48.4	50.8	54.3	54.1	54.7	+0.6
Any illicit drug, other than marijuana[a]										
8th grade	14.3	15.6	16.8	17.5	18.8	19.2	17.7	16.9	16.3	–0.6
10th grade	19.1	19.2	20.9	21.7	24.3	25.5	25.0	23.6	24.0	+0.4
12th grade	26.9	25.1	26.7	27.6	28.1	28.5	30.0	29.4	29.4	0.0
Any illicit drug, including inhalants[a,b]										
8th grade	28.5	29.6	32.3	35.1	38.1	39.4	38.1	37.8	37.2	–0.6
10th grade	36.1	36.2	38.7	42.7	45.9	49.8	50.9	49.3	49.9	+0.6
12th grade	47.6	44.4	46.6	49.1	51.5	53.5	56.3	56.1	55.9	–0.2
Marijuana/hashish										
8th grade	10.2	11.2	12.6	16.7	19.9	23.1	22.6	22.2	22.0	–0.2
10th grade	23.4	21.4	24.4	30.4	34.1	39.8	42.3	39.6	40.9	+1.3
12th grade	36.7	32.6	35.3	38.2	41.7	44.9	49.6	49.1	49.7	+0.6
Inhalants[b,c]										
8th grade	17.6	17.4	19.4	19.9	21.6	21.2	21.0	20.5	19.7	–0.8
10th grade	15.7	16.6	17.5	18.0	19.0	19.3	18.3	18.3	17.0	–1.3
12th grade	17.6	16.6	17.4	17.7	17.4	16.6	16.1	15.2	15.4	+0.2
Nitrites[d]										
8th grade	—	—	—	—	—	—	—	—	—	—
10th grade	—	—	—	—	—	—	—	—	—	—
12th grade	1.6	1.5	1.4	1.7	1.5	1.8	2.0	2.7	1.7	–1.0
Hallucinogens[e]										
8th grade	3.2	3.8	3.9	4.3	5.2	5.9	5.4	4.9	4.8	–0.1
10th grade	6.1	6.4	6.8	8.1	9.3	10.5	10.5	9.8	9.7	–0.1
12th grade	9.6	9.2	10.9	11.4	12.7	14.0	15.1	14.1	13.7	–0.4
LSD										
8th grade	2.7	3.2	3.5	3.7	4.4	5.1	4.7	4.1	4.1	0.0
10th grade	5.6	5.8	6.2	7.2	8.4	9.4	9.5	8.5	8.5	0.0
12th grade	8.8	8.6	10.3	10.5	11.7	12.6	13.6	12.6	12.2	–0.4
Ice[h]										
8th grade	—	—	—	—	—	—	—	—	—	—
10th grade	—	—	—	—	—	—	—	—	—	—
12th grade	3.3	2.9	3.1	3.4	3.9	4.4	4.4	5.3	4.8	–0.5

TABLE 1 (continued)

Trends in Lifetime Prevalence of Use of Various Drugs for Eighth-, Tenth-, and Twelfth-Graders (Entries are Percentages)

	1991	1992	1993	1994	1995	1996	1997	1998	1999	'98–'99 Change
Barbiturates[g]										
8th grade	—	—	—	—	—	—	—	—	—	—
10th grade	—	—	—	—	—	—	—	—	—	—
12th grade	6.2	5.5	6.3	7.0	7.4	7.6	8.1	8.7	8.9	+0.2
Tranquilizers[g]										
8th grade	3.8	4.1	4.4	4.6	4.5	5.3	4.8	4.6	4.4	–0.2
10th grade	5.8	5.9	5.7	5.4	6.0	7.1	7.3	7.8	7.9	+0.1
12th grade	7.2	6.0	6.4	6.6	7.1	7.2	7.8	8.5	9.3	+0.8
Alcohol[i], any use										
8th grade	70.1	69.3	67.1	—	—	—	—	—	—	—
10th grade	83.8	82.3	80.8	—	—	—	—	—	—	—
12th grade	88.0	87.5	87.0	—	—	—	—	—	—	—
Been drunk[h]										
8th grade	26.7	26.8	26.4	25.9	25.3	26.8	25.2	24.8	24.8	0.0
10th grade	50.0	47.7	47.9	47.2	46.9	48.5	49.4	46.7	48.9	+2.2
12th grade	65.4	63.4	62.5	62.9	63.2	61.8	64.2	62.4	62.3	–0.1
Cigarettes, any use										
8th grade	44.0	45.2	45.3	46.1	46.4	49.2	47.3	45.7	44.1	–1.6
10th grade	55.1	53.5	56.3	56.9	57.6	61.2	60.2	57.7	57.6	–0.1
12th grade	63.1	61.8	61.9	62.0	64.2	63.5	65.4	65.3	64.6	–0.7
Smokeless tobacco[d]										
8th grade	22.2	20.7	18.7	19.9	20.0	20.4	16.8	15.0	14.4	–0.6
10th grade	28.2	26.6	28.1	29.2	27.6	27.4	26.3	22.7	20.4	–2.3
12th grade	—	32.4	31.0	30.7	30.9	29.8	25.3	26.2	23.4	–2.8
Steroids[h]										
8th grade	1.9	1.7	1.6	2.0	2.0	1.8	1.8	2.3	2.7	+0.4
10th grade	1.8	1.7	1.7	1.8	2.0	1.8	2.0	2.0	2.7	+0.7ss
12th grade	2.1	2.1	2.0	2.4	2.3	1.9	2.4	2.7	2.9	+0.2
Hallucinogens other than LSD										
8th grade	1.4	1.7	1.7	2.2	2.5	3.0	2.6	2.5	2.4	–0.1
10th grade	2.2	2.5	2.8	3.8	3.9	4.7	4.8	5.0	4.7	–0.3
12th grade	3.7	3.3	3.9	4.9	5.4	6.8	7.5	7.1	6.7	–0.4
PCP[d]										
8th grade	—	—	—	—	—	—	—	—	—	—
10th grade	—	—	—	—	—	—	—	—	—	—
12th grade	2.9	2.4	2.9	2.8	2.7	4.0	3.9	3.9	3.4	–0.5

TABLE 1 (continued)

Trends in Lifetime Prevalence of Use of Various Drugs for Eighth-, Tenth-, and Twelfth-Graders (Entries are Percentages)

	1991	1992	1993	1994	1995	1996	1997	1998	1999	'98–'99 Change
MDMA (Ecstasy)[d]										
8th grade	—	—	—	—	—	3.4	3.2	2.7	2.7	0.0
10th grade	—	—	—	—	—	5.6	5.7	5.1	6.0	+0.9
12th grade	—	—	—	—	—	6.1	6.9	5.8	8.0	+2.3s
Cocaine										
8th grade	2.3	2.9	2.9	3.6	4.2	4.5	4.4	4.6	4.7	+0.1
10th grade	4.1	3.3	3.6	4.3	5.0	6.5	7.1	7.2	7.7	+0.5
12th grade	7.8	6.1	6.1	5.9	6.0	7.1	8.7	9.3	9.8	+0.5
Crack										
8th grade	1.3	1.6	1.7	2.4	2.7	2.9	2.7	3.2	3.1	−0.1
10th grade	1.7	1.5	1.8	2.1	2.8	3.3	3.6	3.9	4.0	+0.1
12th grade	3.1	2.6	2.6	3.0	3.0	3.3	3.9	4.4	4.6	+0.2
Other cocaine										
8th grade	2.0	2.4	2.4	3.0	3.4	3.8	3.5	3.7	3.8	+0.1
10th grade	3.8	3.0	3.3	3.8	4.4	5.5	6.1	6.4	6.8	+0.4
12th grade	7.0	5.3	5.4	5.2	5.1	6.4	8.2	8.4	8.8	+0.4
Heroin[f]										
8th grade	1.2	1.4	1.4	2.0	2.3	2.4	2.1	2.3	2.3	0.0
10th grade	1.2	1.2	1.3	1.5	1.7	2.1	2.1	2.3	2.3	0.0
12th grade	0.9	1.2	1.1	1.2	1.6	1.8	2.1	2.0	2.0	0.0
Other narcotics[g]										
8th grade	—	—	—	—	—	—	—	—	—	—
10th grade	—	—	—	—	—	—	—	—	—	—
12th grade	6.6	6.1	6.4	6.6	7.2	8.2	9.7	9.8	10.2	+0.4
Amphetamines[g]										
8th grade	10.5	10.8	11.8	12.3	13.1	13.5	12.3	11.3	10.7	−0.6
10th grade	13.2	13.1	14.9	15.1	17.4	17.7	17.0	16.0	15.7	−0.3
12th grade	15.4	13.9	15.1	15.7	15.3	15.3	16.5	16.4	16.3	−0.1

Note: Level of significance of difference between the two years indicated: ss = .01, sss = .001.

�క Adolescent Cigarette Smoking

Similar to the patterns of adolescent drug use, in the Monitoring the Future study, cigarette smoking peaked in 1996 among eighth- and tenth-graders nationwide and in 1997 among twelfth-graders. In 1999, there was a gradual decline in cigarette smoking by adolescents (Table 2).

It is in the college-bound sector of secondary students that reports of declines in smoking are noted. Unfortunately, in 1999 there were the same levels of cigarette

TABLE 2

Long-Term Trends in Prevalence of Cigarettes for Eighth-, Tenth-, and Twelfth-Graders

	1975	1976	1977	1978	1979	1980	1981	1982	1983	1984	1985	1986
Lifetime												
8th grade												
10th grade												
12th grade	73.6	75.4	75.7	75.3	74.0	71.0	71.0	70.1	70.6	69.7	68.8	67.6
30-day												
8th grade												
10th grade												
12th grade	36.7	38.8	38.4	36.7	34.4	30.5	29.4	30.0	30.3	29.3	30.1	29.6
Daily												
8th grade												
10th grade												
12th grade	26.9	28.8	28.8	27.5	25.4	21.3	20.3	21.1	21.2	18.7	19.5	18.7
1/2 pack+ per day												
8th grade												
10th grade												
12th grade	17.9	19.2	19.4	18.8	16.5	14.3	13.5	14.2	13.8	12.3	12.5	11.4
Approximate Ns												
8th grade												
10th grade												
12th grade	9,400	15,400	17,100	17,800	15,500	15,900	17,500	17,700	16,300	15,900	16,000	15,200

Source: The Monitoring the Future Study, The University of Michigan.
Note: Level of significance of difference between the two years indicated: s = .05.

smoking in the noncollege-bound students (who traditionally have higher smoking percentages). It follows that the decline in cigarette smoking by eighth- and tenth-graders is concentrated among children from more educated families. Lloyd D. Johnston observes, "Despite these recent improvements, over one-third of today's young people are active smokers by the time they leave high school. In fact, more than one in every six is an active smoker as early as eighth-grade."

Consistent with the Michigan study, the Centers for Disease Control report that tobacco use is the leading cause of preventable death in the United States, and more than 3,000 teens in the United States became established daily smokers each day. The study "How Many Adolescents Start Smoking Each Day in the United States?" conducted by Gilpen, Choi, Berr, and Pierce, 1999, suggests that "smoking uptake by adolescents is at levels that warrant aggressive public health efforts to circumvent a continued epidemic of smoking-related diseases."

1987	1988	1989	1990	1991	1992	1993	1994	1995	1996	1997	1998	1999	'98–'99 Change
				44.0	45.2	45.3	46.1	46.4	49.2	47.3	45.7	44.1	–1.6
				55.1	53.5	56.3	56.9	57.6	61.2	60.2	57.7	57.6	–0.1
67.2	66.4	65.7	64.4	63.1	61.8	61.9	62.0	64.2	63.5	65.4	65.3	64.6	–0.7
				14.3	15.5	16.7	18.6	19.1	21.0	19.4	19.1	17.5	–1.6s
				20.8	21.5	24.7	25.4	27.9	30.4	29.8	27.6	25.7	–1.9
29.4	28.7	28.6	29.4	28.3	27.8	29.9	31.2	33.5	34.0	36.5	35.1	34.6	–0.5
				7.2	7.0	8.3	8.8	9.3	10.4	9.0	8.8	8.1	–0.7
				12.6	12.3	14.2	14.6	16.3	18.3	18.0	15.8	15.9	+0.1
18.7	18.1	18.9	19.1	18.5	17.2	19.0	19.4	21.6	22.2	24.6	22.4	23.1	+0.7
				3.1	2.9	3.5	3.6	3.4	4.3	3.5	3.6	3.3	–0.3
				6.5	6.0	7.0	7.6	8.3	9.4	8.6	7.9	7.6	–0.3
11.4	10.6	11.2	11.3	10.7	10.0	10.9	11.2	12.4	13.0	14.3	12.6	13.2	+0.6
				17,500	18,600	18,300	17,300	17,500	17,800	18,600	18,100	16,700	
				14,800	14,800	15,300	15,800	17,000	15,600	15,500	15,000	13,600	
16,300	16,300	16,700	15,200	15,000	15,800	16,300	15,400	15,400	14,300	15,400	15,200	13,600	

References

"Cigarette Smoking Among American Teens Continues Gradual Decline." Press Release, University of Michigan, 412 Maynard, Ann Arbor, Michigan 48109-1399, December 17, 1999.

"Drug Trends in 1999 Among American Teens Are Mixed." Press Release, University of Michigan, 412 Maynard, Ann Arbor, Michigan 48109-1399, December 17, 1999.

Monitoring the Future Study, University of Michigan Institute for Social Research (ISR) (The 25th National Survey of High School Seniors And the Ninth National Survey of Eighth- and Tenth-graders), 1999.

Understanding Substance Abuse

Etiology

A Better Understanding of Drug Use— Models, Functions, and Meanings

Chapter Objectives

1. Explain alcohol/drug use as a drive to alter one's consciousness.

2. Describe alcohol/drug use as a passive activity.

3. Identify the three criteria that establish alcoholism as a disease.

4. Cite the research that supports the genetic model of alcoholism, including twin studies and adoption studies.

5. Identify personality traits and personality disorders related to problems with alcohol/drugs.

6. Explain the role of mood and feeling (affective) disorders and substance abuse.

7. Explain the relationship among risk-taking behavior, impulsivity, and disinhibition to alcohol/drug use.

8. Identify the dimensions of the tension-reduction models of substance abuse and the relation of attention deficit hyperactivity disorder (ADHD) to substance abuse.

9. Describe the family model of substance abuse.

10. Explain the role of conditioning in substance abuse.

11. Describe the psychosocial, sociocultural, and psychoanalytic models of substance abuse.

12. Explain the role of hopelessness, pessimism, and poor future orientation in developing substance abuse problems.

13. Describe the functions and meanings of drugs in the context of power, self-destruction, and seduction/sexuality.

✵ Why Do People Abuse Alcohol/Drugs?

It's peer pressure. . . . No, it's poor self-concept. . . . It's just because it's fun and pleasurable. . . . It's the hopelessness of our society. . . . It's due to the dishonesty and hypocrisy of our institutions. . . . No, it's our inability to connect with each other and establish effective relationships. . . . It's the parents. . . . It's the media that promote instant pleasure, short-term goals, and alcohol use. . . . It's the ineffectiveness of the school system and other institutions. . . . It's the avoidance of pain and hedonism of modern society. . . . It's the lack of caring for our fellow humans. . . . It's stress, pressure, and the breakdown of the family. . . . It's socioeconomic inequities. . . . It's just available. . . . Why not?

Our Innate Drive to Alter Consciousness

There is a belief that there are four primary drives. The drives are hunger, thirst, sex, and our desire to alter our consciousness. Drugs have been a major

---

* The case studies in this chapter are based on a composite of many clients. Names and circumstances have been changed to maintain anonymity.

way of altering consciousness. Drugs have been used throughout history to alter consciousness and will continue to be used in this way in the future.

Some feel drugs open avenues to unconscious issues, conflicts, and possibly an awareness or perception new to their life. On the downside, drugs can easily become traps that keep our minds from being used in positive ways. Drug use becomes unrealistic and neurotic when used in an addictive manner. Individuals often are passively dependent and destructive. Their nervous system is less able to work in active, constructive and interesting ways. Our society is becoming more aware of positive ways to alter consciousness while avoiding addictions to alcohol/drugs, food, gambling, television, work, and many other activities.

All people consciously or subconsciously alter their state of consciousness. Some common ways children achieve this are through daydreaming, rolling downhill, tumbling, and spinning.

Drug Use as a Passive Activity

Many people are passive procrastinators and conflict avoiders. In my private counseling practice, I often see clients who deny the painful issues that initially brought them to counseling. Once they get some immediate relief, they avoid the real issues. Nonetheless, growth involves working through painful conflicts. Our search for the magic pill or cure for the pain of the human condition has created a modern marketplace for alcohol and drug elixirs.

Alcohol and drug use is a passive activity; individuals take pills, powders, or liquids and wait for the desired effect—an alteration of their consciousness. In some cases, such as freebasing cocaine or injecting drugs (e.g., heroin), the desired effect is almost instantaneous. Too frequently, feelings of boredom, sadness, stress, and loneliness are not actively worked through; instead, the individual passively changes what he or she feels by using alcohol/drugs. Changing your mood by more active approaches involves more effort and motivation. This is frequently a learning process, especially if the individual has a life-long pattern of either avoiding feelings or self-medicating feelings with alcohol/drugs. More on proactive approaches is outlined in the Prevention chapter of this book.

We cannot isolate one specific cause of alcoholism and drug addiction. There are often multiple, confounding reasons for addiction, just as there are numerous causes for cancer and other medical diseases. Many theories and models of causality exist. Early alcoholism models labeled alcoholics as inherently weak or unable to control or tolerate their consumption of alcohol. One test of manliness was the ability to "really hold his

✄ Models of Alcohol/Drug Dependence and Addiction

liquor." Other early models focused on the individual as psychologically pathological. Alcoholics used alcohol in a pathological manner to block out memories of unpleasant, traumatic personal experiences, which brought with them unmanageable feelings. As time went on, a physiological model of alcoholism developed as scientists searched for a biochemical link to, or genetic marker of, alcoholism.

Today, those of us in the alcohol/drug field generally accept the fact that alcoholism and drug addiction have multiple causes, or etiologies. Clearly, a matrix of both genetic and environmental factors can cause an individual to develop problems with alcohol and drugs. "Evidence has accumulated to indicate that alcoholism is a heterogenous entity arising from multiple etiologies" (Tabakoff and Hoffman 1988). We will discuss some of the causality models later in this chapter.

Disease Concept of Alcoholism

In 1957, the American Medical Association declared alcoholism a disease on the basis of three criteria: alcoholism has (1) a known etiology (cause), (2) the symptoms get worse over time, and (3) alcoholism has known outcomes. The outcomes of alcoholism are dependence, physical symptoms, and eventual death. For more than 30 years, research has indicated an increasingly strong case for a genetic component of alcoholism; this validates the disease model as shown in Table 1.1.

The disease model is the foundation of Alcoholics Anonymous and many other self-help programs. The increased acceptance of this disease model is due to continuing research linking alcoholism to genetic markers, the model's effectiveness as a recovery tool, and its reduction of the shame-based stigma associated with problems of alcohol/drug dependence and addiction. (See Chapter 11 for more information on the advantages and drawbacks of Alcoholics Anonymous.)

Genetic Model of Alcoholism

In January 1990, researchers at the University of California, Los Angeles, and University of Texas, San Antonio, identified a link between the receptor gene for the neurotransmitter dopamine and alcoholism (Blum et al. 1990). Although these findings need to be replicated with a larger sample, they establish more clearly the significance of a genetic factor predisposing people to alcoholism. Ernest Noble of U.C.L.A. said that this research "more firmly establishes alcoholism as a disease, and adds to evidence that genetic factors are as important as environmental factors in predisposing people to the disease." The general opinion is that alcoholism is related to several genes, however, and no one gene can be a genetic marker to identify individuals at risk for alcoholism.

TABLE 1.1

Alcoholism as a Disease

A disease is defined as having the following:
1. A known etiology (cause)
2. A known progression of symptoms, which get worse over time
3. A known outcome

Devor (1994) describes a developmental-genetic model of viewing alcoholism. He proposes that "alcoholism must no longer be thought of as a single disease with a cause that is either genetic or environmental but as a group of illnesses in which the influences of genes and the environment ebb and flow over the course of the at-risk lifetime". The logical conclusion is that treatment for alcoholism would be individually designed and fine tuned to consider both pharmacological and behavioral therapies.

Adoption Studies

Donald W. Goodwin (1971) conducted a series of adoption studies in Denmark, indicating that sons of alcoholics are four times more likely to become alcoholics than are sons of nonalcoholics. In the study, the results held true whether the sons were raised by nonalcoholic foster parents or their own biological parents, thus supporting the genetic component of alcoholism. C.R. Cloninger, M. Bohman, and S. Sigvardsson (1981) conducted the most detailed and extensive adoption studies. Their work confirmed the earlier work of Goodwin in demonstrating the following:

1. Adopted sons of alcoholic biological parents are four times more likely to become alcoholics than adoptees whose biological parents are not alcoholics.
2. Sons of alcoholic biological parents are more likely to be classified as alcoholics at an earlier age than their peers.
3. Daughters of alcoholic fathers, although not demonstrating a greater incidence of alcoholism, exhibit a high incidence of somatic anxiety and frequent physical complaints.

Twin Studies

Studies of identical (monozygotic, or MZ) and fraternal (dizygotic, or DZ) twins have supported a genetic factor. Because identical twins share 100 percent of their genes, while fraternal twins share only 50 percent, research should show a higher rate of alcoholism in MZ twins than in DZ twins. L. Kaij (1960) examined 174 sets of twins and demonstrated that, indeed, the MZ twins had a 71 percent concordance rate, and the DZ twins had only a 32 percent concordance rate. In 1981, Z. Hrubec and G.S. Omenn again demonstrated a higher concordance rate in MZ twins (26 percent) than in DZ twins (12 percent). A more recent study by Gurling and associates (1984), however, did not support the previous studies' results.

Currently, no significant genetic research is exploring drug abuse due to the many research design problems with illicit drugs. The assumption is that the genetic factors for drug addiction are comparable with the genetic research findings on alcoholism.

Personality and Substance Abuse

It's my personality. . . . I'm compulsive. . . . I drink/drug to quiet my temper. . . . It quiets my moodiness. . . . I use because I'm bored.

Addictive Personality

For quite some time, the media have emphasized the concept of an **addictive personality.** This simplistic approach makes the mistake of labeling all alcoholics and addicts as somehow possessing a particular personality that leads to addictive and compulsive behavior. It is more accurate to recognize that many personality traits can make an individual vulnerable to the disease of alcoholism and drug addiction, but to conclude there is a particular addictive personality is beyond the scope of modern medicine. **Psychological vulnerability** is a better term to use and is defined as a prior psychological factor that makes a pattern of substance dependence more likely to develop (Jellinek 1960).

It is difficult to identify the relationship of alcoholism and drug addiction to particular dimensions of personality, because many personality traits overlap. Cloninger's (1987) three-dimensional model of personality has been applied to the research literature on alcohol use disorders. He identifies three temperament constructs that correlate with alcohol use disorders:

1. Harm avoidance—cautious, apprehensive, fatiguable, inhibited
2. Reward dependent—ambitious, sympathetic, warm, industrious, sentimental, persistent, moody
3. Novelty seeking—impulsive, excitable, exploratory, quick-tempered, fickle, extravagant

Personality Traits

Many researchers and clinicians have described various personality traits of alcoholics/addicts. These personality traits include the following:

- High emotionality
- Anxiety and overreactivity
- Immaturity in interpersonal relationships
- Low frustration tolerance
- Inability to express anger adequately
- Anger over dependence and ambivalence to authority
- Low self-esteem with grandiose behavior
- Perfectionism
- Compulsiveness
- Feelings of isolation
- Sex role confusion
- Depression
- Dependence in interpersonal relationships
- Hostility
- Sexual immaturity
- Rigidity and inability to adapt to changing circumstances
- Simplistic, black-and-white thinking

Personality Disorders

> I'm angry and drugs quiet me. . . . It's hard for me to get close to others without drugs. . . . I feel anxious and fearful, so the drugs relax me.

Of all the personality disorders, the one with the strongest relationship to substance abuse is antisocial personality disorder (ASPD). The second most common personality disorder that has a high incidence of substance abuse is borderline personality disorder (Table 1.2). (For more information, see Chapter 10.)

TABLE 1.2

Comorbidity Between Alcoholism and Personality Disorders in a Sample of Recent Studies

Study	Sample	% Comorbid Diagnosis
Alnaes and Torgersen (1988) (*N* = 38)	Outpatient	AvPD, DPD, OCD, P-BPD, NPD, HPD, API 92%
Casey and Tyrer (1990) (*N* = 41)	Presenting for Tx to GP	Unsp. = 67%
DeJong et al. (1993) (*N* = 178)	Inpatient	BPD = 17%
Derksen (1990) (*N* = 15)	Outpatient	BPD = 53%
Drake and Vaillant (1985) (*N* = 62)	Community	DPD, P-A, HPD, Unsp. = 37%
Drake et al. (1988) (*N* = 62)	Community	BPD = 3%
Haver and Dahlgren (1995) (*N* = 60)	Inpatient, outpatient	BPD = 12%, Unsp. = 1%
Jonsdottir-Baldurson and Horvath (1987) (*N* = 51)	Inpatient	BPD = 27%
Morgenstern et al. (1997) (*N* = 366)	Inpatient, outpatient	APD = 23%, BPD = 22%, NPD = 21%
Nace et al. (1986) (*N* = 74)	Inpatient	BPD = 18%
Nace et al. (1991) (*N* = 100)	Inpatient	BPD = 17%, PPD = 7%, HPD = 6%
Nurnberg et al. (1993) (*N* = 50)	Outpatient	PPD = 44%, APD = 20%, P-A = 18%, BPD = 16%
Poldrugo and Forti (1988) (*N* = 404)	Alcoholics presenting for Tx	APD = 9%, BPD = 4%
Stravynski et al. (1986) (*N* = 167)	Abstinent alcoholics presenting for Tx	AvPD = 20%
Tousignant and Kovess (1989) (*N* = 21)	Community	BPD = 19%
Vaglum and Vaglum (1985) (*N* = 64)	Inpatient	BPD = 66%, Unsp. = 22%
Zimmerman and Coryell (1989) (*N* = 145)	Community	APD = 14%, P-A = 10%, HPD = 8%, BPD = 7%, OCD = 5%

Source: 2nd edition edited by Kenneth E. Leonard & Howard T. Blane, Guilford, 1999.
Note: PD, personality disorder; APD, antisocial PD; AvPD, avoidant PD; BPD, borderline PD; D, dependent PD; HPD, histrionic PD; NPD, Narcissistic PD; PPD, paranoid PD; OCD, obsessive-compulsive disorder; P-A, passive-aggressive PD; Unsp., personality disorder not otherwise specified; Tx, treatment; GP, general practitioner. Sample sizes (*N*s) refer to numbers of participants in original study diagnosed with alcoholism, which does not necessarily equal the study *N*.

Mood and Feeling (Affect) Disorders

Drugs quiet the pain of my depression. . . . Drugs are catalysts to my mania.

Disturbances in affect, mood, and depression are common causes of substance abuse and addiction to medical and nonmedical psychoactive substances, especially in women (Whitlock et al. 1967).

Individuals who are experiencing problems in regulating their affect and mood may self-medicate with alcohol/drugs. Alcohol/drugs may be used to alleviate and self-medicate feelings of anxiety or panic, as well as other negative emotional states, including melancholia, depression, and even mania. Major depression, dysthymic disorder, cyclothymic disorder, atypical depression, and bipolar disorder (manic-depressive illness) are the primary affective, or feeling, disorders associated with self-medicating with alcohol/drugs (for more information, see Chapter 10).

Major depression and dysthymia occur one and a half to two times more commonly in alcoholics (Helzer and Pryzbeck 1988). Female alcoholics have a tenfold increased incidence of mania, and male alcoholics have a threefold increased incidence of mania (Hesselbrock, Meyer, and Keener 1985).

Patients with major depression who experience intermittent or chronic dysphoria may come to value the powerful, though brief, euphorigenic effects of opioids or cocaine. Patients with bipolar or cyclothymic disorder who use cocaine may discover that the drug can not only bring them out of their depressive episodes but also can enhance their endogenously produced highs (Marin and Weiss 1986). Seasonal affective disorder (SAD) is another form of depression that leads to increased alcohol/drug use, especially during the "sunless" winter months in certain environments.

Whatever the underlying mood or feeling disorder, alcohol/drugs begin to be relied on to assuage those negative affects. Unfortunately, the drugs often contribute to a spiraling pattern of isolation and interpersonal distancing. This isolation exacerbates the affective disorder. The pattern can continue to social phobia and paranoid ideations.

Risk-Taking Behavior—Impulsivity/Disinhibition

It seemed like a good idea at the time.

Impulsivity/disinhibition includes personality traits such as sensation seeking and aggressiveness. I refer to some substance abusers as "edgewalkers"—living on the edge of danger or risk. Impulsive/disinhibited individuals are at increased risk for alcohol-related problems (Caspi et al. 1997, Schukit 1998), and the traits of impulsivity/disinhibition are elevated in the children of alcoholics (Alterman et al. 1998, Scher 1991).

Alcohol/drug use involves taking the risk of use. There have always been individuals who, when told "no," are curious and perhaps contrary and translate that "no" into "yes." This is especially true of adolescents. Alcohol/drug use affects each individual's physical and emotional balance; for some, that balance is very delicate, even before they start to use alcohol/drugs. Because some individuals have a need to be in control, when they use alcohol/drugs, they usually have a negative reaction. Others, who enjoy losing control and are looking for an altered state of consciousness that approaches their outer limits of effective functioning, become more involved in alcohol/drug use. Some thrill seekers may go further, to substance dependence and addiction.

The alcoholic/drug addict lifestyle, subculture, and environment are often the most alluring feature of addiction for some. Scoring drugs, hanging out in bars, associating with users, stealing, and engaging in other antisocial behaviors all reinforce the actual use of alcohol/drugs. The risk-taking behavior itself creates feelings of rebellion, aggression, rage, self-destructiveness, and "aliveness" (i.e., the adrenaline rush accompanying danger and fear).

The vicious cycle of problems that results from these risk-taking behaviors then leads to more abuse of alcohol/drugs to alleviate the feelings of pain, anxiety, and depression. This debilitating cycle continues until individuals recognize their own powerlessness and destructive behavior, or until they are in jail or dead.

Tension-Reduction Models

> It's stress. . . . I just drink to calm down. . . . I need to relax. . . . I'm so tense. . . . It lets me worry less. . . . I can avoid the conflicts. . . . It makes decisions easier. . . . I can do the tedious work easier. . . . I can summon energy. . . . It reduces the tension. . . . It allows me not to think so much. . . . It makes me feel better. . . . It is pleasurable.

These are common thoughts and verbalizations that individuals have for using drugs to reduce tension, whether with a martini at the end of a busy workday, some marijuana, or some cocaine or another drug.

The tension-reduction theory (TRT) of drug use is one of the most widely researched. Early research focused on tension reduction and relief from stress as a primary reason for alcohol and drug use. Today, the tension-reduction theory is considered one aspect of drug use. Individuals consume drugs for a variety of reasons, including the sheer pleasurable feelings that accompany drug use.

> Not only has tension reduction theory (TRT) been successful in the amount and range of research that it has engendered, but also it is clearly the theoretical progenitor of many of the theories that have developed over the past 50 years. The progress and extensions of TRT encompass most of the psychological approaches to alcohol. As a field, we seem to have accepted the notion that alcohol is reinforcing because it reduces tension, and we have been undaunted in our pursuit of evidence of this basic precept. . . .

The tension-reduction model involves the concept of homeostasis, or balance. The individual will use alcohol/drugs to counteract stress, anxiety, emotional tension, and conflict—any aversive emotional state. Alcohol/drugs are therefore used as tension reducers.

Tension has been defined as a variety of states that are aversive sources of motivation, causing feelings of fear, anxiety (vague fear), conflict, and frustration due to blocked goals (see Figure 1.1). Stress is just a modern version of the same description. Merriam-Webster's collegiate dictionary defines stress as "a physical, chemical, or emotional factor that causes bodily or mental tension and may be a factor in disease causation" (by permission. From *Webster's Ninth New Collegiate® Dictionary,* Tenth Edition © 1993 by Merriam-Webster, Inc., publisher of the Merriam-Webster® dictionaries). The tension-reduction theory has two major assumptions: alcohol reduces tension, and individuals drink alcohol for its tension-reducing properties (Blane and Leonard 1988). Genetically predisposed individuals may find stress-buffering effects from alcohol or drugs.

Convulsions

S**

ATL*

Comatose

Hours→ 0 1 2 3 4 5 6 7 8 9 10 11 12 13 14

*Average tension level (ATL) varies with each individual.
**Average amount of stimulation(s) required to produce convulsion.

FIGURE 1.1   *Average Tension Level*

SOURCE: From *Facts About Drug Abuse, 1975,* National Institute on Drug Abuse, U.S. Department of Health and Human Services.

A noted authority on alcohol/drugs, Stanley Gitlow, emphasizes an etiological model that focuses on discomfort and tolerance to stress as a major factor in the decision to use alcohol/drugs. Gitlow believes that we have biological variations in our levels of tolerance to stress and stimulation. "The initiating stimulus could well be perceived by one individual as minimally inconvenient, while another individual would perceive that same stimulus as agonizingly urgent. The overriding determinant and major variable of appetite regulation is most likely the intensity of the individual's perception of need for relief" (Gitlow 1985). A. Petrie (1960) identified three basic classifications in dealing with stimuli: (1) *stimulus reducers* perceive and react to a stimulus as if that stimulus were less than it is; (2) *stimulus moderators* perceive and react to the stimulus as it is; (3) and *stimulus augmenters* perceive and react as if that stimulus were more than it is. "A perceptual characteristic, such as stimulus augmenting, leading to an overly sensitive need for relief from any discomfort, appeared to be a possible and intriguing genetically determined CNS factor" (Gitlow 1985). In 1984, Lynne Hennecke reported a significantly higher incidence of stimulus augmenters in the sons of alcoholic fathers than in the sons of nonalcoholic fathers. Hennecke suggests that, in stimulus augmenters, alcohol is used to shut down the stimulation overload from the environment.

Gitlow (1972) describes alcoholism as a biochemical defect. The individual possessing this defect is easily agitated by stimuli, becomes uncomfortable, and, therefore, uses alcohol for its sedating effect. Unfortunately, withdrawal from alcohol creates an agitating effect, and the individual must drink again to relieve this discomfort.

Figure 1.2 shows various reactions to alcohol and their relationships to stress. Anyone ingesting alcohol or other sedative hypnotics goes from the normal level of

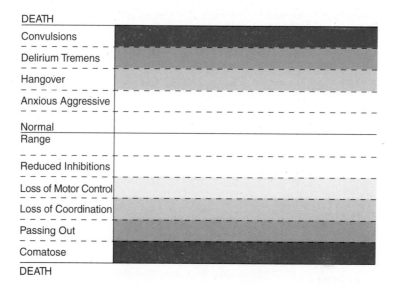

FIGURE 1.2 *Reaction to Sedative Hypnotics (Particularly Alcohol)*

SOURCE: From *Facts About Drug Abuse, 1975,* National Institute on Drug Abuse, U.S. Department of Health and Human Services.

functioning to a level of reduced inhibitions. As that person continues to consume alcohol, the effect becomes more pronounced, as indicated by loss of motor control and loss of coordination. Excessive levels of alcohol ingestion can cause alcoholics to pass out, become comatose, and die. As an alcoholic stops using alcohol, the withdrawal symptoms follow the same progression. At low ingestion levels, the withdrawal may be minor anxiety or aggressive behavior. Figure 1.3 describes the changes after approximately an hour of alcohol consumption. There is a reduced inhibition (change S^1), followed by anxious/aggressive behavior from withdrawal (change S^2). After one hour of alcohol consumption, the human body takes from six to eight hours to get back to its normal average tension level.

When more alcohol is consumed, the withdrawal symptoms are stronger— hangovers, delirium tremens, convulsions, and death. Figure 1.4 shows that, after 5 to 7 hours of alcohol consumption, the human body takes 16 to 20 hours to get back to its average tension level. Figure 1.5 describes a 48-hour binge pattern of alcohol consumption, which requires a recovery time of approximately 600 hours, or 25 days.

Withdrawal from alcohol is far more dangerous than withdrawal from other drugs (see Chapter 3). As Figure 1.6 illustrates, each time the drinker is about to go to the normal range and suffer withdrawal, he or she consumes more alcohol to avoid experiencing withdrawal. To ward off withdrawal, alcoholics often resort to the "hair of the dog." Figure 1.7 shows how, after an entire evening of alcohol consumption, drinking the traditional Bloody Mary the next morning temporarily takes the edge off a hangover. We could develop similar figures for stimulants, hallucinogens, marijuana, and a variety of other drugs to illustrate the effects on an individual's stress levels and normal functioning.

S^1 Reduced tension level due to sedative/hypnotic consumption.
S^2 Increased tension due to psychomotor stimulation.

FIGURE 1.3   *Tension Changes Due to Alcohol Consumption*

SOURCE: From *Facts About Drug Abuse, 1975,* National Institute on Drug Abuse, U.S. Department of Health and Human Services.

FIGURE 1.4   *Effects of Higher Dosages of Alcohol*

SOURCE: From *Facts About Drug Abuse, 1975,* National Institute on Drug Abuse, U.S. Department of Health and Human Services.

FIGURE 1.5   *Tension Levels Produced by 48 Hours of High-Level Alcohol Consumption*

SOURCE: From *Facts About Drug Abuse, 1975,* National Institute on Drug Abuse, U.S. Department of Health and Human Services.

FIGURE 1.6   *The Built-Up Effects of Additional Alcohol Consumption*

SOURCE: From *Facts About Drug Abuse, 1975,* National Institute on Drug Abuse, U.S. Department of Health and Human Services.

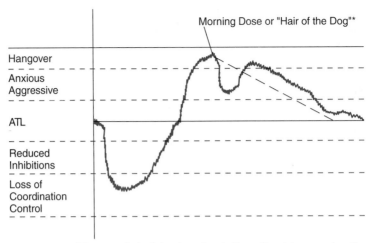

Morning Dose or "Hair of the Dog"*

Hangover

Anxious
Aggressive

ATL

Reduced
Inhibitions

Loss of
Coordination
Control

*The term *hair of the dog* refers to the colloquial expression, "to recover, take a hair of the dog that bit you."

FIGURE 1.7   *Hair-of-the-Dog Effect*

SOURCE: From *Facts About Drug Abuse, 1975,* National Institute on Drug Abuse, U.S. Department of Health and Human Services.

Attention Deficit Hyperactivity Disorder (ADHD)

There has been recent focus in the public media on ADHD in adults, especially those adults who might be substance abusers. The three key features of ADHD are inattention, impulsivity, and hyperactivity. The syndrome more commonly affects males (the male to female ratio is estimated at between 3 to 1 to 10 to 1). It is very possible that individuals with ADHD will use alcohol/drugs to self-medicate and manage their symptoms.

The symptoms of inattention include not completing tasks, being easily distracted, being unusually disorganized, forgetting daily activities, and losing things. Signs of impulsivity can include saying and doing things without considering others' feelings, interrupting others, and generally acting without considering the consequences. The symptoms also describe hyperactivity.

There have been thousands of studies of ADHD in children and adolescents, but relatively few involving adults. In establishing a diagnosis of ADHD in adults, it is imperative to determine if the symptoms were present during childhood. Christopher Varley in his article "Hyperactive Adults" (*Professional Counselor Magazine,* December 1995) states, "To qualify for a diagnosis of ADHD, the key features should be persistently present, pervasive and causing a substantial impairment to the individual's life. This is different from the occasional inattentiveness, restlessness, or impulsivity that everyone experiences."

More research is clearly needed to demonstrate the linkage between adult ADHD and alcoholism/drug addiction.

TABLE 1.2

Risk for Alcoholism/Addiction

Parents	Probability of Becoming an Alcoholic/Addict
One alcoholic/addict	Four times higher
Two alcoholics/addicts	Eight times higher

Family Model

I drink/drug because I come from a "dysfunctional family.". . . My mom drank a lot. . . . I felt neglected. . . . I was abandoned. . . . I was abused. . . . I was shamed, violated, and traumatized.

The family model is the model most emphasized throughout this book; it includes all aspects of family life. Some examples of factors contributing to alcohol/drug use in the family include the following:

- Imbalance in parenting
- Marital discord
- Alcoholic/addict behavior
- Imbalanced and dysfunctional family interaction
- Significant trauma and stress in the family
- Physical, emotional, sexual, and psychological violation
- Inappropriate boundaries
- Shame, abandonment, rejection

The family model of chemical dependency is developed in more detail throughout this book.

Family

Alcohol and drug addiction and dependence are **family diseases.** The genetic predisposition to alcoholism is well documented. The probability of developing the disease of alcoholism and drug addiction is four times higher for those individuals who have one alcoholic or drug-addicted parent. The probability increases to eight times higher if both parents are alcoholics or addicts. (see Table 1.2.)

Children from alcoholic, dysfunctional, and shame-based family systems are at greater risk for developing problems with alcohol/drugs. The modeling of family members who use alcohol/drugs also greatly influences the development of alcohol/drug dependence. Exhibiting poor communication, the alcoholic/addict family has specific "no talk, no feel, no trust" rules (see Chapter 7). Such a family system breeds childhood traumas of fear, rejection, abandonment, and sometimes violation. (see Chapters 5 and 6.)

Parents with substance abuse problems have extreme difficulty in being effective parents. "Parenting is a difficult, time-consuming, complicated task. Staying on top of the situation requires quick, sensitive, and intuitive judgment of that which works best" (Kempher 1987). Parents with alcohol/drug problems are ill-equipped to provide the kind of patient, dedicated care necessary for children to develop and grow. Their parenting styles tend to be rigid and insensitive to the needs of children. These parents tend not to be nurturing and available. They often use the coercive or abusive parenting techniques they learned from their parents.

Self-Concept

The most frequently generalized at-risk factor for problems with alcohol/drugs is a poor self-concept. Parents and schools talk about children's general underachievement, shyness, and aggressive or antisocial behavior as being a result of this lack of self-concept. Report cards and progress reports include comments such as "does not work up to his/her potential," "has difficulty finishing assignments and staying on task," "fails to participate in class, daydreams," and "more concerned with peers than teacher." It should be no surprise that the same evaluations occur for adults who have difficulty with work relationships and general achievement.

There are so many different definitions of self-concept that isolating this variable as a causative factor for alcohol/drug problems is impossible. While exploring all of these definitions of self-concept, I developed a more workable behavioral definition that better explains what we are talking about. Instead of using the label *self-concept,* which implies something one gets from outside of oneself and is, therefore, beyond one's internal ability to develop, I relabeled it as a **sense of self.** A sense of self is less static than self-concept, involves more choices by the individual, and is active rather than passive. A sense of self comes from within to the outside world, rather than the outside world's defining who the individual is. This important point has implications for individuals who develop codependent relationships with addicts and alcoholics. (See Chapter 7.) Under this definition, a person with a sense of self is

1. A unique, worthwhile individual with emerging talents and skills
2. An individual who can accomplish things (e.g., develop, prioritize, and achieve goals; solve problems; resolve conflicts; accept and carry out responsibilities; and have the maturity to develop and grow)
3. An individual who can trust and be trusted, one who sets appropriate boundaries for intimacy in relationships

In his article "Beyond Drug Education," Paul Robinson (1975) states that the goal is "not to convince people not to do drugs" but to empower them to enhance their development of self. Robinson suggests that we need to emphasize educational programs that help students acquire this sense of self, by developing the skills to

- Control their destructive impulses
- Understand their values, needs, and desires
- Make wise decisions
- Resist peer pressure when it endangers their welfare or inhibits their growth
- Find nonchemical means of fulfillment and satisfaction
- Think intelligently and rationally

By focusing on programs that teach children and adults to develop and enhance a sense of self, we make them less at-risk for alcohol and drug problems.

The more time I spend working in the alcohol/drug recovery and mental health fields, the more clearly I see that a poor sense of self is a strong predictor of problems with alcohol/drugs. Families that do not promote the child's sense of self cause those children to be emotionally disabled (i.e., develop a poor sense of self). In later chapters, these specific family issues are discussed in more detail.

Encouraging potential alcoholics and addicts to develop a sense of self is just one aspect of the problem; other factors must also be addressed. Even children and adults who possess a wonderful and creative sense of self are at-risk. Improving the sense of self is a preventive inoculation but is neither a cure nor a guarantee against having alcohol/drug problems. (See Chapter 10.)

Adolescence

As children enter adolescence, they are at risk for alcohol/drug problems. In *Drugs and Drinking* (1985), Jay Strack classifies five major factors in adolescent abuse of drugs, using the mnemonic PEACE:

P—pressure (peer pressure)
E—escape
A—availability (of alcohol/drugs)
C—curiosity
E—emptiness

Conditioning and Substance Abuse

> I use drugs because it feels good. . . . Drugs make for a goodtime. . . . I expect to feel good under the influence. . . . There is no "guesswork" here—take the drug for the desired effect. . . . It's modern chemistry. . . .

A strong reinforcing factor in alcohol/drug use is the memorable feeling attached to the first use. A first-time experience with a drug or alcohol-induced altered state of consciousness is a new and unforgettable awareness. This first or early experience with alcohol/drugs is so reinforcing that time after time the individual attempts to reproduce or recapture that original memorable experience. Those smoking heroin describe it as "chasing the dragon." This can be similar to one's first romantic involvement or to the extremely pleasurable yet painful romantic associations of unrequited love. Alcohol/drugs can become that first love, like no other experience ever felt before. Unfortunately, it is impossible to duplicate that feeling. The cycle of addiction has begun: the individual tries to repeat an experience that cannot be recaptured because by definition it was the first. This is the reason addicts continue using alcohol/drugs even though the feeling and behavioral experiences are clearly negative and unpleasant. They hope that somehow the next time will be different.

Frequently, alcoholics and addicts have **euphoric recall** of the pleasant experiences they had during earlier, excessive uses of alcohol/drugs. They forget the negative consequences and dangerous situations that they barely escaped. The human mind defends against the overwhelming fear and shock of these negative experiences and, instead, recalls the good times. Thus, alcoholics and addicts forget how destructive and dangerous their experiences with alcohol/drugs can be.

If they were legal, imagine the unlimited advertising campaigns that could be developed for the sale of drugs based on these characteristics:

> Feeling down and depressed? Lack the energy to do even the most basic things? Suffer from lowered sex drive, sleep disturbances, or have difficulty with interpersonal relationships? Not making the kind of money you would like to, need a vacation, a general lift? Wondering what life is all about or if it is even worth it? Try Zippy, the new nonnarcotic wonder medication brought to you by the What's Happening Now, Don't Worry, Be Happy Institute of Living Life.

The expectancy and cognitive model asserts that alcohol/drug use is an anticipatory response to a pleasure state, conditioned by previous use. This may describe the obsessive-compulsive aspect of chemical dependency.

The biobehavioral models focus on the conditioning, reinforcement, stimulus situations (triggers), and pleasure and withdrawal states associated with alcohol/drugs.

Psychosocial Models—Social-Learning Theory (SLT)

> It's fun to use and be with friends. . . . It's peer pressure. . . . It's cool to use and chill out. . . . I can use drugs and belong. . . . I can connect with others when we are together. . . . Sex is better. . . .

There are a variety of models that could fit under this category. The key element of these models is the social-learning aspect of alcohol/drug use. The social-learning theory also incorporates other models, such as tension-reduction. For example, the young child who sees Dad drink his martini at the end of the day and witnesses the relief of tension may come to see drinking alcohol as an extremely positive experience. Children often experience their parents as more approachable and positive after they have used drugs or alcohol. Nathan (1983), describes alcohol use as a socially acquired, learned behavior pattern, maintained by antecedent cues (classical conditioning and expectancies), consequent reinforcements (operant conditioning and tension reduction), cognitive factors, modeling influences, and the interaction of behavioral and genetic mechanisms.

Marlatt and Gordon (1985), emphasize certain social learning and cognitive-behavioral points about addiction:

- Addictive behaviors represent a category of "bad habits" (or learned maladaptive behaviors). Biological factors may contribute to predisposing an individual to alcohol problems, but specific patterns of use are learned.
- Addictive behaviors occur on a continuum of use—that is, behavior such as alcohol abuse is not seen in a categorical way (e.g., present or absent) but, rather, exists on quantity and frequency of occurrence.
- All points along the continuum of addictive behavior are influenced by the same principles of learning. Therefore, the same mechanism that may be applied to explaining alcohol use can be invoked to explain alcohol use disorder.
- Addictive behaviors are learned habits that can be analyzed in the same way as any other habit.

- The determinants of addictive behaviors are situational and environmental factors, beliefs and expectations, and family history and prior learning experiences with the substance or activity. Emphasis also is placed on the consequences of addictive behavior to understand its reinforcement and punishing features.
- Besides the effects of alcohol (or another substance or activity in question), it also is important to discern the social interpersonal reactions that the individual experiences before, during, and after engaging in the addictive behavior. Social factors are important, both in the acquisition and later performance of the addictive behavior.
- Frequently, addictive behaviors are exhibited under conditions that are perceived as stressful. To that degree, they represent maladaptive coping behaviors.
- Addictive behaviors are strongly affected by the individual's expectations of achieving desired effects of engaging in the addictive behavior. Furthermore, self-efficacy expectancies (i.e., expectations of being able to use behavioral skills to cope with a situation without engaging in the addictive behavior) are important. If self-efficacy in a situation is low, and the individual believes (expects) that engaging in the addictive behavior would help him or her cope with it, then the likelihood of engaging in the behavior increases.
- The acquisition of new skills and cognitive strategies in a self-management program can result in changes in addictive behavior to new, more adaptive behaviors, which come under control of cognitive processes of awareness and decision making. Accordingly, the individual can assume and accept a greater degree of responsibility for changing the addictive behavior.

Sociocultural Models

In his review of cultural and cross-cultural studies, R. Bales (1946) identified the following ways culture and sociological organization influence rates of alcoholism:

1. The degree to which a culture causes acute needs for adjustment of inner tension in its members
2. The attitudes toward drinking that the culture produces in its members
3. The degree to which the culture provides substitute means of satisfaction

Societies, cultures, communities, socioeconomic groups, and even neighborhoods offering few or limited alternatives to drinking and drugging as tension relievers are more susceptible to addiction. The more these groups produce acute inner tensions (shame), suppressed or acted-out aggression, extreme conflict, dilemmas, mixed messages, sexual tensions, and the condoning of attitudes about alcohol/drugs as the normal, accepted way of relieving these tensions, the more prone individuals are to develop alcohol/drug dependence. When there is no limit on supply and distribution, attitudes are liberal, and cost is relative, the incidence of alcohol and drug abuse is high.

The attitude of the culture and ethnic customs may also facilitate patterns of alcohol/drug use. "The Irish and the American Indian groups positively sanction men's drinking to intoxication away from home; in these cultures the rates of alcoholism are high. Drug/alcohol dependence and addiction are influenced by sociological factors such as age, occupation, social class and subculture, and religious affiliation. In the United States, for example, young, single, unemployed urban men have a high incidence of abuse" (Donovan 1986).

Individuals who feel alienated from a larger society and who have no sense of belonging may feel that society's rules and values about alcohol and drugs don't apply to them. This feeling of alienation from a larger social body may result in more favorable attitudes about alcohol/drugs. The application of this social model of alcohol/drug use is evidenced by the crack cocaine epidemic.

The lack of opportunity or hope that one can achieve the American Dream can contribute to feelings of despair that lead to alcoholism and/or drug addiction. This despair is most prevalent in the ghettos in America's inner cities. However, this sense of despair can occur in any locale, in any socioeconomic setting. From the blue-collar bars, to the shooting galleries in abandoned buildings, to middle-class suburban high schools, to the plush boardrooms of major corporations, drugs and alcohol infest our society.

Psychoanalytic Models

The traditional psychoanalytic view of alcohol/drug dependence focused on a fixation at the oral stage of development, resulting in an oral and narcissistic premorbid personality. Otto Fenichel (1945) theorized that individuals use psychoactive drugs "to satisfy the archaic oral longing which is a sexual longing, a need for security, and need for the maintenance of self-esteem simultaneously." K. Menninger (1963) believed that alcohol may function as a coping device to alleviate stress and that the primary psychoanalytic root is a mother's denial of milk (security) in infancy. Other psychoanalytic theories suggest drinking as a strategy for allaying anxiety over masculine inadequacy (Machover et al. 1959). Analytical theories also suggest that abusers use alcohol/drugs to suppress latent homosexuality and ego-dystonic feelings of homosexuality (i.e., the person's ego is not compatible with the possibility of being homosexual).

The major psychoanalytic theory today is "a structural deficit in object relations." This means that individuals have a hard time establishing effective interpersonal relationships due to their difficulty in managing their affect (feeling) and impulse controls. They often establish their defense mechanism of denial by defensive grandiosity. In his 1986 article "Etiological Model of Alcoholism," James Donovan outlined psychoanalytic descriptions used by various researchers in identifying this difficulty in object relations:

H. Krystal and H.A. Raskin (1970)—indicated a defective stimulus barrier and an inability to desomatize emotions

Chein et al. (1964)—described drug use to cope with painful feelings and overwhelming responsibilities in the outside world

L. Wursmer (1974)—emphasized the maladaptive narcissism of the addict, a defensive stance against the potentially overwhelming feelings of rage and loneliness

E.J. Khantzian (1978)—pointed to the impoverished self-esteem, the lack of capacity for self-care, and the poor emotional regulation of the alcoholic

Khantzian (1982), Khantzian, Halliday, and McAuliffe (1990)—described an
     inability to handle emotions, and behavior characterized by swings from over
     control to under control. Feelings are often vague, ill defined, and confusing
     when expressed

Wursmer (1987)—suggested drugs may be used to deny or "overthrow" a
     particularly burdensome and chafing inner authority figure

Hopelessness, Pessimism, and Poor Future Orientation

> There is no hope! Why try? It will never get better! It will always be this way!

This final model of substance abuse and addiction is based on the past 25 years of
my counseling of individuals and alcohol/drug recovery groups. I have identified
some common themes that arise from these sessions. The three themes are feelings
of hopelessness, on attitude of pessimism, and a negative vision of the future.

Feelings of Hopelessness

It is hard to identify a single factor that leads to feeling hopeless, so hopeless that
you give up, even temporarily, and stop trying to grow, achieve, and develop.
Many clients feel as if they are getting nowhere, despite continued efforts. It could
be the hopelessness of poverty or financial disaster or of other socioeconomic loss.
It could be the shattering of idealism in one's work or relationships. It could be the
frustration of blocked goals and aspirations in employment, career, or interpersonal
relationships. It could be the devastation of physical health, disease, physical injury
or the loss of a loved one. It could be the hopelessness of not knowing how to read
or blocks in learning or achievement. It could be the continual shame and loss of
pride from emotional, physical, and sexual violation (see Table 1.3). It could be a
single or continued exposure to a traumatic event or great loss, which leads to feelings of hopelessness. One or all of these can lead to hopelessness, which can lead to
increased drug use, alcohol/drug problems, and addiction.

Pessimism

Many of my clients recovering from alcohol/drugs described their fathers as "cur-
mudgeons." Their fathers (and sometimes their mothers) were extremely negative,
sarcastic, shaming, critical of others, judgmental of their spouses and other family

TABLE 1.3

Incest and Chemically Dependent Women

44% reported incest (Benward and Densen-Gerber 1975)

40% reported incest contacts (Hammond, Jorgenson, and Ridgeway 1979)

40–50% reported past incest (Evans and Schaefer 1987)

63% of women at Women's Center for Alcoholism in a three-year study report incest
contacts before the age of 14 (Turner and Colao 1985)

members, and pessimistic about the world in general. This pessimistic attitude was not limited to fathers. Some family members were fearful and worried, expressing the philosophy that others would take advantage of people and "rip you off," either financially or emotionally. They viewed the world as hostile. As a result, they approached the world defensively, expecting to get hurt, looking for the negative. Some of these parents were alcoholics/addicts; some led lives that were limited, isolated in social and emotional connection, not trusting or getting close to others.

Unfortunately, this pessimistic attitude contributes to alcoholism/addiction. This internalized pessimism often blocks the quality of recovery. Individuals can maintain abstinence from alcohol/drugs, but they have difficulty trusting others, being vulnerable and real enough to get close to others, and they struggle with giving to others or attaining a spiritual sense of self. Developing and maintaining a support system for alcoholism/drug addiction is an integral element of recovery. However, developing the skills to overcome pessimism, and the mistrust of others and the world in general, is an ongoing developmental process.

Martin Seligman, in his book *Learned Optimism* (1991), describes pessimists as having a very negative view of the world, which interprets events as being **permanent, pervasive, and personalized.** These three *P*s of pessimism color the individuals' thoughts, beliefs, and attitudes about themselves and the world. Pessimists have these distorted thoughts about the world and over time continually approach situations with this distorted thinking process. They interpret a loss as permanent, verbalizing the all-or-none perception that "it will never get better, always be this way," evoking shaming self-statements, and viewing a world that is projected to be hard, cruel, and uncaring. The pessimist takes one negative incident or a few negative situations or encounters to generalize that it is pervasive (e.g., one or a few rejections lead to "no one loves me, there is nothing lovable about me, all of me is ugly"). Of course, the pessimist personalizes everything ("It was my fault," "If only I were . . ."). Most cognitive-behavioral therapists encourage their clients to take up these distorted thoughts by *disputing* the distorted reality and by *distracting* from the incessant cycle or focus of these thoughts. This process of disputing and distracting from the distorted thoughts is a common strategy for cognitive-behavioral change. Seligman describes some disputes to some universally distorted thoughts:

Distorted thought—"I can never be loved or find love."
Dispute—"Love is precious but rare."
Distorted thought—"No matter how hard I try, I can't ever be successful."
Dispute—"Success is doing my best."

Seligman defines success as "talent/skill + drive + optimism." In his book, he has a test on optimism. I was very proud of how well I did on the test, soon to find out as I read the next page that even a little bit of pessimism can sabotage all the optimism you have.

Seligman says that an optimistic individual views setbacks, mistakes, and failure as *very temporary,* often confined to a *specific* situation, and *external,* or outside of oneself (i.e., not an internal personalized flaw). Another term that many prevention specialists use to describe the optimistic personality is *resiliency.* Despite negative situations, the individual "challenges" him- or herself rather than

Case Study 1.1

George reported thinking that he was not going to live very long. His father had died of a heart attack at age 50. George turned 50 in February 2000. He had always thought that he would die before the new millennium. He had been in recovery from alcohol/drug use for two years and saw the benefits—his financial situation had improved, he was losing weight gradually, and he had a better relationship with his daughter, and even tolerated his exwife. He was beginning to think that he might live longer than his father. When confronted about his continued habit of smoking cigarettes, George maintained that he was going to smoke one more year. If he didn't die by the age of 51, he rationalized, it might be worth giving up cigarettes.

feeling like a victim. Optimists develop a plan to overcome the negative obstacles in their lives. They persevere through adversity.

You can certainly see how pessimism is a major characteristic of and contributing factor to alcoholism/addiction. The alcoholic/addict's sarcasm, and sarcastic sense of humor underly a negative world view. The procrastination of organizing, cleaning up, or dealing with one's life is an ongoing aspect of this pessimistic view.

Poor Future Orientation

Michael Yapko, in his book *Patterns of Depression* (1997), describes depression as having its roots in a "poor future orientation." It follows that, if you see your future as negative, you might abuse drugs, having a short-range view. Many addicts/alcoholics self-report that they don't expect to live very long. It follows that, if you think your life span is limited, you are not concerned about good physical health. As one client put it, "I might as well party hearty, since I will die young, anyway."

Many adolescents have a poor future orientation because of a continued pattern of academic failure or a difficult family situation. Academic failure, especially in late elementary grades, highly correlates with early antisocial behavior and alcohol/drug abuse (Johnston et al. 1978, Kandel, Kessler, and Margulies 1978, Robins 1978). Many of these children fail to develop the skills necessary to learn, integrate concepts, and succeed in school. Many exhibit learning disabilities, emotional problems, and attention deficit disorders. Parents are frequently in denial of these emotional and learning disabilities, and the school system may not adequately address these problems, resulting in educational failure for children. Some children do well during adolescence, some barely escape alcohol/drug problems, some develop addictions, and some die in alcohol/drug–related accidents and overdoses.

Some young adults might be frustrated that their careers are not developing. Middle-aged persons may be realizing that there are limitations, and they may not accomplish what they had intended. Older adults may have the existential despair about aging, future health problems, or death itself.

All of these issues may cause a person to have a poor future orientation. The adolescent, the young adult, the middle-aged person and the elder may choose to abuse alcohol/drugs to cope with these discouraging issues. The obvious goal, whether it is poor future orientation, pessimism, or hopelessness, is to address these issues and to find new ways to enjoy life and relationships.

✕ Functions and Meanings of Drugs

Functions of Drugs

The individual's choice of a particular drug is related to the function that drug has for the individual. People are looking for a desired effect. Users of opiates (heroin, morphine, and others) take them to kill physical and emotional pain; these users want to be numb to life. Users of central nervous system (CNS) depressants (alcohol, tranquilizers, and barbiturates) take them to decrease activity. Or they may use stimulants (cocaine, amphetamines, coffee, nicotine, and others) to increase activity. The hallucinogens and marijuana change the way users view the world and manipulate their perception of reality. Whatever the desired effect, a drug exists to serve that function. (See Table 1.4.) This powerful combination of individuals' seeking altered states of consciousness, the passive nature of drug use, and the vast array of drugs that can almost immediately provide various desired effects has resulted in many individuals' developing problems with alcohol and drugs.

TABLE 1.4

Drugs and Their Functions

Drug Category	Function
Narcotic analgesics or opiates	Kill pain
CNS depressants	Decrease activity
CNS stimulants	Increase activity
Hallucinogens, marijuana	Change the user's view of the world

 Case Study 1.2

Jerry did not fit in. As an adolescent, he was a social outcast. He was a poor athlete, the last one chosen for any athletic game. He didn't want to stand out, but he was tall and very overweight, bespeckled, and smarter than the rest. He tried to hide his intelligence in class, but the teachers knew how bright he was. At home, his alcoholic parents were unavailable and unaware of Jerry's feelings of depression.

Drugs seemed to be the natural answer to his problem. He knew some college kids down the block, and with their help he began using and dealing marijuana. He was transformed overnight from Jerry the "fat nerd" to Jerry the dope dealer. He began to dress differently and was invited to parties because he always took some good dope. Jerry could function at the parties by getting so wasted he just sat and observed everyone. He developed a reputation as a stoner and a guy who could get you any drugs you wanted. This empowered Jerry, and for the first time in his life he felt as if he belonged. He felt powerful.

Meanings of Drugs

Sometimes the choice of a particular drug is related to the meaning that drug has, both consciously and subconsciously, for that person. As we explained in the following sections, the drug also has a symbolic meaning.

Alcohol/Drugs as Power

Alcohol/drugs frequently denote power or feeling powerful to users. The expression *getting high* symbolizes feeling above others or above one's usual sense of self. Ironically, despite the original reason for using

Although cocaine may give users feelings of power, cocaine use can actually have many negative effects on personality and can quickly lead to addiction for some people.

drugs to feel powerful, the ultimate state in the cycle of addiction makes the individual powerless. Cocaine is a drug that has a symbolic meaning of power. As a power drug, cocaine is attractive because of its status as well as its physical and psychological effects. An energizing stimulant, cocaine produces a sublime feeling of well-being; users describe being on top of the world, in control, able to accomplish a great deal, able to have tremendous capabilities and insights, and able to stimulate sexual arousal and performance. However, the reality today is that cocaine is one of the most addicting drugs, and it takes the least time to develop an addiction, which ultimately renders users powerless.

Alcohol and other drugs symbolize power in the forms of sensuality and sexuality; potency; the feeling of being supernatural, pleasure, sensitivity, insensitivity, or not feeling pain; productivity; rebelliousness; high energy; and so forth. Our review of the research on why adolescents initially used marijuana indicated the following reasons: for pleasure; contentment; the joy of being high; relaxation and recreation; to facilitate social interactions; to achieve status in one's peer group; friendship leading to better understanding; to defy authority, seek thrills, and flirt with danger; for curiosity and excitement; escapism; enhancement of activity; to enhance aesthetic appreciation or sexual stimulation; to alleviate a sense of alienation; to make life better and more tolerable; to understand or find oneself; to expand one's mind for religious insights; to improve oneself.

Table 1.5 shows studies on daily marijuana use among adults. These users report similar reasons for marijuana use.

Alcohol/Drugs as Self-Destruction

Alcohol/drugs can also have a powerful meaning as weapons of self-destruction and ultimately death. In *Family Therapy of Drug Abuse and Addiction,* M. Duncan Stanton and associates (1982) describe the addict "as part of a continuum of self-destruction." Stanton reports that, when compared with the general public, addicts have a higher death rate, shorter than average life expectancy, and greater than normal incidence of

TABLE 1.5

Aspects of Life Experience Adult Daily Users Most Frequently Described as Positively Affected by Marijuana

- Ability to relax and enjoy life
- Enjoyment of food
- Ability to overcome worry and anxiety
- Ability to sleep well
- Ability to avoid feeling bored
- Enjoyment of sex
- Understanding of others
- Creativity
- Ability to avoid feeling angry
- Ability to enjoy varied activities
- Self-understanding
- Overall happiness
- Ability to avoid feeling depressed
- Ability to be tolerant and considerate of others

From Herbert Hendin et al., *Living High: Daily Marijuana Use by Adults,* Copyright © 1987 Human Sciences Press. Reprinted by permission of Insight Books, New York, NY.

sudden death. Addicts also view death as more positive and potent than their peers and are more likely to express a wish for death.

A number of clinicians have described alcoholism and drug addiction as an unconscious death wish. Self-destructiveness is the failure of ego functions involving self-care and self-protection. "We are all subject to our instincts, drives, and impulses, and if they are expressed indiscriminately, we are subject to hazard and danger" (Gottheil 1983).

Alcohol/Drugs in Seduction and Sexuality

Alcohol/drugs have important symbolic seduction and sexuality meanings. Practically all drugs and alcohol have been described at some time as aphrodisiacs. Unfortunately, no drug is truly an aphrodisiac. Alcohol/drugs may reduce inhibitions and stimulate sexual arousal at low doses; however, alcohol and other drugs impair sexual performance, especially with prolonged use.

The symbolic seduction and sexuality meanings of alcohol/drugs are exploited in advertisements for tobacco and alcohol products. If such advertising were legal, it would probably be used to advertise illicit drugs, too.

Whether celebrating an important event with a traditional toast of wine, champagne, or alcohol; passing around a pipe filled with marijuana; or sharing cocaine, heroin, or other drugs, the symbolic meaning is a shared altered state of consciousness.

Case Study 1.3

Heroin Overdose: Rock 'n' Roll

Allan was the most likeable of guys. Everyone liked him. It was this quality that eventually killed him. His fans adored him. He was the lead singer in the band, and it was going places. They had just signed the record contract and were planning a new road tour.

His heroin use had gotten worse with his success. The more popular he was, the more free dope he got. People liked to say, "I shot dope with Allan." The other band members were seeing the signs of how out of control he was getting, so his agent sent him for evaluation. Allan was up front about his use and admitted he was out of control. He agreed to go to an inpatient program for treatment.

He did great in treatment and followed up with his aftercare. He was drug free and feeling great, having 100 days sober. The band was skyrocketing. Allan talked about the success with feelings of guilt. He never thought he would succeed. It was the challenge of trying to make it in a difficult business that was the attraction, not the success. He had a traditional "fear of success." Perhaps it was this fear, or his people-pleasing nature, or just the fact that he loved heroin, that caused him to relapse. Despite the fact that he was doing well, with excellent support, he tried shooting dope, just one more time, and it was his last. A fan gave him some heroin. The heroin was of high purity and Allan's tolerance was low, having been drug free for 100 days. He overdosed and never regained consciousness.

Case Study 1.4

A Drug's Meaning—Seduction
Lyn

A female patient of mine successfully stopped her dependence on marijuana for 10 months. During a party, a male acquaintance was flirting with Lyn. He established eye contact across the proverbial crowded room; she was very interested, so she returned the seductive eye contact. When they eventually found themselves in the same part of the room, they began talking, and he invited her out to the balcony. Even though Lyn had not smoked marijuana in over 10 months and was determined not to start again, she accepted and smoked the marijuana he offered. The symbolic meaning of her accepting the marijuana was that she was available and open to his seduction.

Summary

This chapter explores the many reasons for, models of, functions of, and meanings of alcohol/drug use, abuse, and addiction.

The chapter emphasizes that (1) there is an innate human drive to alter consciousness and (2) alcohol/drug use is a passive activity.

The innate drive to alter consciousness is one of several natural human drives, such as hunger, thirst, and the drive to survive, as well as the sex drive with the goal of procreation. Using alcohol/drugs is often an attempt to alleviate feelings of boredom, melancholia, sadness, or fatigue, or is just something to do to break up the monotony of everyday activities.

Alcohol/drug use is a passive activity in that the individual takes in the chemical and waits for the physiological reaction. The person is not actively involved in changing anything but, instead, looks to the drugs as a means of changing feelings, observations, and interactions.

Several models of alcoholism and drug addiction are explored in the chapter. The most widely known is the disease model of alcoholism. The American Medical Association in 1957 recognized alcoholism as a disease based on three criteria: alcoholism has (1) a known etiology (cause), (2) symptoms that get worse over time, and (3) known outcomes.

The genetic model of alcoholism has been supported in adoption and twin studies. Twins from alcoholic parents raised in nonalcoholic families have a higher rate of alcoholism than normal, and children adopted from alcoholic families have a higher incidence of alcoholism than adopted children from the nonalcoholic home. Devor proposes a developmental-genetic model, which views alcoholism as a group of illnesses in which the influences of genes and the environment interplay throughout the individual's lifetime.

The personality model debunks the ideal of an "addictive personality"; instead, there are personality traits that correlate with alcoholism. The strongest relationship with substance abuse is found with antisocial personality disorder. The second most common personality disorder with a high incidence of substance abuse is borderline personality disorder.

The mood and feeling (affect) disorder model identifies depression and mood disorders as causes of substance abuse and addiction.

Risk-taking behavior, impulsivity, and disinhibition are identified as contributing factors to substance abuse.

The tension-reduction theory (TRT) is the most widely researched model of substance abuse. Stress and tension are certainly contributing and confounding factors in a person's use and abuse of alcohol and other drugs.

Other models outlined in this chapter include the family, conditioning, psychosocial, sociocultural, and psychoanalytic models. Additional factors discussed in this chapter that contribute to substance abuse are feelings of hopelessness, pessimism, and poor future orientation.

The chapter concludes with an emphasis on three major functions and meanings of drugs as "power," "self-destruction," and "seduction/sexuality," with accompanying case studies.

References

Alterman, A.I. et al. "Personality Pathology and Drinking in Young Men at High and Low Familial Risk for Alcoholism." *Journal of Studies on Alcohol* 59, (1998): 495–502.

Bales, R. "Cultural Differences in Rates of Alcoholism." *Quarterly Journal of Studies of Alcohol* 6 (1946): 480–99.

Benward, J., and J. Densen-Gerber. "Incest as a Causative Factor in Antisocial Behavior: An Exploratory Study." *Contemporary Drug Problems* 4 (1975): 323–40.

Blane, Howard T., and Kenneth E. Leonard, eds. *Psychological Theories of Drinking and Alcoholism.* New York: Guilford Press, 1988.

Blum, Kenneth, et al. "Allelic Association of Human Dopamine D2 Receptor Gene in Alcoholism." *Journal of American Medical Association* 263, no. 15 (April 1990): 2055–60.

Caspi, A. et al. "Personality Differences Predict Health-Risk Behaviors in Adulthood: Evidence from a Longitudinal Study." *Journal of Personality and Social Psychology* 73, (1997): 1052–63.

Chein, I. et al. *The Road to H.* New York: Basic Books, 1964.

Cloninger, C.R. "A Systematic Method for Clinical Description and Classification of Personality Variants." *Archives of General Psychiatry,* 44 (1987): 573–88.

Cloninger, C.R., M. Bohman, and S. Sigvardsson. "Inheritance of Alcohol Abuse." *Archives of General Psychiatry* 38 (1981): 861–68.

Devor, Eric. "A Developmental-Genetic Model of Alcoholism: Implications for Genetic Research." *Journal of Consulting and Clinical Psychology* 62, no. 6 (1994): 1108–15.

Donovan, James M. "Etiological Model of Alcoholism." *American Journal of Psychiatry* (1986): 1–11.

Fenichel, Otto. *The Psychoanalytic Theory of Neurosis.* New York: W.W. Norton, 1945.

Gitlow, S.E. "The Pharmacological Approach to Alcoholism." *Journal of Drug Issues* 2, no. 3 (1972): 32–41.

Gitlow, S.E. "Alcoholism: A practical treatment guide." (edited by Stanley E. Gitlow, Herbert S. Peyser). Philadelphia: Grune and Stratton, 1988.

Goodwin, D.W. "Is Alcoholism Hereditary: A Review and Critique." *Archives of General Psychiatry* 25 (1971): 545–49.

Gottheil, Edward, ed. *Etiological Aspects of Alcohol/Drug Abuse.* Springfield, IL: Charles C. Thomas, 1983.

Gurling, H.M. et al. "Genetic Epidemiology in Medicine—Recent Twin Research." *British Medical Journal* 288 (1984): 3–5.

Hammond, D.C., G.Q. Jorgenson, and D.M. Ridgeway. *Sexual Adjustment of Female Alcoholics.* Salt Lake City: University of Utah, 1979.

Helzer, J.E., and T.R. Pryzbeck. "The Co-occurence of Alcoholism with Other Psychiatric Disorders in the General Population and Its Impact in Treatment." *Journal of Studies on Alcohol* 49 (1988): 219–24.

Hennecke, Lynne. "Stimulus Augmenting and Field Dependence in Children of Alcoholic Fathers." *Journal of Studies on Alcoholism* 45 (1984): 486–92.

Hesselbrock, M.N., R.E. Meyer, and J.J. Keener. "Psychopathology in Hospitalized Alcoholics." *Archives of General Psychiatry* 42 (1985): 219–24.

Hrubec, Z., and G.S. Omenn. "Evidence of Genetic Predisposition to Alcoholic Cirrhosis and Psychosis Twin Concordance for Alcoholism and Its End Points by Zygosity Among Male Veterans." *Alcoholism* 5 (1981): 207–15.

Jellinek, E.M. *The Disease Concept of Alcoholism.* New Haven, CT: Hillhouse Press, 1960.

Johnston, L.O. et al. "Drugs and Delinquency: A Search for Causal Connections." In *Longitudinal Research on Drug Use,* D.B. Kandel, ed. Washington, DC: Hemisphere, 1978.

Kaij, L. *Alcoholism in Twins. Studies in the Etiology and Sequelae of Abuse of Alcohol.* Stockholm: Alonquist and Winkell, 1960, p. 24.

Kandel, D.B., R. Kessler, and R. Margulies. "Antecedents of Adolescent Initiation into Stages of Drug Use: A Developmental Analysis." In *Longitudinal Research on Drug Use,* D.B. Kandel, ed. Washington, DC: Hemisphere, 1978.

Kempher, Carol. "Special Populations: Etiology and Prevention of Vulnerability to Chemical Dependency in Children of Substance Abusers." In *Youth at High Risk for Substance Abuse.* Washington, DC: U.S. Department of Human Services, 1987.

Khantzian, E.J., K.S. Halliday, and W.E. McAuliffe. *Addiction and the Vulnerable Self.* New York: Guilford Press, 1990.

Khantzian, E.J. "Psychopathology, Psychodynamics, and Alcoholism." In E.M. Pattison and E. Kaufman, eds., *Encyclopedia Handbook of Psychiatry.* New York: Gardner Press, 1982, pp. 581–97.

Krystal, H., and H.A. Raskin. *Drug Dependence: Aspects of Ego Functions.* Detroit: Wayne State University Press, 1970.

Machover, S. et al. "Clinical and Objective Studies of Personality Variables in Alcoholism. An Objective Study of Homosexuality in Alcoholics." *Quarterly Journal of Studies in Alcohol* 20 (1959): 528–42.

Marin, Steven, and Roger D. Weiss. "Psychiatric Comorbidity in Drug and Alcohol Addiction." *Journal of Drug Education,* 1986.

Marlatt, A., and Gordon, J. *Relapse Prevention: Maintenance Strategies in the Treatment of Addictive Behaviors.* New York: Guilford Press, 1985.

Menninger, K. *The Vital Balance.* New York: Viking Press, 1963.

Miczek, K., Elise M. Weerts, and Joseph F. Debold. "Alcohol, Aggression, and Violence: Biobehavioral Determinants." In *Alcohol and Interpersonal Violence: Fostering Multidisciplinary Perspectives,* Susan E. Martin, Ph.D., ed. NIAA, Research Monograph 24, U.S. Department of Health and Human Services, 1992.

Petrie, A. "Some Psychological Aspects of Pain and the Relief of Suffering." *Annals of the New York Academy of Sciences* 86 (1960): 13–27.

Robins, L.W. "Sturdy Childhood Predictors of Adult Antisocial Behavior: Replication from Longitudinal Studies." *Psychology Medicine* 8 (1978): 617–22.

Robinson, Paul E. "Beyond Drug Education." *Journal of Drug Education* 5, no. 1 (1975): 183–91.

Scher, K.J. *Children of Alcoholics: A Critical Appraisal of Theory and Research.* Chicago: Chicago University Press, 1991.

Scher, K.J., and T.H. Trull. "Personality and Disinhibitory Psychopathology: Alcoholism and Anti-social Personality." *Journal of Abnormal Psychology* 103 (1994): 92–102.

Schukit, M.A. "Biological, Psychological, and Environmental Predictors of the Alcoholism Risk: A Longitudinal Study." *Journal of Studies in Alcohol* 59, (1998): 485—94.

Seligman, Martin E.P. *Learned Optimism: How to Change Your Mind and Your Life.* New York Pocket Books, 1991.

Stanton, M. Duncan, Thomas C. Todd, and associates. *The Family Therapy of Drug Abuse and Addiction.* New York: Guilford Press, 1982.

Strack, Jay. *Drugs and Drinking—What Every Teen and Parent Should Know.* Nashville: T. Nelson, 1985.

Tabakoff, Boris, and Paula L. Hoffman. "Genetics and Biological Markers of Risk for Alcoholism." *Public Health Report* 103, no. 6 (1988): 690–98.

Turner, S., and F. Colao. "Alcoholism and Sexual Assault: A Treatment Approach for Women Exploring Both Issues." *Alcoholism Treatment Quarterly* 2, no. 1 (1985): 91–101.

Whitlock, F.A. et al. "Drug Dependence in Psychiatric Patients." *Medical Journal of Australia* 1 (1967): 11–57.

Wursmer, L. "Flight from Conscience: Experience with the Psychoanalytic Treatment of Compulsive Drug Abuser." *Journal of Substance Abuse Treatment* 4 (1987): 169–79.

Wursmer, L. "Psychoanalytic Considerations of the Etiology of Compulsive Drug Use." *Journal of American Psychoanalytic Association* 22 (1974): 820–43.

Yapko, Michael D. *Breaking the Patterns of Depression.* New York: Doubleday, 1997.

Alcohol/Drugs and Our American Society
At-Risk Factors

Chapter Objectives

1. Identify the problems related to alcohol abuse and alcoholism (e.g., child abuse, accidents, teenage drinking and driving, aggression and violence).

2. Identify the scope of problems and risks related to nicotine dependence and cigarette smoking.

3. Classify the at-risk factors for developing problems with alcohol and drugs.

4. Explain trauma, violence, and violation as at-risk factors for developing substance abuse and addiction.

5. Explain the problem of using a supply-side approach to the drug problem while neglecting the demand side.

6. Identify the importance and meeting the special alcohol/drug treatment needs of people of color and those suffering from systemic socioeconomic inequities.

7. Describe the impact of academic failure and the educational system's struggle to motivate young people.

8. Classify the characteristics of the four basic perspectives of alcohol/drug use and abuse (moral-legal, medical/public health, psychosocial, sociocultural). Cite examples of each perspective and problems inherent in each perspective.

9. Complete the Fifth Perspective Worksheet and identify the dimensions of your personal perspective about alcohol/drugs.

⚔ Alcohol and Nicotine— the Two Largest Problem Drugs in the United States

The general tendency has been to emphasize the war on drugs and to exclude alcohol and nicotine (cigarette smoking) as a target of that war. Throughout this text, we make reference to "alcohol/drugs" instead of the category of "drugs," because people forget to include alcohol and nicotine as drugs. Many established institutions in the United States agree that we must do something about the "drug problem," yet they deny, ignore, or neglect addressing the larger problems of alcohol abuse and alcoholism and cigarette smoking and addiction to nicotine.

Many individuals are in recovery from alcohol and drug use but continue to kill themselves by smoking cigarettes. Treatment centers are helping people overcome their addictions to drugs but not strongly addressing another source of addiction that will kill them—cigarettes. Ironically, the research indicates that the best time to address smoking is when people go in for alcohol/drug treatment. The misconception that many people have is that you first must address the drug problem, that it would be too much for the individual to handle withdrawal from nicotine at the same time. This misconception is perpetuated by addicts/alcoholics themselves and is enabled by the treatment centers. Both the public and private treatment centers have the "habit" of ignoring this issue, for fear that their clients might leave if they insisted that the addiction to nicotine and cigarettes is a drug that will kill them and must be addressed right away.

Alcohol Use, Abuse, and Addiction

Alcohol is integrated into the fabric of America's lifestyle, causing people to deny the impact it has on our society. The strong alcohol lobby and the economic realities created by America's developed taste for alcohol often blind our legislators to new and creative efforts in addressing the problems related to alcohol abuse and addiction.

Failure to Recognize Alcohol Problems

Alcohol is the most devastating drug we know of today in the sheer number of people that it affects; estimates indicate that there are more than 12 million alcoholics in the United States. This would also mean that there are more than 28 million children of alcoholics, who will suffer some form of dysfunction in their adult lives as a result of growing up in alcoholic family systems.

Estimates are that more than $136 billion are lost each year in business and industry due to lost employment, reduced productivity, and health care costs related to alcohol.

Child Abuse and Alcohol Drugs

Families with alcohol and drug problems are involved in 90 percent of the cases of child abuse (see Figure 2.1). The National Committee for the Prevention of Child Abuse (1990) reported that cases of child abuse in the United States rose 10 percent in 1989 to 2.4 million. This increase is the largest since 1985 and is caused by

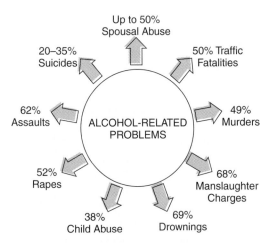

FIGURE 2.1   *Americans have a big problem with alcohol, the number one drug of abuse*

SOURCE: Office for Substance Abuse Prevention, modified. Data derived from the National Institute on Alcohol Abuse and Alcoholism. In Carroll, Charles R., Drugs in Modern Society, Brown & Benchmark, 1993.

parents' substance abuse, an increase in crack cocaine use, and changes in child abuse reporting requirements. In that timeframe, deaths due to child abuse were also up 3 percent to 1,237.

In a study by Bijur et al. (1992) the children of mothers categorized as problem drinkers had twice the risk of serious physical injury as the children of mothers who were nondrinkers. The children of women who were problem drinkers married to men rated as moderate to heavy drinkers had a 2.7 times higher risk of serious physical injury compared with the parents who were nondrinkers.

A study entitled "Parental Substance Abuse and the Nature of Child Maltreatment" by Famularo et al. (1992) concluded that "alcohol abuse is specifically associated with physical maltreatment (of children), while cocaine exhibits a specific relationship to sexual maltreatment (of children)."

Alcohol—Aggression and Violence
Table 2.1 outlines the number of studies reviewed and the percentage of those individuals under the influence of alcohol (measured by blood alcohol levels, police reports of driving, witness reports, or self-reports).

Alcohol and Accidents—Drinking and Driving
Following are some standard facts that highlight the impact of drinking and accidents, particularly driving (automobiles) under the influence of alcohol (see Table 2.2):

- Alcohol is implicated in the four leading causes of accidental death in the United States—motor vehicle crashes, falls, drownings, and fires and burns (*Alcohol and Health* 1990).
- In 1997, someone in the United States died in an alcohol-related motor vehicle crash every 32 minutes (see Figure 2.2) (GAO Report to Congress June 1999).
- More than 1.8 million people are arrested for driving under the influence each year in the United States.
- There were 16,189 alcohol-related fatalities in 1997, representing 38.6 percent of the nearly 42,000 people killed in fatal crashes that year.

See Figure 2.3 for a comparison of alcohol consumption and blood alcohol level.

Cigarettes kill more Americans than AIDS, accidents, fires, illegal drugs, and suicides combined. Twenty percent of all deaths in the United States, approximately 419,000, are related to cigarette smoking, and almost 90 percent of lung cancer deaths are caused by smoking. According to the Centers for Disease Control and Prevention, a smoker loses seven minutes of life with each cigarette smoked. There are approximately 700 ingredients in cigarettes, and at least five of these are hazardous and can be considered carcinogenic (Gold 1995).

Addiction to nicotine is one of the most difficult addictions to overcome. "Nicotine, as any smoker or any physician who's treated a smoker can tell you, is one of the most virulent of all addictions" (Gold 1995). The relapse rate is extremely high. Only

⚔ Tobacco—the Most Deadly Drug

TABLE 2.1

Alcohol—Aggression and Violence

Area	Number of Studies	Percentage Range	Area	Number of Studies	Percentage Range
Crime			Fire/burns	19	9–83
Arrested populations			Falls	8	17–70
Homicide offenders	13	28–86	Work	1	15
Assault offenders	3	24–37	Other accidents	7	9–45
Robbery offenders	3	7–72	Coroner's studies	13	14–64
Sex offenders	18	13–60	Nonfatal		
Homicide victims	29	14–87	Fire/burns	7	12–62
Assault victims	5	25–60	Falls	3	13–25
Robbery victims	2	12–16	Work	2	1–16
Sex victims	5	6–40	Other accidents	5	21–83
Prison populations			Emergency room/	3	23–63
Offenders	17	14–100	trauma studies		
Suicide			*Traffic Accidents*		
Attempters	6	30–70	Fatal		
Completers	13	18–66	Drivers	33	32–64
Family Abuse			Passengers	8	16–49
Marital violence	6	6–57	Pedestrians	26	21–83
(men's drinking)			Motorcycle	8	25–63
Marital violence	2	10–27	Drivers		
(women's drinking)			Single vehicle	19	41–72
Child abusers/neglecters	1	13	Multivehicle	15	8–51
Child molesters	6	32–54	Responsible		
Casualty			All fatal accidents	6	45–75
Accidents			Multivehicle accidents	3	31–44
Fatal			Nonresponsible		
Aviation	15	0.7–44	Nonfatal		
Drowning	14	12–80	Drivers	6	3–25

From Judy Roizen. *The Epidemiology of Serious Events: Alcohol, Casualties and Crime.* Alcohol Research Group, as printed in Kinus Miczek et al., *Alcohol Aggression, and Violence: Behavioral Determinants,* in Alcohol and Interpersonal Violence: Fostering Multidisciplinary Perspectives, U.S. Department of Health and Human Services Research Monograph 24, 1992.

3 percent of the 20 million smokers in the United States who try to quit each year are successful. See Table 2.3 for clinical opportunities to talk about smoking.

Smoking has a long history of being associated with a particular image, dating back to the Marlboro Man and Virginia Slims. The tobacco industry is a powerful lobby that has been successful for years at discounting the harmful effects and trying to make people think positively about a deadly drug. "The tobacco industry is a powerful lobby with $48 billion in annual revenues. Despite the Surgeon General's report in 1988 that nicotine is an addictive substance similar to cocaine or opiates, smoking has leveled off

T A B L E   2 . 2

Teenage Drinking and Driving

1. The leading single cause of death among 15- to 24-year-olds is drunk driving.
2. Close to 9,000 teenagers from 15 to 19 are killed in motor vehicle accidents each year.
3. Approximately 14 teenagers die each day in drunk driving accidents.
4. Close to 130,000 teenagers are injured per year in drunk driving accidents.
5. Of all fatal crashes involving young drivers, 40 percent are alcohol-related.
6. For all traffic crashes, young drivers are more likely to have been drinking than older drivers.
7. Of the 25,000 people who die each year in drunk driving accidents, 5,000 of the victims are teenagers.
8. One year after the state of Michigan raised its drinking age from 18 to 21, research showed a 31 percent reduction in alcohol-related car accidents. (National Council on Alcoholism 1988)

Source: Data from the *NCADD Fact Sheet: Youth in Alcohol,* by the National Council on Alcoholism and Drug Dependence, Inc., New York.

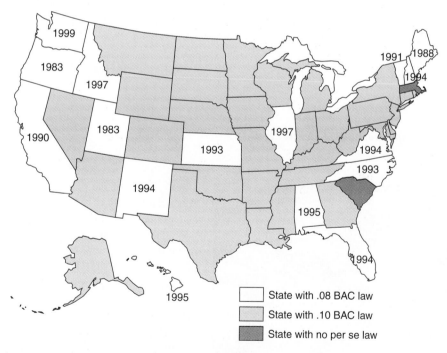

FIGURE 2.2   *State Blood Alcohol "per State" Laws*

From GAO Report *Highway Safety: Effectiveness of State .08 Blood Alcohol Laws,* 1999.

Drinks Consumed in a Two-Hour Period

FIGURE 2.3   *Alcohol Consumption and Blood Alcohol Levels*
GAO

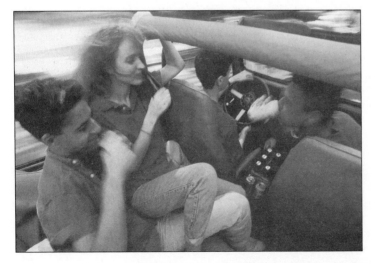

at about 25% of the population. The American Society of Addiction Medicine estimates that no less than 40 million adults are active smokers." Many of these smokers will be from the 3 million teenagers who currently smoke on a regular basis.

Eight out of every ten alcoholics are smokers. Ironically, Alcoholics Anonymous founders, Bill Wilson and Dr. Bob, both were able through mutual support to overcome their alcoholism and maintain sobriety but died from smoking cigarettes. Bill Wilson died of emphysema and Dr. Bob of oral pharyngeal cancer. Alcoholics account for 25 percent of the population of smokers, and many of those in recovery from alcoholism will die of smoking-related illnesses. This creates a challenge for most

TABLE 2.3

Clinical Opportunities to Talk About Smoking with Patients

Symptoms

Cough
Sputum production
Shortness of breath

Tests

Electrocardiography
Pulmonary function tests
Total leukocyte counts
Blood pressure measurements
Hematocrit
Auscultation of heart and lungs = blood lipid studies
Blood coagulation studies
Serum alpha$_1$ antiprotease determinations
Pregnancy tests
Carboxyhemoglobin determinations

Diagnosis of Disease and Risk Factors

Coronary heart disease
Peripheral vascular disease
Angina pectoris
Hypertension
Emphysema
Chronic bronchitis
Pneumonia
Asthma
Acute bronchitis
Recurrent respiratory infection
Diabetes mellitus
Hypercholesterolemia
Peptic ulcer
Allergy

Drug Prescriptions

Drug-tobacco-smoke interactions
Pharmacological aids to smoking cessation

Source: *Clinical Opportunities for Smoking Intervention: A Guide for the Busy Physician.* U.S. Department of Health and Human Services, Public Health Service, National Institutes of Health, 1986.

chemical dependency treatment programs in recognizing that they may be saving alcoholics but ignoring treatment for smoking, which causes their clients to die prematurely.

The risks of smoking are numerous. Prevention approaches with young people, education and treatment for those already addicted to smoking and nicotine (see Table 2.4), increasing the tax on cigarettes, and fighting the alcohol lobby

Kicking the Habit

To wean oneself from cigarettes means denying the central nervous system a substance that induces pleasure. There are a variety of methods to break the habit, but experts say wanting to break the habit is half the battle.

Method	Description	Duration	Pros/Cons
Acupuncture Cost: About $200 but depends on program	Needles are placed primarily in the scalp and ears to stimulate production of enkephalins, the chemical messengers found at nerve endings. These chemicals have a morphinelike effect on the brain and theoretically override desire for nicotine.	From one month to six weeks. Patients come in once a week for a treatment. Relaxation tapes also are used.	Some people have an aversion to needles. But, if patients can stomach it, the technique is 80 percent successful, practitioners say.
Cold Turkey Cost: None	The oldest method of breaking the smoking habit involves giving up cigarettes altogether.	Can take a week for some people, months for others. The time it takes to break the habit depends on how often the smoker "sneaks" a cigarette.	Because of a lack of supervision, there is often a tremendous desire to smoke, and each cigarette enhances the desire for nicotine. The technique can be 100 percent successful for individuals. There have been no studies conducted on this method versus medically supervised techniques.
Hypnosis Cost: $50 to $100 per session	The smoker is hypnotized to enhance the power of suggestion.	Some people need just a single session, while others need more.	National studies have not established the effectiveness of hypnosis. Smokers who have tried the technique often turn to medically supervised nicotine patch or nicotine gum programs.
Nicotine gum Cost: $36.99 for 96 pieces of gum	Smokers chew gum laced with nicotine to replace the substance found in cigarettes. The gum is often offered as part of behavioral-modification programs.	From 10 to 12 pieces of the prescription gum are recommended per day, with a maximum of 30. Each piece is chewed for 30 minutes. The program lasts 3–6 months.	There have been complaints about the taste and texture of the gum, which some say is like cardboard. The effectiveness rate is 40 percent to 50 percent.
Nicotine patch Cost: $56.99 for a two-week supply	Smokers receive decreasing doses of nicotine from a patch that adheres to the body. A different patch is worn daily and is rotated to different parts of the body to prevent skin irritation.	Generally involves a six-week program in which patches with decreasing amounts of nicotine are worn	The patch has to be worn faithfully. Some people will forget to put on a patch; others on occasion sneak a cigarette, defeating the purpose because the amount of nicotine is increased in the body. National studies place the overall effectiveness at 60 percent.
Self-Help with Behavioral Modification Cost: $10 refundable deposit for a four-week program on how to quit	The American Medical Association and the American Cancer Society offer a "How to Quit" program of audio- and videotapes. The program focuses on four areas: How to Keep My Mouth Busy; How to Keep My Hands Busy; Calm My Nerves; and Focus My Concentration.	A four-week program	The success of the program depends largely on the smoker's desire to quit. It is endorsed by the AMA and the ACS because it changes the smoker's need to have a cigarette. AMA studies show that the program is more effective than behavior modification alone.

Source: D. Ricks. "What a Drag: How Nicotine Gets Its Hammerlock on Users." *Salt Lake Tribune* 251 (21 March 1996): B1, B8.
Note: A 1994 study by the University of Iowa showed that: (1) two methods—hypnosis and acupuncture—worked well and 36 percent of smokers using hypnosis and 30 percent who underwent acupuncture quit for approximately three months; (2) 16 percent of smokers using nicotine gum were not smoking three months later; (3) smokers who were told verbally to quit without any other assistance had a 7 percent success rate after three months; and (4) the best smoking cessation aid was the nicotine patch, with a 60 percent success rate.

T A B L E 2 . 5	
At-Risk for Alcoholism/Addiction	
Parents	**Probability of Becoming Alcoholic/Addict**
One alcoholic/addict	Four times higher
Two alcoholics/addicts	Eight times higher

when it misrepresents the harmful effects of cigarette smoking are just a few of the approaches to reduce adolescent cigarette smoking.

There are a number of genetic, familial, psychological, environmental, socioeconomic, and community factors that contribute to risk for developing alcohol/drug problems. There are also factors that decrease risk of substance abuse and addiction.

✄ At-Risk Factors for Problems with Alcohol/Drugs

Denial of Family Problems—Parental Alcoholism and Addiction

The longer a family denies its alcohol/drug problem, the more vulnerable the family members become to experiencing the destructive consequences of substance abuse. Early assessment of alcohol/drug problems and dysfunctional behavior may prevent a problem from getting out of control. Parental alcoholism and drug addiction make the children in that family four to eight times more likely to develop problems with alcohol/drugs (see Table 2.5). Children who grow up in families that exhibit dysfunctional behaviors such as physical and emotional abuse, sexual violation, and other traumas are at a greater risk for developing problems with alcohol/drugs.

Public media are beginning to address the issues of child abuse, sexual violation, and other abuses by parents. However, increased public awareness and multimedia programs need to be further developed to address these issues, as well as information on early assessment and referral for treatment.

Before addressing these systemic problems, one must recognize that systems are often threatened by change, are resistant to change, or change too slowly. The pressures of public opinion and the influence of vested interests may cause systems not to respond to the need for change or to respond inappropriately in trying to solve the problem.

Academic Failure—an At-Risk Factor

Alcohol/drug problems may occur when there is academic failure. Particularly in late elementary grades, early antisocial and other problem behaviors may correlate with academic failure. Frequently, these children fail to develop the skills necessary to learn, integrate concepts, and succeed in school. Many have learning disabilities, emotional problems, and attention-deficit disorders. Parents often deny these emotional and learning disabilities until the children are much older. The school system may also fail to adequately address these problems, resulting in educational failure for these children. Failure at school causes children to disregard school as a viable option for success in the real world. Alcohol and drugs are often the choice for these young people. Discouraged by their failure in school, the additional shame of being labeled poor learners (i.e., stupid) leads to rebellious behaviors and alcohol/drug use.

Some children do well during adolescence, some barely escape alcohol/drug problems, some develop addictions, and some die in alcohol/drug–related accidents and overdoses.

The Office for Substance Abuse Prevention (OSAP) developed a monograph on risk factors correlation to alcohol/drug use (see Table 2.6).

Hawkins, Catalano, and Miller (1992) identified 17 at-risk factors for adolescents and young adults:

1. Laws and norms
2. Availability of alcohol and drugs
3. Extreme economic deprivation
4. Neighborhood disorganization
5. Physiological factors
   a. Biochemical
   b. Genetic
6. Family drug behavior
7. Family management practices
8. Family conflict
9. Low bonding to family
10. Early and persistent problem behavior
11. Academic failure
    a. Intelligence
    b. School failure
12. Low commitment to school
13. Peer rejection in elementary grades
14. Association with drug-using peers
15. Alienation and rebelliousness
16. Attitude favorable to drug use
17. Early onset of drug use

More information on these at-risk factors and prevention strategies can be found in Chapter 8, "Prevention of Substance Abuse Problems."

Trauma, Violence, and Violation—At-Risk Factors

Trauma, violence, and violation are all factors that contribute to the incidence of substance abuse. Tables 2.7 and 2.8 illustrate the relationship of substance abuse to these factors, making it imperative to address them in treatment.

TABLE 2.6

Risk Factors and Correlates to Alcohol/Drug Use

Parental Discord

Parental divorce and separation associated with drug use and delinquent behaviors (Baumrind 1983, Penning and Barnes 1982, Robins 1980)

Parental conflict associated with drug abuse (Simcha-Fagan and Gersten 1986)

Large absence of family rituals in homes of alcohol/drug abusers (Bennett and Wolin 1985, Wolin et al. 1979, 1980)

Parental Supervision

Disorganization, home/family management skills less evident in homes of alcohol/drug abusers, less time with children, less evidence of support (Kumpfer 1987, Kumpfer and DeMarsh 1986)

Less monitoring and parental involvement in homes of alcohol abusers (Patterson and Dishion 1985, Dishion et al. 1985)

Alcohol and drug abuse strongly correlated with number of evenings per week outside the home (Bachman et al. 1981)

Peer Influence

Peers' attitudes toward drug use and use of drugs related to adolescents' own use (Kandel 1978, 1985)

Beliefs about drug use by peers and orientation to peers associated with own use (Jessor and Jessor 1978, Robins and Ratcliff 1979)

Associations with drug-using peers associated with own use (Johnson et al. 1991, Elliot et al. 1985, Jessor et al. 1980, Kaplan et al. 1982, Norem-Hebeisen et al. 1984, O'Donnell and Clayton 1979)

Psychological Temperament

Sensation seeking related to marijuana use and to number of drugs used in adolescence (Pennign and Barnes 1982, Spotts and Shontz 1984, Zuckerman 1979)

Risk taking by child associated with expectations to use and later use of tobacco and alcohol (Ahmed et al. 1984)

Decreased attention span associated with alcoholism (Tartar et al. 1985)

Decreased ability to return to emotional homeostasis with alcoholism (Rosenberg 1969)

Hypersensitivity in children with alcoholic parent(s) (Cartwell 1972, Morrison and Stewart 1983)

Emotional lability and hypersensitivity associated with alcoholism (Goodwin et al. 1975)

Depression, low frustration, and emotional immaturity in sons of alcoholic fathers (Aronson and Gilbert 1963)

Deviance

Early antisocial behavior associated with later adolescent drug use (Elliot et al. 1985, Johnston et al. 1978, Kandel et al. 1978, Robins 1978, Weschler and Thum 1973)

Rebelliousness associated with later drug use (Bachman et al. 1981)

Early (first-grade) aggressiveness in males, particularly in combination with shyness, associated with adolescent drug use (Kellman and Brown 1982)

Early use of drugs associated with later regular use (Kandel 1982, Kaplan et al. 1986, Robins and Przbeck 1985)

Early use of drugs associated with later criminal activity (Brunswick and Boyle 1979, Kleinman 1978, O'Connell and Clayton 1979)

TABLE 2.6 (*continued*)

Risk Factors and Correlates to Alcohol/Drug Use

School Behaviors

Alienation from school and school peers and decreased attendance associated with later alcohol and drug abuse (Kumpfer and Demarsch 1986)

School dropout related to adolescent drug use (Anhalt and Klein 1976, Annis and Watson 1975, Johnston 1973, Robins 1980)

Low commitment to school associated with alcohol and drug abuse and delinquency (Catalano et al. 1985, Johnston et al. 1986)

Academic problems and behavioral difficulties in early grades associated with drug use (Herjancic et al. 1977, Rimmer 1982)

Tardiness and truancy associated with later drug use (Homberg 1985)

Plans to attend college associated with lower levels of drug use (Hohnston et al. 1985)

Absenteeism, class cutting, and poor performance associated with drug abuse (Bachman et al. 1981, Brooks et al. 1977, Kandel 1982, Kim 1979)

Low academic performance in early grades associated with initiation of drug use (Jessor and Jessor 1977, Johnston 1973, Kandel et al. 1978)

Attitude toward school and time spent on homework associated with drug use (Friedman 1983, Johnston and Bachman 1980)

School failure associated with subsequent use and level of use (Smith and Fogg 1978)

Aggressive, antisocial behavior in early grades associated with later delinquency and drug use (Spivak 1983)

Community Deprivation

Community disorganization related to higher levels of delinquency (McCord and McCord 1959, Schlossman et al. 1984)

Poverty and inadequate housing and living conditions associated with delinquency and drug use (Blumstein et al. 1985, Farrington 1985, Robins 1979, West and Farrington 1973)

Neighborhood Involvement

Residential stability associated with lower rates of initiation of drugs and lower frequency of drug use (Catalano et al. 1985)

More mobile adolescents felt more alienated from family and school and were more likely to have friends using drugs. (Kaplan et al. 1984)

Delinquency and crime associated with low stability of neighborhood population (Sampson et al. 1981)

Religious Commitment

Adolescents attending religious services more frequently and rating religion important in their lives were less likely to use any substance. (Bachman et al. 1981, Johnston and Bachman 1980)

Source: Adapted from the Office for Substance Abuse Prevention (OSAP), *Monograph 1—Risk Factors and Correlates to Alcohol/Drug Use, 1989.*

TABLE 2.7

Incest and Chemically Dependent Women

44% reported incest (Benward and Densen-Gerber 1975)

40% reported incest contacts (Hammond, Jorgenson, and Ridgeway 1979)

40–50% reported past incest (Evans and Schaefer 1987)

63% of women at the Women's Center for Alcoholism in a three year study report incest contacts before the age of 14 (Turner and Colao 1985)

TABLE 2.8

Epidemiological Data on Alcohol and Violence

Type of Violence	Individuals Drinking Alcohol (%)	References
Rape	50	Shupe 1954
Rape	53	McCaldon 1967
Rape	35	Rada 1975
Rape	57	Rada et al. 1978
Rape	72	Johnson et al. 1978
Rape	65	Barnard et al. 1979
Incest	49	Virkkunen 1974
Incest	50	Browning and Boatman 1977
Family violence	40	Gaylord 1979
Family violence	15–20	Erberle 1982
Murder and homicide	36	Wilentz and Brady 1961
Murder and homicide	10	Scott 1968
Murder and homicide	57	Grunberg et al. 1978
Murder and homicide	56–83	Bloom 1980
Murder and homicide	56	Lindquist 1986
Murder and homicide	61	Tinklenberg and Ochberg 1981
Felonies	33	Guze et al. 1968
Felonies	57	Mayfield 1976

Source: From Klaus Miczek, Elise M. Weerts, and Joseph F. Debold. "Alcohol, Aggression, and Violence: Biobehavioral Determinants," in *Alcohol and Interpersonal Violence: Fostering Multidisciplinary Perspectives,* NIAA Research Monograph 24, U.S. Dept. of Health and Human Services, 1992.

❧ Emphasis on the Supply Side and Neglect of the Demand Side of the Drug Problem in the United States

Approximately 70 percent or more of the federal money available to fight the drug problem is being spent on programs and agencies that focus on reducing the supply of drugs in the United States. Despite these efforts, there appears to be no real reduction in the availability of drugs. The lucrative profits are such a strong incentive at every level of the illegal drug trade that government efforts to decrease drug trafficking have not been successful.

As a result, this strong emphasis on the supply side has caused a neglect in funding for demand-side programs of drug prevention, intervention, and treatment. The problem has escalated to such levels that respected government officials and other prominent individuals are considering the legalization of illicit drugs. In 1988, Mayor Kurt Schmoke of Baltimore, Maryland, asked for a "national debate on the question of decriminalizing marijuana." Schmoke's suggestion was not well received by supply siders in the war on drugs, because it dramatically highlighted the ineffectiveness of the supply-side approach. Even considering legalizing drugs clearly points to the frustration of a segment of the American society with the lack of progress being made by the supply-side approach.

Most publicly funded agencies are seeing their funding base diminishing, caseloads increasing, and severity of their patients needs increasing. The March 1990 survey by the National Association of State Alcohol and Drug Abuse Directors indicated that publicly financed programs had long waiting lists for both inpatient and outpatient treatment services. The average waiting time for publicly funded outpatient alcohol/drug treatment was 22 days. The average waiting time for publicly funded inpatient alcohol/drug treatment was 45 days. Nationally, more than 65,000 people are waiting to enter public alcohol/drug treatment programs. Once the alcoholic/addict is ready for treatment and breaks through denial, there is such a long waiting list that relapse is inevitable. This costs taxpayers additional money in increased crime and public health care costs.

The same survey reported that, in 1988, states outspent the federal government in supporting chemical dependency treatment programs. Only 23 percent of the $2.1 billion spent on state-supported treatment programs comes from the federal government. In the 1991 federal budget, the $700 million in treatment grants represented only an 11 percent increase, despite backlogs in treatment services and dramatic funding needs to expand alcohol/drug treatment services.

There is a gap between the demand for substance abuse treatment and its availability. The 1996 National Household Survey on Drug Abuse (NHSDA) estimated that 5.3 million people, age 12 and over, needed drug treatment but only 37 percent of that number received it in the same year.

In 1997, the U.S. Census Bureau reported that 16 percent (43,448,000) of U.S. residents did not have health insurance, making it very difficult for large numbers of people (who need alcohol/drug treatment) to receive it because they lack the resources to pay for it.

Money alone cannot necessarily solve the problem. However, it can alleviate delays in providing treatment for those desperately seeking and needing treatment.

Funding for innovative programs addressing the needs of the inner-city crack addict and programs for the prevention of addiction in pregnant women are high priorities. Funding is also needed for alcohol/drug prevention programs for high-risk youth in their communities, with a special early focus on kindergarten to sixth grade. To make a major impact, longitudinal prevention projects with funding for several years are needed. Innovative yet realistic methods of funding are also necessary to attract the support of big business.

Historically, there has been prejudice and oppression of people of color, a scapegoating of minorities, and a neglect of substance abuse problems in the inner city. Legislation on drug policy was often formed more on racial scapegoating prejudices than a concern for the harmful impact of the drug on people. "People's attitudes toward a specific drug became inseparable from their feelings about that group of people with which the drug's use was associated" (White 1976). For instance, in 1875, the goal of suppressing opium smoking and opium dens had little to do with the control of opium but more to do with the fear of interracial contact and a fear of interracial mixing of the Chinese with American women and the white working class. The Chinese question dominated California politics in the 1870s. The tremendous racial and class conflicts resulted in many racial riots, the lynching and killing of Chinese, and the burning of their dwellings in numerous West Coast cities. The California Working Man's Party was organized under the cry of "The Chinese must go."

The association between opium and the Chinese into the 1900s was part of the national legislation to prohibit opium smoking and opium dens, even though, at the time, opium was a primary ingredient in most over-the-counter medications and elixirs for physical ailments (White 1976).

The same held true for the association between cocaine and African Americans during the late 1800s and early 1900s. Hamilton Wright, a State Department official considered by many as the father of American narcotics laws, went before Congress in 1910 and gave the following warning about cocaine.

> It has been authoritatively stated that cocaine is often the direct incentive to the crime of rape by the Negroes of the South and other sections of the country.
>
> Once the Negro has reached the stage of being a "dope taker" [dope here referring to cocaine] . . . he is a constant menace to his community until he is eliminated. . . . Sexual desires are increased and perverted, peaceful Negroes become quarrelsome, and timid Negroes develop a degree of "Dutch courage." . . . Many of these officers in the South have increased the caliber of their guns for the express purpose of stopping the cocaine fiend when he runs amuck. (Williams 1914)

These racial associations with drugs were documented in a *New York Times* newspaper article that reflected the anti-Semitic feelings of the time: "There is little doubt that every Jew Peddler in the South carries the stuff (cocaine)."

This historical association of drugs with hated minority groups includes

- Opium with the Chinese
- Cocaine with African Americans
- Alcohol with urban Catholic immigrants
- Heroin with urban immigrants, African Americans
- Marijuana and PCP with Latinos

⚔ Neglect of the Alcohol/Drug Treatment Needs of People of Color

The underlying assumption was that minorities were not able to control or tolerate the use of alcohol and drugs because they were inherently lazy and physically, emotionally, and morally/ethically weak. Of course, it was thought, most self-respecting white men could control their alcohol/drug use. This prejudice and association of drugs with hated minority subgroups caused politicians and others to use these emotional feelings in gaining support for antidrug legislation.

Unfortunately, as long as drugs were confined to minority populations, funding and treatment resources were limited. It wasn't until the 1960s, when white middle-to-upper class young adults and college students were using marijuana, hallucinogens, and other drugs, that the modern drug war began.

Until we resolve the more dramatic issues of socioeconomic inequities, racial prejudice and the oppression of minorities, inequities in pay and occupational opportunities, and other related issues, the inner city will continue to be the breeding ground for the abuse of alcohol/drugs (see Table 2.9).

❧ Academic Failure and the Failure of the U.S. Educational System in Motivating and Educating Young People to Strive for Productive Lives

In 1959, the former U.S.S.R.'s launching of the first manned spacecraft caught the United States by surprise. As a result, the United States took up the challenge for space by rededicating energy and resources to the study of science and math as well as the general education of our young people. Perhaps the current failure of the U.S. educational system and the high incidence of alcohol/drug use by young people will be the impetus to implement reform and innovation in school systems, much like that of the 1960s.

We have seen the educational system in the United States neglected to the point of an increasing level of academic failure and dropout rates. The academic standards for students who do graduate are inferior. The ripple effect of this lowering of academic standards is also seen in colleges and education in general. Illiteracy has increased, and the quest for knowledge and general personal and intellectual improvement is a standard that is not emphasized or valued by the average American citizen. This complacency in education also pervades other standards in American business and industry. Attitudes about doing high-quality work and performing with productive energy at work are diminished when the motivation for personal improvement is not there. The quality and pride in American workmanship are also decreased, resulting in inferior goods and services and a general public attitude that accepts these standards. The industries that employ individuals with good educational backgrounds and positive self-motivating attitudes tend to experience fewer of these problems.

The current failure of the educational systems of the United States is a result of a variety of problems. The biggest problems are poor administration, teacher burnout, lack of adequate funding, and a bureaucratic system that promotes complacency.

The factor that contributes the most to teacher burnout is the lack of support from the principal and school board. Innovation is threatening to some school administrations, and the fear of parents' complaints and litigation often results in a political administration that is more concerned with how parents and the school board may respond than the effective development and education of the child.

Another factor is the lack of incentives—other than the genuine desire to work with young people—for teachers to invest themselves in their profession. The

TABLE 2.9

Substance Abuse in Brief

Hispanics—The 31,166,000 Hispanics in the United States represent 11.4% of the total population; 34% lack health insurance, compared with 16% of all Americans, and 27% earn below the poverty level, compared with 13% for all others. In 1997, 23% of Hispanics living in households and self-reporting their need for treatment received it; Hispanics comprised 11% of admissions to publicly funded treatment in 1996.

African Americans—The nation's 33,051,000 African Americans represent 12.1% of the total population; 22% lack health insurance, compared with 16% for all citizens; 27% live below the poverty line, compared with 13% for all citizens; 26% of African American household residents reporting their need for treatment actually received it, and 25% of admissions to publicly funded treatment programs were African Americans.

Native Americans—The 2,020,000 Native Americans constitute 0.7% of the total national population; 19% of their families receive public assistance, compared with 5% of all others; and 31% earn salaries below the poverty level, compared with 13% for all others combined. The total alcohol-related discharge rate for Indian Health Service or tribal-run hospitals was 31.0 per 100,000 persons, compared with 19.3 per 100,000 for all other general, short-stay hospitals. According to an analysis conducted in 1991–1993, Native Americans report the highest rates of needing treatment, at 8% vs. 2–4% for other racial/ethnic groups. Their need for treatment is underscored by the alcohol-related death rate among Native Americans: 39.4 per 100,000, compared with 6.7 per 100,000 for all U.S. racial groups combined.

Asians/Pacific Islanders—The 10,186,000 people of Asian/Pacific Island descent represent 3.7% of the total population; 21% of that number lack health insurance, compared with 16% of all Americans; and 14% earn below the poverty level, compared with 13% for all others. Data on treatment needs among Asians are hampered by cultural taboos. Admitting to problems and seeking help outside the family unit. However, 1.7% living in households self-reported their need for substance abuse treatment, and an estimated 7,697 received treatment for illicit drug use in 1998. Washington State estimated 5,160 of its Asian residents, or 3% of its total population, needed substance abuse treatment and that 33% of those in need lived below the poverty level.

Rural residents—25% of the national population live in rural areas and find the lack of finances and transportation, shortage of treatment providers, limited service hours, and the local or family attitudes about treatment to be obstacles to receiving it. Arizona found the highest unmet need for publicly funded treatment among adults was in its rural areas. Ohio found that 21% of adult male and female arrestees reported a need for "alcohol only" treatment, compared with 9% for all others.

Homeless—An estimated 50%, or 1 million, of all homeless adults have substance abuse disorders requiring treatment. Alameda County, California, found substance abuse at a ratio of 31.3% among homeless persons, compared with 3.6% for all others. New Jersey found that 41% of its homeless shelter residents wanted treatment but did not receive it.

Source: *Substance Abuse in Brief,* Center for Substance Abuse Treatment (CSAT), U.S. Dept. of Health and Human Services, September 1999.

teacher who repeats the same lesson plan over and over without making any invest-ment in the job receives the same salary as the teacher who is attentive, is involved, and spends time and energy in educating students.

The combination of inadequate pay, lack of support from administration, and no financial incentives or other motivations has resulted in dedicated and talented teachers' leaving educational systems. This puts students in the hands of teachers who lack the talent or motivation to help them overcome academic failure and a poor sense of self.

Reforms such as site-based management, parent involvement, shared decision making, accountability, and alternative schools have been successful in turning school systems around. We need to apply these principles in educational reform to provide children the opportunity for academic and personal success. The develop-ment of our children as a natural resource is essential in developing a future genera-tion strong enough not to succumb to dependence and addiction to alcohol/drugs.

✠ Socioeconomic Inequities Undermining the American Dream

The inequities in socioeconomic opportunities have created bitterness, racial con-flict, and a general rebelliousness and hopelessness, which fuel the desire to use alcohol/drugs. *The American Dream is a nightmare for those who are unable to de-velop feelings of competency and pride in their lives.*

The reality is that hard work and dedication can be rewarded with the attain-ment of each person's American Dream. Many successful people have refused to be limited by the prejudice of others to the color of their skin, their sex, their reli-gious or ethnic background, or their lack of membership in the inner circles of our society. Many individuals positively strive to reach their full potential by overcom-ing the prejudices of others and work to correct these inequities when they have an opportunity to change them. Other individuals become so embittered by socioeco-nomic injustices that they give up, become alienated from society, and lack a per-sonal commitment to strive in life. Alcohol/drugs numb and shut down these feel-ings of embitterment, anger, and pain. Instead of working through these issues and resolving the conflict, a bitter hopelessness devours their meaningfulness in life.

Elizabeth Schnoor, in her book *Within Our Reach: Breaking the Cycle of Disad-vantage* (1988), identifies poverty as the greatest risk factor for chemical dependency and other destructive behaviors. Violent crime, school-age childbearing, and school failure are outcomes that need "early interventions to prevent rotten outcomes," and "high-risk families need high-intensity services." Changes in economic policy, health care reform, and welfare reform can help in "breaking the cycle of disadvantage."

American society needs to acknowledge and address these issues of disparity in opportunity. Other factors contributing to the alcohol/drug problem are the breakdown of the neighborhood, changes in the traditional nuclear and extended family system, limited support systems, stress, and trauma.

✠ The Major Perspectives of Alcohol/ Drug Use

In *Drugs Demystified*, Helen Nowlis (1975) described four major perspectives of drug use: (1) the moral-legal perspective, (2) the medical-health perspective, (3) the psychosocial perspective, and (4) the social-cultural perspective.

Moral-Legal Perspective

The moral-legal perspective is primarily the viewpoint of law enforcement and the criminal justice system. The major focus of this perspective is to keep specific drugs away from people and people away from specific drugs. This approach reduces the availability of drugs and uses punishment as a deterrent in addressing the supply side of drugs, not the demand side.

The agencies in this perspective have not been able to significantly affect the availability of drugs. Although they are doing their best with limited resources, these agencies are unable to substantially affect the price of drugs by reducing their availability. The criminal justice system is a deterrent for some people, but few people stop drug use and drug dealing because they fear criminal-justice interventions. The antisocial personality of the people caught by the system makes rehabilitation difficult. The weak rehabilitative components of the criminal-justice system have resulted in minimal changes in the attitudes of those convicted or caught by the system.

The moral-legal perspective is the one emphasized by most politicians, yet this perspective alone cannot be effective. Unless we address the demand side, the moral-legal perspective is ineffective. With so many buyers in the marketplace, sellers are motivated to deal, despite the risks.

The moral-legal perspective also encompasses the value judgments that people have about drugs and alcohol. This often takes the form of the licit versus illicit debate, personal biases about punishment for illegal use, and values about moral/ethical decisions about alcohol/drug use.

Medical-Health Perspective

The medical-health perspective is held by physicians, nurses, and the medical and health treatment fields. In this perspective, alcohol and drug use is a public health problem. Treatment focuses on the physical damage related to alcohol/drug use, abuse, and dependence.

The medical-health perspective assumes that people seek good health. The perspective is also based on the assumption that health information influences attitudes and behaviors. However, information alone does not change attitudes about the use of alcohol/drugs.

Psychosocial Perspective

The psychosocial perspective is a common viewpoint shared by a variety of alcohol/drug agencies that specialize in addressing the demand side of alcohol/drugs. The services they provide are

- Recovery from substance dependence
- Intervention and treatment services
- Early intervention approaches with adolescents
- Prevention services for young children, adolescents, adults, and seniors

The goals of this perspective are to prevent, intervene, and treat alcohol/drug problems. Inadequate funding for chemical dependency treatment programs and alcohol/drug prevention programs has created problems in obtaining treatment services and in maintaining prevention programs long enough to see conclusive results. (See Chapter 8)

Social-Cultural Perspective

The social-cultural perspective is held by most social agencies and institutions. The basic goal of this perspective is to adapt the environment to meet the individual's needs. The underlying assumption of this perspective is that alcohol/drug use is due to the frustration and hopelessness of people's lives. If users had any hope that they could attain the American Dream, they would be motivated to achieve and establish a constructive place in society.

Unfortunately, most social agencies are impersonal, bureaucratic, and rigid in dealing with their clients' needs. Such agencies are poorly funded and, therefore, poorly staffed; their employees are overworked, underappreciated, and underpaid. As a result, the agencies are reticent to change, change too slowly, or may even lack a mechanism to change.

Edward Brecher, the renowned author of *Licit and Illicit Drugs* (1992), believes we should "stop viewing the drug problem as primarily a national problem to be solved on a national scale. In fact, . . . the drug problem is a collection of local problems." By supporting neighborhood and community efforts, we could provide an environment that could prevent the development of alcohol/drug problems.

The Fifth Perspective—Your Perspective

What is your perspective on alcohol/drugs? Complete the following Fifth Perspective Worksheet to clarify your perspective on alcohol/drugs.

Moral-Legal Perspective

1. Should drugs be legalized? Explain.
2. Is the supply-side approach to the drug problem an effective approach? Explain.
3. Is alcoholism/drug addiction a defense for irresponsible and/or criminal behavior? Explain.

Medical-Health Perspective

1. Is alcoholism/drug addiction a disease? Explain.
2. Describe the physician's role in making a patient aware of problems with alcohol/drugs.
3. Do people need more information about the health risks of alcohol/drug use? Does this information change attitudes? Explain.

Psychosocial Perspective

1. What role does parenting play in the development of alcohol/drug problems?
2. Is it important for the entire family system to be involved in alcohol/drug treatment? Explain.
3. How can alcohol/drug treatment be more effective?

Personal Perspective

Circle *true* or *false* and explain the reasoning supporting your answer to each question.

1. Illicit drugs are not necessary, and drug use is harmful.
   True
   False
2. Illicit drugs can play a role in enhancing life experiences.
   True
   False
3. Alcohol is a drug with great abuse potential.
   True
   False
4. My family history does not make me at risk for developing problems with alcohol/drugs.
   True
   False
5. If a family member or close friend had an alcohol/drug problem, I could suggest the person either get help or participate in an intervention.
   True
   False
6. Persons with alcohol/drug problems have to break through their own denial.
   True
   False
7. Alcoholism and drug addiction are family diseases.
   True
   False
8. Parent modeling of alcohol/drug use is an important influence on a child's use of alcohol/drugs.
   True
   False
   Other personal views

A Perspective of Hope

Perhaps the problems that spawn alcohol/drug abuse and addiction seem too difficult to overcome. The negative impact of these problems frequently gives rise to feelings of hopelessness that we can never adequately resolve these issues. There is, however, positive and dramatic success: millions of Americans are in recovery from alcoholism and drug addiction. Family members are changing their own codependent and enabling behavior in relationships. Adult children of alcoholics are overcoming the trauma of their childhoods. Most important, families are successfully developing more functional and healthy systems for the next generation of youngsters. Their children will be less vulnerable to the familial problems of alcohol/drug dependence and addiction.

There is something to be said for thinking small. Initially, this might sound like strange advice. We each must think about our own small contribution to solving problems that seem large and insurmountable. Each of us needs to first think about our own behavior and our own family and address growth and positive development in those areas. Then we can begin to address these issues in our neighborhoods, communities, workplaces, and other interpersonal interactions. My hope is that we can each, in our small way, address the issue of alcohol/drug dependence and other issues in our society by endeavoring to focus on our own and our children's functional growth and development.

Summary

There is still a tendency to ignore, deny, or minimize the problems of alcohol abuse and alcoholism. Expanded awareness of the costly impact of alcoholism on our society is needed through greater efforts in education. An estimated $136 billion is spent each year in business and industry due to lost employment, reduced productivity, and health care costs. More than 1.8 million people are arrested for driving under the influence each year in the United States (*Drugs and Crime Facts—1992*).

By far the biggest systemic problem has been the government's emphasis on the supply side of the drug problem while not adequately addressing the demand side. A second problem has been the lack of cooperation and communication among the mental health and alcohol/drug treatment fields. A third problem has been the historical neglect of the alcohol/drug prevention and treatment needs of people of color. The fourth problem is the failure of the U.S. educational system to motivate and educate young people to strive for productive lives. The fifth problem is socioeconomic inequities that discourage the underclass from having the hope and means to attain the American Dream.

The chapter ends on a more hopeful perspective of encouraging parents and families to work on their relationships and parenting of their children.

References

Alcohol and Health, Seventh Special Report to the U.S. Congress. Rockville, MD: U.S. Department of Health and Human Services, NIAA, 1990.

Bijur, Polly E. et al. "Parental Alcohol Use, Problem Drinking, and Children's Injuries." *Journal of American Medical Association* 267, no. 23 (1992): 3166–71.

Brecher, Edward M. *Licit and Illicit Drugs.* Boston: Little, Brown, 1992.

Drugs and Crime Facts—1992. Washington, DC: U.S. Department of Justice, Bureau of Justice Statistics, 1992.

Famularo, R. et al. "Parental Substance Abuse and the Nature of Child Maltreatment." *Child Abuse and Neglect* 16 (1992): 475–83.

GAO Report to Congress: Highway Safety Effectiveness of State .08 Blood Alcohol Laws, June 1999.

Gold, M. *Tobacco.* New York: Plenum Medical Book Co., 1995.

Hanson, Glenn, and Peter Ventarilli. *Drugs & Society.* Jones & Bartlett, 1998.

Hawkins, J. David, Richard E. Catalano, and Janet Y. Miller. "Risk and Protective Factors for Alcohol and Other Drug Problems in Adolescence and Early Adulthood: Implications for Substance Abuse Prevention." *Psychological Bulletin* 112, no. 1, (1992): 64–105.

Nowlis, H. *Drugs Demystified,* 1975.

Schnoor, Elizabeth B. with Daniel Schorr. *Within Our Reach: Breaking the Cycle of Disadvantage.* New York: Doubleday, 1988.

White, William. "Chemical Prohibition." In *Facts About Drug Abuse,* Participants Manual. Rockville, MD: National Institute on Drug Abuse, 1976.

Williams, Edward Huntington. Editorial in the *Medical Record Newspaper,* 1914. In *Facts About Drug Abuse,* Participants Manual. Rockville, MD: National Institute on Drug Abuse, 1976.

Drug-Specific Information
Drugs on the Street Where You Live

Chapter Objectives

1. Define and apply the following terms: *physical dependence, withdrawal, psychological dependence, routes of administration, set and setting, tolerance, cross-tolerance, synergism, antagonism.*

2. Define and outline the various aspects of the behavioral definition of addiction.

3. Explain the difference between psychoactive and nonpsychoactive drugs.

4. Outline some updated information on crystal methamphetamine, Rohypnol, LSD, heroin, marijuana, inhalants, and MDMA (Ecstacy).

5. Outline the basic classification system of drugs.

6. Classify the drugs in the narcotic analgesics (painkillers) category.

7. Discuss the central nervous system depressants (alcohol, barbiturates, and tranquilizers).

8. Classify the central nervous system (CNS) stimulants.

9. Classify the drugs in the hallucinogens category.

10. Classify the drugs in the cannabis sativa category.

11. Classify the various inhalants and their available forms.

12. Explain the problems in classifying phencyclidine (PCP).

13. Explain the various uses of drugs in sports and athletics, to include a discussion of caffeine, tobacco products, amphetamines, steroids, cocaine, and other drugs.

Every neighborhood and community are affected in some way by problems with alcohol/drugs. No house, farm, tenement, high-rise, or alleyway is immune from alcohol/drugs. Many streets of inner cities are infected with crack cocaine, and other streets are contaminated by heroin. Perhaps families on your own block have problems with alcohol, cocaine, hallucinogens, or marijuana. Perhaps families who live down the street are mixing the highly explosive chemicals to produce methamphetamine. Even in rural areas, children might be inhaling the fumes of gasoline to get high, growing marijuana in secluded areas, or harvesting hallucinogenic mushrooms. Every family in every community is vulnerable to the problems associated with alcohol and drugs.

✂ Drugs in Our Society

The 1960s and 1970s were truly the birth of the modern drug revolution. Marijuana, hallucinogens (especially LSD), and other drugs became a major part of the hippie movement of that time. It was a time when young people rebelled against their parents' traditional values by using drugs, dressing differently, growing their hair long, espousing open love, and listening to rock 'n' roll. Protests against civil rights violations, the war in Vietnam, and the traditional values of our political system further became the cause for young people.

In the 1980s, a new drug was the rage—a drug that was thought to be only "psychologically dependency-producing." We soon found over the next 10 years that this drug would cause us to dramatically change our definition of addiction and our whole outlook on drug abuse. That drug is cocaine. Cocaine was soon being used intravenously and smoked in the form of *freebase cocaine.* Comedian Richard Pryor set himself on fire while smoking freebase cocaine, and John Belushi overdosed by injecting cocaine and heroin (speedballing). Both of these unfortunate tragedies brought cocaine to the forefront. A dramatic and tragic victim of cocaine was Len Bias. Bias, a talented college basketball player, was drafted by the Boston Celtics. The Boston fans were elated at Bias and Larry Bird being on the same team. Unfortunately, on the evening he was drafted by the Celtics, Bias celebrated with freebase cocaine and died.

Soon cocaine was being converted to *crack cocaine* (discussed later in this chapter). Crack addicts in the inner cites became a major addict population that quickly challenged our treatment and criminal-justice system. Babies born to crack cocaine–addicted mothers were another casualty of this new drug.

It is fair to say that cocaine changed our entire outlook about addiction. Even individuals who thought drugs rather benign and only psychologically dependency-producing could not ignore the high addiction potential of cocaine. This short-acting drug created addicts very quickly, with dramatic and disastrous life circumstances. It also affected all socioeconomic levels.

Another drug group that came to our attention in the mid-1980s was synthetically produced drugs. In an attempt to subvert existing controlled substance laws, new drugs were created by underground chemists. These new drugs were chemically different (by a molecule or two) from those banned by existing drug laws.

Donald Wesson, M.D., defined designer drugs as "substances wherein the psychoactive properties of a scheduled drug have been retained, but the molecular structure has been altered in order to avoid prosecution under the Controlled Substance Act." The potency and volume of production of these drugs challenged our perception of illicit drug manufacturing. There was no need for the large production and distribution networks like those used for cocaine and marijuana. There was no harvest of the drug. Instead, one chemist with the basic raw materials could produce enough of the drug to supply the entire United States.

In the early 1990s, another new drug brought to public attention was *ice.* Ice is a transparent, sheetlike crystalline structure that is a purified form of the drug methamphetamine hydrochloride. In the early 1990s, ice was imported to mainland United States by the eastern drug cartels operating out of Oahu, Hawaii. In January 1990, authorities busted the operation of an ice factory in northern California. At that time, the National Institute of Drug Abuse reported the use of ice in cities such as Atlanta, Dallas, Los Angeles, Phoenix, San Diego, and Seattle. Attempts to develop ice on the East Coast did not pan out. Much as crack is to cocaine, ice is to methamphetamine. Ice is a smokable and more powerful form of methamphetamine (hydrochloride). Smoking ice allows more rapid absorption into the blood via the lungs. Unlike the extremely short-acting high of freebase and crack cocaine, the ice high can last from 7 to 30 hours. Dr. David Smith, of the Haight Ashbury Free Clinic, has noted, "Ice did not replace crack, it widened the group of people who use drugs."

✂ Drug Updates— into the New Millennium

Crystal Methamphetamine

The United States is currently experiencing an upward cycle of stimulant abuse, with a dramatic increase in the availability and use of crystal methamphetamine, in a potency, purity, and accessibility unlike any previous time in our history. This is a substance that does not occur in nature and thus must be synthesized in an illicit laboratory.

Street names for this drug are speed, crank, crystal, ice, meth, chalk, chicken powder, peanut butter-crank, go-fast, crystal meth, shabu-shabu, glass, go qip, chris, and christy, depending on the geographical area, the dealer, and the physical form, crystal versus powder.

The name ice has been used by dealers to represent methamphetamine, as well as other substances, including methamphetamine mixed with heroin, cocaine or other adulterants, quarts, and rock salt.

Part of this alarming trend is ascribed to the takeover of the manufacture and distribution of speed, formerly the province of outlaw "Biker"-type fringe individuals, by Mexican nationals, who already had a strong, well-organized distribution network. This has resulted in a much purer, significantly more potent, and lower-priced drug, precipitating a sharp increase not only in the number of users but also in those of a much lower age group.

Methamphetamine enters the brain more rapidly than any other CNS stimulant, rapidly producing a "rush" of euphoria when injected or smoked. Many people who try methamphetamine go on to compulsive abuse of the drug. Typically, small doses can have a profound effect, including stimulated movement and increased speech, feelings of excitement and euphoria, and decreased appetite. A significant rise in pulse rate and blood pressure occurs, as well as a sensation often described by users as "my heart pounding out of my chest." This may progress to irregularities in heart rhythm, a dramatic rise in body temperature, convulsions, cardiovascular collapse, and death.

Populations Using Methamphetamine

- Traditionally associated with white, male, blue-collar workers, methamphetamine is now reportedly being used by diverse groups in all regions of the country.
- Use is increasing among men who have sex with men and use other drugs, making this population more vulnerable to contracting and spreading sexually transmitted diseases, especially HIV/AIDS.
- Young adults who attend "raves" or private clubs are increasingly using methamphetamine.
- Notable increases are occurring among homeless and runaway youth.
- Increasing use of methamphetamine is reported among male and female commercial sex workers who also trade sex for drugs and among members of motorcycle gangs. Also, people in occupations that demand long hours, mental alertness, and physical endurance (such as long-haul truckers) have been using this drug at increased rates. (National Institute on Drug Abuse 1998)

You Can Identify Methamphetamine Users By . . .

- Signs of agitation, excited speech, decreased appetites, and increased physical activity levels. Other common symptoms include dilated pupils, high blood pressure, irregular heartbeat, chest pain, shortness of breath, nausea and vomiting, diarrhea, and elevated body temperature.
- Occasional episodes of sudden and violent behavior, intense paranoia, visual and auditory hallucinations, and bouts of insomnia
- A tendency to compulsively clean and groom and repetitively sort and disassemble objects, such as cars and other mechanical devices (National Institute on Drug Abuse 1998)

Chronic use leads to a state of paranoia, with individuals displaying behaviors strikingly resembling those of someone experiencing an acute episode of paranoid schizophrenia. Tolerance develops quickly, and chronic users must increase their dose, which, in turn, leads to magnification of the side effects and may lead to permanent brain damage.

In addition to the physical symptoms, the chronic user will experience a profound depression, with low energy levels, anhedonia (the total inability to experience any pleasurable feelings), and such a profound craving for the drug, remembering when the drug "worked" for them, that the cycle is often repeated many times, often with tragic results.

Ice, the smokable form of methamphetamine, is of extremely high purity—greater than 90 percent—and can lead to "runs" of four to five days without any sleep and often without food or even fluids. Then a "crash" of four days or so occurs, before the user begins another "run."

The drug, regardless of form, is often used concurrently with alcohol, either to blunt some of the stimulant effect or to help the user "come down" after a protracted period of use. The use of other depressant psychoactive substances leads to a polydrug use pattern that can be extremely dangerous.

Rohypnol

Rohypnol is also known as narcozep, rohipnols, and roiphol. It is the brand name for flunotrazepam, a sleeping pill legally manufactured and prescribed for use in Europe, Mexico, South America, and the Asias. It is from the benzodiazepene class (e.g., Valium, Wanax, Restoril) and is not available on the formulary of drugs that may be legally prescribed in the United States. All rohypnols in the United States are therefore illegally purchased. Common street names are rohies, ropies, roofies, wheels, and row-shapys.

Like other benzodiazepenes, when taken alone, it is unlikely to cause problems. But, if combined even with a small amount of alcohol, the intoxication effects may be extreme, leading to severely impaired judgment and motor skills. Individuals given such a combination often "come to" anywhere from 8 to 24 hours later, with no memory of any events that transpired after the time they ingested the drugs (blackouts).

Teens and young adults often follow the abuse pattern of taking the drug in combination with alcohol, as an "alcohol extender." There is a synergistic effect that increases the impairment of memory and judgment. It may also be used by drug addicts to "boost the high" or to "parachute down" from a cocaine binge. Rohypnols have been widely implicated in "date rape," in which the female victims are seduced or tricked into ingesting the drug plus alcohol. The disinhibition effect, as well as amnesia for the subsequent events, are why they have been given the appellation "leg splitters."

The federal government has begun the process of classifying this drug as a category 1 substance, putting it into the same category as narcotics. This would bring with it severe penalties for dealing and possession of the drug.

LSD

"Designer acid," also know as "cocktail acid," is emerging on the drug scene. This hallucinogen is less potent, shorter acting, and milder than the acid from the 1960s. It is therefore easier to conceal the use of this hallucinogen by young people. It has begun to make its way into the party scene, and one can "drop acid" in the afternoon, party for six to eight hours, and then safely return home and sleep off the residual effects.

Brand names help identify the stronger, more potent preparations, such as Mr. Natural, muscle man, and yin yang, with some brands sporting the "dead head" logo (from the psychedelic band the Grateful Dead), and even a "Mr. Bill" caricature of our thirty-ninth president, President Bill Clinton.

Heroin

The 1990s saw a significant increase in the use of heroin. The number of hard-core users, estimated by the National Institute of Drug Abuse (NIDA), has remained fairly constant over the past 25 years, at 750,000–1,000,0000. However, the past several years have seen a disturbing number of individuals using heroin who are dramatically unlike the stereotypical heroin addict. The profile now contains well-educated, often female individuals, frequently employed in white-collar and even professional capacities. The age of users is also alarming, considering reports of use in high schools and even middle schools.

The reasons for this trend are many. For one, heroin use has assumed the trappings of glamour, often associated with the "arts," fashion, and entertainment world. It is now much purer, and thus more potent, which enables it to be inhaled, either through smoking it, "chasing the dragon," or snorting it in its powder form. The very fact that it does not have to be injected makes it more attractive by alleviating the aversion most people have to needles (i.e., needle phobia, stigma, risk of AIDS virus). There is also the widespread misbelief, and rationalization, that if one smokes or snorts heroin it will be nonaddicting.

To add to its "attractiveness," it is also relatively inexpensive, especially compared with crack cocaine. A bag of heroin containing enough to get the user high for six to eight hours may be purchased for as little as $3 in New York City and will be of significant purity and potency, whereas a $10 bag of heroin purchased on the streets in 1980 was about 4 percent pure. Today it is not uncommon for a sample to be 65 percent pure, or even higher.

Another factor is that the drug is more easily obtained. The neophyte user is no longer forced to venture into dangerous neighborhoods in order to purchase the drug. It may be as easy as paging the dealer, who then delivers it, or it may be available on certain street corners in middle-class or industrial neighborhoods or even at the workplace.

One of the more insidious aspects of the drug is that, unlike cocaine and even alcohol, heroin use may exist for a significant period of time before its use is suspected. Individuals may be fairly high and functioning for quite a while, and, if they are careful, it may take months before they have to increase their dose and risk getting toxic. By the time it becomes obvious, the problem has progressed to the point where medical treatment and appropriate intervention is most often necessary to treat the addiction.

Heroin-related emergency department visits doubled from 33,900 in 1990 to 70,500 in 1996. In 1993, more than 3,805 deaths nationwide were related to heroin. "Both urban and suburban emergency departments treat patients with heroin overdoses daily and hospitalize 3 to 7 percent of these patients for related complications." (Sporer 2000)

Heroin use can no longer be confined along geographic, economic, or social lines. It is in "Heartland USA," as well as in suburbia and in the urban centers of the nation. It is found among the unemployed and disadvantaged, blue-collar workers, professional workers, the economically advantaged, and even homemakers.

Marijuana

The appearance of so-called hybrid superweeds, known in some areas of the country as tastybun or purple tar are 10 times more potent than the marijuana available in the 1960s or 1970s. This marijuana is often smoked in the form of "blunts," which are cheap, hollowed-out cigars filled with this powerful drug.

Inhalants

In addition to glue, paint, room deodorizers (e.g., Glade), butane, and even propane, there are commercial products that are often inhaled to get high. This includes ethyl chloride and nitrous oxide, which are known as "whippets," in the form of whipped cream canisters. It is estimated that there are 10,000 common household products that contain ingredients that can be abused.

Ecstasy

Another drug that fits into our definition of a designer drug is MDMA, better known as Ecstasy, XTC, X, Rave, or Adam. Although MDMA was first synthesized and patented in 1914 as an appetite suppressant, it became popular in the 1980s with college students. Prior to July 1985, when it was illegal to sell MDMA, or Ecstasy, the drug was legally sold in bars in Texas catering to college students. A major factor that contributed to MDMA's emergence in the rest of the country was the publicity associated with a drug being blatantly sold in bars and the publicity in scheduling the drug as a controlled substance. In 1985, *Newsweek, Time, Life,* and other magazines sensationalized the euphoric, therapeutic, and aphrodisiac qualities of the drug. MDMA is related to both mescaline and amphetamines and could be best described as a "mood-enhancing stimulant." It is often perceived as "mild speed," and users often claim that it increases empathy and communication, which is why it is also called the "hug drug." A subculture has evolved around the drug, with resultant Ecstasy and rave parties, which are often clandestine (although most young adults seem to have no problem knowing where they are), changing location as often as every weekend.

Even though it is often referred to as hallucinogenic, it rarely produces delusions. MDMA is most frequently taken orally, with reports of a variety of psychological effects, including the following:

- Positive mood change
- A dramatic drop in defense mechanisms
- Increased empathy for others
- Increased self-esteem and elevated mood

Combined with the stimulant effect, this also may produce an increase in communication, intimacy, and enhanced pleasure of touching, yet it inhibits orgasm and interferes with erection.

Negative effects include overdose potential, extreme fatigue with too much use, dilated pupils, dry mouth and throat, tension in the lower jaw, grinding of the teeth, and too much stimulation.

Although perceived as harmless by the users, there are reports of cases of acute and chronic paranoia associated with usage, and even panic reactions requiring emergency care. As with other central nervous stimulants, a rise in blood pressure accompanies its use, which is often of no consequence to most otherwise healthy young adults but can have a potentially deleterious effect on someone with an underlying problem or a congenital abnormality.

There often appears to be a hangover effect, consisting of muscle aches, especially of the jaw and facial muscles (clenching of the teeth is common); generalized fatigue; decreased concentration; and insomnia. Tolerance to the mood- and mind-altering effect does develop, with subsequent increase in the "unwanted" side effects.

✖ Definitions of Terms

Physical Dependence

Physical dependence is the altered state that develops when a person cannot stop taking a certain drug without suffering from withdrawal.

Withdrawal

Withdrawal symptoms are physical symptoms resulting from stopping the use of a drug (see Table 3.1). These vary according to the specific drug, the amount used, and the length of time over which it has been used. Because the body has actually adapted metabolically to the presence of the drug, when it is withdrawn (or even tapered off too rapidly), the reactions may vary from mild, flulike symptoms for a person coming off of opiates to a severe, potentially life-threatening situation when withdrawing from alcohol or other sedative hypnotics.

Psychological Dependence (Formerly Habituation)

A user with a profound emotional or mental need for the repetitive use of a drug or a class of drugs is **psychologically dependent.** The user becomes so preoccupied with taking the drug to achieve the optimal level of functioning or to maintain a

TABLE 3.1

Diagnostic Criteria for Drug Withdrawal

Opioid	Alcohol	Cocaine	Nicotine
Dysphoric mood	Autonomic hyperactivity	Dysphoric mood	Dysphoric or depressed mood
Nausea or vomiting	Hand tremor	Fatigue	Insomnia
Muscle aches	Insomnia	Unpleasant dreams	Irritability
Lacrimation	Nausea or vomiting	Insomnia or hypersomnia	Anxiety
Rhinorrhea	Hallucinations	Increased appetite	Difficulty concentrating
Pupillary dilation	Illusions	Psychomotor retardation or agitation	Restlessness
Piloerection	Psychomotor agitation		Decreased heart rate
Sweating	Anxiety		Increased appetite
Diarrhea	Seizures		Weight gain
Yawning			
Fever			
Insomnia			

Note: Data are from the *Diagnostic and Statistical Manual of Mental Disorders* (4th ed.); American Psychiatric Association, 1994.

sense of well-being that it becomes extremely difficult to abstain. Psychological dependence is a subjective state that is almost impossible to quantify; therefore, it is of limited usefulness in establishing a diagnosis of chemical dependency.

Routes of Administration

The route of administration is the method by which the alcohol/drug is ingested. Ingestion may be oral, through the skin, by injection, by smoking, or through other orifices (e.g., suppositories). The most rapid reaction occurs after inhalation while smoking a drug; injection is the next most rapid route. Oral administration and absorption through the skin are the slowest routes.

Set and Setting

Set refers to the user's state of mind at the time of use. *Setting* refers to the physical environment or environmental factors surrounding alcohol/drug use.

Tolerance

Tolerance to a drug develops when the individual requires increasingly larger doses to achieve the desired optimal effect. In other words, users require larger doses to achieve the same high produced previously by a smaller dose of the same drug.

Cross-Tolerance

Cross-tolerance is a diminished or reduced response to the effect of a psychoactive drug. This response is due to prior use of other psychoactive drugs, usually in the same drug category.

Synergism

In a synergistic process, one chemical enhances, or adds power to, the effect of another. The combined effect of two or more drugs is greater, therefore, than the effect of each agent added together (e.g., 1 + 1 = 3 or more).

Antagonism

The opposite of synergism, antagonism occurs when the combined effect of two drugs is less than the sum of the drugs' effects acting separately (e.g., 1 + 1 = less than 2). For example, the depressant effects of alcohol are counteracted by the stimulant effects of cocaine.

✷ Definitions of Addiction

Historically, there have been a wide range of definitions of addiction—for example,

A chronic, progressive and potentially fatal disease. It is characterized by tolerance, psychological and physical dependence, pathogenic organ changes, all of which are the direct or indirect consequence of the alcohol ingested. (National Council on Alcoholism)

An illness characterized by preoccupation with alcohol and loss of control over its consequences, which usually leads to intoxication if drinking is begun; by chronicity; by progression; and by the tendency to relapse. Typically associated with physical disability and impaired emotional, occupational, and/or social adjustments as a direct consequence. (American Medical Association, 1957)

As described throughout this textbook, the current definition of addiction used in the alcohol/drug field is the one developed by David Smith. An expanded version of that definition of addiction follows:

1. Compulsion and obsession
   a. The compulsive use of the chemical despite its no longer having the desired effect
   b. The fear of being without the substance
   c. The compulsion to substitute other drugs if that particular substance is unavailable
   d. Thoughts about the drug as a dominant theme or integral part of one's life
2. Loss of control or inability to stop
   a. The inability to limit the amount of use
   b. The inability to refuse the substance if available
   c. The inability to stop using the substance for three months or longer
   d. Binge patterns of use

3. Continued use despite known adverse consequences
   a. Medical complications
   b. Psychiatric complications ranging from mood swings and anxiety to depression, panic disorders, and paranoid-schizophrenic reactions or other psychoses
   c. Social consequences, the deterioration of family and other significant relationships, work status, and legal complications

---

A drug may be most simply defined as a nonfood substance intended to affect the structure and function of the body, most often to diagnose, cure, mitigate, treat, or prevent disease.

There are many ways to classify drugs, such as by chemical structure or specific effects on particular organ systems. Most frequently, drugs are classified as nonpsychoactive and psychoactive. **Nonpsychoactive drugs** are substances that in normal doses do not directly affect the brain, such as vitamins, antibiotics, and topical skin preparations. **Psychoactive drugs** affect brain functions, mood, and behavior and are subdivided primarily on the basis of physiological and psychological effects. The psychoactive drug classification includes the following:

1. Narcotic analgesics: painkillers and designer drugs (fentanyl)
2. Central nervous system depressants: sedative hypnotics, alcohol, tranquilizers, and barbiturates
3. Central nervous system stimulants: amphetamines, cocaine, nicotine, and caffeine
4. Hallucinogens
5. Cannabis sativa: marijuana and hashish
6. Inhalants: volatile solvents
7. Phencyclidine (PCP)

Classification of Drugs

Narcotic Analgesics
Definition
The term *narcotic* comes from the Greek word *narkosis,* which means to numb or to be in a stupor. *Analgesia* means to relieve pain, without producing unconsciousness.

The narcotic analgesics (morphine, codeine, and heroin) come from the poppy plant (*papaver somniferum*). (See Table 3.2.) The narcotic analgesics category also includes synthetic and semisynthetic drugs that have morphinelike action, such as meperidine (Demerol), methadone, Dilaudid, and Percodan.

The term *narcotic* was often incorrectly applied to a wide variety of drugs, including marijuana, alcohol, and cocaine. This was the result of a legal classification system rather than a medical classification. The emotional overtone of *narcotic* was frequently misapplied to those drugs considered dangerous by legislators and policymakers.

The term *narcotic* has a variety of meanings. Its scientific meaning is drugs related botanically to the opium poppy and pharmacologically to opium, morphine, and heroin. Its medical meaning is synthetic drugs having morphinelike effects on a user. Its legal meaning is anything the legislature of a state wants to classify. Its public meaning is anything the general public wants to label as belonging to a particular drug category. In some states, this includes all drugs having morphinelike

TABLE 3.2

Narcotic Analgesics Classification

Natural Opioids	Synthetic	Semisynthetic	Antagonists
Morphine	Demerol	Dilaudid	Narcan
Codeine	Meperidine	Percodan	Naloxone
Opium		Talwin	

The Poppy (*Papaver Somniferum*).
DEA/Department of Justice.

action. Elsewhere the term may also be applied to drugs chemically unrelated to narcotics (e.g., cocaine and marijuana).

Additional analgesics are nonnarcotic and satisfy other functions, such as reducing fever (antipyretic) and reducing inflammation (anti-inflammatory). Other nonnarcotic analgesics include aspirin, phenacetin, and Darvon. Nonsteroidal anti-inflammatory drugs (NSAIDs) include Naprosyn and Motrin.

Heroin

It is estimated that there are 2.1 million lifetime heroin users in the United States (*1994 National Household Survey* 1995), and this is a conservative estimate.

Common street names for heroin include big bag, big H, blanco, bomb, boy, brother, brown, brown rocks, brown sugar, caballo, cat, chich, Chinese red, Chinese white, chiva, crap, dogie, doojee, dope, duji, dust, eighth, flea powder, garbage, good stuff, H, hard stuff, harry, H-caps, henry, him, horse, hombre, jones, joy powder, junk, Mexican mud, mojo, muzzle, pack, poison, powder, pure, red chicken, red rock, rock, scag, schmeck, smack, stuff, tecata, thing, white boy, white junk, and white stuff.

Brief History of the Narcotic Analgesics

The opiates have been used for medicinal purposes and pleasure since prehistoric times. Opium eating has been known in Asia for thousands of years. A brief history follows:

1806: Friedrich Wilhelm Adam Serturner, a German chemist, isolated morphine from opium.

1832: Codeine was isolated.

1845: Alexander Wood invented the hypodermic syringe.

1861–1865: Approximately 45,000 Civil War soldiers were addicted to morphine.

1874: Alder Wright, a London chemist, first synthesized heroin from morphine.

1875: A San Francisco ordinance prohibited the smoking of opium in public houses and opium dens.

1906: Pure Food and Drug Act required all medicines containing opiates and certain other drugs to list them on the labels.

1914: Harrison Narcotics Act required licensure of drug manufacturers, importers, pharmacists, and physicians marketing or prescribing narcotics. Patent medicine manufacturers were exempt from the act, provided that their products did not contain more than two grains of opium, or one-eighth grain of heroin per ounce.

1942–1943: During World War II, a German chemist, Aschenbrenner, synthesized methadone and named it after Adolph Hitler, Dolophine.

1970s: Most addicted soldiers returning from Vietnam withdrew from heroin on the trip back to the United States or shortly thereafter. The anticipated need for heroin treatment was not realized.

1978: Scientists discovered endorphins; these proteins play an important role in the body's pain suppression system.

Chemists first isolated morphine in the early nineteenth century. During the Civil War, doctors widely used morphine in injectable form. Addiction to morphine was very common at that time, resulting in a significant addict population. Fortunately, society attached no stigma to the soldiers' addiction to morphine; it was commonly referred to as "soldiers' disease." Most soldiers withdrew from morphine on their own or under medical supervision, and there was minimal social impact.

Around the 1870s, manufacturers added tincture of opium to many patent medicines sold over the counter for treatment of diarrhea in infants and children. When first introduced at the end of the nineteenth century, heroin was thought to cure opium dependence and morphinism.

Routes of Administration

Users may inject narcotics either intravenously, subcutaneously (under the surface of the skin—known as skin popping), or deep within the muscle. They can also snort narcotics intranasally, smoke it, or absorb it into their bodies via the mucous membrane of the mouth or rectum (using suppositories). The route of administration determines how quickly the drug affects the brain: a drug that is smoked reaches the brain in 5 seconds. A drug injected intravenously reaches the brain 14 seconds later. A drug taken by mouth doesn't hit the brain until 30 to 45 minutes later.

The intensity of the drug effect and the complications are also influenced by the route of administration. Intravenous use can lead to infection, local abscesses, disseminated infections (HIV, hepatitis B, pulmonary emboli), and local damage to the lungs and lining of the nose.

Major Effects

1. Pain relief (analgesia)
2. Euphoria (sense of well-being)
3. Cough suppressant (antitussive)
4. Respiratory depression
5. Sedation or drowsiness
6. Constriction of the pupils (pinpoint pupils)
7. Nausea and vomiting
8. Itching
9. Decrease in gastrointestinal activity (constipation)

Hazards

Even while using low to moderate doses, users face many hazards related to the circumstances of illicit use, such as drug impurities, infection, and the consequences of the addict lifestyle. By using dirty and shared needles, they contract infections (AIDS, hepatitis, and tetanus) and all other blood-borne infections (septicemia) leading to endocarditis, and liver, brain, and skin abscesses.

Other hazards include allergic (anaphylactic) reactions to the narcotic or substances used to cut or dilute the narcotic. Overdosing causes cardiac arrest, lung reaction, and the narcotic's direct actions on the brain, leading to coma, shock, respiratory arrest, and death.

Tolerance

Tolerance develops to a rapid degree with the effects of analgesia, respiratory depression, sedation, and feelings of euphoria. In effect, users must take more and more of the narcotic to get the original effect.

The rate of tolerance depends on the pattern of use, route of administration, and physical aspects of each individual. Even though some addicts build to phenomenally high doses, inevitably there is always a final dose that can produce death from respiratory depression.

Tolerance often returns to normal after withdrawal. Many narcotic addicts have fatally overdosed by returning to their normal and customary doses after detoxification.

Cross-tolerance exists between even chemically dissimilar opioids.

Withdrawal

Withdrawal symptoms and their severity depend on the specifics of the drug being used. With low doses of intermittent narcotic use, withdrawal symptoms may be negligible or perhaps resemble mild, flulike symptoms. Anyone who has ever been seasick can identify with these feelings. Withdrawal symptoms include the following:

- Appetite suppression
- Nausea and vomiting
- Dilated pupils
- Gooseflesh, or increased pylomotor activity—the skin resembles a plucked turkey, hence the expression "going cold turkey"
- Restlessness
- Intestinal spasms
- Abdominal pain
- Muscle spasms
- Kicking movements—hence the expression "kicking the habit"
- Occasional diarrhea
- Increased heart rate and blood pressure
- Chills alternating with flushing and sweating
- Irritability
- Insomnia
- Violent yawning
- Severe sneezing and runny nose (rhinorhea)
- Crying and tearing, nasal inflammation
- Depressive mood and tremor

The peak intensity of withdrawal occurs at 48 to 72 hours (2 to 3 days) for heroin, but for methadone the peak withdrawal is from 5 to 7 days.

Despite these symptoms, the management of withdrawal from opiates is far less dangerous than the management of alcohol withdrawal. The effects of the withdrawal are not life threatening but may need medical attention. The medical conditions worthy of attention may be excessive weight loss, dehydration, body chemistry disturbances, and stress on the cardiovascular system. Without treatment, symptoms usually disappear in 7 to 10 days for heroin but may last 2 to 3 weeks for methadone.

Opiates and Pregnancy

Chronic use of opiates, especially heroin, results in a variety of obstetrical compromises. Because withdrawal in an addicted mother may lead to spontaneous miscarriage, the consensus of the medical community to date is to stabilize the heroin-addicted mother on methadone during the pregnancy. However, these babies tend to be born prematurely, with a lower birth weight. Born addicted, these babies may display withdrawal symptoms and have significant neonatal difficulties, with lifelong negative effects on psychomotor development.

Central Nervous System Depressants

The central nervous system (CNS) depressants category commonly refers to drugs that are sedative hypnotics. The basic sedative-hypnotic category includes alcohol, barbiturates, and tranquilizers.

Alcohol

Alcohol acts as a depressant on the central nervous system. Once absorbed, it is distributed throughout the body, enters the brain easily, and is uniformly found in all body fluids. In pregnant women, alcohol crosses the placental barrier into the fetus.

A blood alcohol level of 0.05 percent or higher produces some driving impairment. In most states, anyone driving with a 0.10 percent blood alcohol level is driving under the influence. Alcohol is metabolized at a relatively constant rate, which depends primarily on the body weight of the drinker. A 150-pound man metabolizes approximately three-quarters to one ounce of alcohol in an hour.

Brief History of Alcohol

1500 B.C.: Book of the Dead mentioned "hek," a form of beer made from grain.

2225 B.C.: The Code of Hammurabi, Assyria, involved rules for the keeping of beer and wine shops and taverns.

400 B.C.: Plato wrote rules for the leader of the "symposia" to try to control the excessive drinking that went on. This was probably an ancient version of the "designated driver" (of course, back then it was the chariot driver).

Eighth century: Numerous taverns and beer houses were established in Britain.

Sixteenth century: Through the distillation process, Irish settlers manufactured and distributed "usquebach," or whiskey.

"I keep forgetting. Is alcohol a depressant or a stimulant?"

Alcohol is a CNS depressant.

© 1980 Richard Guindon. Reprinted by permission.

These alcoholic beverages contain equal amounts of alcohol.

Michael Siluk.

1660: Distilleries were licensed and the popularity of gin became widespread.

1770s: British brought beer and alcohol to the Colonial Americans.

1777: After the American Revolution, there was an increase in rum consumption as a new American freedom, when prior to the revolution there was some success in regulating taverns.

Late 1700s: Dr. Benjamin Rush, champion of the temperance movement and author of *An Inquiry into the Effects of Ardent Spirits,* inspired the nineteenth-century American temperance movement.

1917: Alcohol Prohibition came about with the 18th Amendment to the Constitution.

1920s: The Roaring Twenties brought bootlegging, bathtub gin, homemade beer, and speakeasies.

1932: The 21st Amendment to the Constitution repealed the highly unpopular 18th Amendment.

1970–present: Numerous alcohol products have been developed and marketed, especially to young people (e.g., malt liquors, wine coolers, a variety of beers).

Estimates of Alcoholism   Other than tobacco products containing nicotine, beverage alcohol (ethanol) is the most widely used psychoactive drug known to humanity. In 1994, approximately 113 million persons age 12 and over had used alcohol in the past month, which was about 54 percent of the total population age 12 and older. About 13 million Americans (6.2 percent of the population) were heavy drinkers (*1994 National Household Survey on Drug Abuse* 1995).

Major Effects   The range of physical reactions to varying doses of alcohol is vast. The effects depend on the amount consumed, the circumstances of consumption (set and setting), the drinker's body size, and the experience of the drinker. Someone unaccustomed to alcohol use is more likely to show signs of impairment than a conditioned drinker who has learned to compensate for impaired behavior. One or two alcoholic drinks may induce talkativeness in one individual, along with slight flushing, and reduce the drinker's inhibitions, so he or she appears more expansive and more animated, perhaps grandiose at times. The same amount of alcohol in another individual may induce drowsiness and lethargy.

Alcohol in even moderate doses generally reduces one's performance in tasks that require physical coordination or mental agility, such as driving a car. Larger doses can alter perception and cause staggering, blurred vision, and the manifestations of drunkenness. However, one person may become emotional or amorous, while another becomes aggressive and hostile. Extremely high doses—typical during binges—can knock out a drinker, even kill the person, if the central nervous system is depressed to the point that body functions, such as breathing, cease altogether.

Alcohol is a toxic drug with irritating as well as sedative properties. It can have a negative effect on every tissue in the human body, as shown in the following:

1. Brain
   a. Amnesia—most commonly called blackouts—causes partial, or sometimes temporary, loss of memory, often following binge patterns of alcohol use. Blackouts can occur even after low-dose alcohol

consumption, or first-time alcohol consumption by someone who has a family history of alcoholism. Blackouts may be a significant early indicator of a diagnosis of alcoholism.

   b. Permanent loss of memory and mental confusion, as in Wernicke-Korsakoff's syndrome

   c. Damage to the cerebellum, affecting balance and coordination

2. Peripheral nerves

   a. Usually in the legs and sometimes other extremities, alcoholics experience pain, loss of sensation, and general weakness.

   b. Optic nerves are damaged, causing blurred or dimmed vision.

3. Gastrointestinal tract

   a. Gastritis and esophagitis, irritation of the lining of the esophagus and stomach, causing mild to severe pain; may aggravate an ulcer

   b. Peptic ulcer at the outlet of the stomach (duodenal)

   c. Fatty liver, hepatitis, or cirrhosis (a scarring of the liver that destroys the tissue and is a leading cause of death from alcohol)

   d. Pancreatitis, in which muscle spasms block the duct from the pancreas, causes the acidic juices to back up and start digesting the pancreas. This is often very painful and can also cause death.

4. Heart and blood vessels

   a. Heart muscle becomes weaker, and heart expands because it is working harder. Alcohol complicates problems with heart disease.

   b. Peripheral blood vessels are dilated by alcohol. Initially, this causes a sensation of warmth, followed by serious heat loss in the cold. The old habit of drinking alcohol to fend off the cold actually makes the person more susceptible to the cold.

   c. High blood pressure is often associated with alcoholism, but the relationship is not clearly established.

5. Lungs: emphysema occurs most frequently in the alcoholic who also smokes. Alcohol seems to have a direct toxic effect on the cells lining the alveoli, or small air sacs in the lungs, as the alcohol is excreted into the air.

Sobering Up   Contrary to much public opinion, steam baths, vigorous exercise, black coffee, and other sobering-up agents have no effect on the rate at which alcohol is metabolized. Time is the only thing that works.

Tolerance   Tolerance to most of the immediate effects of alcohol develops with frequent use. Regular heavy drinkers may be able to consume two or three times as much alcohol as novice drinkers. Heavy drinkers have to drink more and more to achieve the desired effect.

Withdrawal Symptoms   ***Stage 1 Withdrawal Symptoms*** Withdrawal from alcohol usually begins 6 to 12 hours after the last drink and may even begin in the presence of significant blood alcohol levels. Table 3.3 lists the Stage 1 withdrawal symptoms. These symptoms, in varying degrees, may last anywhere from 3 to 5 days and are relieved by drinking more alcohol.

T A B L E   3 . 3

Stage 1 Alcohol Withdrawal Symptoms

1. Psychomotor agitation
2. Anxiety
3. Insomnia
4. Appetite suppression
5. Gastrointestinal disturbances
6. Elevated heart rate, blood pressure, sweating, and tremors

Stage 2 Withdrawal Symptoms   The onset of Stage 2 withdrawal symptoms is usually within 24 hours after the last drink but may occur as long as 3 days later. Stage 2 consists of the symptoms in Stage 1, plus hallucinations. These may be visual, auditory, tactile, olfactory (smell), or mixed. Although the visual hallucinations usually predominate, olfactory hallucinations are a particularly more ominous sign and may be accompanied by seizures. The delirium tremens—disorientation to person, place, or time—also can be life threatening; this is a true medical emergency, with a 15 percent mortality rate if untreated.

Related Illnesses   Alcoholics have twice the chance of experiencing premature deaths as nonalcoholic persons. Liver disease of varying types is one of the most prominent manifestations of alcoholism. Among young males 20 to 40 years of age, liver cirrhosis is the third fastest growing cause of death, after heart disease and lung cancer. Alcoholics also show higher than normal rates of peptic ulcers, pneumonia, cancer of the upper digestive and respiratory tracts, heart and artery disease, tuberculosis, and suicide.

Many heavy drinkers also suffer vitamin deficiencies, gastritis, sexual impotence, and infections. The more serious alcohol-related neurological disorders include peripheral neuritis (loss of sensation), Korsakoff's psychosis (loss of memory), and Wernicke's encephalopathy (mental confusion).

Fetal Alcohol Syndrome   Alcohol use and abuse by pregnant women is the third leading cause of birth defects, exceeded only by Down syndrome and spina bifida. The four basic abnormalities characteristic of fetal alcohol syndrome are as follows:

1. Distorted facial features. An FAS baby has short fissures in the eyelids, a small or underdeveloped upper lip with thinned vermilion, and a diminished philtrum, the line running between the upper lip and nose.
2. Prenatal onset growth deficiency. FAS babies are usually two standard deviations below normal in weight and height; they exhibit little or no indication of growth spurts to catch up after birth.
3. Reduced central nervous system performance. As a result, FAS babies have mild to moderate mental retardation; microcephaly, or disproportionately small heads; poor coordination; irritability in infancy; and hyperactivity in childhood.

4. Increased frequency of major abnormalities. Such disorders range from gross cardiovascular abnormalities and congenital heart disease to abnormal and malformed limbs.

Alcohol use during the first trimester is often responsible for stillbirths. Research further supports the position that even small doses of alcohol affect the development of the fetus, especially in the first trimester. The only safe dose of alcohol during pregnancy is no alcohol at all.

Antabuse   Some alcoholics have extreme difficulty in abstaining from alcohol. Usually, they choose Antabuse (disulfiram) when other methods to stop drinking have failed. At early stages of recovery, alcoholics may use Antabuse as a deterrent to drinking alcohol, but it must not be viewed as the only modality. (See Chapter 11.)

Alcohol is metabolized by a liver enzyme (aldehyde dehydrogenose) to form acetaldehyde. Normally, acetaldehyde is rapidly metabolized by another enzyme, which breaks it into inert substances, eventually becoming carbon dioxide and water. Antabuse interferes with the enzyme that breaks down acetaldehyde. A person taking Antabuse and drinking alcohol would have a sharp increase in acetaldehyde, resulting in extreme feelings of discomfort, which include nausea and vomiting, flushing, sweating, palpitations, increased heart rate, breathing difficulty, and anxiety. Blood pressure may first rise and then fall, making the person appear to be in shock. Feelings of drowsiness may occur later. People rarely die from an alcohol-Antabuse reaction, but they feel so sick they think they will die. Nevertheless, some people continue to drink alcohol while on Antabuse.

Barbiturates

Barbiturates also belong to the sedative-hypnotic class of drugs and are widely prescribed to decrease central nervous system activity (e.g., induce sleep, relax the nervous system). Barbiturates and barbiturate-like drugs seem to affect the cortex of the brain or those areas related to sleep more than other sedative hypnotics.

Medical Uses   In low doses of 25 to 50 milligrams, the short- or intermediate-acting compounds such as amobarbital (Amytal), pentobarbital (Nembutal), secobarbital (Seconal), and butabarbital (Butisol) treat or prevent acute convulsions associated with tetanus; epilepsy; and an overdose of stimulants such as strychnine, nicotine, or cocaine and the withdrawal symptoms associated with alcoholism and other sedative drug dependence. (See Table 3.4.)

For years, doctors prescribed barbiturates in the treatment of asthma, premenstrual tension, motion sickness, nausea and vomiting, peptic ulcer and other gastrointestinal disturbances, hyperthyroidism, high blood pressure, and other cardiovascular diseases. Now doctors can prescribe many newer drugs, which have fewer side effects and less potential for abuse.

Estimates of Use and Addiction   After minor tranquilizers, barbiturates are prescribed more than any other psychoactive drug in the United States. Most individuals are introduced to barbiturates by physicians, who prescribe them as mild tranquilizers or sleeping pills.

TABLE 3.4

Classification of Barbiturates and Their Street Names

Short-Acting

Amobarbital (Amytal)—known as blues, blue angels, bluebirds, blue devils, blue bullets
Pentobarbital (Nembutal)—known as yellows, yellow jackets, yellow bullets, nembies
Butabarbital (Butisol)

Intermediate-Acting

Phenobarbital (Luminal, Eskabarb)—know as phennies
Secobarbital (Seconal)—known as reds, pinks, red birds, red bullets, red dolls, seccies, F-40s

Long-Acting

Pento-secobarbital (Tuinal)—known as trees, tootsies, double trouble, gorilla pills, rainbows

---

Many individuals find barbiturates make coping with life easier. As tolerance to the tranquilizing and sedating effects set in, individuals increase their doses, often without their physicians' knowledge. Teenagers and young adults take enough barbiturates orally to produce highs the same way as alcohol might be taken. The sources of the supply for these young people are often the black market, the family medicine cabinet, and sometimes manipulation of otherwise legitimate prescriptions.

Illicit use of barbiturates has been on the decline for the past several years in North America. Because they are still prescribed so often for a variety of medical conditions, however, their pharmaceutical use remains widespread, as is their abuse by those who have obtained legitimate prescriptions.

Routes of Administration   Usually taken orally, barbiturates are readily absorbed by the stomach and small intestine. Absorption into the bloodstream can be rapid, especially on an empty stomach. Most barbiturates are white powders, odorless but with a slightly bitter taste. Most often packed in capsules and tablets of varying colors, they are also available as liquids, injectable solutions, and suppositories.

Major Effects   The short-term effects of barbiturates are very similar to those of alcohol. At low doses, barbiturates tend to induce relaxation, a sense of well-being, and drowsiness. At higher doses, the drug reduces the individual's ability to react quickly and to perform skilled, precise tasks. Often there is a feeling of sedation, and the individual may alternate between feelings of euphoria and hostility and aggressiveness. This is very similar to the high-dose reactions under the influence of alcohol.

At still higher doses, the symptoms may be similar to those of drunkenness, with confusion and difficulty communicating. The person may fall into a stupor or sleep. If the dose is high enough, it may impair the respiratory function so severely that the individual stops breathing and dies.

Barbiturates and Sleep   Barbiturates are generally considered by the public as sleep medication. However, long-term barbiturate use can interfere with the rapid eye movement (REM) phase of sleep. REM sleep is associated with an essential feature of healthy sleep—dreaming. Normal functioning is further disturbed with the disruption of REM sleep. When the individual stops taking barbiturates, there is often a rebound effect and more REM sleep occurs. But the dreaming is more intense and frequently turns into a nightmare. The user interprets this as poor sleeping and again takes sleeping pills, often escalating the dose, and a vicious cycle is put into play.

Barbiturates and Pregnancy   Barbiturates should never be taken during pregnancy, unless advised by a physician, because they could cause birth defects. Also, the baby may be born addicted to barbiturates and have potentially dangerous withdrawal symptoms.

Tolerance   Barbiturates used repeatedly over a long period can induce tolerance and physical and psychological dependence. Tolerance to the euphoric effects of the drug develops quickly in many users, so larger and larger amounts of the drug must be taken to achieve the same high.

   The lethal dose is usually only 10 to 15 times the therapeutic dose, so the margin of safety is low. As tolerance develops, the difference between the amount needed to get high may be only one or two pills away from an overdose; such an amount is also potentially lethal in combination with alcohol use.

Withdrawal   Table 3.5 lists the withdrawal symptoms of barbiturates; these and other symptoms may last for days or even months. Anyone greatly addicted to barbiturates also runs a risk of having a grand mal seizure. Grand mal seizures can occur up to two weeks after the barbiturates are withdrawn and can be fatal. This is

TABLE 3.5

Barbiturate Withdrawal

The withdrawal symptoms may include
1. Physical weakness
2. Dizziness
3. Anxiety
4. Tremors
5. Sleeplessness
6. Nausea
7. Abdominal cramps and vomiting

From the third to seventh day of withdrawal, the user may experience
1. Delirium
2. Delusions
3. Hallucinations

why it is essential that barbiturate addicts withdraw under a doctor's supervision, preferably in a medical facility.

Overdose Signs and Symptoms   The signs and symptoms of an overdose include the following:

1. Mood alteration ranging from depression to euphoria
2. Sedation or drowsiness proceeding to stupor and coma with increasing doses. Paradoxical excitement rather than drowsiness may occur, especially in the young or the old.
3. Confusion and disorientation
4. Slurred speech (dysarthria)
5. Staggering gait (ataxia), indicating that motor coordination is impaired
6. Nystagmus, or involuntary rapid eye movement from side to side
7. Pupils constricting a little at first; later as the level of unconsciousness deepens, they dilate
8. Respiratory depression, with a decrease in the oxygen supply to the brain; this can cause death

Barbiturates Used with Other Drugs   Barbiturates are often used in conjunction with stimulants. Amphetamine users often use barbiturates to come down after a prolonged period of amphetamine use. Barbiturates are also used by heroin addicts when their drug of choice is not available.

Barbiturates plus other central nervous system depressants can have a synergistic effect when taken together. People who drink alcohol and use barbiturates run the risk of accidental overdose. Overdoses on barbiturates plus alcohol are more common than on barbiturates alone. (See Table 3.6.)

Methaqualone   Methaqualone was introduced to the American medical market in the mid-1960s for the treatment of insomnia and anxiety. It was originally believed to have none of the abuse potential of short-acting barbiturates. It was alleged to be a safe, nonaddictive sedative; however, this drug has an extremely high abuse potential.

TABLE 3.6

Nonbarbiturates with Barbiturate-like Action

- Chloral hyudrate (Noctec)—known as Mickey Finn, or knock-out drops when used with alcohol
- Methaqualone (Quaalude, Sopor)
- Flurazepam (Dalmane)
- Glutethimide (Doriden)—known as goofers
- Ethchlorvynol (Placidyl)
- Methyprylon (Noludar)
- Paraldehyde

The popularity of methaqualone grew swiftly, given its enthusiastic medical use and street use. Among its most enthusiastic users were college students in the 1970s. Since then, methaqualone has spread not only to high school and college campuses throughout the United States but also into the adult population. Methaqualone use has also become popular among methadone maintenance patients because of the additive high the drug produces in combination with methadone.

Some street names for methaqualone are sopors, ludes, and love drug.

Principally, younger age groups use this illicit drug, with the heaviest concentration of use between high school age and people in their mid-30s. The cost of illicit methaqualone ranges from $4 to $8 per tablet.

Methaqualone is usually taken orally in pill form. Since 1984, pharmaceutical companies can no longer legally produce methaqualone in the United States. The drug is most often found on the street in bootlegged forms, which look real but may or may not contain actual methaqualone.

Following its ingestion, methaqualone is readily absorbed from the gastrointestinal tract. Once transported into the blood plasma, it is distributed in body fat, the liver, and brain tissue.

Relatively low doses (75 milligrams four times a day) produce sedation; larger doses of 150 to 300 milligrams lead to sleep. Those who use the drug to get high often take far larger doses, sometimes 600 to 900 milligrams and much more if they have been using the drug steadily enough to develop a tolerance.

Users describe the sensation produced by methaqualone as "a peaceful calm, a rush, a drunk." Some describe it as a love drug due to methaqualone's alcohol-like symptoms (e.g., loss of motor and muscle control, loss of inhibitions), although, just as with alcohol, actual sexual performance is reduced.

Basically, intoxication with methaqualone is similar to intoxication with barbiturates or alcohol and subjects the individual to similar risks: death by overdose and accidents due to confusion and impaired motor coordination.

Methaqualone has induced headaches, hangovers, fatigue, dizziness, drowsiness, torpor (extreme sluggishness, apathy, dullness), menstrual disturbances, dry mouth, nosebleeds, diarrhea, skin eruptions, lack of appetite, numbness, and pain in the extremities. Researchers have found that a coma occurs following 2.4 grams of Quaalude. Eight to 20 grams have produced severe toxicity and death.

Methaqualone overdoses are less often associated with cardiac and respiratory depression than are overdoses of the oral barbiturates. However, shock and respiratory arrests may occasionally occur. Methaqualone overdose can also result in delirium, restlessness, hypertonia (excessive tension), and muscle spasms leading to convulsions.

As with barbiturates, tolerance to the intoxicating effects of methaqualone develops more rapidly than does tolerance to the lethal dose. Withdrawal from methaqualone dependence carries approximately the same risks as withdrawal from the short-acting barbiturates and can be quite severe for a large addiction.

Japanese researchers have provided a good deal of the information about methaqualone's addiction potential. In Japan, where this drug was once available over the counter, it was widely abused by young people (Tamura 1989). During 1963 to 1966, a survey of drug addicts in Japan found 176 out of 411 (41.8 percent) were addicted to methaqualone. Withdrawal convulsions occurred in 7 percent of the methaqualone addicts and 9 percent developed delirium tremens symptoms. Subsequent studies in England and in the United States have documented cases of physical dependence as manifested by a withdrawal syndrome. The symptoms include insomnia, abdominal cramps, headaches, anorexia, and nightmares.

Research conducted in Philadelphia and at the Haight-Ashbury Clinic in San Francisco has also documented the high abuse potential and dependence-producing properties of methaqualone, as well as its cross-tolerance with the short-acting barbiturates.

Tranquilizers

Minor tranquilizers are drugs that act primarily as antianxiety agents. They reduce anxiety and tension. Major tranquilizers are drugs used over the long term in the treatment of mental illnesses, such as schizophrenia. They are antipsychotic agents. (See Table 3.7.)

All of the antipsychotic drugs can produce Parkinson-like signs and symptoms with tremor, rigidity, and shuffling gait. To counteract these side effects, one of the following anti-Parkinsonism drugs is often prescribed along with the antipsychotic drug: Artane, Cogentin, Kemadrin, or Benadryl.

Because the major tranquilizers do not produce pleasant psychological effects, they are rarely used nonmedically and have no illicit attraction. (See Table 3.8.) The focus of this section is on the minor tranquilizers, which do have an abuse and dependence potential.

Medical Uses   Doctors prescribe the minor tranquilizers mainly for treatment of tension, insomnia, behavioral excitement, and anxiety. Some treat convulsive disorders, symptoms of barbiturate-alcohol dependence, and the anxiety and panic that sometimes result from the use of hallucinogenic drugs. Although fairly high doses are necessary, some minor tranquilizers are also effective muscle relaxants (e.g., Valium may be used in injectable form for this purpose).

TABLE 3.7

Classification of Minor Tranquilizers (Antianxiety Agents)

Benzodiazepines	Meprobamate	Sedating Antihistamines
Valium (diazepam)	Equanil	Atarax, Vistaril (hydroxyzine)
Librium (chlordiazepoxide)	Miltown	Benadryl (diphenhydramine)
Serax (oxazepam)		Sleep-Eze, Sominex, Nytol
Tranxene (chlorazepate)		
Ativan (lorazepam)		
Xanax (alprazolam)		
Halcion (triazolam)		

TABLE 3.8

Classification of Major Tranquilizers (Antipsychotic Agents)

Phenotiazines	Butyrophenones	Thioxanthenes	Other
Thorazine (chlorpromazine)	Haldol (haloperidol)	Navane (thiothixene)	Serpasil (reserpine)
Mellaril (thioridazine)		Taractan (chlorprothixene)	Moban (molindone hydrochloride)
Stelazine (trifluoperazine)			
Compazine (prochlorperazine)			Loxitane
Trilafon (perphenzaine)			
Prolixin (fluphenazine)			

Estimates of Use   Most Americans are introduced to minor tranquilizers by physicians, and most use them according to prescription, but there are large numbers who do not stay within the physician's guidelines. Recent statistics show that the prescribing of tranquilizers is on a downward trend, and some authorities believe this trend may continue.

Routes of Administration   Most minor tranquilizers are usually taken orally as tablets, capsules, or liquids. Occasionally, they are injected for both medical and nonmedical purposes.

Major Effects   With normal therapeutic doses, individuals usually feel well, feel relaxed, and may lose some of their inhibitions. They feel a lessening of anxiety, tension, and agitation.

As the dosage is increased, patients usually feel more sedated and may have a sensation of floating. Many individuals at this dosage level experience some depression of nervous and muscular activity, mental confusion, and physical unsteadiness. High doses may produce the following:

- Drowsiness
- Loss of muscle coordination
- Lethargy
- Disorientation and confusion
- Low blood pressure
- Memory impairment
- Rage reactions
- Moodiness and personality alterations
- Symptoms resembling drunkenness

Obviously, the ability to drive a car under high-dose levels is also impaired. Other side effects may include skin rashes, nausea, loss of sex drive, and menstrual and ovulatory irregularities.

The margin of safety of minor tranquilizers is so wide that death rarely results from use of these drugs alone, with the lethal dose being 100 or more times the effective dose. Where death has occurred, it has often been due to an interaction be-tween the tranquilizer and other drugs, such as alcohol.

Tolerance   With regular use, tolerance can develop to most of the effects of these sedatives. This means that the user has to take increased doses to get the desired effect.

Dependence and Withdrawal   Even though physical dependence and withdrawal can occur with most tranquilizers, these effects are infrequent in relation to the large number of people who take these drugs. On a therapeutic dosage level, addiction may still occur. Escalation of the amount and frequency of the dose without a doctor's orders increases the chance of physical dependence.

Withdrawal from a large habit may involve anxiety states, apprehension, tremors, insomnia, rapid pulse, fever, loss of appetite, nausea, vomiting, stomach cramps, sweating, fainting, and other symptoms. Withdrawal from high-dose tran-quilizer dependence is often done gradually as the individual is tapered off of the medication. A quick withdrawal can produce life-threatening withdrawal symptoms.

Addiction Potential with Alcoholics/Addicts   Physicians should not prescribe minor tranquilizers for patients who are addiction-prone. Pharmaceutical manufacturers warn physicians through medical journal ads and the *Physicians' Desk Reference* that tranquilizers are capable of abuse and dependence, especially when prescribed to addiction-prone individuals. Many patients deny or are unaware of their problems with alcohol and/or drugs, however, and fail to report this to their physicians. A thorough assessment for alcohol/drug problems is necessary before prescribing minor tranquilizers. "Non-medical use of benzodiazepines in the general population is rare and of little or no consequence; on the other hand, benzodiazepines are used with some frequency among populations with histories of drug abuse" (Woods et al. 1988).

Central Nervous System Stimulants
Amphetamines
Overview   Amphetamines are central nervous system stimulants which—until recent years—were widely prescribed by physicians for conditions such as obesity, depression, and narcolepsy (uncontrolled fits of sleep). For certain kinds of hyperactive behavior in children, Ritalin is most commonly prescribed.

Doctors also prescribe amphetamines for Parkinson's disease, epilepsy, nau-sea during pregnancy, bed-wetting, asthma, sedative overdoses, and hypotensive states associated with anesthesia. Because amphetamines relieve sleepiness and fa-tigue, they are widely used nonmedically by students cramming for exams, long-distance truck drivers, nightshift workers, and individuals seeking general stimula-tion. (See Table 3.9.)

In the mid-1960s, a phenomenon new to North America emerged: intra-venous use of massive doses of amphetamines (usually methamphetamines) by chronic abusers, or speed freaks. This abuse pattern had been common in Japan and some parts of Europe following World War II, when stockpiles of amphetamines used by the military were diverted to more general use.

TABLE 3.9

Classification of Stimulants

Amphetamines	Cocaine (Benzoylmethylecognine)	Other Stimulants
Benzedrine (amphetamine)		Ritalin (methylphenidate)
Dexedrine (dextroamphetamine)		Preludin (phenmetrazine)
Methedrine, Desoxyn (methamphetamine)		Tenuate (diethylpropion)
		INH (isoniazid)
		Coffee, colas, tea (caffeine)
		Tobacco (nicotine)

As a result of amphetamines' abuse potential, physicians have sharply restricted their use. Now they prescribe amphetamines primarily for narcolepsy, hyperkinetic syndrome in children, certain mental conditions, and short-term weight control. David Smith and Donald Wesson (1988) note that in 1972, when the U.S. government put federal control over stimulants in the same category as narcotic control, legitimate production of stimulants was reduced by 80 percent.

Street Names for Amphetamines   Common street names are A, AMT, bam, beans, bennies, black beauties, black mollies, brain ticklers, brownies, bumblebees, cartwheels, chalk, chicken powder, crank, Christmas trees, crossroads, cross tops, crystal, dexies, diet pills, dolls, double cross, eye openers, fives, footballs, forwards, hearts, jam, jellybeans, leapers, lid poppers, lightning, meth, pep pills, purple hearts, rippers, sparkle plenties, sparklers, speed, splash, sweets, tens, thrusters, truck drivers, turnabouts, uppers, uppie, ups, wake-ups, water, and white crosses.

Estimates of Use   The Domestic Council Drug Abuse Task Force estimates that close to 500,000 American adults are now using stimulant drugs (primarily amphetamines) regularly and nonmedically. A new and emerging population of methamphetamine users is developing in adolescents and young adults (15 to 30 years of age) (National Institute on Drug Abuse 1989).

Routes of Administration   Amphetamines are available in a variety of forms; tablets and capsules are the most common. Amphetamines are usually taken orally or injected intravenously.

Methamphetamine (speed) is usually in powder or crystal form and is made illicitly. The solid form of methamphetamine with the street name ice was first cooked up in Hawaii. Ice is smoked much like freebase or crack cocaine.

Major Effects   Typical therapeutic doses of amphetamines stimulate the central nervous system, increase blood pressure, widen the pupils, increase respiration rate, depress the appetite, relieve sleepiness, and decrease fatigue and boredom. Other effects include increased awareness and alertness, slight euphoria, elevation of mood and self-confidence (although the ability to perform complex tasks is usually diminished), increased talkativeness and excitement, reduced nausea and gastrointestinal upset, and dry mouth.

Adverse Effects   In some individuals, even a moderate dose of amphetamines can have adverse effects, such as agitation, an inability to concentrate, anxiety, confusion, blurred vision, tremors, and heart palpitations. Higher doses of amphetamines can produce quite severe adverse reactions, which include the following:

- Tremors, palpitations
- Dilated pupils (mydriasis)
- Sweating and flushing, abdominal cramps, nausea
- Tachycardia (rapid heartbeat), heart abnormalities
- Hypertension (later hypotension), circulatory collapse
- Anxiety, agitation, and panic
- Aggression and violent behavior often associated with paranoia
- Rapid breathing, respiratory collapse
- Hallucination (visual and auditory), delirium
- Extremely high fevers
- Convulsions and seizures

Although death reports from amphetamine use are rare, some individuals who are unusually sensitive to these drugs have died as a result of burst blood vessels in the brain, heart failure, or high fever. Amphetamine psychosis, a mental disturbance similar to paranoid schizophrenia, is sometimes associated with high-dose amphetamine use, but many of its symptoms have been observed with moderate dose levels.

Injecting amphetamines causes other complications: unsterile and shared needles cause problems with tetanus, AIDS, abscesses, and hepatitis. The injection of insoluble particles in street speed also causes many problems.

Dependence and Withdrawal   Abruptly stopping amphetamines after chronic heavy use is often followed by symptoms such as fatigue, brain wave abnormalities, prolonged sleep, voracious appetite, stomach cramps, muscle pains, lethargy, and severe emotional depression. Some of these symptoms seem just as dramatic as withdrawal symptoms from depressant drugs.

Withdrawing amphetamines from chronic users does not seem as physically distressing as withdrawal from depressant drugs. There is little evidence of any physical dependence on moderate doses of amphetamines, but researchers frequently report psychological dependence on even low doses.

Prolonged use of amphetamines leads to a broad range of illnesses. Chronic users suffer dehydration, weight loss, and vitamin deficiency. Their reduced resistance to disease allows sores, nonhealing ulcers, and chronic chest infections. Users have a higher than normal rate of liver and cardiovascular disease, hypertensive disorders, and psychiatric problems.

Bootlegged Amphetamines   The newer, tighter regulations imposed on the legitimate prescribing of amphetamines have caused the widespread bootlegging of

Coca Leaves and Cocaine.

DEA/Department of Justice.

amphetamines and substitution of other substances to mimic the amphetamine high. The most common substitutes include ephedrine—a mild stimulant found in some over-the-counter asthma remedies—and phenylpropanolamine, or PPA, the ingredients in most legal diet capsules. The moderate to large amounts of caffeine in most illicit amphetamines sometimes account for the bulk of the ingredients.

Cocaine

Cocaine is a central nervous system stimulant that has gained great popularity in a variety of drug forms. At first, cocaine was expensive; only the wealthy could afford it. Today, crack cocaine is used by every socioeconomic class, making it the scourge of humanity.

Brief History of Cocaine

2500 B.C.: Coca leaves were found in burial sites in Peru.

500 B.C.: In Columbia, South America, large stone monolithic idols possessed puffed-out cheeks, representative of a coca chewer.

Tenth century: Incans started to use the plant referred to as "Mama Coca," and the coca tree was pictured as a beautiful woman.

Eighteenth century: The Spanish took coca leaves back to Europe. However, there was general disinterest in coca by Europeans. One can speculate that the sample of coca leaves taken from South America lost their potency during the trip.

1786: Lamarck named the species of the coca plant *Erythroxylum coca.*

1844: Conflicting reports stated that either Albert Nieman or Gaedecke isolated cocaine.

1878: W.H. Bentley espoused cocaine as a cure for morphine addiction.

1883: Aschenbrandt prescribed the use of cocaine to counteract the battle fatigue of the Bavarian troops.

1883: Sigmund Freud wrote *Uber Coca* praising the medicinal effects of cocaine.

1887: Sigmund Freud recognized cocaine addiction and wrote a book titled *Fear of and Craving for Cocaine.*

Cocaine is obtained from the leaves of *Erythroxylum coca,* a bush grown in parts of South America. Mountain Indians of Peru and Bolivia have chewed coca leaves as a social ritual for more than a thousand years.

The coca leaf was taken to Europe in the nineteenth century and became quite popular in certain circles. Sigmund Freud, the father of psychoanalysis, used cocaine extensively. In 1883, he recommended cocaine for treatment of morphine addiction, alcohol dependence, asthma, digestive disorders, and depression and fatigue. Freud frequently recommended the drug for what was then called neurasthenia (i.e., nervous anxiety). Freud soon realized cocaine was addictive; in 1887, he wrote *Fear of and Craving for Cocaine,* describing dependence on cocaine.

One of the most popular soft drinks of all time, Coca-Cola, originally contained extracts of the coca leaf. Coca was also present in wines such as Vin Mariani, a wine that was extremely popular with the pope and the royal families in Italy and other countries. Today, a little more than 100 years after the cocaine problems of the 1880s, we have another cocaine problem caused by coca products that are far more addicting than those of the past.

Street Names for Cocaine   There are several street names for cocaine: Bernice, bernieds, big C, blow, bombita, bouncing powder, burese, C, charles, charlie, coke, cola, corrine, dream, dust, flake, fly, girl, gold dust, heaven, heaven dust, her, ice (not to be confused with the form of methamphetamine), incentive, jay, joy powder, lady, lady snow, nose candy, nose powder, paradise, poison, powder, rock, schoolboy, snow, star dust, sugar, white, white lady, white powder, and white stuff.

Estimates of Use   In 1994, an estimated 1.4 million Americans were cocaine users. This represents 0.7 percent of the population aged 12 and older, while the estimated number of crack users was about one-half million (*1994 National Household Survey on Drug Abuse* 1995).

This late nineteenth-century ad for Mariani wine, which contained cocaine, portrays the beverage as a panacea for all ills.

Bettmann Archive.

Routes of Administration   Cocaine can be inhaled, injected, or smoked. Cocaine hydrochloride is snorted or injected, while crack cocaine is smoked.

Freebase cocaine is another smokable form of cocaine. Heating up cocaine hydrochloride with a volatile solvent (usually ether) and a base (baby laxative) results in cocaine free of its hydrochloride base, with by-products of water and salt.

Cocaine HCl + ether + base + heat = pure cocaine + NaCl (salt) + H$_2$O (water)

Because this cocaine is extremely pure, the volatile point, or the temperature at which cocaine burns, is raised. This allows freebase cocaine to be smoked without burning it. Simply burning cocaine does not produce a high. Freebase cocaine smoke goes from the lungs to the brain in 6 seconds, resulting in an immediate and intense high. This high lasts only 40 to 50 seconds and requires

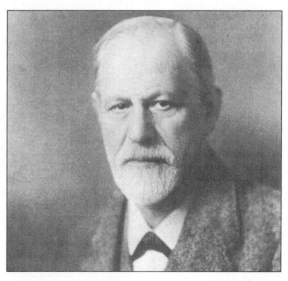

Sigmund Freud.

TABLE 3.10

Cocaine Clinical Syndromes

Cocaine Euphoria	Cocaine Dysphoria	Cocaine Schizophreniform Psychosis
Euphoria	Sadness	Anhedonia (inability to feel pleasure from what would have normally given pleasure)
Affective Lability	Melancholia	
Increased intellectual function	Apathy	Disorientation
Hyperalertness	Inability to concentrate	Hallucinations
Hyperactivity	Painful delusions	Concern with minutia
Anorexia	Anorexia	Stereotyped behavior
Insomnia	Insomnia	Paranoid delusions (parasitosis)
Hypersexuality		Insomnia
Proneness to violence		Proneness to violence

repeated doses, making it extremely expensive to maintain a habit. Crack cocaine is formed by combining cocaine with baking soda; this overrides the hydrochloride acid and allows the crack to be smoked. Crack is sold in small rocks at lower prices to lower economic populations.

Major Effects   The cocaine user experiences 15 to 30 minutes of excitation and euphoria, tends to talk a lot, and feels energetic and self-confident. The effect of cocaine often gives the individual a supreme feeling of well-being, control, and enjoyment of activities that may previously have been mundane. At early stages of use, men report feeling a stimulation of sexuality. Cocaine is very short-acting because it has an extremely short half-life; after the euphoria, psychological depression, nervousness, fatigue, and irritability set in. (See Table 3.10.)

Adverse Effects   With heavy regular use, depression and anxiety can be so severe that the user continues to snort, smoke, or inject cocaine every 20 minutes or so for several hours to avoid the onset of depression. This pattern may develop into binges—or 24 to 48 hours of cocaine use.

Another method to take the edge off cocaine is to inject heroin with cocaine (speedballing). This form of cocaine use was implicated in the death of comedian and actor John Belushi. Addicts frequently turn to the sedative hypnotics (alcohol, tranquilizers, and barbiturates) to counteract the downside after using cocaine. This pattern of sedative hypnotic use may also cause a dependence on drugs in this classification. Acute toxicity can occur from any method of cocaine use. In the past, cocaine was thought of as a rather benign drug. Today, we know that cocaine-related deaths are more common than once thought. Cases of sudden death from cocaine use are increasing. Large doses of cocaine may cause shallow breathing, fever, restlessness, anxiety, and confusion. Even small doses of cocaine can cause a slowing of the heart rate. High doses also have an impact on the motor systems in the brain and spinal cord, resulting in tremors and convulsive movements. Long-term chronic snorting of large amounts of cocaine can destroy

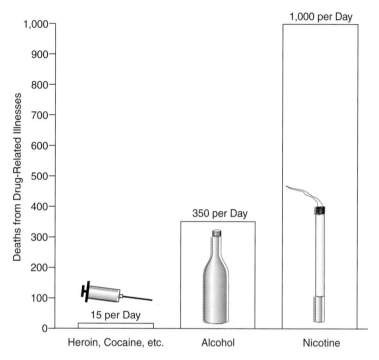

This graph shows the number of deaths from drug-related illnesses for illicit drugs (heroin, cocaine, etc.) and licit drugs (alcohol and nicotine).

tissue in the nose. Nausea, vomiting, and abdominal pains can occur. Death from cocaine overdose is usually due to convulsions, respiratory arrest, and/or the Casey Jones reaction, a condition during which the body acts like a runaway train exceeding its own metabolic limits. People have done and seen some bizarre things under the influence of cocaine. Case studies in Chapter 5 describe these in more detail.

Tolerance and Withdrawal According to our behavioral definition of addiction, cocaine is the most addicting drug known today, especially freebase cocaine. However, a physical tolerance to cocaine does not develop. When cocaine is used, the dopamine neurotransmitters are blocked from reuptake, stranding them in the synaptic clefts. This causes a cessation of stimulant response. However, this is not a classical tolerance reaction. This was one of the factors that led to the tragic miscalculation that cocaine was not an addicting drug. Its intense high and the user's need to avoid the crash or depression makes cocaine highly addicting and contributes to the binge patterns of cocaine use. Cocaine is one of the few chemicals (other than amphetamines and other stimulants) that exist outside of the body and stimulate catecholamine. Catecholamines are responsible for extraordinarily intense reactions to stressful situations (e.g., a father lifts a car to release his child pinned beneath it). The Casey Jones reaction previously mentioned is directly related to this catecholamine-enhancing property of cocaine. Once this reaction is set in motion, it usually results in death. Some people die from nontoxic doses of cocaine due to a phenomenon known as the kindling effect. The brain is primed for, sensitized to, the effect of cocaine, so that one additional dose may trigger firing or discharge, leading to sudden death.

Cocaine Additives   Cocaine purchased on the illicit market is very seldom, if ever, pure by the time it reaches the consumer. As it makes its way from the original source down to the illicit market, the drug's purity is cut with various substances. These additives include mannitol (a mild baby laxative), lactose (milk sugar), or the psychoactive drugs procaine (Novocain), Lidocaine (Xylocaine), benzocaine, tetracaine, and amphetamine. Some individuals have allergic reactions to these substances.

Tobacco

Ironically, although tobacco is the last drug category discussed in this section, it is the most widely abused drug. Despite warnings regarding the health hazards, approximately one-fifth of adults in the United States continue to use tobacco products; tobacco use is the single leading cause of preventable death in this country (U.S. Surgeon General 1988). In comparing deaths related to alcohol and other drugs, smoking tobacco contributes to far more deaths.

Diseases Related to Smoking Tobacco

1. Heart disease (coronary heart disease, increased artherosclerotic disease). Smoking elevates low-density lipoproteins (LDL, or bad cholesterol), while reducing high-density lipoproteins (HDL, or good cholesterol).
2. Peripheral vascular disease
3. Cerebrovascular disease
4. Cancer (lung cancer; cancer of the larynx, mouth, esophagus; contributing factor in urinary cancer, kidney cancer, and pancreatic cancer)
5. Chronic obstructive lung disease and colds (chronic bronchitis and emphysema)

Health Consequences   Some alarming health consequences of tobacco products are

- More women die from lung cancer than breast cancer each year.
- Twenty to 25 percent of female smokers don't stop during pregnancy.
- Over three-fourths of smokers start during the developmental teenage years.
- One out of every five high school seniors smoke cigarettes on a daily basis.
- Chewing tobacco (smokeless tobacco) is the leading cause of oral cancer.
- Approximately 75–80 percent of recovering alcoholics smoke cigarettes.

In recent years, there has been a decrease in use of tobacco products by the general public, yet the use of tobacco, especially by young people, makes them a significant population at-risk for the development of smoking-related diseases.

Hallucinogens
Definition
The term *hallucinogen* is derived from the Latin word *hallucinari,* which means to dream or to wander in the mind. Other terms describing hallucinogens are *psychedelic,* which alters consciousness; *psychotomimetic,* which mimics psychosis; and *psychotogenic,* which produces psychosis. (See Table 3.11.)

Hallucinogens are capable of altering time and space perception; of changing feelings of self-awareness and emotion; of changing one's sense of body image; and of increasing sensitivity to textures and shapes, sounds, and taste. In addition, these drugs bring visions of luminescence, flashes of light, kaleidoscopic patterns, and landscapes. They can also induce hallucinations and feelings of enlightenment and spiritual or religious awakening.

In the past, any substance whose function is to change the habitual way of perceiving and orienting oneself toward one's physical, psychological, and social environment was considered a hallucinogen. As a result, many drugs such as marijuana, PCP, and even cocaine are inappropriately classified as hallucinogens because that is the category they seem to fit best.

In the 1960s, Timothy Leary advocated LSD as a means of "turning on, tuning in, and dropping out" of mainstream lifestyles and thinking. Of the many natural and synthetic hallucinogens, LSD is the most potent by weight and the most thoroughly researched.

Other hallucinogens include mescaline, which is derived from the dried buttons or heads of the peyote cactus; peyote buttons, which can be eaten or made into a tea; and psilocybin, which is found in a wide range of American and Mexican mushrooms. Some street names for peyote are bad seed, big chief, buttons, cactus, P, peyotl, and topi. Common street names for mescaline include beans,

---

TABLE 3.11

Classification of Hallucinogens

LSD-25 (lysergic acid diethylamide)
Dimethyltryptamine (DMT)
Psilocybin (mushrooms)
Psilocin
Bufotenine
Harmine
Mescaline (active part of peyote cactus)
Diethytryptamine (DET)
Dipropryltryptamine (DPT)
Dimethoxymethamphetamine (DOM/STP)
Methylenedioxyamphetamine (MDA)
Belladonna alkaloids (atropine, scopoliamine, and stramonium are found in many medicines for asthma and stomach cramps)
Nutmeg (myristicin)

The Panther Mushroom.

DEA/Dept. of Justice.

big chief, buttons, cactus, cactus buttons, mesc, mescal, and moon topi.

LSD

Common street names for LSD are acid, barrels, beast, Big D, blotter, blue acid, blue cheer, blue heaven, blue mist, brown dots, California sunshine, cap, chocolate chips, contact lens, cubes, cupcakes, D, deeda, domes, dots, electric Kool-Aid, flash, ghost, hawk, haze, L, lysergic, mellow yellows, microdots, orange cubes, paper acid, peace, pearly gates, pellets, pink owsley, purple haze, sacrament, strawberries, strawberry fields, sugar, sugar cubes, sunshine, tabs, ticket twenty-five, wedges, white lightning, window pane, and yellow.

Brief History of LSD

1000 B.C. or earlier: Hallucinogenic mushrooms were used in religious and tribal use.

700 B.C.: Hallucinogenic mandrake root was referred to by the Assyrians and mentioned in the Bible as a fertility substance.

38: Datura was used by the early Incas and other Indians of South America. Peyote cactus (mescaline) was used by Incas and later by Native Americans.

1899: Oklahoma was the first state to outlaw the use of peyote.

April 16, 1943: Albert Hoffman, a chemist who discovered aspirin, working at Sandoz Laboratories in Basel, Switzerland, discovered LSD-25 and experienced the first LSD-25 trip.

Until mid-1960s: LSD was used in experiments in mental hospitals and laboratories to explore the treatment of mental disorders and as a means of studying psychotic behavior.

1960: Timothy Leary, Ph.D., a research professor in the Department of Social and Human Relations at Harvard University, reported in 1960 a "full-blown conversion experience" after eating psilocybin mushrooms. He and Richard Alpert, Ph.D. (today known as lecturer Ram Dass), distributed psilocybin.

1961: Leary and Alpert distributed LSD.

1963: Leary and Alpert were dismissed from Harvard, giving them tremendous publicity. They coined the famous phrase "Turn on, tune in, and drop out."

1965: At an LSD conference, Sidney Cohen summarized the research on LSD use with psychiatric patients and other experiments.

1969: The Woodstock Festival took place in Woodstock, New York.

1960s and 1970s: LSD was extremely popular on the streets, especially among young people and college students.

1992–93: An increase in the trend of LSD use by young people became evident.

Estimates of Use

In comparison with the use of hallucinogens in the late 1960s, today's use rate is smaller. But, contrary to media reports, that use has not all but died out. These

LSD Blotter Paper

Psilocybe Mushroom

Phencyclidine (PCP)

Peyote Cactus

drugs continue to be taken by millions of people in the United States each year. LSD is shown to be the most commonly used hallucinogen. In 1994, LSD use was 1.0 percent for persons 18 to 25 years old and 0.5 percent for youth (*1994 National Household Survey on Drug Abuse* 1995). LSD is easily manufactured, and hallucinogenic mushrooms grow wild in many states, as do many plants with hallucinogenic or toxic-hallucinogenic properties. (See the drug update section earlier in this chapter.)

Routes of Administration

Hallucinogens are usually ingested orally, but they may be smoked, snorted, or injected. Because such small amounts are required at any one time (25 to 150 millionths of a gram), LSD is often impregnated in sugar pills, blotter paper, or small gelatin squares. The nasty taste of some hallucinogens requires mixing them with other substances to counteract their taste. Teas and broths are a common method of ingesting hallucinogens.

Major Effects

The effects of hallucinogens are influenced by the personality of the user, the expectations of use, the user's general experience with drugs, the mind set of the individual, and, most important, the setting. The right group of trusting friends, a comfortable, soothing environment (e.g., dim lights and soft music), and someone experienced with hallucinogens are described as integral in developing a good hallucinogenic trip.

As a result of all these variables, users of hallucinogens report a wide range of reactions. Some individuals feel an insight and expanded consciousness, while others report a discomfort and fear of losing control that is quite disturbing. Generally, low to moderate doses of hallucinogens produce mood and perceptual alterations. LSD and other hallucinogens can produce profound effects on the user's thinking, self-awareness, and emotions. Hallucinogens distort time and space perception and induce hallucinations.

Adverse Effects

Hallucinogenic experiences can sometimes add to existing neuroses, or character disorders, and can produce transient waves of mild anxiety, paranoia, or severe panic. Flashbacks (recurrences of negative hallucinogenic experiences) usually occur within a year or less from the previous use of hallucinogens. However, the incidence of flashbacks occurring is relatively small. Flashbacks can occur in individuals who have used hallucinogens excessively and in the occasional or first-time user.

Accidents are very common under the influence of hallucinogens. The high degree of suggestibility and perceptual distortions and hallucinations often lead to accidents. Such accidents include walking through a plate glass window; jumping from a roof due to the coaxing of a friend (high degree of suggestibility); and suffering accidental falls, drownings, and car accidents.

Tolerance and Dependence

Researchers have observed psychological dependence in long-term LSD users but have rarely reported dependence as a consequence of other hallucinogenic use. Hallucinogenic trips can be of long duration, compared with other drug use. Users tend to trip for from 4 to 6 hours to 12 to 24 hours. Following these trips, users are usually quite tired. This often necessitates periods of getting back to normal functioning before again using hallucinogens. Because of this pattern of occasional or intermittent use of hallucinogens, physical dependence is unlikely under most conditions. Tolerance has been shown to develop to some of the psychological and physiological effects of LSD. Quite frequently, there is cross-tolerance to other hallucinogens. For example, an individual who has recently been taking LSD generally shows a reduced response to mescaline and psilocybin.

Marijuana Plant.

Cannabis Sativa

Cannabis refers to any product of the plant *Cannabis sativa,* which grows in most parts of the world. In North America, the most commonly used products derived from this plant are marijuana and hashish. Marijuana is the unprocessed, dried leaves, flowers, seeds, and stems of the plant. Hashish is a more potent product processed from the resin of this herb. Researchers have obtained more than 300 cannabis products (cannabinoids) from cannabis. They have isolated and synthesized the most active ingredient in marijuana. This product, tetrahydrocannabinol (THC), is the psychoactive compound found in the greatest amount in the plant; it is thought to produce most of the high.

Street Names

Common street names for marijuana include Acapulco gold, ace, African black, aunt mary, baby, bale, bomb, boo, brick, broccoli, bush, Canadian black, charge, Colombian, doobie, dry high, fatty, fingers, flowers, gage, ganga, gauge, giggleweed, grass, green, grefa, greta, grifa, grillo, grunt, hay, hemp, herb, homegrown, Indian hay, Indian hemp, J, jane, jay smoke, joint, joy stick, juanita, kick sticks, kif, killer, killer weed, kilter, loco, mary, maryann, maryjane, mary warner, mary weaver, meserole (messerole), Mexican brown, Mexican green, Mexican locoweed, MJ, mooca, moota, mooters, mootie, mota, mother, mu, muggles, muta, number, Panama gold, Panama red, panatella, pin, pode, pot, ragweed, rainy day woman, red dirt, reefer, roach, root, sassafras, sinsemilla, smoke, snop, stick, sweet lucy, tea, Texas tea, twist, weed, wheat, yerba, and Zacatecas purple. Street names for hashish include black hash, black Russian, blond hash, canned sativa, hash, Lebanese, and mahjuema.

Brief History of Marijuana

2737 B.C.: The earliest reference to marijuana by a Chinese treatise on pharmacology was attributed to Emperor Shen Nung.

Second century B.C.: The Scythians, a warlike and mobile Middle Eastern tribe, spread cannabis into Egypt and then northward to Russia and Europe. They had a ritual of throwing hemp seeds on heated stones and inhaling the vapors (funeral rite).

650 B.C.: The use of cannabis was mentioned in Persia and Assyria.

400 B.C.: The use of cannabis was mentioned in Rome.

1545: The first record of a marijuana plant in the New World occurred when Spanish traders introduced marijuana to Chile.

1611: Sir Walter Raleigh was ordered by the British to grow hemp in his Virginia colony. Hemp was much needed for the strong shipbuilding industry of the time.

1765: George Washington grew marijuana hemp and is said to have experimented with the medicinal or intoxicating potency of the plants.

1804–1844: Jacques-Joseph Moreau of France used marijuana in the treatment of melancolia, hypomania, and other forms of mental disorder.

1839: W.B. O'Shaughnessy, a young chemistry professor, used marijuana for medicinal use as an anticonvulsant and an appetite stimulant.

1846: A group of French writers formed the "Club des Hachichias," meeting in Paris once a month, where they often smoked marijuana. The meetings were attended by Victor Hugo, Baudelaire, Dumas, Gautier, and De Nerval.

Early 1900s: It is believed that the drug and use of the word *marijuana* were introduced to the United States by migrant Mexican laborers.

1937: Henry Anslinger, commissioner of the Bureau of Narcotics, campaigned on the dangers of marijuana.

1937: The federal government developed the Marijuana Tax Act and used taxes to outlaw the drug.

October 1969: A Gallup Poll estimated that 10 million Americans, half of them under 21 years of age, have smoked marijuana.

1970: The Controlled Substance Act, supported by the American Medical Association, reported that marijuana had no potential medicinal use, ignoring years of medical evidence to the contrary.

Estimates of Use

Marijuana is the most widely used of all illicit drugs. By various estimates, 35–50 million Americans have tried this drug, and 12–18 million are regular users of two or more joints per week (National Institute on Drug Abuse 1989).

Medical Uses

Cannabis, primarily in the form of synthetic THC, has been under scientific investigation in recent years to ascertain its potential therapeutic uses. One approved therapeutic use is as an antiemetic (antivomiting) agent for the nausea and vomiting associated with chemotherapy treatment for cancer patients. It is also medically used to relieve the intraocular pressure accompanying glaucoma. Both of these medical uses are the most well researched. Other potential medical uses of marijuana researched thus far include spasm relief, asthma relief, anxiety reduction, and relief of alcohol withdrawal symptoms. Studies in these areas have not been as prolific, or as conclusive, as those regarding chemotherapy and glaucoma (Solomons and Neppve 1989).

Thirty-four states currently have statutes on the books allowing marijuana, typically in the form of THC, to be used in medical research and/or medical treatment as a part of a clinical investigation. The number of states that have actually implemented these procedures is much smaller. The political and moral/ethical emotionality of our times may further hinder these investigations into the effectiveness of marijuana in medical research. For this reason, other synthetically produced cannabis derivatives are also under investigation.

Routes of Administration

Marijuana can be smoked in hand-rolled cigarettes or joints. Today's higher-potency marijuana is usually smoked in a pipe—most frequently, a water pipe. This allows the most intense high with the least waste of the marijuana.

Generally, hashish has a much higher THC content, though it varies widely in potency. Hashish can be crumbled and rolled into a cigarette for smoking; often, it is mixed with a lower-grade marijuana or tobacco. In this country, hashish is normally smoked in a water pipe.

Marijuana and hashish can also be eaten in cookies, brownies, and other food or made into a tea. In this form, the high lasts longer, since it is slowed down by the digestive processes.

Cannabis resin is not water soluble, so the drug cannot be injected. The few who have tried using it this way usually experienced violent convulsions.

Major Effects

The effects of cannabis depend on the potency of the drug, the method of use, and the experience and expectations of the user regarding what will happen. For low-dose periodic use, the common effects of marijuana use are

- Feelings of exhilaration, relaxation, giddiness
- Minor increase in heart rate
- Drowsiness, dry mouth and throat, bloodshot eyes
- Impaired short-term memory
- Altered states of time and space
- Dilated pupils

Increased Potency of Marijuana

You might remember hearing about types of marijuana such as Acapulco gold, Maui Wowi, or Panama red. Most of the potent marijuana in the 1960s was imported from these places. Today, homegrown marijuana is the staple of American pot smokers. The more than 22 million pot smokers in the United States prefer the high-potency sinsemilla grown in hidden caches throughout the United States. Humboldt County in California is an example of this homegrown cultivation. The California gold rush still goes on there in the form of marijuana crops, despite increased eradication efforts.

In the 1960s, the THC content of marijuana was 1–2 percent in potency. Most users would smoke half a joint to get high. Two or three joints passed among friends could get everyone high. Today, the THC content of marijuana averages 6 percent. One hit is enough to keep an individual loaded. Today, hashish is 10 percent THC, and hash oil is 20 percent THC. This increase in the potency of marijuana means we are looking at a new drug with new problems. The research of the past with marijuana in the 1–2 percent THC level does not apply to marijuana now in use.

Subjective effects of cannabis intoxication have been reported in hundreds of different ways. Common reports include happiness, warmth, conviviality, camaraderie, and the ability to enjoy music and art better than when sober. Reactions to marijuana depend a great deal on the attitude of the user and the compatibility of the surroundings (set and setting). Cannabis is sometimes classified as a mild hallucinogen. With the increase in potency of marijuana, this classification may be warranted.

Adverse Effects

The long-term effects of chronic cannabis use are at the heart of the current medical debate on this drug. Strong psychological dependence does develop in many regular users of marijuana, as evidenced by a need for cannabis use every day to perform certain tasks, to relax and unwind, or to sleep. The individual's life begins to revolve around the use of marijuana as a primary activity. The user tends to use marijuana more frequently throughout the day and evening.

Withdrawal symptoms after steady use may include irritability, decreased appetite, restlessness, sleep disturbances, sweating, nausea, or diarrhea. Hangovers the next morning are not uncommon. However, unlike the alcohol hangover, which causes headaches and sensitive optic nerves, the cannabis hangover is more likely to be light-headedness characterized by the inability to gather thoughts. When the drug is ingested, the effect can linger on for an entire day, along with nausea, body aches, and other symptoms.

Despite the lack of classic withdrawal symptoms, some patterns of marijuana use fit the behavioral definition of addiction. Researchers have well established the fact that chronic marijuana use can cause physical dependence by identifying full-blown withdrawal symptoms in the newborn babies of marijuana-dependent mothers. Treatment for the addiction to marijuana requires the support of an outpatient treatment counselor knowledgeable about alcohol/drug recovery and marijuana dependence. Marijuana Anonymous groups have also developed to meet the rising incidence of dependence on marijuana.

Anxiety and panic reactions are common with chronic marijuana use. Many individuals who have used marijuana to self-medicate affective disorders, such as depression and bipolar disorder, can experience severe anxiety and panic reactions. Individuals experiencing psychologically negative reactions may require temporary hospitalization so they don't get out of control and hurt themselves or others.

Damage to the Respiratory System

The tars in cannabis smoke are 50 percent greater by weight than tobacco tars and 70 percent higher in cancer-producing substances. Considering that marijuana is deeply inhaled and the smoke is held in the lungs, instead of passively inhaled, as in cigarette smoking, the cancer-causing risk is increased by marijuana smoking.

Long-term, heavy smoking of cannabis is associated with bronchial problems, sore throat, and chronic coughing. These conditions may be more severe in chronic hashish users. In addition, those who smoke tobacco as well as cannabis products have an added risk of bronchial problems and cancer.

Immune System Effects

Research suggests that cannabis, particularly when used regularly, tends to suppress the body's immune response and ability to combat infections (Cohen 1986). Marijuana temporarily arrests the maturation of developing t-cells, which protect the body from colds and other bacterial infections. This increases the chances of illness due to either bacteria or viruses. The most prominent indication of this effect is the higher incidence of bronchial infections, coughing, bronchitis, and pneumonia noted among chronic, heavy marijuana users.

Reproductive System Effects

Chronic use of cannabis decreases sperm motility and serum testosterone in men and interferes with the menstrual cycle in women, thus affecting fertility. Most of these effects are reversed after marijuana use is discontinued. Marijuana is suspected to be harmful to the fetuses in pregnant women; research with rhesus monkeys has shown pregnancy problems such as stillbirth and spontaneous abortion. Reduced birth weight is also a characteristic of surviving fetuses.

Brain System Effects

Considerable debate continues over the effects of cannabis on the brain. A certain percentage of users develop lethargy, apathy, and disorientation, which persist long after chronic use has been discontinued. Fortunately, these effects appear to wear off gradually. Some researchers claim that long-term changes occur in some brain wave patterns; these claims are being investigated further.

Impairment of Maturation Process

Most researchers agree that cannabis use, during the primary developmental years of 11 to 15, in particular, interferes with physical and mental maturation processes and impedes emotional development. Research describes an amotivational syndrome with symptoms of apathy, lethargy, and a general lack of involvement and motivation in growth and developmental activities.

Marijuana and Driving

Cannabis intoxication and chronic marijuana use impair short-term memory, alter the user's sense of time and space, and impair overall coordination and motor functioning. The ability to track other vehicles is also impaired and is a major problem in driving a car. Tracking involves judging time, distance, and the speed of other cars. Skills such as merging into traffic, making U-turns, and performing other driving tasks require tracking skills. Adding another drug, such as alcohol, only makes the situation worse. Many persons insist that their driving performance is improved under the influence of marijuana. This is due to their increased sensitivity to enjoying driving, not to a realistic evaluation of driving ability.

Smoking marijuana also makes it very dangerous to operate machinery and other equipment, since perception and timing are off, and the drug may also produce fatigue and drowsiness.

A study of airplane pilots reported that, after smoking marijuana, performance was impaired up to two to three days later, despite the pilots' thinking that they did extremely well on simulated tests (Rohr 1989). Other problems include (1) true allergic reactions to cannabis for a small minority of users; (2) gastrointestinal disturbances and weight loss among a small percentage of heavy users; and (3) difficulty in medical control of some diabetic users.

Inhalants

From time to time, the phenomenon of inhalant use is brought to public attention. In the 1960s, there was an epidemic of glue sniffing. Nowadays, there is still a consistent use of various solvents, aerosols, and other gases that people inhale to get high. For young people, people of color, and minorities who do not have the money to buy drugs, inhalant use is more prevalent. And, in certain locations, the problem is much more serious because of the number of young people who use inhalants to get high, yet this is hardly a modern-day phenomenon. Table 3.12 lists some common inhalants.

Brief History

Some inhalants and anesthetics, such as nitrous oxide, ether, and chloroform, were used recreationally in the nineteenth century, especially during times of liquor scarcity. This occurred in Europe, Great Britain, and North America, where ether inhalation parties were common among students and physicians.

In the 1960s, the inhalation of volatile substances such as plastic model glue, nail polish removers, and aerosol sprays occurred frequently among adolescents. A wave of antiglue-sniffing publicity at the time resulted in many local and state laws prohibiting minors from buying such substances. In spite of these laws, inhalant vapors and sprays continue to be used to this day, partially because of the widespread

---

TABLE 3.12

Classification of Inhalants

A wide variety of names apply to inhaled substances. Many liquids also contain alcohol and petroleum distillates.

Naphtha	Fluorocarbon propellants
Benzene	Nitrous oxide
Acetone	Amyl nitrite, butyl nitrite
Toluene	Anesthetic gases (e.g., ether, chloroform)
Carbon tetrachloride	Gasoline

application of such products in household use and partially because of ineffective legislation and enforcement.

In the 1970s and 1980s, paint became the primary inhalant of abuse. Users sprayed cans of paint, preferably gold and silver, into rags which they stuffed under their noses to inhale the fumes. These huffers (paint inhalers) were often inner-city Latinos and other young people of color. Native American youth have an extremely high incidence of gasoline inhalant use. In 1994, the 12- to 17-year-old age group had the highest rate of current inhalant use—1.6 percent (*1994 National Household Survey on Drug Abuse* 1995).

Route of Administration

Inhalation is accomplished in any number of ways, depending on the ingenuity of the user. Inhaling fumes can be accomplished by placing the substance on a rag; placing or spraying the substance in a plastic bag; or, in the case of some pressurized gases, filling up a balloon, then waiting for the frozen vapor to warm up (if necessary) before inhaling. Users also sometimes go into a food market, smash the bottom of whipped cream cans, and squirt the gas from the broken containers into the backs of their throats. This aerosol freon gives them a cheap high.

Absorption of gases and volatile liquids is efficient and rapid. Absorption into tissues begins with the nasal mucous membranes. The major absorption site is the lungs, where substances enter the bloodstream. From the lungs, substances are distributed directly to the brain and other organ systems. They also enter fatty tissue.

Available Forms of Inhalants

Glue, model cement, fingernail polish removers, various cosmetics, various cleaning solvents, gasoline, paint, paint thinners, lighter fluids, antifreeze, aerosol cans, and white correction fluids can all be inhaled.

Major Effects

Users report a feeling of well-being, a reduction of inhibitions, and an elevated mood. In many respects, the effects are similar to those produced by alcohol and other sedatives. Higher doses often produce laughing and giddiness, feelings of floating, dizziness, time and space distortions, and illusions. (See Table 3.13.) Some substances induce psychedelic effects. An inhalant's effects may last anywhere from five minutes to an hour, depending on the substance and the dose.

Many people do not understand why anyone would actively seek a high from inhalants. They forget how young children often twirl to feel the effect of dizziness and how children, adolescents, and even adults are exhilarated by the rides at amusement parks, especially the rides that give them feelings of vertigo. These effects are altered states of consciousness that are reinforcing to many individuals. Such is the case with inhalant abusers. Other reasons for using inhalants include (1) recreation (fun, mood elevation, the high); (2) peer group influence ("it was what everyone was doing"); (3) cost effectiveness (a quicker and cheaper high); and (4) easy availability.

TABLE 3.13

Signs and Symptoms of Inhalant Use

1. Slurred speech
2. Odor of the substance being used
3. Mental disorientation or confusion
4. Headaches, dizziness, and weakness
5. Muscle spasms in the neck, chest, or lower extremities
6. Euphoria, exaggerated feeling of well-being
7. Loss of balance and ataxia (uncoordinated walk)
8. Nystagmus (eye movement from side to side)

Tolerance and Dependence

When use of volatile substances continues for a long time and becomes heavy, tolerance may develop. Physical dependence with withdrawal symptoms has also occurred among some chronic users. These withdrawal symptoms include hallucinations, headaches, chills, delirium tremens, and stomach cramps. Hangovers lasting several days have also occurred.

There is cross-tolerance between some solvents and central nervous system depressants. For example, skid row alcoholics inhale hydrocarbon vapors from kerosene or spray paint when they run out of liquor. These solvents forestall withdrawal symptoms from the alcohol, especially delirium tremens.

Alcohol and barbiturates potentiate some of the adverse effects of certain solvents. Consequently, users risk unconsciousness or even heart failure if they add the effects of alcohol to the effects of volatile solvents.

Acute Adverse Effects

Acute use of solvents often brings on confusion, drunkenness, slurred speech, numbness, runny nose, tears, headache, and muscular incoordination. Frequently, there is nausea and vomiting. Due to impaired judgment from solvent use, users often feel confusion, panic, irritation, tension, and hyperactivity and become physically aggressive.

In cases of high dosage, the general sedative-anesthetic effects take over, resulting in drowsiness, stupor, respiratory depression, and unconsciousness. Extremely heavy use can inhibit breathing and bring on death.

Many of these substances are capable of sensitizing the heart to adrenaline. Since the early 1960s, heart failure due to this effect has been suspected in hundreds of users. This has been referred to as sudden sniffing death syndrome (SSD).

Some deaths have been directly attributed to solvent use. Most of them are due to suffocation when the users faint from inhalation and their noses and mouths remain covered by the plastic bags or when they suffocate in their own vomit. Additional acute adverse effects depend on the specific products and their chemical makeup.

Long-Term Effects

Some temporary abnormalities take place in liver and kidney function and bone marrow activity; gastritis, hepatitis, jaundice, blood abnormalities, and peptic ulcers also occur.

Chronic users have exhibited slow-healing ulcers around their mouths and noses. Other effects are loss of appetite, weight loss, and nutritional disorders. Brain damage also results from regular solvent use; most of the time, this has been reversible (without permanent effect) once the use was stopped. Reports of chromosome damage and blood abnormalities as a result of solvent inhaling have not yet been conclusively proven and remain under study (Ashton 1990).

With so many different kinds of solvents and hydrocarbons with chemically different structures, it is impossible to predict the long-term effects of the inhalation of all possible substances. Recent information suggests that some substances, such as toluene, may actually be less harmful than previously believed. On the other hand, long-term use of other substances, such as n-hexane, which is commonly found in some plastic cements, gasoline, various adhesives, and rubber cements, may cause permanent damage to the muscles. Because spray paint, aerosols, glues, and other such substances often contain a half-dozen or more ingredients in combination, researchers have had a great deal of difficulty ascertaining the exact damage potential for humans (Ashton 1990).

Phencyclidine

Phencyclidine (PCP) is a drug that cannot be classified properly as a hallucinogen, a stimulant, or a depressant, causing it to be listed in a separate drug category. Originally, PCP was developed in the 1950s as a sedative, general anesthetic, and analgesic. In clinical testing, it worked fine as a painkiller, although subjects often developed visual disturbances, severe agitation, and other unpleasant side effects. These side effects caused its discontinued use with humans. Until 1978, phencyclidine was sold as a veterinary medication for immobilizing primates and other large animals. Its use as an illicit drug began in the mid-1960s.

Street Names for PCP

Common street names for PCP are angel dust, animal trank, aurora borealis, DOA, dust, elephant, hog, peace, peace pill, rocket fuel, supergrass, and tic tac.

Estimates of Use

The geographic patterns of PCP use are haphazard. It has long been popular on the West Coast and in certain large cities; recently, the geographical pattern of use has become more widespread.

The majority of users are young, approximately 12 to 18 years of age, though there is use by young children and adults. (PCP users inadvertently exposed infants to PCP when they stored their drugs in empty milk bottles.) Few users have been involved for as long as 10 years, probably due to negative effects, resulting in discontinuance or a switch to another intoxicant (Thombs 1989).

Routes of Administration

PCP is a white, crystalline powder, soluble in water. Most commonly smoked or ingested, it may occasionally be injected. As tablets or capsules, PCP commonly comes in various sizes and colors. When PCP is smoked, users sprinkle the drug over mint leaves, marijuana, tobacco, or other substances, or they spray PCP liquid onto the substance to be smoked. One popular method is to dip cigarettes into liquid PCP. Given all these possibilities, this drug may appear as a drug or be disguised to look like any number of other substances.

Major Effects

With a moderate or low dose, PCP produces a state of euphoria lasting three to five hours when smoked or five to eight hours when eaten. Reactions to the drug vary greatly; much depends on the personality of the user and the circumstances surrounding the use (set and setting). Users who have bought this drug thinking it was THC have sworn that the high was like a heavy marijuana intoxication. When PCP is misrepresented as a hallucinogen, users report LSD experiences. Users who believe they are getting PCP, however, seldom have these convictions.

The most common reactions from moderate to low doses are auditory, visual, time, and other sensory disturbances. The most consistent effect is deadening of the extremities. Due to the drug's anesthetic properties, users lose control of their muscles. Depending on the individual, the overall reaction may vary anywhere from hyperactivity to complete immobility. The drug, though not a true hallucinogen, may mimic hallucinogenic drugs in some ways. It has been described by one authority as a *delusionogen,* a term that may more accurately describe its effect on the user.

Intoxication by PCP produces an experience of tranquilization, euphoria, inebriation, dissociation, and usually tactile and auditory hallucinations. The most common effects are changes in body imagery, perceptual distortions, and feelings of apathy and estrangement. The experience often includes drowsiness, inability to verbalize, and feelings of nothingness or emptiness. Reports of difficulty in thinking, poor concentration, and preoccupation with death are frequent.

Adverse Effects

As with most other drugs, for some users occasional recreational or social use of small amounts of PCP does not cause undesirable side effects. However, this situation is likely to change when users take or smoke larger doses or smaller amounts consistently day after day. Users often smoke or ingest other drugs in addition to PCP, causing many unusual reactions.

Accidents

With high doses of PCP, accidents are common. Because PCP produces a loss of feeling, users frequently report cuts, bruises, and torn muscles and ligaments. The dissociative effects of PCP may make users believe these injuries are happening to someone else at the time.

In the heyday of PCP use in southern California in the 1960s, high doses resulted in many drownings. In those drownings, the individuals under the influence of PCP became disoriented; once underwater, they did not know which way was up. Drownings also result when users are so anesthetized that they forget to breathe; friends who are also stoned may not realize what is taking place (Thombs 1989).

Violence

Higher or consistent doses of PCP have also led to incidents of violence. These vary widely, but many are characterized by the user's inability to feel pain. The result is a situation where the user feels extraordinary strength and immunity to pain. Police have reported high-dose PCP users breaking out of steel handcuffs, failing to stop an attack even though shot several times, coming forward and attacking police, or bleeding to death because of an inability to feel the injury inflicted during an attack. Despite several hundred reports of incidents like these, in relation to the millions who use this drug, they are considered rare.

More common adverse reactions include the following:

- Paranoia
- Severe agitation
- A severe withdrawn or isolated feeling
- Bizarre delusions
- Increases in heart rate, blood pressure
- Sweating, salivation, and flushing of the skin (these increase according to the dose)
- Nystagmus (jerky eye movements) and other reactions

PCP is unsafe to use during pregnancy, though the exact potential for damage to the fetus is unknown. PCP may also interfere with the hormones governing normal growth and development in the adolescent user. The principal proven negative effects on youthful users, however, relate to a decreased learning capacity, difficulty in concentration, poor grades, and poor social adjustment.

Unpredictable episodes of panic may occur. Latent psychopathology may be unmasked or triggered either by acute doses or by patterns of chronic use, as evidenced by episodes of violence, paranoia, and so forth. With prolonged regular PCP use, the effects can linger after the intoxication has worn off, necessitating therapy or rehabilitation. Flashbacks are also reported from prolonged PCP use. With very large doses, convulsions or coma may occur.

Several PCP deaths have been due to the direct effects of the drug. Other deaths have been attributed to PCP combined with other drugs, particularly central nervous system depressants. As mentioned earlier, deaths are more frequently due to accidental causes while under the influence.

Tolerance and Dependence

PCP does not appear to be physically addictive, even though some tolerance does develop in regular users. When used orally, PCP is most often used only occasionally. When smoked, it is very often used more frequently and can create a very strong psychological dependence. Few data substantiate a withdrawal syndrome with PCP, though the drug often produces aftereffects lasting many months after use is discontinued. One of these aftereffects is depression, which can last up to a year; if untreated, it can lead to relapse and suicide.

⚔ Athletes and Drugs

Athletes have been using drugs to enhance their performance since ancient times. The use of drugs by athletes is almost as old as the Olympic games themselves.

In the marathon event of the 1904 Olympic games in St. Louis, Missouri, the winning runner was American Thomas Hicks, who was aided by a heady cocktail of brandy and strychnine (a stimulant at low doses, a poison at high doses). Today, more than 50 psychomotor stimulant drugs are banned from use during an Olympic competition.

Caffeine

Comedian George Carlin once described coffee as "the low end of the speed spectrum." The International Olympic Committee found that this joke contains a grain of truth. After high concentrations of caffeine were found in several competitors' urine during the 1976 summer Olympic games, studies were conducted to see if caffeine affects athletic performance.

Controlled studies involved both athletes and nonathletes using cycle ergometers. Results showed that the caffeine present in two and a half cups of coffee is sufficient to increase endurance, as measured by maximal oxygen consumption when cycling to exhaustion. A further study involving five young athletes concluded that small doses of caffeine significantly increase the power of leg muscle contractions. The enhancement, however, is limited to endurance athletes. Caffeine does not significantly improve performance during maximal short-term bursts of exercise (Lombardo 1990).

Based on this information and other reports, the International Olympic Committee banned caffeine in amounts greater than 12 ug-ml. An average of four cups of coffee could produce this level.

Caffeine is also produced synthetically, used in some pain-killing preparations, and sold over the counter in diet preparations and caffeine tablets.

The adverse effects of caffeine are mainly dose-related. Depending on the individual's sensitivity, symptoms may include headaches, tremors, nausea, and irregular heartbeat, especially in the 200 to 500 milligram dose range.

A particular effect that may have significance to athletes is the increase in urine output. This might not only increase the number of involuntary bathroom stops during an endurance event but also have potential implications for the athletes' hydration status.

Caffeinism is now a recognized entity. People have gone to emergency rooms complaining of heart palpitations, restlessness, anxiety, insomnia, and myriad other symptoms directly attributable to their high caffeine intake. People who consume significant amounts of coffee daily and then taper off too rapidly suffer from caffeine abstinence syndrome. Withdrawal symptoms include headaches, drowsiness, lethargy, irritability, and depression.

Chewing Tobacco

Epidemiologically, the percentage of smokers among athletes in the United States has declined, along with the decreasing trend in the general population. The use of chewing tobacco, however, remains inordinately high among athletes. Part of this can certainly be ascribed to new marketing and promotion campaigns by the tobacco companies, as well as the almost mythic, traditional relationship of "chewing" tobacco to the great American pastime of baseball. Ironically, the original baseball cards advertised tobacco. Long ago, politicians recognized the health hazards and declared chewing and spitting tobacco illegal in most places—except the baseball park.

From 1978 to 1985, celebrity athletes promoted chewing tobacco. Free supply programs and heavy advertising at sporting events stimulated the sale of chewing tobacco. As a result, chewing tobacco saw a 55 percent rise in sales at a time when cigarette sales dropped off. In 1970, men 55 and older were the heaviest users of chewing tobacco. By 1985, males under the age of 20 displaced them. Smokeless tobacco, a marketing label for chewing tobacco, is used by kindergarten children in Arkansas and Alaska; in Texas, reportedly, up to one-third of varsity football and baseball players use smokeless tobacco (Lombardo 1985).

Many people have been misled into thinking that smokeless tobacco is a safe alternative to smoking. The surgeon general's *Report on the Health Consequences of Smokeless Tobacco Use* concluded that smokeless tobacco is causally related to oral cancer and gum recession, that it can lead to dependence on nicotine, and that it is not a safe alternative to cigarettes (U.S. Surgeon General 1988).

Nonetheless, some athletes use nicotine products for their perceived stimulating effect before their events, while others paradoxically use the tobacco for its calming effect. Still others state they use nicotine for its effect on the satiety center ("I'll gain weight if I stop smoking"). Some just use tobacco products for personal rather than performance reasons.

Regarding the widely held misconception that smokeless tobacco enhances performance, it is critical to make known that nicotine does not heighten energy or strength. In reality, the user who smokes, chews, or snorts nicotine is simply experiencing elevation in heart rate and blood pressure. The perceived relaxation is actually relief from the craving associated with nicotine withdrawal.

Clearly, young people will continue chewing smokeless tobacco unless professional athletes, coaches, and managers act as role models and point out the negative effects of all tobacco products.

The relationship between caffeine consumption and athletic performance has been studied extensively. Although small doses of caffeine increase endurance, there are adverse effects (e.g., dehydration) on athletic performance.

America's Favorite Pastime: Baseball. Players still chew tobacco.

Bettmann Archive.

Amphetamines

The first widespread abuse of drugs in professional sports occurred in the late 1960s and early 1970s, when professional football players used amphetamines. Mandell (1979) reported this as a so-called Sunday syndrome of amphetamine use to enhance performance. However, athletes in many other sports—notably, those involved in endurance events—also have used amphetamines.

Amphetamines have an appetite-suppression effect attractive to a variety of athletes for whom making and keeping a required weight is essential (e.g., jockeys, gymnasts, wrestlers, and boxers). Numerous studies have attempted to document the effects of amphetamines on performance. Some have looked at psychomotor tasks, others have examined certain variables related to overall performance, and still others have studied athletic performance (Derlet and Heischober 1990).

Smith and Beecher (1959) reported that approximately 75 percent of trained swimmers, weight lifters, and runners showed improvements in performance after administration of amphetamines. However, Karpovich (1969) found improvement in only 3 of 20 athletes, and 1 athlete actually performed more poorly. A review in 1981, using criteria based on knee-extension strength and running to exhaustion, showed that performance usually improved by only a small percentage. However, in highly competitive sports, even a 1 percent improvement can mean the difference between victory and defeat.

Most people also would probably agree that the alertness of the fatigued person, whether an athlete, a truck driver, a student, or a subject of an experiment, increases with the use of amphetamines. However, Chandler and Blair concluded in 1980 that "amphetamines do not prevent fatigue but rather mask the effects of fatigue and interfere with the body's fatigue-alarm system which could lead to disastrous results, especially under extreme environmental conditions."

Deaths caused by amphetamine use have involved cerebral vascular accidents (strokes) secondary to hemorrhages in the brain, acute heart failure with arrhythmias, and hyperthermia. The elevation of body temperature, if not fatal, can combine with heat exhaustion and circulatory collapse to cause heat stroke, because amphetamines obscure the athlete's normally protective physiologic fatigue level.

By diminishing pain thresholds, amphetamines allow athletes to continue to compete despite injury, thus potentially causing more tissue damage to the injured areas. Finally, there is an added potential for injury to others in contact sports because of the increase in aggressiveness caused by amphetamine use.

Steroids

All of the previously described drugs used in sports and athletics can be labeled *ergogenic* because they are performance-enhancing substances. By far, the most controversial ergogenic drug used by many athletes—especially young, developing boys and girls—is steroids.

Brief History

Steroids were developed in the 1930s for the treatment of anemia and a variety of diseases that wasted away muscles. Physicians have also used steroids to treat cancer, burn victims, intestinal problems, asthma, and emaciation. After World War II, steroid use restored body tissue to victims of starvation. The increased aggressiveness caused by steroid use was one of the benefits sought by German soldiers in World War II.

In 1988, Canadian sprinter Ben Johnson lost the gold medals he won in the Olympic games because he tested positive for steroids. Today, steroid use is not only a problem with world-class Olympic athletes but also with teenagers. Steroid use became the adolescent rage of the 1990s. Studies indicate that 6 to 10 percent of high school boys will use steroids by graduation, as will 1 percent of girls. Unfortunately, two-thirds of these young people will start to use steroids prior to the age of 16. Most young people who use steroids do so to enhance their performance in sports, yet a surprisingly large percentage (25 percent) use steroids for appearance. The skinny boy on the beach who gets sand kicked in his face no longer chooses the old Charles Atlas weight-training program to bulk up. Instead, steroid use with weight training and diet create the hulking bodies that young men desire. Beefing up and strengthening their bodies give these young people added self-confidence because they feel attractive (Hough 1988).

Steroids are illegal without a prescription. Federal officials estimate the illicit steroid market at $400 million.

Terminology

Androgenic steroids, which include testosterone, primarily develop and maintain male sex characteristics. So-called **anabolic** steroids are synthetic derivatives of testosterone developed in an attempt to minimize testosterone's androgenic or masculinizing effects on the individual while promoting protein synthesis and muscular growth.

Because none of these compounds is purely anabolic or purely androgenic in their effects, and since athletes usually stack, or use the steroids in combination, technically the more correct designation is "anabolic-androgenic steroids (A-AS)" rather than just anabolic steroids (AS).

Major Effects

Many of the early studies regarding the effectiveness of steroids produced conflicting results. More recent studies have clearly indicated significant increases in strength as a result of steroid use. The American College of Sports Medicine in its position statement on steroids in 1989 concluded that "gains in strength can occur through a variety of mechanisms in the highly trained athlete who takes steroids."

Increases in lean body mass do occur in A-AS steroid use. In the past, this was thought to be the result of water retention. It is now clear that there is an actual increase in muscle tissue and enhancement of muscle contractility. In addition, some reports cite an increase in actual bone density. However, most of these changes do not increase strength unless their use is combined with high-intensity weight training and a properly balanced diet.

A-AS steroids also increase the ability to perform high-intensity training sessions. In part, this is due to increased protein metabolism as well as the inhibition of the metabolic (breaking down) effects of corticosteroids, which are released in increased amounts whenever the body is stressed. The result is that the body requires less recuperation time between intensive workouts to repair itself. However, most studies have also shown that aerobic capacity is not affected or improved at all with steroid use.

Adverse Effects

The problem with steroids is that they do not act exclusively on one muscle or tissue group. Therefore, they stimulate all muscles and tissues, making the individual at risk for other adverse effects. The body's homeostasis is disrupted with the use of steroids, causing a variety of physical problems. "Heart disease will probably be the most widely noted side effect with anabolic steroid abuse. Blood pressure elevates significantly when an individual takes anabolic steroids due to the retained fluid and increased blood volume. . . . High Density Lipoproteins (HDL-C) that aid the body in removing cholesterol, and are important to cardiac longevity, are drastically reduced with the use of androgens" (American Osteopathic Academy of Sports Medicine 1989).

For adolescents, the drug can cause stunted growth and the premature closing of growth plates. Other problems resulting from steroid abuse by men include the following:

- Liver and kidney damage
- Breast development
- Acne, baldness
- Cysts
- Shrinking of the testicles and sterility
- Reduced sex drive
- Headaches, nausea, and dizziness

For women the drug can cause the following:

- Infertility
- Clitoral enlargement
- Breast atrophy
- Menstrual irregularities
- Male pattern baldness and voice change

More and more evidence is accruing that the most significant effect of A-AS use may be psychiatric. Psychological reactions such as extreme aggressiveness, mood swings, depression, and delusions are reported in some individuals. Signs and symptoms similar to drug and alcohol dependence (e.g., loss of control; continued use despite known adverse consequences, tolerance, and withdrawal) suggest that both physical and psychological dependence can occur with A-AS use.

Other Drugs/Alcohol in Sports

The pressures of professional athletic competition and the accompanying lifestyle can create a situation in which athletes seek both relief and the enhancement of performance by using alcohol or other drugs. Many high school, college, and even professional athletes are ill prepared for these pressures.

The widespread use of cocaine, marijuana, alcohol, amphetamines, and other drugs in professional sports came to the attention of the general public in the drug scandals of the past three decades. This was an indicator of the high level of denial and enabling behavior by players, coaches, and management. Today, teams are making more concerted efforts at education, assessment, and treatment. They have programs that help athletes develop the skills to deal with the pressures. However, alcohol/drug problems are still enabled and/or denied at many levels of athletic competition. Additional efforts are needed to resolve the issue of alcohol/drug abuse and addiction at all levels of athletic endeavor.

Summary

Alcohol/drugs are found everywhere in our society, and every family is vulnerable to the problems associated with alcohol/drugs. The following terms are commonly used in the chemical dependency field to describe the nature of these problems:

- *Physical dependence*
- *Withdrawal*
- *Psychological dependence*
- *Metabolism, absorption, excretion*
- *Routes of administration*
- *Set, setting*
- *Tolerance, cross-tolerance*
- *Synergism, antagonism*
- *Toxicity*

The behavioral definition of addiction includes the compulsive use of a chemical, an obsession with the drug, the loss of control or, inability to stop using, and continued use despite known adverse consequences. A drug is a nonfood substance that affects the structure and function of the body.

Drugs are classified as either nonpsychoactive or psychoactive. Nonpsychoactive drugs are the substances that in normal doses do not directly affect the brain. Psychoactive drugs affect brain functions, mood, and behavior and are subdivided primarily on the basis of physiological and psychological effects.

The major psychoactive drug categories are the following:

1. Narcotic analgesics—painkillers and designer drugs (Fentanyl)
2. Central nervous system depressants—sedative hypnotics (alcohol, tranquilizers, and barbiturates)
3. Central nervous system stimulants—amphetamines, cocaine, nicotine, and caffeine
4. Hallucinogens
5. Cannabis sativa—marijuana and hashish
6. Inhalants—volatile solvents
7. PCP

Each of these psychoactive drugs has specific major effects, hazards, withdrawal symptoms, and problems.

The substances that athletes use to enhance athletic performance discussed in this chapter include caffeine, chewing tobacco, amphetamines, and steroids. The current problem of steroid use by athletes, especially young people, can be a major tragedy.

References

American Osteopathic Academy of Sports Medicine. 1989.

Ashton, C.H. "Solvent Abuse, Little Progress After 20 Years." *British Medical Journal* 300 (January 1990): 135–38.

Chandler, J.V., and S.N. Blair. "The Effect of Amphetamines on Selected Physiological Components Related to Athletic Success." *Medicine and Science in Sports and Exercise* 12 (Spring 1980).

Cohen, S. "Marijuana Research: Selected Recent Findings." *Drug and Alcohol Newsletter, Vista Hill Foundation* 15, no. 1 (January 1986).

Derlet, R., and B. Heischober. "Methamphetamine, Stimulant of the 1990s." *Western Journal of Medicine* (December 1990): 153, 625–28.

Hough, D. "Anabolic Steroids and Ergogenic Aids." *Academy of Family Practice* 41, no. 4 (April 1988): 1157–64.

Karpovich, P.V. "Effect of Amphetamine Sulfate on Athletic Performance." *Journal of American Medical Association* 170 (1969).

Lombardo, J. "Stimulants and Athletic Performance, Amphetamine and Caffeine." *The Physician and Sports Medicine* 4, no. 11 (April 1990): 1157–64.

Mandell, A.J. "The Sunday Syndrome: A Unique Pattern of Amphetamine Abuse Indigenous to American Professional Football." *Clinical Toxicology* 15, no. 2 (1979).

National Institute on Drug Abuse. *Community Drug Alert Bulletin.* Rockville, MD: Author, 1998.

National Institute on Drug Abuse. *Drug Use Among American High School Students, College Students, and Other Young Adults. National Trends Through 1988.* Rockville, MD: Author. 1989.

1994 National Household Survey on Drug Abuse, Advance Report 10, U.S. Department of Health and Human Services, Substance Abuse and Mental Health Services Administration, September 1995.

Rohr, V. "Withdrawal Sequelae to Cannabis Use." *The International Journal of the Addictions* 24, no. 7 (1989): 627–31.

Smith, David, and Donald Wesson. *Treating Cocaine Dependence.* Center City, MN: Hazeldon Foundation, 1988.

Smith, G.M., and H.G. Beecher. "Amphetamine Sulfate and Athletic Performance." *Journal of American Medical Association* 170, no. 5 (1959).

Solomons, K., and V.M. Neppve. "Review Article, Cannabis—Its Clinical Effects." *S.A.M.T.* 76 (August 1989).

Sporer, Karl A. "Acute Heroin Overdose." *Annals of Internal Medicine,* April 6, 1999, 130: 584–90 in Heroin Overdose: Research & Interventions, Linden Ctr., SF, CA, January, 2000.

Tamura, M. "Japan: Stimulant Epidemics, Past and Present." *Bulletin on Narcotics* XLL, no. 1 and 2 (1989).

Thombs, D. "A Review of P.C.P. Abuse, Trends and Perceptions." *Public Health Reports* 104, no. 4 (July/August 1989): 325–28.

U.S. Surgeon General. *The Health Consequences of Smoking, Nicotine Addiction.* Rockville, MD: U.S. Department of Health and Human Services, 1988.

Woods, James H. et al. "Use and Abuse of Benzodiazepines." *Journal of American Medical Association* 260, no. 23 (December 1988).

Screening and Assessment of Alcohol/Drug Problems

Chapter Objectives

1. Identify the three elements in the behavioral definition of addiction.

2. Establish guidelines for parents in trying to discourage initial use of alcohol/drugs by their children.

3. Describe factors that can decrease alcohol/drug use by adolescents.

4. Define and describe the impact of set and setting on alcohol/drug use.

5. Describe the stages and progressive cycle of alcohol/drug use: initial contact, experimentation, integrated use, excessive use, and addiction.

6. Explain the different types of alcoholism Jellinek identified and the behavioral characteristics of the progression of the disease.

7. Outline the stages of alcohol/drug recovery.

8. Identify three diagnostic criteria for both substance abuse and substance dependence based on the diagnostic and statistical manual *(DSM-IV)*.

9. Describe the role of family in assessment and recovery from alcohol/drugs.

10. Identify the tests for the screening and assessment of alcohol/drug problems.

11. Identify two or three questions about the physical, psychological, sexual, relationship, job, financial, and legal consequences of substance abuse.

12. Identify some physical, psychological, and emotional responses that might indicate a problem with the use of marijuana.

13. Identify some physical, psychological, and emotional responses that might indicate a problem with the use of cocaine.

14. Explain how denial is an obstacle to an accurate alcohol/drug assessment.

15. Identify and describe 11 common areas that may help identify an adolescent alcohol/drug problem.

16. Identify several assessment questions for suicide.

17. Describe how individual, family, and societal denial contribute to problems in alcohol/drug assessment.

The most difficult assessment question is differentiating those individuals who fall in the gray area between occasional, or nonproblematic, use of alcohol/drugs and those who use excessively and/or have an alcohol/drug problem. Assessment is also complicated by the fact that people strongly deny problems with alcohol and drugs. Individual, family, and societal perceptions of alcohol/drugs are distorted by this denial system.

This chapter defines addiction and describes the stages of alcohol/drug use (Figure 4.1) and stages of recovery. The major goal of this chapter is to help the reader develop a more focused perception of chemical dependency.

❧ Definition of Addiction

In the early 1980s, the rise in cocaine use challenged the basic framework of our definition of

*The names and circumstances of case studies in this chapter have been changed to maintain anonymity.

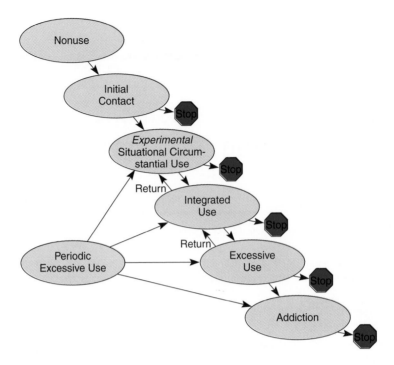

FIGURE 4.1 *Stages of Alcohol/Drug Use*

Richard Fields Ph.D. 1986, revised, 1988.

alcohol/drug addiction. Cocaine was previously thought to be a drug that incurred psychological dependence with no physical dependence. At that time, we defined addiction as a physical dependence measured by a significant and noticeable medical withdrawal symptom. Although cocaine had no significant medically noticeable withdrawal symptoms, users reported a severe addiction to it. David Smith (Smith and Wesson) was aware of this discrepancy and proposed a more behavioral definition of addiction. Because this definition is more functional, counselors in the fields of chemical dependency treatment and addictionology use it. In fact, counselors can apply this behavioral definition of addiction to a wide variety of types of disorders, including eating, gambling, sex, workaholism, television, smoking, video games, spending/consumerism, and other activities.

Alcoholism and drug addiction are best described metaphorically as "the dragon in the corner, eating its own tail."

The three basic components of the behavioral definition of addiction are the three *Cs*—*compulsion, control,* and *consequences.*

1. **Obsessive-compulsive behavior** with alcohol/drugs. Users think about alcohol and drugs in a vicious negative cycle; their obsessive concern and preoccupation follow an incessant use of alcohol/drugs in a continuous pattern and compulsive lifestyle.
2. **Inability to stop** using the substances. Users cannot stop using alcohol/drugs for at least three months and/or make feeble attempts to cut back in a stop-then-start pattern. They are unable to refuse readily available drugs.

3. **Continued use despite adverse consequences.** Users are caught up in their addictions, illustrating the pervasive defense mechanisms of denial (rationalization and minimization). Eventually, the alcoholic/addict suffers family, social and interpersonal, economic, and spiritual bankruptcy.

Defining addiction is a challenge; however, defining the stages and patterns of alcohol/drug use that precede addiction is even more challenging.

Nonuse of Alcohol/Drugs by Children

The most successful preventive approach is not to use drugs and alcohol, especially at early ages. Not smoking cigarettes at early ages highly correlates with not developing addictions later in life. Children are less likely to develop chemical dependencies later in life, if parents

1. Do not model alcohol/drug use and encourage a healthy approach to life
2. Encourage children to participate in activities that enhance the development of a strong sense of self
3. Promote positive alternative activities to alcohol/drug use (see prevention chapter)
4. Are sensitive to what children feel while parents are setting appropriate boundaries
5. Provide structure, discipline, and consistency
6. Develop a climate of discussion, which facilitates an effective exploration of values and the development of coping skills in goal setting, decision making, and conflict resolution

Parents can establish nonuse of drugs and alcohol by teaching children to make positive lifestyle choices that they can maintain throughout adult life. Although the drive or desire to alter one's consciousness is innate, learning to alter one's consciousness with alternatives other than chemicals is a developmental task of childhood. Children can be encouraged to be more active in choosing things to do that change their mood and develop their sense of self, instead of choosing a passive solution, the use of alcohol/drugs.

Nonuse of Alcohol/Drugs by Adolescents

Some young people are able to use alcohol and drugs and not suffer any significant problems. For others, especially those who have family histories of alcoholism and drug addiction, such a trial could be the beginning of a life-long pattern of addiction.

To help their at-risk adolescents, parents should

1. Establish clear, consistent guidelines and rules regarding alcohol/drugs
2. Model nonuse of alcohol/drugs
3. Establish clear, consistent communication of the hazards and potential harm of alcohol/drugs, especially at early ages of adolescence
4. Encourage the development of alternative activities to alleviate feelings of boredom, depression, and isolation and to promote the development of a strong sense of self

⚔ Stages of Alcohol and Drug Use

5. Promote active involvement in school, athletics, social situations, church, and other activities
6. Encourage active development of skills and talents
7. Promote trust and establish healthy boundaries in relationships
8. Support adolescents in their perseverance through their developmental tasks of identity and individuation

Initial Contact with Alcohol/Drugs

The initial contact stage is defined as the first time one tries alcohol/drugs. Usually, this stage is thought to be relatively harmless, yet there are potential hazards from initial contact, such as the following:

- Anaphylactic (allergic) reactions, which can cause death
- Toxic and lethal doses
- Loss of control and emotional overreactions
- Physical and psychological problems
- Accidents and/or dangerous situations

The three major components of alcohol and drug use are the individual, the drug, and the set and setting in which the drug is taken. Set and setting often determine the individual's reaction to alcohol/drugs.

As mentioned in an earlier chapter, **set** refers to the psychological and emotional frame of mind of a person when using alcohol/drugs. Those who are relaxed, comfortable, and secure in the knowledge that they can handle possibly losing control usually have less trouble with the initial use of alcohol/drugs. Individuals who have a set that can be described as anxious, extremely nervous, or overly concerned with maintaining control are more prone to a negative drug reaction. If a person is not emotionally stable and/or has psychiatric problems, alcohol/drug use can exacerbate those problems. (See Chapter 10.) This is especially true for hallucinogens and marijuana. Set can also be influenced by the person's mood or emotional state at the time of alcohol/drug use. The individual who has just received some bad news or has had a negative experience might be feeling down or depressed; this may result in a negative set and a negative experience with alcohol/drugs. Significant trauma, shame, and embarrassment can also contribute to a negative experience with alcohol/drugs.

Setting involves not only the physical environment but also the social and interpersonal environment. Negative drug reactions may be the result of being in an uncomfortable setting, with unknown people who are not trusted.

Alcohol/Drug Use—a Progressive Disease

Certainly, the beginning of alcohol/drug use starts with initial contact. Because alcohol/drug use is a progressive disease, individuals get more involved as they progress through the stages. A positive initial contact usually leads to the next stage of drug use—experimentation. Experimentation may lead to the subsequent stages, which end in addiction. Richard Rawson (1989) has written about his outpatient treatment of cocaine addicts. He describes the progressive themes at vari-

TABLE 4.1

Phases of Cocaine Addiction

Initial contact	"Isn't this a great drug?"
Experimentation	"It's sure expensive, but it's worth it."
Excessive use	"I really should cut down."
Addiction	"I know I have to stop, but I can't."

ous stages of cocaine addiction, as shown in Table 4.1. These descriptions can easily be adapted to alcohol and other drugs and illustrate the progressive nature of addiction.

As was stated earlier, a positive initial contact may be the beginning of a progressive cycle to addiction. This is especially true for those who grew up in alcoholic/addict and/or dysfunctional family systems.

Experimentation

Experimentation is the stage of using alcohol/drugs in different situations and circumstances. People explore and experiment with a drug, testing their own capacity to use alcohol/drugs in different situations and circumstances. Users learn about alcohol/drugs by experimenting with various doses, frequencies of use, methods of ingestion, and sometimes combinations (polydrug use). Each individual's reaction to a drug is also affected by physiological, psychological, and emotional factors. Some factors include not eating prior to use, fatigue, and levels of physical and emotional well-being. During experimentation, individuals change and adjust the drug, the set, and the setting and then determine their reaction.

Experimenters use drugs during this stage in different settings, with different people, and in different frames of mind, or set. A triangular relationship exists among the individual (set), the drug, and the environment (setting). During the experimentation stage, the user adjusts the three elements of this equation to determine the drug's effect.

Many systems that classify the stages of alcohol/drug use often call the experimental stage a *recreational* or *social use* stage. These terms tend to put alcohol/drugs in a more positive, emotion-laden frame of reference. The implication of the term *recreational* is that alcohol/drug use is no more than harmless recreational/social fun. This view overlooks the potential hazards and problems that may occur.

Parental guidelines during the experimental stage should include the following:

1. Talking with other parents and exchanging information about their children's behavior in the neighborhood, at neighboring homes, at school, or in the general community
2. Knowing where children are and who their friends are, as well as meeting the parents of their friends
3. Developing initiative, responsibility, and appropriate consequences for behavior

4.   Evaluating the dynamics of the family and seeking professional help for early alcohol/drug educational advice and assessment

5.   Being aware that a child is at-risk and seeking family counseling for alcohol/drug education, prevention, and treatment if there is a history of alcohol/drug problems in the family

Integrated Use

At the integrated stage of alcohol/drug use, the person spends more time, thought, and energy in the use of alcohol/drugs. It has become an integrated part of the individual's life. Whether adolescent or adult, the person begins to associate with others who use the same drug. At parties, the marijuana smokers congregate, the alcohol users belly up to the bar, and the polydrug users are the life of the party, drinking at the bar and smoking dope in the backyard.

The individual at the integrated stage buys the drug to make sure that the drug is available. For example, at this stage a person must have the alcohol/drug available when away from home for a vacation or a business trip. Obviously, alcohol/drugs are well integrated into the user's style of life.

Excessive Use

Even for experts, the excessive use stage is difficult to describe because there are different kinds of excessive use. Some people call this stage drug abuse; however, drug abuse is very arbitrary, emotion-laden, and difficult to define. The second Commission on Marijuana (1973) found that the term *drug abuse* had "no functional utility" and "had become no more than an arbitrary code word for that drug use which is presently considered wrong." The commission concluded that the facts of actual drug use are often not distinguished from feelings and opinions. The commission recommended that the term *drug abuse* be discontinued because of the emotion-laden, subjective interpretation of the term.

Excessive use is an increase in alcohol/drug use that results in significant problems or negative consequences. Users are putting increased time, thought, and energy into buying—perhaps selling—and using alcohol/drugs.

Some people use alcohol/drugs excessively in a periodic pattern, sometimes in the form of binges, which are excessive drug use within a period of 24 to 72 hours. Periodic excessive alcohol/drug use can occur just on weekends, every other week, once in a month, or even as infrequently as once every three months. When all the criteria for addiction are met, periodic excessive use is also defined as addiction.

Addiction

Addiction is the last stage. Based on our definition of addiction and the disease model, an addict cannot return to any of the previous stages of alcohol/drug use. The best recovery strategy is to abstain from alcohol/drug use and to participate in a 12-step recovery program. This usually involves an inpatient program; strong development in self-help support groups, such as Alcoholics Anonymous, Narcotics Anonymous, and Cocaine Anonymous; a relationship with a sponsor; and an aftercare treatment program on completion of the inpatient program. (See Treatment chapter.)

Chronic alcoholics and drug addicts spend major portions of their lives addicted to alcohol/drugs. In this late stage of chronic addiction, they are extremely difficult to treat. (See Table 4.2.) Some new approaches are required for this population. Such programs provide basic needs for shelter, food, other health-related services, and educational and counseling services. These programs for

An alcoholic's arm sinking into a glass of booze.

AP/Wide World Photos.

TABLE 4.2

Early and Late Stages of Alcohol/Drug Use

Early Stage	Late Stage
More freedom	Lack of freedom
Fewer risks and less damage	More damage
Possible abuse	Present abuse
No illness	State of illness
Linear operating factors	Vicious cycles

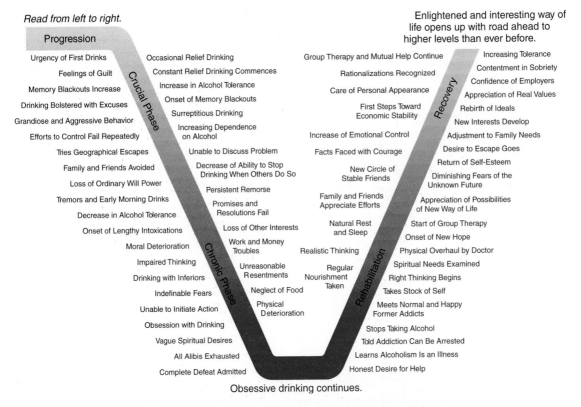

Read from left to right.

Progression

Enlightened and interesting way of
life opens up with road ahead to
higher levels than ever before.

Urgency of First Drinks
Feelings of Guilt
Memory Blackouts Increase
Drinking Bolstered with Excuses
Grandiose and Aggressive Behavior
Efforts to Control Fail Repeatedly
Tries Geographical Escapes
Family and Friends Avoided
Loss of Ordinary Will Power
Tremors and Early Morning Drinks
Decrease in Alcohol Tolerance
Onset of Lengthy Intoxications
Moral Deterioration
Impaired Thinking
Drinking with Inferiors
Indefinable Fears
Unable to Initiate Action
Obsession with Drinking
Vague Spiritual Desires
All Alibis Exhausted
Complete Defeat Admitted

Crucial Phase

Occasional Relief Drinking
Constant Relief Drinking Commences
Increase in Alcohol Tolerance
Onset of Memory Blackouts
Surreptitious Drinking
Increasing Dependence
on Alcohol
Unable to Discuss Problem
Decrease of Ability to Stop
Drinking When Others Do So
Persistent Remorse
Promises and
Resolutions Fail
Loss of Other Interests
Work and Money
Troubles
Unreasonable
Resentments
Neglect of Food
Physical
Deterioration

Chronic Phase

Group Therapy and Mutual Help Continue
Rationalizations Recognized
Care of Personal Appearance
First Steps Toward
Economic Stability
Increase of Emotional Control
Facts Faced with Courage
New Circle of
Stable Friends
Family and Friends
Appreciate Efforts
Natural Rest
and Sleep
Realistic Thinking
Regular
Nourishment
Taken

Recovery

Rehabilitation

Increasing Tolerance
Contentment in Sobriety
Confidence of Employers
Appreciation of Real Values
Rebirth of Ideals
New Interests Develop
Adjustment to Family Needs
Desire to Escape Goes
Return of Self-Esteem
Diminishing Fears of the
Unknown Future
Appreciation of Possibilities
of New Way of Life
Start of Group Therapy
Onset of New Hope
Physical Overhaul by Doctor
Spiritual Needs Examined
Right Thinking Begins
Takes Stock of Self
Meets Normal and Happy
Former Addicts
Stops Taking Alcohol
Told Addiction Can Be Arrested
Learns Alcoholism Is an Illness
Honest Desire for Help

Obsessive drinking continues.

FIGURE 4.2   *Progression and Recovery of the Alcoholic in the Disease of Alcoholism*

From *Understanding Personality Problems and Addictions and Understanding Mood Disorders and Addictions,* 1993, Hazelden Foundation, Center City, MN.

chronic alcoholics have an emphasis on maintaining the individual's dignity while
providing access to recovery services.

⚑ Jellinek's Types of Alcoholics

E.M. Jellinek (1960) believed that persons with certain types of alcoholism suffer
through declining stages of functioning. He described five distinct types of alcoholism:

1. Alpha alcoholism: psychological dependence, in which alcoholics use
   drinking increasingly to help with their problems
2. Beta alcoholism
   a. Physical problems, such as cirrhosis of the liver or stomach problems,
      resulting from the consumption of alcohol
   b. No physical or psychological dependence
3. Gamma alcoholism
   a. Physical addiction, with withdrawal symptoms occurring whenever
      drinking is stopped
   b. Loss of control to regulate alcohol use
   c. Severe damage to health, financial, social, and interpersonal functioning
   d. Periods of abstinence (going on the wagon)

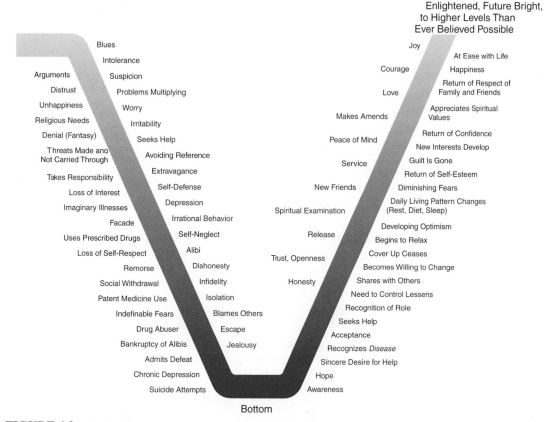

FIGURE 4.3   The progression and recovery symptoms listed are based on the *most repeated experiences* of family members in the disease of alcoholism or other chemical dependencies. While not every symptom in the chart occurs in every member of every family, or in the same sequence, it does portray an *average* chain reaction. The entire process may take years, or it may occur in a very short time.

From *Understanding Personality and Addictions and Understanding Mood Disorders and Addictions,* 1993, Hazelden Foundation, Center City, MN.

4.   Delta alcoholism
   a.   Similar to gamma; however, the individual can control intake in given situations
   b.   High degree of physical and psychological dependence, making abstinence, even for brief periods, impossible
5.   Epsilon alcoholism: periodic, unpredictable drinking binges

Once an alcohol/drug problem is identified, the next step is recovery (Figure 4.2). Richard Rawson (1989) described a model for the stages of cocaine recovery, as seen in Table 4.3. This model also applies to alcohol or other drugs, although the time periods for each stage can be different and variable. Each stage of recovery is fully explained in Chapter 11.

TABLE 4.3

Stages of Recovery

Stage	Time Course*
Withdrawal	0–15 days
Honeymoon	15–45 days
The Wall	45–120 days
Adjustment	120–180 days
Resolution	180–360 days

From Richard Rawson et al., "Neurobehavioral treatment for cocaine dependency" in *Journal of Psychoactive Drugs* 22 (2): 159–71. Haight-Ashbury Publications, San Francisco, CA. Reprinted by permission.
*These generalized categories are rough estimates for periods of time when alcohol/drugs are not used. The actual time course for each stage of recovery may be quite different for each individual and alcohol or drug used.

The alcoholic's life is limited, with significant negative consequences, as if he or she "is trapped in a shot glass."

AP/Wide World Photos.

⚓ Diagnostic Criteria of Substance Abuse and Dependence

The *Diagnostic and Statistical Manual (DSM-IV)* is a major reference used by psychologists, mental health and alcohol/drug counselors, psychiatrists, and most health professionals to identify psychiatric diagnoses. The manual describes criteria for substance dependence and substance abuse, as well as other substance-related disorders. The manual is available in most college bookstores or can be ordered through the American Psychiatric Association in Washington, DC. The following material is from the *Diagnostic and Statistical Manual of Mental Disorders,* fourth edition, copyright 1994 American Psychiatric Association.

Substance Abuse

Substance abuse is described by the following diagnostic criteria in *DSM-IV:*

A. A maladaptive pattern of substance use, leading to clinically significant impairment or distress, as manifested by one (or more) of the following, occurring within a 12-month period
   1. Recurrent substance use, resulting in a failure to fulfill major role obligations at work, school, or home (e.g., repeated absences or poor work performance related to substance use; substance-related absences, suspensions, or expulsions from school; neglect of children or household)
   2. Recurrent substance use in situations in which it is physically hazardous (e.g., driving an automobile or operating a machine when impaired by substance use)
   3. Recurrent substance-related legal problems (e.g., arrests for substance-related disorderly conduct)
   4. Continued substance use despite having persistent or recurrent social or interpersonal problems caused or exacerbated by the effects of the substance (e.g., arguments with spouse about consequences of intoxication, physical fights)
B. The symptoms have never met the criteria for substance dependence for this class of substances.

Substance Dependence

Substance dependence is described by the following diagnostic criteria in *DSM-IV* (see Table 4.4).

A maladaptive pattern of substance use, leading to clinically significant impairment or distress, as manifested by three (or more) of the following, occurring at any time in the same 12-month period:

1. Tolerance, as defined by either of the following:
   a. A need for markedly increased amounts of the substance to achieve intoxication or desired effect
   b. Markedly diminished effect with continued use of the same amount of the substance
2. Withdrawal, as manifested by either of the following:
   a. The characteristic withdrawal syndrome for the substance
   b. The same (or a closely related) substance is taken to relieve or avoid withdrawal symptoms.
3. The substance is often taken in larger amounts or over a longer period than was intended.
4. There is a persistent desire or unsuccessful efforts to cut down or control substance use.

TABLE 4.4

DSM-IV and *ICD-10* Diagnostic Criteria for Alcohol and Drug Dependence

	DSM-IV	ICD-10
Clustering criterion	A. A maladaptive pattern of substance use, leading to clinically significant impairment or distress as manifested by three or more of the following occurring at any time in the same 12-month period:	A. Three or more of the following have been experienced or exhibited at some time during the previous year:
Tolerance	(1) Need for markedly increased amounts of a substance to achieve intoxication or desired effect; or markedly diminished effect with continued use of the same amount of the substance	(1) Evidence of tolerance, such that increased doses are required in order to achieve effects originally produced by lower doses
Withdrawal	(2) The characteristic withdrawal syndrome for a substance or use of a substance (or a closely related substance) to relieve or avoid withdrawal symptoms	(2) A physiological withdrawal state when substance use has ceased or been reduced as evidenced by the characteristic substance withdrawal syndrome, or use of substance (or a closely related substance) to relieve or avoid withdrawal symptoms
Impaired control	(3) Persistent desire or one or more unsuccessful efforts to cut down or control substance use (4) Substance use in larger amounts or over a longer period than the person intended	(3) Difficulties in controlling substance use in terms of onset, termination, or levels of use
Neglect of activities	(5) Important social, occupational, or recreational activities given up or reduced because of substance use	(4) Progressive neglect of alternative pleasures or interests in favor of substance use; or a great deal of time spent in activities necessary to obtain, to use, or to recover from the effects of substance use
Time spent	(6) A great deal of time spent in activities necessary to obtain, to use, or to recover from the effects of substance used	
Inability to fulfill roles	None	None
Hazardous use	None	None
Continued use despite problems	(7) Continued substance use despite knowledge of having a persistent or recurrent physical or psychological problem that is likely to be caused or exacerbated by use	(5) Continued substance use despite clear evidence of overtly harmful physical or psychological consequences
Compulsive use	None	(6) A strong desire or sense of compulsion to use substance
Duration criterion	B. No duration criterion separately specified. However, several dependence criteria must occur repeatedly as specified by duration qualifiers associated with criteria (e.g., "often," "persistent," "continued")	B. No duration criterion separately specified
Criterion for subtyping dependence	With physiological dependence: Evidence of tolerance or withdrawal (i.e., any of items A(1) or A(2) above are present) Without physiological dependence: no evidence of tolerance or withdrawal (i.e., none of items A(1) or A(2) above are present)	None

Source: McCrady, Barbara S., and Elizabeth E. Epstein. *Addictions: A Comprehensive Guide Book.* Cary, NC: Oxford University Press, 1999.

5. A great deal of time is spent in activities necessary to obtain the substance (e.g., visiting multiple doctors or driving long distances), use the substance (e.g., chain-smoking), or recover from its effects.

6. Important social, occupational, or recreational activities are given up or reduced because of substance use.

7. The substance use is continued despite knowledge of having a persistent or recurrent physical or psychological problem that is likely to have been caused or exacerbated by the substance (e.g., current cocaine use despite recognition of cocaine-induced depression, or continued drinking despite recognition that an ulcer was made worse by alcohol consumption).

At each of the stages of recovery, individuals are vulnerable to relapse, or a return to alcohol/drug abuse or addiction. Therefore, all chemical dependency treatment programs must address relapse issues. Many experts agree that a longer-term inpatient or residential program is much needed (although financially difficult, due to limitations in insurance reimbursement and managed care). Experts agree that a six- to nine-month inpatient program would be most effective, considering the high relapse rates. In addition, a one-year outpatient aftercare program would further enhance the probability of recovery without relapse. It is not surprising that the relapse statistics are high following the traditional 28-day inpatient stay, making it even more important to counsel patients in relapse prevention. (See Treatment Chapter.)

⊀ **Vulnerability to Relapse**

Many people find it extremely difficult to stop using alcohol/drugs. B.G. Danaher and E. Lichtenstein (1978) describe the natural cycle of smoking, which is similar to the cycle of alcohol/drug use (see Table 4.5).

Recovery from alcohol/drugs also involves the family of the alcoholic/addict. The family system is an integral part of the development of the disease. The most difficult work in recovery is dealing with family issues and relationships to help family members recover from dysfunctional patterns in the family system. (See Chapter 5.)

⊀ **Family and Recovery**

The most important task in assessing the potential for problems with alcohol/drugs is determining if there is a family history of alcohol or drug abuse and addiction. Family members may deny the extent of alcohol/drug use in their family. It might take additional questioning to clarify the true dimensions of family use of alcohol/drugs.

Alcohol/Drug History

Some education for family members and the individual who may have a drug problem also might be necessary to establish a clear perception of the dimensions of substance abuse and addiction (see Table 4.6). To assess an individual's alcohol/drug problem, counselors need the following information:

- Age of initial drug and alcohol use
- Frequency of use, amounts used, set and setting of use

TABLE 4.5

Natural Cycle of Cigarette Smoking

Reasons for Starting

Availability	Social confidence
Curiosity	Modeling of peers, siblings, parents
Rebelliousness	Other reasons in the psychosocial domain
Anticipation of adulthood	

Reasons for Continuing

Nicotine addiction	Avoidance of negative effects (withdrawal)
Immediate positive consequences	Other reasons in the physiological
Signals (cues) in the environment	and psychosocial domains

Reasons for Stopping

Health	Aesthetics (feeling that it is bad, ugly,
Expense	and/or unbecoming)
Social pressure	Example to others
Self-mastery	Other reasons in the psychosocial domain

Reasons for Resuming

Stress	Alcohol consumption
Social pressure	Other reasons in the psychosocial domain
Abstinence violation effect	

From Brian G. Danaher and Edward Lichtenstein. *Becoming an Ex-Smoker,* copyright © 1978 Brian G. Danaher and Edward Lichtenstein. Reprinted by permission.

TABLE 4.6

Factors Enhancing the Reliability and Validity of Self-Reports Among Substance Abusers

The client is alcohol- and drug-free when interviewed.

Sufficient time has passed since last drink/drug use to allow clear responses.

Confidentiality is assured.

The setting is nonthreatening and nonjudgmental and encourages honest reporting.

The client does not feel pressure to respond in a particular way.

The client has no reason to distort reports (e.g., abstinence being a condition of parole).

The client is aware that corroborating information is available and will be collected (e.g., breath test, report of spouse) and that this information from other sources will be used to confirm what he or she reports.

Care is taken to ensure that questions are clearly worded and valid measurement approaches are used.

The assessment worker or therapist has a good rapport with the client.

The person administering the measures should be able to communicate clearly with the client.

Adapted from National Institute on Alcohol Abuse and Alcoholism (1990) and the Addiction Research Foundation (1994).

- Patterns of use, binges, periods of nonuse
- Stage of current use—experimentation, integrated use, excessive use, addiction
- History of negative consequences—physical, psychological, financial, familial, and spiritual
- Medical history—conditions that might affect use of drugs/alcohol
- Use of coffee, cigarettes, and medication

Individual Vulnerability to Alcohol/Drugs

What evidence is there of individual vulnerability?

- Primary alcoholism/drug addiction in the family system of origin
- Inherited or acquired mood disorder
- Psychosis
- Rejection or insensitivity to norms of behavior

What is the individual's attitude toward alcohol/drug use?

- Favorable, unfavorable, nonexistent

What are the environmental factors?

- Family, other

Are drugs available?

- Legally available, readily available illegally
- Individual has the necessary finances for drugs (Rankin 1978)

Counselors should also identify any other significant problems, especially other compulsive behaviors in the family—a family history of

- Alcohol/drug problems, gambling, workaholism
- Eating disorders—anorexia, bulimia, obesity
- Employment and financial problems
- Marital problems
- Psychiatric disorders—depression, anxiety, affective (feeling) disorders, and others

---

An extremely important area of assessment is the consequences of alcohol/drug use. Remember, the third criteria of addiction is "continued use despite adverse consequences."

A client, who was referred for outpatient counseling after 120 days in a residential and extended care program, was now dealing with significant criminal, civil and other legal problems, financial, marital, business, and relationship problems. He said, "You can do all the drinking and drugging you want as long as you are willing to pay the consequences."

Perhaps this is a straightforward way of looking at addiction, but it does point out the significant consequences that come with substance abuse and addiction. Pointing out the consequences may be a valuable tool in breaking through denial. A very common exercise used in most drunk driving programs is to have

✄
Consequences of Alcohol/ Drug Use

TABLE 4.7

Consequences Related to Alcohol or Drug Use

Check below any PHYSICAL problems caused by or worsened by your use of alcohol or drugs:

- Convulsions with loss of consciousness
- Nasal sores, bleeding
- Chest congestion, wheezing
- Hepatitis or other liver problems
- Severe or frequent headaches
- Drug overdose requiring treatment in an emergency room or hospital
- Coughing up black phlegm
- Severe weight loss (without dieting)
- Sinus problems
- Ulcers or other stomach problems
- Heart palpitations
- Other (specify)

Check below any PSYCHOLOGICAL problems caused by or worsened by your use of alcohol or drugs:

- Irritability, short temper
- Panic attacks
- Violent thoughts
- Severe depression
- Memory problems
- Paranoia, suspiciousness
- Suicidal thoughts
- Other (specify)

Check below any SEXUAL problems caused by or worsened by your use of alcohol or drugs:

- Loss of sex drive
- Sex with strangers
- Sexuality out of control
- Sexual obsession or preoccupation
- Risking of AIDS through sexual behavior
- Other (specify)

Check below any RELATIONSHIP or SOCIAL problems caused by or worsened by your use of alcohol or drugs:

- Arguments with spouse or mate
- Thrown out of household
- Loss of friends
- Arguments with parents, brothers, or sisters
- Spouse or mate has threatened to leave or has already left
- Social isolation
- Other (specify)

Check below any JOB or FINANCIAL problems caused by or worsened by your use of alcohol or drugs:

- In jeopardy of losing my job
- Late to work
- Less productive at work
- In debt
- Already lost at least one job
- Missed days of work
- Missed opportunity for promotion or raise
- Behind in paying bills
- Other (specify)

Check below any LEGAL problems caused by or worsened by your use of alcohol or drugs:

- Arrested for possession of illicit substances
- Arrested for forging prescriptions
- Auto accident while driving under the influence
- Arrested for assaulting someone
- Arrested for embezzlement or check forgery
- Arrested for sale of illicit substances
- Arrested for DWI or DUI
- Arrested for violent or disorderly conduct
- Arrested for theft or robbery
- Other (specify)

From Arnold Washton, Washton Institute, New York, NY.

clients figure out how much their conviction has cost them. For some, the amount is staggering when they stop to consider the cost of legal fees, the diversion program, loss of work, and so on.

Arnold Washton (1995) asks several questions in the assessment stage about consequence covering—physical, psychological, sexual, relationship, job, financial, and legal consequences of alcohol/drug use (Table 4.7).

The denial of alcohol/drug problems is a major factor in the difficulty of assessment. There is widespread denial, not only by individuals who have drug problems but also by family and friends, as well as society at large. It is often difficult to break through denial and have the courage to admit a problem with alcohol/drugs. Family members often experience a sense of shame or embarrassment or feelings of responsibility for the alcohol/drug problem of a family member.

⚔ **Denial— Problems in Accurate Assessment**

The two major defense mechanisms used to deny problems with alcohol and drugs are minimization and rationalization. Common examples of minimizations and rationalizations of alcohol/drug problems follow:

Minimizations and Rationalizations

"Now, if I drank and drugged like Shawn, then I would really have a problem."
"I use alcohol and drugs only on weekends; a person with a problem uses everyday."
"I never miss work, no matter how much [alcohol/drugs] I've used."
"The media are just trying to get you scared."
"I don't have a problem. Now, Tiffany has a problem. Why don't you get her into treatment?"

Additional consequences of minimization and rationalization include the following:

- Neglect; emotional, physical, or sexual abuse
- Loss—death, trauma, divorce, separation
- Numerous relocations and unstable home environment
- Parental dysfunction, creating feelings of parental unavailability and/or feelings of abandonment, rejection, or shame

The following 11 questions can help in identifying an adolescent alcohol/drug problem:

⚔ **Identification of Adolescent Alcohol/Drug Problems**

1. *Mood.* Has the child been extremely moody or more upset than usual? Adolescence is a time of fluctuations in mood. A child might be as happy as a lark one minute and quite despondent the next. Therefore, it is difficult to isolate change in mood as being related to alcohol/drug use. However, if a child's mood seems more intense than usual, it could be related to the irritability associated with withdrawal from marijuana, alcohol, or other drugs.
2. *Changes.* Are there some significant changes in the child's choice in friends, grades, dress, general hygiene, and responsibilities? Adolescence is a time of change, a time to explore different aspects of one's identity and personality. However, when these changes are self-damaging and seem more than just the trying on of a different role, it could be a sign for concern.
3. *Responsibility.* Is the child more irresponsible about his or her commitments (e.g., chores, schoolwork, friends)? Is he or she not coming home on time or disregarding rules? It is common for young people to push limits and boundaries. However, doing this on a consistent basis or pushing boundaries beyond reasonable expectations may be a sign of alcohol/drug abuse.

4. *Motivation.* Is there a noticeable decrease in motivation, interest, or activity? Has the child shown disinterest in things he or she is normally interested in (e.g., friends, school, sports, extracurricular activities)? Loss of motivation is indicative of regular marijuana use. Alcohol and other drugs can also impair interest and/or performance in activities normally seen as pleasurable.

5. *School.* Are there signs of problems at school and difficulty in studying, completing assignments, and so on? Has the teacher complained that the youngster is sleeping or inattentive in class? Some common signs of problems are ditching school, having problems with teachers, acting out behavior, getting failing or lowered grades, and having fights and arguments with friends. School problems are usually the first sign of negative consequences that may be related to an alcohol/drug problem.

6. *Negative activities.* Is the child engaging in activities that are not healthy or productive and potentially damaging? Such activities include those that might provoke physical violence; emotional abuse of others; disregard for others' property; dangerous use of motor vehicles; weekend-long parties or excessive isolation and secrecy about activities; and no accountability or supervision of time. A youngster having problems with alcohol or other drugs will abandon old friends and seek out those with similar attitudes and behaviors.

7. *Lying, stealing, and cheating.* Is money, household objects, or personal property missing? Is alcohol, prescription medication, or perhaps a parent's own stash of drugs missing? Does the child make up stories and lie compulsively? The expense of alcohol/drugs can be overcome by taking things that can be used for cash or bartered for alchohol/drugs. It is probably not forgetfulness or memory loss that has caused things to be either "misplaced" or "missing."

8. *Community.* Has the child been in trouble with neighbors, storekeepers, or other community members? Have concerned friends, neighbors, relatives, or others talked about this child's behavior? Have former friends, teachers, or parents of the child's friends expressed concern or given information that indicates this child may have a problem with alcohol/drugs? You can't go on ignoring the problem when others in the community have seen the child's misbehavior or actual alcohol/drug abuse.

9. *Criminal justice problems.* Has the child been involved in an activity that has caused investigation or charges being made by the police? Examples of some of these behaviors include disorderly conduct, drunkenness, driving under the influence, stealing, bouncing checks, shoplifting, vandalism, fighting, and breaking and entering. As previously outlined, alcohol/drug use and antisocial behavior are highly correlated.

10. *Physical signs.* Are there physical signs of alcohol or drug use? Have some of the following been noticed?

- The smell of alcohol or marijuana on the breath or body
- Dilated pupils
- Increase in activity
- Grandiosity
- Talkativeness
- Extreme quietness
- Slurred or incoherent speech

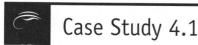

Case Study 4.1
The Marijuana Search

Despite Mr. and Mrs. Green being aware of signs of drug use by their 13-year-old son, John, he kept denying he was using. John seemed to have an answer for everything. He would make them feel guilty for doubting his word and not trusting him. As time went on, the deceptions and lies got more and more complicated. John, despite being caught in these lies, insisted that he was not smoking marijuana. The parents were frustrated and felt the only way they could have their son acknowledge his problem was for them either to catch him using marijuana or to find his marijuana.

One day, while their son was out of the house, they both searched his room. Despite looking everywhere in the room, they couldn't find any tangible evidence of marijuana use. Curiously, the room seemed cleaner and neater than usual—almost as if their son suspected a search was imminent. Perhaps he heard them talking on the phone to the neighbors when they suggested a search. By chance, the father decided to expand the search to other rooms in the house—the bathrooms, family room, bedrooms. They were searching the hall closet when they found what they were looking for. They unscrewed the rubberized handle of the vacuum cleaner and found a small stash of marijuana.

When their son came home, the parents calmly held a family meeting. They asked their son if he had any marijuana in the house. Again, he said he didn't. When they produced the marijuana and told him where they found it, the son didn't blink an eye while saying, "Oh, that stuff. I forgot all about it. I've been holding that for the kid down the block for months now—you know, the one who went into drug treatment. I forgot all about it."

- Bizarre behavior
- Moodiness
- Aggressiveness and show of temper
- Fatigue, lethargy

Has drug paraphernalia been found in the child's room (e.g., rolling paper, syringes, pipes [water pipes], mirrors, razors, baggies)?

11. *Parents.* Do you find yourself justifying your child's behavior? Are you saying things like the following?

- "He or she will grow out of it."
- "This is just a stage."
- "Kids will be kids."
- "I went through the same kind of behavior when I was a kid."

If so, you may be denying signs of alcohol/drug abuse. Remember: *Believe the behavior,* not necessarily what the person says. See Table 4.8 for statistics regarding adolescent and adult drug use.

What we learn from Case Study 4.1 is that it is not necessary to catch your children red-handed using alcohol/drugs. If there is enough evidence of possible alcohol/drug abuse, seek professional help early—don't wait until the problem gets out of hand.

TABLE 4.8

Percentage of U.S. Household Population 12 Years of Age and Older Reporting Past 30-Day Illicit Drug and Alcohol Use According to Age Group: 1997

Drug	Age Group				
	12 to 17 Years	18 to 25 Years	26 to 34 Years	35 years and Older	Total 12 Years and Older
Any illicit drug[a]	11.4	14.7	7.4	3.6	6.4
Marijuana and hashish	9.4	12.8	6.0	2.6	5.1
Cocaine (including crack)	1.0	1.2	0.9	0.5	0.7
Crack	0.4	0.4	0.3	0.2	0.3
Inhalants	2.0	1.0	0.4	*	0.4
Hallucinogens	1.9	2.5	0.5	0.3	0.8
Heroin	0.3	0.5	0.2	0.2	0.3
Nonmedical use of psychotherapeutics[b]	2.1	2.4	1.4	0.8	1.2
Stimulants	0.6	0.7	0.2	0.2	0.3
Sedatives	.01	0.2	0.1	0.1	0.1
Tranquilizers	0.5	1.0	0.7	0.2	0.4
Analgesics	1.3	1.3	0.6	0.5	0.7
Any alcohol use	20.5	58.4	60.2	52.8	51.4
Binge alcohol use[c]	8.3	28.0	23.1	11.7	15.3
Heavy alcohol use[c]	3.1	11.1	7.5	4.0	5.4

Source: *1997 National Household Survey on Drug Abuse Main Findings* (Substance Abuse and Mental Health Services Administration, 1999).

*Low precision; no estimate reported

[a]"Any illicit drug" indicates use at least once of marijuana or hashish, cocaine (including crack), inhalants, hallucinogens (including PCP and LSD), heroin, or any prescription-type psychotherapeutic used nonmedically.

[b]Nonmedical use of any prescription-type stimulant, sedative, tranquilizer, or analgesic; does not include over-the-counter-drugs

[c]"Binge alcohol use" is defined as drinking five or more drinks on the same occasion on at least 1 day in the past 30 days. "Occasion" means at the same time or within a couple of hours of each other. "Heavy alcohol use" is defined as drinking five or more drinks on the same occasion on each of 5 or more days in the past 30 days; all heavy alcohol users are also binge alcohol users.

⚔ Alcohol/ Drugs and Suicide

Another key assessment issue with alcohol/drugs is the potential for suicide. M. Duncan Stanton and Judith Landau-Stanton (1985) state that the "recognition of substance abuse as a suicidal endeavor stems from as far back as 1938 when Menninger likened addiction to chronic suicide." Others have since concluded that the high rate of deaths among addicts "is more than a result of living in dangerous environments and is to a great extent—if not primarily—" (Stanton and Coleman 1980). Table 4.9 highlights key questions related to alcohol/drug use and suicide.

Some common assessment questions for suicide are:

1. Is there a family history of alcohol/drug problems, suicide, or depression?
2. Do you use alcohol/drugs to
   a. overcome bad/shameful feelings?
   b. deal with sleeping problems, depression, or stress?
   c. quiet suicidal or self-destructive thoughts?

TABLE 4.9

The Facts About Suicide

1. Suicide is preventable. Most suicide victims do not want to die.
2. Suicide is the eighth leading cause of death and ranks ahead of homicide.
3. Talking about suicide does not cause someone to be suicidal.
4. Suicidal behavior is not inherited, but the risk is higher for family members who have lost a close relative to suicide.
5. The suicide rate is higher for the elderly than any other age group.
6. Suicide is the second leading cause of death among young people. Accidents are number one, but even some of these accidents could be suicides.
7. Suicide claims the lives of at least 30,000 people annually in the United States.
8. Five states have passed legislation providing for school suicide prevention programs. Federal legislation is still pending.
9. The incidence of suicide among young people has nearly tripled during the past three decades.
10. Three times as many men as women kill themselves, yet three times as many women as men attempt suicide.
11. More than 80 percent of people communicate their intent to kill themselves before they attempt to do so. They leave clues as to their distress and/or plans.

From the American Association of Suicidology, 4201 Connecticut Ave. NW, Suite 310, Washington DC 20008, (202) 237–2280.

3. Do you have suicidal thoughts?
4. How will you do it? Do you have a plan? (Assess the availability or means to commit suicide and the lethality of the means.)
5. Have you previously had suicidal thoughts and have you attempted suicide before? How frequently do these thoughts occur?
6. What role does alcohol/drug use have in relation to suicide? Does it make you more likely or less likely to follow through?
7. On a scale of 1 to 10, how likely are you to kill yourself?
8. How much do you want to die? to live?
9. What would prevent you from committing suicide?
10. What might occur to make life worth living?

Some questions to assess the intention of potential suicide are:

- Have you been thinking about suicide?
- Do you have a plan to take your life?
- Do you feel hopeless about the future?
- Do you think you are a burden to your loved ones?
- Are you feeling so bad you are considering ending your life?
- Do you ever wish you could go to sleep and never wake up?
- Have you ever wanted to stop living?

If a client is suicidal, an extremely important question to ask is "What would prevent you from committing suicide?" This will often lead to a dialogue and plan

Case Study 4.2
Alcohol, Depression, and Suicide

The names and details of this case study have been changed to maintain anonymity.

Cheryl, a 43-year-old manager of a telecommunications company, struggled with bouts of alcoholism and depression. She originally called, seeking help for marital problems. During the assessment session, Cheryl reported her struggles with alcohol and drugs. She admitted that she was probably addicted to cocaine. She was convinced that she could no longer use cocaine. She still struggled to control her drinking. Cheryl had been through one inpatient treatment program and sporadically attended AA but was able to sustain only short periods of abstinence. Her job was extremely stressful, demanding more of her time and energy. She frequently lost her temper with people she worked with. The counselor listened to her "gripes" about her husband and their marital problems but astutely brought the conversation back to Cheryl's alcohol abuse.

In the third session, Cheryl acknowledged the need to strengthen her efforts to seek recovery from alcohol. She began attending AA and was encouraged to obtain an AA sponsor and attend counseling sessions once a week, yet, as time went on, she got distracted from committing to AA and chose a sponsor whom she rarely interacted with. Despite the counselor's efforts to get her to develop a stronger recovery program, she resisted. In future sessions, Cheryl began to talk about overwhelming feelings of depression and suicidal thoughts. She was referred to a psychiatrist for evaluation and was put on antidepressant medication. At the same time, the counselor and Cheryl wrote a contract that she would not attempt suicide and, if she felt suicidal, she would call the counselor or the suicide helpline.

Several months into treatment, Cheryl's depression was stabilizing and she was attending AA meetings more regularly, but she still had not established an active relationship with a sponsor or others in the program. The counsel suggested a woman's recovery therapy group. Cheryl agreed and attended the therapy group each week. At this time, her marriage was headed for a divorce, and her job was getting worse. She eventually moved out of her house and rented an apartment. During this time, she lapsed back to using alcohol and was more depressed. The counselor and group encouraged her to get more active in AA and to continue with her medication. Unfortunately, Cheryl did the opposite. She stopped taking her medication, rarely went to AA, and immersed herself in her work. She spent excessive hours working overtime and eventually dropped out of group counseling, stating that her schedule and finances made it impossible to attend. Despite efforts by her counselor to have her continue in group at a reduced fee, Cheryl decided against it. She continued, only briefly, with her individual counseling. Despite the counselor's best efforts to point out the need for counseling and renewed recovery efforts, Cheryl did not follow through. She began to miss counseling appointments. The counselor pointed out her pattern of "isolating" and continued to try to reengage her into counseling and recovery. Despite the counselor's best efforts, Cheryl went to counseling less frequently and eventually stopped going.

It was nine months later when the counselor received news that Cheryl had killed herself. The combination of alcoholism, depression, marital problems, stress at work, and Cheryl's inability to seek connection with others had led to her suicide.

of action that will prevent suicide. Fortunately, the vast majority of suicidal people do not want to die so much as they want to find a way to live. Quinnett emphasizes the importance of the quality of the relationship between the counselor and the client as being pivotal to suicidal risk assessment. "Even clients in very high-risk groups will choose to live and will agree not to hurt themselves. However, if the counselor is perceived as frightened, angry or disinterested, the risk for suicide may be increased." A common practice involves a written contract with a client who may be suicidal. The client agrees to not take action or to call the therapist or a suicide hot line before making an attempt.

"Silence is the enemy of recovery" (Alcoholics Anonymous proverb).

The task of screening is to determine if an alcohol/drug problem exists. Screening inventories are often used by alcohol/drug counselors and mental health professionals, substance abuse treatment agencies, employee assistance programs, and other agencies to help identify a potential alcohol/drug problem.

⚓ Alcohol/ Drug Screening Inventories

Michigan Alcohol Screening Test (MAST) and Drug Use Screening Inventory (DUSI)

The Michigan Alcohol Screening Test (see test on pages 132 and 133), better known as the MAST, is a brief, easily scored questionnaire. The MAST gives consistent and reliable (alpha of .95) results with a high validity ($r = .90$). The Drug Use Screening Inventory (DUSI) is a bit longer than the MAST. However, it not only helps identify adolescents and adults with alcohol/drug problems but also identifies areas of disturbance and their severity. These areas can then be addressed by referral to appropriate treatment. In addition to substance abuse, the major problem areas identified include behavior, health, psychiatric disorders, social competency, family system, school adjustment (for adolescents), work, peer relationships, and leisure/recreation (see screening inventory on pages 133–138).

Marijuana and Cocaine Screening Questionnaires

The questionnaires on pages 138 and 139 are designed to sensitize individuals to symptoms that might indicate they have problems with either marijuana or cocaine. Individuals check those items that might apply to their use of either marijuana or cocaine. A "yes" answer to several questions may indicate problems requiring further assessment by a professional trained in alcohol/drug treatment.

Part of the problem in identifying drug dependence and addiction is the black-or-white perception many people have about drugs. People tend to put drugs into simplistic categories of good drugs versus bad drugs, licit drugs versus illicit drugs, and soft drugs versus hard drugs (Nowlis 1975). Public perceptions of drugs are based on limited information and personal, often emotional, viewpoints.

MICHIGAN ALCOHOL SCREENING TEST (MAST)

Points		YES	NO
	0. Do you enjoy a drink now and then?	___	___
(2)	*1. Do you feel you are a normal drinker? (By normal we mean you drink less than or as much as most other people.)	___	___
(2)	2. Have you ever awakened the morning after some drinking the night before and found that you could not remember a part of the evening?	___	___
(1)	3. Does your wife, husband, a parent, or other near relative ever worry or complain about your drinking?	___	___
(2)	*4. Can you stop drinking without a struggle after one or two drinks?	___	___
(1)	5. Do you ever feel guilty about your drinking?	___	___
(2)	*6. Do friends or relatives think you are a normal drinker?	___	___
(2)	*7. Are you able to stop drinking when you want to?	___	___
(5)	8. Have you ever attended a meeting of Alcoholics Anonymous (AA)?	___	___
(1)	9. Have you gotten into physical fights when drinking?	___	___
(2)	10. Has your drinking ever created problems between you and your wife, husband, a parent, or other relative?	___	___
(2)	11. Has your wife, husband (or other family members) ever gone to anyone for help about your drinking?	___	___
(2)	12. Have you ever lost friends because of your drinking?	___	___
(2)	13. Have you ever gotten into trouble at work or school because of drinking?	___	___
(2)	14. Have you ever lost a job because of drinking?	___	___
(2)	15. Have you ever neglected your obligations, your family, or your work for two or more days in a row because you were drinking?	___	___
(1)	16. Do you drink before noon fairly often?	___	___
(2)	17. Have you ever been told you have liver trouble? Cirrhosis?	___	___
(2)	**18. After heavy drinking have you ever had Delirium Tremens (D.T.s) or severe shaking, or heard voices or seen things that really weren't there?	___	___
(5)	19. Have you ever gone to anyone for help about your drinking?	___	___
(5)	20. Have you ever been in a hospital because of drinking?	___	___
(2)	21. Have you ever been a patient in a psychiatric hospital or on a psychiatric ward of a general hospital where drinking was part of the problem that resulted in hospitalization?	___	___
(2)	22. Have you ever been seen at a psychiatric or mental health clinic or gone to any doctor, social worker, or clergyman for help with any emotional problem, where drinking was part of the problem?	___	___
(2)	***23. Have you ever been arrested for drunk driving, driving while intoxicated, or driving under the influence of alcoholic beverages? (IF YES, How many times? _____)	___	___
(2)	***24. Have you ever been arrested, or taken into custody, even for a few hours, because of other drunk behavior? (IF YES, How many times? _____)	___	___

    * Alcoholic response in negative
    ** 5 points for delerium tremens
    ***2 points for *each* arrest

MICHIGAN ALCOHOLISM SCREENING TEST (MAST) (*continued*)

Scoring System: In general, five points or more would place the subject in an "alcoholic" category. Four points would be suggestive of alcoholism, three points or fewer would indicate the subject was not alcoholic.

Programs using the above scoring system find it very sensitive at the five point level and it tends to find more people alcoholic than anticipated. However, it is a screening test and should be sensitive at its lower levels.

References

Selzer, M.L. "The Michigan Alcoholism Screening Test (MAST): The Quest for a New Diagnostic Instrument." *American Journal of Psychiatry* 3 (1971): 176–81.

Selzer, M.L., A. Vinokur, and L. van Rooijen. "A Self-Administered Short Version of the Michigan Alcoholism Screening Test (SMAST)." *Journal of Studies on Alcohol* 36 (1975): 117–26.

DRUG USE SCREENING INVENTORY

DOMAIN I: SUBSTANCE USE

    A. Drug Preference

1.   How many times have you used each of the drugs listed below in the last month? Put an "X" in each box that applies to you.

	0 times	1–2 times	3–9 times	10–20 times	More than 20 times
Alcohol					
Cocaine/crack					
Marijuana/pot					
Stimulants/uppers					
LSD/mescaline					
Tranquilizers					
Pain killers					
Heroin/opiates					
PCP					
Sniff gases or fumes					
Other					

2.   Circle the drugs that you think you may have a problem with.
3.   Shade in the circle of the drug that you prefer the most.

Instructions: Answer *all* of the following questions. Even if a question does not apply exactly, answer according to whether it is mostly yes (true) or mostly no (false). Answer the questions as if they apply to you within the past year and leading up to the present time. Put a check mark (✓) in the box for each question.

DRUG USE SCREENING INVENTORY (*continued*)

B. Drug Involvement

	Yes	No
1. Have you ever had a craving or very strong desire for alcohol or drugs?	___	___
2. Have you ever had to use more and more alcohol or drugs to get the effect you want?	___	___
3. Have you ever felt that you could not control your alcohol or drug use?	___	___
4. Have you ever felt that you were "hooked" on alcohol or drugs?	___	___
5. Have you ever missed out on activities because you spent too much money on alcohol or drugs?	___	___
6. Did you ever break rules, miss curfew, or break the law because you were high on alcohol or drugs?	___	___
7. Do you change rapidly from very happy to very sad or from very sad to very happy because of drugs?	___	___
8. Have you ever had a car accident after using alcohol or drugs?	___	___
9. Have you ever accidentally hurt yourself or someone else after using alcohol or drugs?	___	___
10. Have you ever had a serious argument or fight with a friend or family member after drinking or drug use?	___	___
11. Have you ever had trouble getting along with any of your friends because of alcohol or drug use?	___	___
12. Have you ever experienced any *withdrawal symptoms* following use of alcohol or drugs (e.g., headaches, nausea, vomiting, shaking)?	___	___
13. Have you ever had a problem remembering what you had done when you were under the effects of alcohol or drugs?	___	___
14. Do you like to play drinking games when you go to parties?	___	___
15. Do you have trouble resisting using alcohol or drugs?	___	___

DOMAIN II: BEHAVIOR PATTERNS

	Yes	No
1. Do you argue a lot?	___	___
2. Do you brag a lot?	___	___
3. Do you tease or do harmful things to animals?	___	___
4. Do you yell a lot?	___	___
5. Are you stubborn?	___	___
6. Are you suspicious of other people?	___	___
7. Do you swear or use dirty language a lot?	___	___
8. Do you tease others?	___	___
9. Do you have a bad temper?	___	___
10. Are you very shy?	___	___
11. Do you threaten to hurt people?	___	___
12. Do you talk louder than other kids?	___	___
13. Are you easily upset?	___	___
14. Do you do things a lot without first thinking about the consequences?	___	___
15. Do you do risky or dangerous things a lot?	___	___
16. Do you take advantage of people if you can?	___	___
17. Do you generally feel angry?	___	___
18. Do you spend most of your free time by yourself?	___	___

DRUG USE SCREENING INVENTORY (*continued*)

	Yes	No
19. Are you a loner?	___	___
20. Are you very sensitive to criticism?	___	___

DOMAIN III: HEALTH STATUS

	Yes	No
1. Have you had a physical exam or been under a doctor's care in the last year?	___	___
2. Have you had any accidents or injuries that still bother you?	___	___
3. Do you sleep too much or too little?	___	___
4. Have you recently lost or gained more than 10 pounds?	___	___
5. Do you have less energy than you think you should have?	___	___
6. Do you have trouble with your breathing or with coughing?	___	___
7. Do you have any concerns about sex or trouble with your sex organs?	___	___
8. Have your ever had sex with someone who shot up drugs?	___	___
9. Have you had trouble with abdominal pain or nausea in the past year?	___	___
10. Have your eyewhites ever turned yellow?	___	___

DOMAIN IV: PSYCHIATRIC DISORDER

	Yes	No
1. Have you ever intentionally damaged someone else's property?	___	___
2. Have you stolen things on several occasions?	___	___
3. Have you gotten into more fights than most kids?	___	___
4. Are you a fidgety person?	___	___
5. Are you restless and can't sit still?	___	___
6. Do you get frustrated easily?	___	___
7. Do you have trouble concentrating?	___	___
8. Do you feel sad a lot?	___	___
9. Do you bite your fingernails?	___	___
10. Do you have trouble sleeping?	___	___
11. Are you nervous?	___	___
12. Do you get easily frightened?	___	___
13. Do you worry a lot?	___	___
14. Do you have trouble getting your mind off things?	___	___
15. Do people stare at you?	___	___
16. Do you hear things that no one else around you hears?	___	___
17. Do you have special powers nobody else has?	___	___
18. Are you afraid to be around people?	___	___
19. Do you often feel like you want to cry?	___	___
20. Do you have so much energy that you don't know what to do with yourself?	___	___

DOMAIN V: SOCIAL COMPETENCY

	Yes	No
1. Do kids your own age dislike you?	___	___
2. Are you usually unhappy with how well you do in activities with your friends?	___	___
3. Is it difficult to make friends in a new group?	___	___
4. Do people take advantage of you?	___	___
5. Are you afraid to stand up for your rights?	___	___
6. Is it very hard for you to ask for help from others?	___	___
7. Are you easily influenced by other kids?	___	___
8. Do you prefer doing things with kids much older than you?	___	___

DRUG USE SCREENING INVENTORY (*continued*)

	Yes	No
9. Do you worry about how your actions will affect others?	——	——
10. Do you have difficulty standing up for your opinions?	——	——
11. Do you have trouble saying "no" to people?	——	——
12. Do you feel uncomfortable if someone gives you a compliment?	——	——
13. Do people see you as not being a friendly person?	——	——
14. Do you avoid eye contact when talking to people?	——	——

DOMAIN VI: FAMILY SYSTEM

	Yes	No
1. Has a member of your family (mother, father, brother, or sister) ever used marijuana or cocaine?	——	——
2. Has a member of your family used alcohol to the point of causing problems at home, at work, or with friends?	——	——
3. Has a member of your family ever been arrested?	——	——
4. Do you have frequent arguments with your parents or guardians which involve yelling and screaming?	——	——
5. Does your family hardly ever do things together?	——	——
6. Are your parents or guardians unaware of your likes and dislikes?	——	——
7. Are there no clear rules about what you can and cannot do?	——	——
8. Are your parents or guardians unaware of what you really think or feel about things that are important to you?	——	——
9. Do your parents or guardians argue a lot with each other?	——	——
10. Are your parents or guardians often unaware of where you are and what you are doing?	——	——
11. Are your parents or guardians away from home most of the time?	——	——
12. Do you feel that either of your parents or guardians don't care about you?	——	——
13. Are you unhappy about your living arrangements?	——	——
14. Do you feel in danger at home?	——	——

DOMAIN VII: SCHOOL PERFORMANCE/ADJUSTMENT

	Yes	No
1. Do you dislike school?	——	——
2. Do you have trouble concentrating in school or when studying?	——	——
3. Are your grades below average?	——	——
4. Do you cut school more than two days a month?	——	——
5. Are you absent from school a lot?	——	——
6. Have you thought seriously about quitting school?	——	——
7. Do you often not do your school assignments?	——	——
8. Do you often feel sleepy in class?	——	——
9. Are you often late for class?	——	——
10. Do you have different friends at school than you did last year?	——	——
11. Do you feel irritable and upset when in school?	——	——
12. Are you bored in school?	——	——
13. Are your grades in school worse than they used to be?	——	——
14. Do you feel in danger at school?	——	——
15. Have you ever failed a grade in school?	——	——
16. Do you feel unwelcome in school clubs or extracurricular activities?	——	——

DRUG USE SCREENING INVENTORY (*continued*)

	Yes	No
17. Have you ever missed or been late to school because of alcohol or drugs?	___	___
18. Have you ever been in trouble at school because of alcohol or drugs?	___	___
19. Have alcohol or drugs ever interfered with your homework or school assignments?	___	___
20. Have you ever been suspended?	___	___

DOMAIN VIII: WORK ADJUSTMENT

	Yes	No
1. Have you ever had a paying job that you were fired from?	___	___
2. Have you ever stopped working at a job because you just didn't care?	___	___
3. Do you need help from others to go about finding a job?	___	___
4. Have you been frequently absent or late for work?	___	___
5. Do you find it difficult to complete work tasks?	___	___
6. Have you ever made money doing something that is against the law?	___	___
7. Have you ever used alcohol or drugs while working on a job?	___	___
8. Have you ever been fired because of drugs?	___	___
9. Do you have trouble getting along with bosses?	___	___
10. Do you mostly work so that you can get money to buy drugs?	___	___

DOMAIN IX: PEER RELATIONSHIPS

	Yes	No
1. Do any of your friends regularly use alcohol or drugs?	___	___
2. Do any of your friends sell or give drugs to other kids?	___	___
3. Do any of your friends cheat on school tests?	___	___
4. Do your parents or guardians dislike your friends?	___	___
5. Have any of your friends ever been in trouble with the law?	___	___
6. Are most of your friends older than you?	___	___
7. Do your friends cut school at lot?	___	___
8. Do your friends get bored at parties when there is no alcohol served?	___	___
9. Have your friends brought drugs or alcohol to parties in the past year?	___	___
10. Have your friends stolen anything from a store or damaged school property on purpose during the past year?	___	___
11. Do you belong to a gang?	___	___
12. Are you bothered now by problems you are having with a friend?	___	___
13. Is there no friend you can confide in?	___	___
14. Compared to most kids, do you have few friends?	___	___

DOMAIN X: LEISURE/RECREATION

	Yes	No
1. Compared to most kids, do you do fewer sports?	___	___
2. Do you go out for fun on school nights without permission?	___	___
3. On a typical day, do you watch more than two hours of TV?	___	___
4. Are the parents absent at the parties you have gone to recently?	___	___
5. Do you exercise less than most kids you know?	___	___
6. Is your free time spent just hanging out with friends?	___	___
7. Are you bored most of the time?	___	___
8. Do you do most of your recreation or leisure activities alone?	___	___
9. Do you use alcohol or drugs for recreational reasons?	___	___
10. Compared to most kids, are you less involved in hobbies or outside interests?	___	___

Drug Use Screening Inventory (*continued*)

	Yes	No
11. Are you dissatisfied with how you spend your free time?	——	——
12. Do you get tired very quickly when you exert yourself?	——	——

Instructions: Go back over the answers and make sure that every question has either the "yes" or "no" box filled in with a check mark.

Cocaine Screening Questionnaire

Check the box before any question to which you would answer yes.

❑   1. Are you using more cocaine than you plan to use and do you find that you are enjoying it less? That is, your tolerance is developing and despite not feeling very well, you continue to use.

❑   2. Are you experiencing three or more of the following physical signs?
   ❑ Excessive periods of fatigue
   ❑ Sinus problems and nose bleeds
   ❑ Chest pains and palpitations
   ❑ Tremors and poor coordination
   ❑ Light spots on the periphery of your vision
   ❑ Sleep disturbances, sleepiness,
      or excessive sleeping
   ❑ Itching, scratching, and/or skin lesions
   ❑ Trouble breathing and/or catching your breath
   ❑ Decreased appetite or weight loss
   ❑ Headaches
   ❑ Hoarseness

❑   3. Do you feel apathetic, disinterested, depressed; have you lost the ability to concentrate?

❑   4. Do you experience mood swings, irritability, short temperedness, emotional outbursts, rage or excessive sadness, paranoid and/or frantic bizarre behavior?

❑   5. As a result of cocaine use, have you been absent, late, or exhibited inappropriate behavior at work?

❑   6. Are family members and friends suggesting that you have a problem with cocaine and/or are you lying about your frequency of cocaine use?

❑   7. Are you reducing outside interests, withdrawing from, or in conflict with friends and family members?

❑   8. Are you experiencing financial and/or legal problems as a direct or indirect result of cocaine use?

❑   9. Are you injecting or freebasing cocaine?

❑   10. The morning after cocaine use are you feeling depressed, remorseful, guilty, and/or shameful about your behavior the night before?

If you checked the boxes before two or more of these questions you may have a potentially serious cocaine problem. Pursue further evaluation with a chemical dependency professional.
© Copyright, July 1988, Richard Fields.

Marijuana Screening Questionnaire

Denial of marijuana dependence and addiction stems from misconceptions of the harmlessness of this drug. Current research clearly documents the physical, psychological, and emotional harm of marijuana in the 1990s.

This questionnaire is a tool to help those who might have a problem, or those individuals and family members concerned with others who might have a problem with marijuana. Check the box before any question to which you would answer yes.

❑   1. Are you smoking marijuana
   ❑ in the morning
   ❑ on a daily basis
   ❑ during work/school time
   (one or more checks is a yes answer)

❑   2. While under the influence of marijuana, do you experience any of the following symptoms?
   ❑ irritability
   ❑ anxiety
   ❑ tremors
   ❑ insomnia
   ❑ restlessness
   ❑ sweating
   ❑ feeling loss of control
   ❑ nausea, vomiting

❑   3. As a result of marijuana use, do you experience a loss of initiative and ambition and/or a withdrawal from customary interests and interpersonal relationships?

❑   4. After using marijuana have you experienced any of the following?
   ❑ a clouding of mental processes
   ❑ flashbacks
   ❑ delusions
   ❑ impaired thinking and confusion
   ❑ fear of brain damage

❑   5. Have others commented on your poor driving skills while under the influence of marijuana, and/or have you noticed impairment in perceptual motor skills, driving, decision making, and/or tracking and reaction time?

❑   6. As a result of using marijuana, have you experienced any adverse negative consequences (e.g., problems at work/school, accidents, difficulty in relationships, or mood swings)?

❑   7. Do you think about using marijuana often (i.e., do events, time of day, or particular daily situations trigger the desire to use marijuana)?

❑   8. Have you been unable to stop using marijuana for three months or longer without substituting other drugs, alcohol, or medication?

❑   9. Do you use marijuana with cocaine, alcohol, and/or other drugs?

❑   10. Do other members of your family have problems with marijuana, alcohol, and/or other drugs?

❑   11. Do you use marijuana to alleviate stress, loneliness, depression, boredom, and/or problems in relationships?

❑   12. Did you start using marijuana at a young age and/or have you been using marijuana regularly for several years?

If you checked three or more of these questions, consult a specialist in alcohol and drug assessment and treatment for further evaluation.

© Copyright, July 1988, Richard Fields.

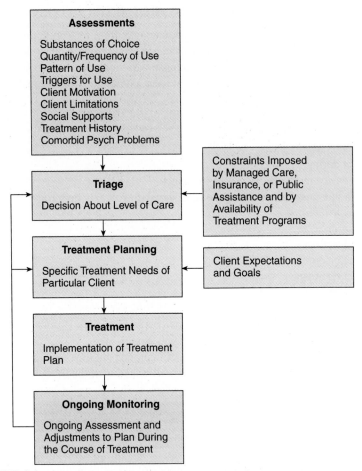

FIGURE 4.4   *Key Elements of Treatment Decision Making*

⚔ Assessment   Once screening has established that a substance abuse problem exists, the next step is to assess the nature, scope, and severity of the problem. A seasoned alcohol/drug treatment professional who specializes in alcohol/drug assessment and treatment services can conduct a basic assessment and establish a diagnosis. More time and energy are involved in further assessing the dimensions and depth of the substance abuse problem (see Figures 4.4 and 4.5). The negative consequences—deficits in developmental skills, mood and personality disorders, family and marital impact of substance abuse, and other psychosocial factors—need to be assessed. This is essential in order to establish a clinical decision about treatment. A listing of assessment tools is found in Table 4.10.

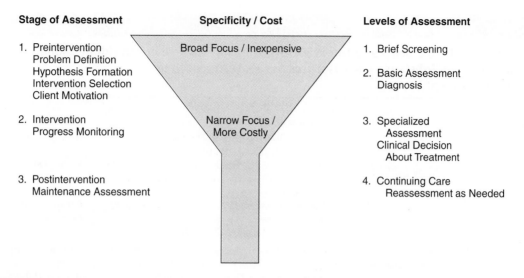

Stage of Assessment

1. Preintervention
   Problem Definition
   Hypothesis Formation
   Intervention Selection
   Client Motivation

2. Intervention
   Progress Monitoring

3. Postintervention
   Maintenance Assessment

Specificity / Cost

Broad Focus / Inexpensive

Narrow Focus /
More Costly

Levels of Assessment

1. Brief Screening

2. Basic Assessment
   Diagnosis

3. Specialized
   Assessment
   Clinical Decision
   About Treatment

4. Continuing Care
   Reassessment as Needed

FIGURE 4.5   *Assessment*

TABLE 4.10

Examples of Instruments and Interviews Appropriate for Use in Multidimensional Assessments of Substance Use Disorders Across Different Stages of the Assessment Process

Stage of Assessment	Assessment Domain	Examples of Instruments	References
Screening	Alcohol use	CAGE Questions	Mayfield et al. 1974
		Two Item Alcohol Screening Questions	Cyr and Wartman 1988
		NET	Russell 1994
		T-ACE	Sokol et al. 1989
		TWEAK	Russell et al. 1991
		Alcohol Use Disorders Identification Test (AUDIT)	Saunders et al. 1993
		Michigan Alcohol Screening Test (MAST)	Selzer 1971
		Brief Michigan Alcohol Screening Test (bMAST)	Pokorny et al. 1972
		Short Michigan Alcohol Screening Test (sMAST)	Zung 1984
	Drug use	Two Item Alcohol and Drug Screening Questions	Brown et al. 1997
		Drug Abuse Screening Test (DAST)	Skinner 1982
Problem assessment	Alcohol use patterns	Time-Line Follow Back	Sobell and Sobell 1992
		Form-90	Miller 1996
		Comprehensive Drinker Profile (CDP)	Miller and Marlatt 1984
		Alcohol Use Inventory (AUI)	Wanberg et al. 1977
	Drug use patterns	Addiction Severity Index (ASI)	McLellan et al. 1992
		Drug History Questionnaire (DHQ)	Sobell et al. 1995
		Individual Assessment Profile (IAP)	Flynn et al. 1995

TABLE 4.10 (continued)

Examples of Instruments and Interviews Appropriate for Use in Multidimensional Assessments of Substance Use Disorders Across Different Stages of the Assessment Process

Stage of Assessment	Assessment Domain	Examples of Instruments	References
	Diagnoses	Psychiatric Research Interview for Substance and Mental Disorders (PRISM)[a]	Hasin et al. 1996
		Diagnostic Interview Schedule (DIS)	Robins et al. 1981
		Schedules for Clinical Assessment in Neuropsychiatry (SCAN)	Wing et al. 1990
		Composite International Diagnostic Interview (CIDI)	Robins et al. 1988
		Alcohol Use Disorders and Associated Disabilities Interview Schedule (AUDADIS)	Grant and Hasin 1990
	Outcome expectancies—alcohol	Negative Alcohol Expectancy Questionnaire (NAEQ)	Jones and McMahon 1993
		Alcohol Expectancy Questionnaire (AEQ)	Brown et al. 1987
		Drinking Expectancy Questionnaire (DEQ)	Young and Knight 1989
		Alcohol Beliefs Scale (ABS)	Connors and Maisto 1988
		Effects of Drinking Alcohol (EDA)	Leigh 1987
		Comprehensive Effects of Alcohol Scale (CEAS)	Fromme et al. 1993
	Outcome expectancies—drugs	Cocaine Expectancy Questionnaire (CEQ)	Jaffe and Kilbey 1994
		Cocaine Effect Expectancy Questionnaire—Likert (CEEQ-L)	Schafer and Fals-Stewart 1993
		Cocaine Effect Expectancy Questionnaire (CEEQ)	Schafer and Brown 1991
		Marijuana Effects Expectancy Questionnaire (MEEQ)	Schafer and Brown 1991
	Relapse risk	Substance Abuse Relapse Assessment (SARA)	Schonfeld et al. 1993
		Cocaine Relapse Interview (CRI)	McKay et al. 1996
		Cocaine High-Risk Situations Questionnaire (CHRSQ)	Michalec et al. 1992
		Situational Competency Test (SCT)	Chaney et al. 1978
		Reasons for Drinking Questionnaire (RFDQ)	Zywiak et al. 1996
		Reasons for Heroin Use Questionnaire (RFHUQ)	Heather et al. 1991
		Relapse Situation Appraisal Questionnaire (RSAQ)	Myers et al. 1996
	Coping: substance-related	Coping Behaviors Inventory (CBI)	Litman et al. 1983
		Problem Skills Inventory (PSI)	Hawkins et al. 1986
		Alcohol Specific Role Play Test (ASRPT)	Monti et al. 1993
	Coping: general	Ways of Coping Checklist (WOC)	Folkman and Lazarus 1980
		COPE	Carver et al. 1989
		Coping Responses Inventory (CRI)	Moos 1995
	Self-efficacy—alcohol	Alcohol Abstinence Self-Efficacy Scale (AASE)	DiClemente et al. 1994
		Drinking Refusal Self-Efficacy Questionnaire (DRSEQ)	Young et al. 1991
		Individualized Self-Efficacy Survey (ISS)	Miller et al. 1994
		Inventory of Drinking Situations (IDS)	Annis et al. 1987
		Situational Confidence Questionnaire (SCQ)	Annis and Graham 1988

TABLE 4.10 (continued)

Examples of Instruments and Interviews Appropriate for Use in Multidimensional Assessments of Substance Use Disorders Across Different Stages of the Assessment Process

Stage of Assessment	Assessment Domain	Examples of Instruments	References
	Self-efficacy—drugs	Inventory of Drug-Taking Situations (IDTS)	Annis and Graham 1991
		Drug Abuse Self-Efficacy Scale (DASES)	Martin et al. 1995
		Situational Confidence Questionnaire—Heroin (SCQ-Heroin)	Barber et al. 1991
Personal assessment	Personality	California Psychological Inventory (CPI)	Gough 1975
		NEO Personality Inventory	Costa and McCrae 1992
		Personality Research Form (PRF)	Jackson 1994
	Psychopathology	Minnesota Multiphasic Personality Inventory (MMPI-2)	Hathaway et al. 1989
		Millon Clinical Multiaxial Inventory (MCMI-II)	Millon 1992
		Psychological Screening Inventory (PSI)	Lanyon 1970
	Emotional state	Symptom Checklist-90 (SCL-90)	Derogatis 1977
	Anger	State-Trait Anger Inventory	Spielberger et al. 1983
		Multidimensional Anger Inventory	Siegel 1986
	Anxiety	State-Trait Anxiety Inventory	Spielberger et al. 1970
		Beck Anxiety Inventory	Beck et al. 1988
	Depression	Beck Depression Inventory (BDI)	Beck et al. 1961
		Center for Epidemiologic Studies Depression Scale (CES-D)	Radloff 1977
		Inventory to Diagnose Depression (IDD)	Zimmerman and Coryell 1987
	General life/social function	Addiction Severity Index (ASI)	McLellan et al. 1992
		Psychosocial Functioning Inventory (PFI)	Feragne et al. 1983
Treatment-related factors	Readiness to change	Stages of Change Readiness and Treatment Eagerness Scale (SOCRATES)	Miller and Tonigan 1996
		Readiness to Change Questionnaire (RTCQ)	Rollnick et al. 1992
		University of Rhode Island Readiness to Change Assessment (URICA)	McConnaughy et al. 1983
		Desire for Help Scale (DHS)	Simpson and Joe 1993
		Intrinsic/Extrinsic Motivation to Quit Questionnaire (IEMQ)	Curry et al. 1990 McBride et al. 1994
	Barriers to treatment	Barriers to Treatment Instrument (BTI)	Allen 1994
		Reasons for Delaying Seeking Treatment (RDST)	Cunningham et al. 1993
		Fears About Treatment Questionnaire (FTQ)	Oppenheimer et al. 1988

TABLE 4.10 (continued)

Examples of Instruments and Interviews Appropriate for Use in Multidimensional Assessments of Substance Use Disorders Across Different Stages of the Assessment Process

Stage of Assessment	Assessment Domain	Examples of Instruments	References
	Reasons for seeking treatment	Treatment Seeking Scale (TSS)	Cunningham et al. 1994
		Treatment Motivation Questionnaire (TMQ)	Ryan et al. 1995
		Readiness for Treatment Scale (RTS)	Simpson and Joe 1993
		Reasons for Giving Up Drugs and Alcohol	Murphy and Bentall 1992
		Reasons for Coming to Treatment Questionnaire (RCTQ)	Oppenheimer et al. 1988
		Circumstances, Motivation, Readiness, and Suitability Scales (CMRS)	DeLeon et al. 1994
	Treatment goals	Treatment Goals Inventory (TGI)	Glaser and Skinner 1981
	Treatment services utilization	Treatment Services Review (TSR)	McLellan et al. 1992
Collateral information	Collateral reports	Form-90	Miller 1996
		Comprehensive Drinker Profile (CDP)	Miller and Marlatt 1984, 1987

aPRISM was formerly known as the SCID-A
Source: McCrady, Barbara S., and Elizabeth E. Epstein. *Addictions: A Comprehensive Guide Book*. Cary, NC: Oxford University Press, 1999.

Summary

The new behavioral definition of addiction was developed by David Smith to better classify addiction to cocaine. Currently, counselors use this behavioral definition in assessing an addiction to alcohol/drugs. The three basic components of the definition of addiction are (1) obsessive-compulsive behavior with alcohol/drugs; (2) an inability to stop using chemicals; and (3) continued use despite negative or adverse consequences. Another way to remember this definition is to focus on the three Cs—*compulsion, control,* and *consequences.*

The first of five key points in describing this stage model of alcohol/drug use is that, at early stages of use, set and setting greatly influence the individual's reaction to the chemicals used; throughout use, these factors continue to be dominant. *Set* refers to the psychological and emotional frame of mind of the individual when using alcohol/drugs. Setting involves not only the physical environment but also the social and interpersonal environment at the time of taking alcohol/drugs.

Second, alcohol/drug use is progressive; individuals get more involved as they progress through the stages. Third, the alcohol/drug effect is based on the drugs used, the individual (set), and the environment (setting).

Fourth, the experimental stage is using alcohol/drugs in different situations and under different circumstances situational or circumstantial use. Referring to drug use as recreational during the experimental stage is misleading and minimizes the hazards of use at this stage. Fifth, the term *drug abuse* has limited functional utility and is often no more than an arbitrary code word for that drug use which is presently considered wrong.

Jellinek defines five distinct types of alcoholism, ranging from psychological dependence to periodic, unpredictable drinking binges. The popular Jellinek charts in this section emphasize the progressive nature of the disease of alcoholism.

Assessment involves not only taking a good alcohol/drug history but also assessing the individual's vulnerability to alcohol/drugs, the consequences of alcohol/drug use, and the person's suicide potential. During recovery, denial is the major perceptual problem, due to users' minimizations and rationalizations of their involvement with alcohol/drugs.

The stages of cocaine recovery are fairly similar to alcohol and other drug recovery periods. They include the following:

- Withdrawal (0 to 15 days)
- Honeymoon (15 to 45 days)
- The Wall (45 to 120 days)
- Adjustment (120 to 180 days)
- Resolution (180 to 360 days)

The length of each stage of recovery, however, can be quite variable for alcohol and other drugs.

These perspectives are a bleak reality to the multifaceted problems of alcoholism and drug addiction. Ideally, if all of these perspectives worked cooperatively and had the necessary support, we might be better able to address the alcohol/drug epidemic.

References

Danaher, B.G., and E. Lichtenstein. *Becoming an Ex-Smoker.* Englewood Cliffs, NJ: Prentice Hall, 1978.

Diagnostic and Statistical Manual of Mental Disorders, 4e, American Psychiatric Association, 1994.

Jellinek, E.M. *The Disease Concept of Alcoholism.* New Haven, CT: Hillhouse Press, 1960.

McCrady, Barbara S., and E. Epstein. *Addiction: A Comprehensive Guide Book.* Cary, NC: Oxford University Press, 1999.

Michigan Alcoholism Screening Test (MAST), developed by Melvin L. Selzer, M.D.

Nowlis, Helen. *Drugs Demystified.* Paris: UNESCO Press, 1975.

Quinnett, Paul. "The 'S' Question." *Professional Counselor Magazine* (December 1995): 15–16, 64–68.

Rankin, James G. *Core Knowledge of the Drug Field: A Basic Manual for Trainers.* Toronto: Addiction Research Foundation, 1978.

Rawson, Richard. *Cocaine Recovery Issues: The Neurobehavioral Model.* Beverly Hills, CA: Matrix Institute on Addictions, 1989.

Smith, David, and Donald Wesson. *Treating Cocaine Dependence.* Center City, MN: Hazeldon Foundation, 1988.

Stanton, M.D., and Judith Landau-Stanton. "Treating Suicidal Adolescents and Their Families." In *Handbook of Adolescents and Family Therapy,* ed. Marsha Pravder Mirkin and Stuart L. Koman. New York: Gardner Press, 1985.

Stanton, M.D., and S.B. Coleman. "The Participatory Aspects of Indirect Self-Destructive Behavior." In *The Many Faces of Suicide,* ed. N.L. Farberow. New York: McGraw-Hill, 1980.

Washton, Arnold M. *Psychotherapy and Substance Abuse: A Practitioner's Handbook.* New York: Guilford Press, 1995.

Family

Substance Abuse and Family Systems

Chapter Objectives

1. Describe families as systems.
2. Describe the need for the entire alcoholic/addict family system to seek recovery.
3. Explain the use of the term *imbalanced* instead of *dysfunctional* when describing maladaptive family behavior.
4. Describe the family roles in an alcoholic/addict family system.
5. Identify rules, values, motto, communication, drugs of choice, and functions of drugs in a rigid, ambiguous, overextended, and distorted family system.
6. Identify and describe the survival roles in an alcohol/addict and imbalanced family system (Wegscheider-Cruse model).
7. Define enabling behavior and give examples of each of the five types of this behavior.
8. Identify the stages of family recovery in an alcoholic/addict family system.

❧ Families as Systems

Initially, one must look at the family as a system. Some key elements of family systems are that they all have rules, values, verbal and nonverbal methods of communicating, boundaries, roles, and patterns of interaction. Systems always seek some level of homeostasis, or balance. Alcoholism and drug dependency is a dysfunctional element in family life. The result is a disequilibrium, or imbalance, forcing family members to compensate and give up aspects of their own sense of self in an attempt to keep the family in balance. One could describe the alcoholic/addict family as a top-heavy top that tries to spin in a functional pattern but, instead, swerves to one side and skids in a diagonal direction until it stops. The individuals in this system are all compensating in different yet similar ways. It's as if they are walking around with a heavy weight on one shoulder; they have to either lean to one side to walk properly or use all their energy to try to compensate and look as if they are walking upright. Both positions require a great deal of energy. Family therapist Carl Whitaker (Whitaker and Napier 1978) has described the family as the source of all kinds of electrical energy, with positive and negative voltages.

Virginia Satir (1967), a famous family therapist, was the first to describe the family using the metaphor of a mobile: if the wires on one of the pieces of the mobile are twisted, the mobile spins improperly. Instead of a delicately balanced mobile, each piece gets entangled and out of balance at the slightest breeze. A well-balanced mobile, or family system, sways and flexes with the strong gusts and heavy winds of life. The family with alcohol/drug problems is described as an imbalanced, or dysfunctional, family system. In a healthy family, the system is flexible and fluid, open (not rigid), predictable (not inconsistent), and balanced in meeting both the individual's and the family's needs.

Looking at the family as a system is imperative in addressing the problem of alcohol/drug de-

---

*The names and circumstances of case studies in this chapter have been changed to maintain anonymity.

pendence and addiction. If the family system does not change and the family members do not do their recovery work, the same dysfunctional styles of communication and interaction make the alcoholic/addict at risk for alcohol/drug relapse or the development of another dysfunctional behavior.

To effectively treat the alcoholic/addict, the rest of the family system also needs treatment. The dysfunctional aspect of the disease has affected all family members. The high alcohol/drug relapse rate is often attributable to the lack of recovery by the family members. Too frequently, the alcoholic/addict is the focus of help, and the family members deny their own enabling and codependent behavior. The messages from the family are "Just fix the alcoholic/addict" and "Just get him or her to stop using alcohol/drugs and then everything will be O.K."

Functional and Dysfunctional Systems

Annie Bauger.

Family members avoid being active in treatment because they resist looking at their own behavior; they fear getting in touch with painful feelings, which may be overwhelming.

Another fear is whether the family system can survive reexperiencing these feelings. They wonder, "Has the family been hurt beyond repair?" and "Will the family be able to work through the violations of the past?" These questions and others need to be addressed for the effective recovery of the alcoholic/addict and the family members.

The expression *dry drunk* refers to alcoholics/addicts who are abstaining from alcohol/drug use but either are unaware of other behavioral, personality, and relationship problems or are choosing not to address these maladaptive behaviors. Their overall behavior and personality styles are very similar to when they were using alcohol/drugs. Essentially, they have chosen not to deal with the underlying issues that contributed to the negative aspects of their personalities. For some, it is certainly enough that they are sober. Others who are still experiencing feelings of depression, fear, rage, and anxiety may decide to get help and address the problem.

After one to five years of being sober, recovering alcoholics/addicts often realize that they are still having problems, especially in interpersonal relationships. This is often described as the addicts' "second bottom." The first bottom is the realization that they can no longer continue to use alcohol/drugs. The second bottom is the realization that they are still not having fun, due to unresolved personality issues. They ask themselves the question "Now that I am years sober, am I having fun yet?" The answer frequently is "No, my life is more manageable but I'm still not feeling better."

The family of the alcoholic/addict also goes through a kind of dry drunk. The family may glow in the joy of the alcoholic/addict's initial sobriety and may now feel validated that he or she is, indeed, okay. From the viewpoint of friends, neighbors, and community, "he or she did the right thing." There is no discounting that the family members were courageous in struggling to get the alcoholic/addict into treatment. However, they must continue the struggle to develop a healthier family system. In many cases, the family returns to old dysfunctional patterns. It is fair to say that recovery from the diseases of alcoholism and drug addiction is an ongoing process for the individual and the family.

⚔ Family Rules

Each family makes decisions and choices based on the rules, boundaries, and alliances of family members. Families have rules about who, when, and how feelings are expressed.

Family rules often involve rules of communication—who is allowed to express feelings, how they are expressed, and how they are received.

Rules in the alcoholic/addict family system often focus on ways to communicate and believe in order to deal with the substance abusing person. This often involves secret keeping, or what Claudia Block (1981) referred to as the three rules that children of alcoholics often learn to live by: "Don't talk. Don't trust. Don't feel."

"Talking, especially about the substance abuse, might cause even more problems. Trusting usually leads to disappointment when parents do not come through with their promises. Feeling is too painful, and expression of feelings is not allowed because it might cause more trouble." (Lawson and Lawson 1998)

⚔ *Imbalanced vs. Dysfunctional*

Nathan Ackerman first coined the term dysfunctional family in 1958, when referring to alcoholic family systems. Throughout the literature of the alcohol/drug and mental health fields—and even in this textbook—we frequently use the term *dysfunctional* in describing families, systems, relationships, parenting, behavior, and individuals. The term *dysfunctional* is frequently a shame-based, negative label, with a negative emotional tone. Labeling them as dysfunctional discourages families and individuals who are struggling with the problems of alcohol/drug dependence. Many people have been annoyed and discouraged at being told they are dysfunctional. It sounds hopeless. For example, what good does it do to tell a patient, relative, or friend, "You come from a shame-based, dysfunctional family system" or "You have a codependent enabling, dysfunctional relationship with your spouse and children"? This doesn't really help the person and shames him or her, making the person feel helpless and hopeless. Most people feel a sense of betrayal in even thinking about their families in such a derogatory manner.

Instead of using *dysfunctional,* replace it with the term *imbalanced,* for this is truly what we are looking at—an imbalance in the individual, and family members' lives. Remember Satir's image of an out-of-balance mobile. It is so much more hopeful to seek treatment if one has the expectation of becoming balanced. It is also a far more positive approach.

There is truly an emotional systems imbalance in the alcoholic/addict family. The term *imbalance* gives hope that there is a way to get help and better manage the system. The goal is to establish balance and order by addressing the problems in the family.

There are different kinds of imbalance in family systems. Alcohol/drugs serve a different function in each of these imbalanced systems. Next we will examine rigid, ambiguous, overextended, and distorted family systems to better understand imbalanced family systems. In each family system, the drug of choice and its function are for illustration, not an empirically proven fact.

Rigid Family Systems

Rules—Strict interpretation of the rules with no exceptions; inflexibility with no extenuating circumstances. The rules keeper (usually a critical/judgmental father or mother) is exempt from the rules.

Values—"There is only one way to do things and that is the right way—my way." Things are always black or white, right or wrong.

Motto—"Do it right, or else."

Communication—Linear, hierarchical. The father is usually dominant, powerful, and unapproachable. The mother softens the impact of the father's harshness. Or the mother is critical-judgmental, often moralistic and controlling, and the father goes along with the mother, deceptively avoiding conflict and the rage of the mother.

Drugs of choice—Alcohol and/or heroin, other sedative hypnotics, and narcotic analgesics

Functions of drug—Suppress feelings, especially anger, and stay numb to the trauma in this family system

Ambiguous Family Systems

Rules—We have rules but we don't enforce them, and we change them if someone is annoyed or inconvenienced.

Values—Forever changing, based on the situation

Motto—"Keep peace at all costs; avoid conflict."

Communication—Mixed messages that are confusing. "Do what you know we want, without us letting you know what it is we want."

Drugs of choice—Alcohol and/or heroin, marijuana, and hallucinogens

Functions of drug—Suppress feelings of discomfort, kill pain, shut out reality, and/or distort reality

Overextended Family Systems

Rules—Be productive, get busy, stay on the move.

Values—Look good, achieve, do it with willpower, feelings are for wimps.

Motto—"We can achieve anything we set our minds to," "The right stuff."

Communication—Feelings are not expressed or integrated; decisions are based on results and what will please the parents.

Drugs of choice—Cocaine, methamphetamine, and other stimulants, alcohol

Functions of drug—Keep on working/doing, even though feelings are not congruent with work or intimate relationships

Distorted Family Systems

Rules—Don't let outsiders know we are crazy. Act as if we were a normal family, just a bit eccentric.

Values—Maintain an illusion of normalcy, despite significant physical, emotional, and interpersonal problems of the family. Keep outsiders guessing about us.

Motto—"Aren't most families like ours?"

Communication—Mixed messages; parents and children are unavailable and have limited common perceptions of situations.

Drugs of choice—Alcohol, hallucinogens, marijuana, and inhalants

Functions of drug—Distort reality, which is already distorted, to try and make sense, or no sense, of it

---

✕ Satir's Family Pattern of Communication

Virginia Satir, author of *Conjoint Family Therapy* (1967) and *Peoplemaking* (1972) and co-author of *Helping Families to Change* (1976), emphasizes the feeling component of family patterns of communication. She describes a dysfunctional family as one that maintains rules that do not fit the reality of what is felt and believed.

Satir's work is monumental and popular. According to Satir, individuals with poor self-concepts see pots that are half-empty. Individuals with the ability to differentiate (i.e., those with good self-concepts) see their pots as half-full. The former group feels hopeless and negative; the latter group is positive and hopeful.

Satir identified the following dysfunctional styles as well as a functional style of communicating:

1. Placaters discount themselves. Their goal is frequently to avoid conflict and to avoid others' anger. Their communication patterns feature the following:
   a. Words that agree and avoid conflict: "Whatever you want is O.K." The placaters' worth is based on others accepting, not rejecting, what they say.
   b. Bodies that placate: "I am helpless." The placaters' worth is based on being physically available, even when that may not be consistent with what they feel.
   c. Feelings: "I am worthless." Placaters believe they have no choices but to be dependent in dysfunctional relationships because there is no way out, and they are not strong enough or worth the struggle.

2. Blamers elevate themselves by discounting others. Their goal is to avoid looking at themselves, their own issues, and their own responsibility. Others' feelings are often discounted. If others would only do it the right way—which is their way—then things would work out. Their communication patterns feature the following:
   a. Words that are critical, judgmental, shaming put-downs: "You never do anything right." "It's all your fault."
   b. Bodies that blame: "I am more powerful, more dominant."
   c. Feelings: "It is your fault that I am unhappy."

3. Intellectualizers discount their own feelings. Their goal is to place rigid emphasis on the cognitive to figure out problems, to deny the role feelings play in relationships and decisions, and to avoid the emotional impact of feelings. Intellectualizers are the brains, the computers, the cognitive persons who think,

"If I can only understand this, I'll be OK." They often feel that, if they can only find that missing piece of the puzzle, they will find the cause of their problems. They fail to integrate the key elements of the puzzle—their feelings—and fail to realize that the puzzle may not be solvable, especially with their linear approach. Their communication patterns feature the following:

a. Words that are extremely logical: "That makes sense and is reasonable."
b. Bodies in control or shut down
c. Feelings: "I am vulnerable and feel threatened when I get in touch with my feelings, especially feelings of vulnerability."

4. Distracters discount context. Their goal is to keep others and themselves away from painful feelings, to distract and avoid conflict. Distractors are the elusive, sometimes charming, magicians. They are difficult to hold accountable or responsible because they keep the focus elsewhere, not on themselves. Many alcoholics and addicts are masters of this style of communication and avoid or deny their problems with alcohol and drugs. Their communication patterns feature the following:

a. Words that are confusing and irrelevant. They are unable to establish clarity or to set specific goals.
b. Bodies that act as if they are somewhere else when the content gets too specific and focused. They want to frustrate, discount, and escape from others.
c. Feelings: "Nobody cares. I am not happy."

According to Satir, **leveling** is the healthy state of communication. Words, body, and feelings are consistent with the message. The individual is congruent and acts in a congruent fashion.

Sharon Wegscheider-Cruse was trained by and has worked closely with Virginia Satir. Wegscheider-Cruse is best known for her books *The Family Trap* (1976) and *Family Reconstruction Therapy—the Living Model* (1994). She is a leader in the field of adult children of alcoholics and family reconstruction and has popularized the concept of survival roles in the alcoholic/addict family system. These roles describe the coping mechanisms members use to survive in a dysfunctional alcoholic/addict family. They include the following: chief enabler, family hero, family scapegoat, lost child, and family mascot.

The *chief enabler* assumes primary responsibility for the chemically dependent family member. The chief enabler shelters and protects, even denies, the dysfunctional aspects of a family member's alcohol/drug use. The major enabling approaches are the following:

1. Avoiding and shielding
2. Attempting to control
3. Taking over responsibilities
4. Rationalizing and accepting
5. Cooperating and collaborating (Nelson 1988)

The *family hero* is the achiever, the responsible child, the good child, the model child. The family hero is often the firstborn, who escapes the dysfunctional

✄ Wegscheider-Cruse's Alcoholic/ Addict Family System Survival Roles

Case Study 5.1

The Lost Child

Michelle

Michelle was beginning her senior year in high school when her family began therapy. At that time, her stepbrother, Jack, was heavily into drugs (marijuana, hallucinogens, speed, and cocaine) and alcohol. Her other sisters were extremely angry with Jack's attitude and behavior. Michelle was an *A* student and student body president. She was on the cross-country team and very popular. She had a quiet, affable presence and acted older than her 17 years. She was the only one in the family to whom Jack related. During the course of treatment, it was very difficult for Michelle to express any feelings. Even in individual sessions, she would deny feeling any pain or negative emotions.

Later that year, Michelle was accepted to a college a few hours' drive from home. During her first semester away at school, despite good study habits, she ended up dropping a course and receiving *C* grades. Also, she didn't make any friends at school. Michelle was running on the college track team but was unmotivated and not running to her true potential. This was quite traumatic for Michelle because she had been so popular and such a good student and athlete in high school. Michelle set up an individual counseling appointment during her college break. For the first time, she was in touch with her pain and grief. If she had not reached out for help, Michelle would have been another college student unable to cope with the pressures or to deal effectively with backlogged feelings, which eventually might have caused her to take her own life.

---

aspects of the alcohol/drug family through personal achievement. The family's sense of self-worth is often the conscious or unconscious responsibility of this family member. Unfortunately, the family hero achieves for the family and ignores personal feelings, values, and goals. The family hero in adulthood often experiences a depression or sense of loss due to the incongruency of internal feelings with external behaviors. The hero may be outwardly successful but feel like a charlatan, or empty inside. When this conflict is not dealt with, the family hero is vulnerable to alcohol/drug problems and/or problems in interpersonal relationships.

The primary function of the *family scapegoat* is to divert the family members away from the real issues in the family (e.g., marital discord, marital infidelity, or parental alcohol/drug problems) and the painful emotionality of these family issues. The family members can then blame the scapegoat for all of the family problems. The family scapegoat often exhibits acting-out behavior in school and at home, antisocial behavior, and substance abuse due to underlying feelings of anger and resentment.

The *lost child's* role is often the most tragic. This is the child whose primary function is to allow the dysfunctional family—especially the parents—to expend less energy. This child often identifies with the pain of his or her parents and other siblings and wants to decrease the family members' level of pain by not contributing to the problem, perhaps even taking on the family's pain. The family inadvertently reinforces this child for not having needs. The child denies feelings and needs, frequently disconnecting emotionally and even physically from the family. At some point, the child can no longer deny personal feelings and pain. Thus, lost children frequently get overwhelmed with emotions and are at risk for suicide.

The primary function of the *family mascot* is to divert attention away from the family issues and family pain. The mascot uses humor, silliness, and even self-disparaging ineptness (making fun of oneself) as a way of diverting the family from its pain. Frequently, the mascot discounts a sense of self as the price to pay for calm in the family. As a result, the mascot may feel unworthy of love, unless able to alleviate someone's pain.

These are just a few family roles. The roles are stereotypic classifications for purposes of identifying some common role features in dysfunctional, or imbalanced, family systems. Please note that the roles are illustrations of dysfunctional patterns of family interaction and should not be used to pigeonhole someone into a static classification. Usually, people maintain a variety of traits from each of the roles. Family roles may also change based on different family situations and adjustments in the family process.

Other important family therapists—Salvador Minuchin, Theodore Lidz, Lieman Wynne, James Framo, Ron Jackson, and Jay Haley—emphasize a systems approach in their work with families and changing dysfunctional patterns of family communication and interaction. These family therapists have different styles, theories, and methods of working with families. Some see the entire family together in a counseling session. Others may see family members separately or sometimes see the father and son, mother and daughter, or just the children. Family therapists even use a multigenerational approach which includes grandparents, or an expanded family approach of including other relatives. The key element of all of these approaches is looking at the family as a system, a system that is affected and changed by the actions and events in the lives of each of the family members.

Family Roles Played Out at the Dinner Table

The Green family, like many families, had the ritual of having dinner together. When the children were younger, the minor irritations of "spilled milk" (literally and metaphorically) gave rise to Dad's rage. Mr. Green was usually exhausted at dinner time, stressed out by his job. Mr. Green's father was a mean-tempered, negative, emotionally disconnected and nasty alcoholic, who didn't model any form of connection or caring toward his children. Mr. Green, like his father, had little patience with his children and would lose his temper easily. As the children got older, the dinner table became a battle zone. The youngest daughter was the "lost child," the middle son the "scapegoat," and the oldest son the "hero."

The middle son (the scapegoat) would spark the battle by antagonizing his father, challenging him. The son would argue politics, religion, current events, and so on, taking a position that would irritate his father. The middle son was the brightest child, aware and well read, and would use these skills to mock his father's ignorance on issues.

Mr. Green would soon escalate and explode. The youngest daughter (lost child) would plead for a truce, which was ignored. She would burst into tears and retreat to her room. The oldest son (the hero) would make jokes and tell the family they were too serious about all this. Sometimes this approach worked, but many times it didn't. Mr. Green would usually explode, grab his dinner plate, and retreat to the den. The oldest son was aligned and enmeshed with his mother. Mom would then sit down by the oldest son and blame the middle son (scapegoat) for causing the conflict.

This is just one scenario of family roles and alliances. The family imbalance is played out night after night at the dinner table.

Enabling Behavior

In an attempt to avoid recognizing problems, the family enables the continued use of alcohol/drugs and other dysfunctional behaviors. Enabling is described as an unhealthy doing for, or killing with kindness (Table 5.1). Parents may have good intentions in enabling their children. Their lack of insight into the dynamics of the enabling process, however, causes problems to continue and to get progressively worse.

"Protecting one's child is normal and appropriate, but overprotection can cause problems. Enablers overprotect and find it difficult to separate what their child needs from what their child wants. The price of overprotection is prolonging the dependency of immaturity and thereby aiding the progression of chemical dependency" (MacDonald 1984).

TABLE 5.1

Enabling Behavior

Charles Nelson (1988) identified the following four styles of enabling behavior.

Avoiding and Shielding

Avoiding and shielding constitute any behavior by a family member that covers up or prevents the user or the family member from experiencing the full impact of the harmful consequences of the drug use. Enabling behavior includes
- Making up excuses to avoid social contact during drinking and drugging periods
- Side-stepping or avoiding participation in discussions about drugs
- Taking alcohol, sedatives, and/or other drugs to try to lower one's own anxiety or stress about a family member's problems with drugs
- Not standing up for one's rights in fear of the family member going into a binge cycle of drug use
- Cleaning up the family member's vomit after an alcohol/drug episode
- Staying away from home as much as possible to get away from the situation
- Shielding the addict from a crisis that could send her/him into therapy
- Telling the alcoholic to leave until he/she quits drinking but then immediately going out and looking for that family member
- Helping the addict keep up appearances or cover up around relatives, friends, neighbors, or her/his employer

TABLE 5.1 (continued)

Enabling Behavior

Attempting to Control

Attempting to control is any behavior by a family member that is performed with the intent of taking personal control over the alcoholic/addict's use of the drug. Enabling behavior includes

- Trying to buy things that might divert the addict from drug use (sports equipment, tools, car, house, etc.)
- Spending the night at a hotel or motel to get the user to quit
- Spending the night at a friend's house to get the user to quit
- Screaming, yelling, swearing, or crying in an attempt to get a family member to stop drinking or drugging
- Threatening to hurt oneself in an attempt to get a family member to quit
- Threatening physical violence to get the user to quit
- Checking or measuring the addict's drug stash to determine how much he has been using
- Encouraging the addict to do the drug at home to avoid more problems away from home
- Using or withholding sex as a way to control a partner's alcohol/drug use
- Throwing away, hiding, or destroying the family member's stash or paraphernalia

Taking over Responsibilities

Taking over responsibilities is any behavior by the family member designed to take over the user's personal responsibilities (e.g., finances, household chores, or employment). Enabling behavior includes

- Cleaning the family member's drug paraphernalia when left out
- Waking the alcoholic in time for work
- Reminding the user to eat at times
- Staying home from work to take care of the family member's problems resulting from drug use
- Preaching to the addict about her failures as a warning about the personal effects of the drug use
- Doing the family member's chores
- Waiting hand and foot on the family member
- Paying all the bills
- Taking a second job to cover the bills piling up after money has been diverted to drugs
- Covering the alcoholic/addict's bad checks

Rationalizing and Accepting

Rationalizing and accepting are any behavior by the family member that conveys a rationalization or acceptance of the alcoholic/addict's use of the drug. Enabling behavior includes

- Believing and/or communicating that the family member's episodes of drug use were only isolated instances and not patterns of use
- Believing and/or communicating that the use of the drugs was safe
- Believing and/or communicating that the family member's use of drugs increased that person's self-confidence

Enabling behavior has been defined as taking responsibility for someone else's lack of responsibility, or softening the consequences for someone's irresponsibility. Enablers are under the delusion that no one knows about the problems and they can continue to cover them up. The reality is that others are aware of the problems and are directly and indirectly letting the family know they need help. Only the family maintains this denial to the real dimensions of the problem.

✗ Stages in Family Recovery from Substance Abuse Problems

Families have a wide range and variety of reactions to alcohol/drug problems, yet there are some common, generalizable patterns to a family's response.

One model describes the following stages in the family's adjustment to the substance abuse problem:

1. Denial and minimizing
2. Tension and isolation
3. Frustration and disorganization
4. Attempts to reorganize, Shifts in family member alliances
5. Separation, in roles, Escape
6. Reorganization without the addict/alcoholic
7. Recovery and reorganization with the addict/alcoholic

The application of the stages of grieving can also be used as a model to describe the stages in recovery for the alcoholic/addict and their family members.

1. Denial
2. Anger
3. Bargaining
4. Feeling (or depression)
5. Acceptance

Often the stages are positioned differently or combined. Remember, this is a model to demonstrate different aspects of the recovery process.

Denial's Linkages to Society

At the denial stage, family members rarely acknowledge that something is wrong, although they sense something might be different about their family. The spouse or family members may seek help in an indirect, nonspecific manner, such as talking to friends and/or relatives. Unfortunately, those friends and relatives often reinforce the denial. One such example is the following:

Denial Transaction Between Mary and Her Sister-in-Law, Maureen

Mary: The other night at the party, do you think Harry drank too much?
Maureen: Oh, that happens to everyone once in a while.
Mary: You don't think he has a problem with alcohol, do you?
Maureen: No, of course not. He drinks like most of us in the family, and we certainly don't have a problem. You're overreacting.

In reality, Harry and Maureen grew up in alcoholic family systems and they both have drinking problems.

Anger

Anger is an effective defense to keep family members from talking about issues and feelings that might indicate an alcohol/drug problem in the family. Anger can be expressed as verbal, physical, emotional, and/or sexual threats, abuse, and/or violation. Anger can be actual or threatened rejection and abandonment. Alcoholics/addicts use anger to blame and shame other family members as inadequate and responsible for their predicament. In reality, the anger is a way for the alcoholic/addict to avoid feelings of shame, to control others in the family, and to deny responsibility for problems in the family system.

The Garden of Eden: Enabling Behavior

Callahan, distributed by Levin Represents.

Once in recovery, many adolescent and adult patients/clients admit that causing a conflict or big fight was a way to get out of the house and use alcohol/drugs. Many clients rationalized that they were already in trouble with the family, so what was the difference if they got into more trouble?

An adolescent patient/client once described her alcoholic/addictive family system as "raging and ragging" (nagging): "Dad is the one who rages around the home, and Mom attempts to control him by ragging at Dad and everyone else. It is no wonder that I don't spend much time at home."

The combined effect is an unsafe, unpredictable family system with underlying feelings of confusion, fear, anxiety, and shame and sometimes immobilizing trauma.

This conflict among family members creates a climate of confusion and a lack of clarity as to what is an appropriate approach to the problem of alcohol/drugs. The result is often a trial-and-error approach. At first, family members try extreme control or rigid threats: "The next time you use alcohol/drugs, I will . . ." (not let you in the house, confine you to your room for one month, get a divorce or separation). When this doesn't work, the next approach might be to let go, or to try to ignore the addictive behavior completely, as if the addict didn't exist. The resulting pattern of control-release is chaotic. This trial-and-error approach creates further anger, confusion, and feelings of hopelessness.

At this stage, the family might go beyond relatives and friends and talk to a minister, priest, rabbi, family physician, or school counselor. The family members may be vague in disclosing the degree to which alcohol/drugs are used. At this stage, family members are still not quite sure they need help and are embarrassed in

Case Study 5.2

Anger in an Alcoholic Family System

John

John, a 43-year-old insurance salesman, described having a few drinks after work one day and then realized he was late for an important dinner with his family. He rationalized that, since he was already in trouble, what was the use in calling; he would just get yelled at.

Since he was already late and wanted to delay the pain of his wife's anger, he might as well continue drinking and be really late. Once he was drinking, the hours passed quickly. When the bar closed, John went home.

TABLE 5.3

Anger Stage in Imbalanced Family Systems

Feelings—confusion, fear, anxiety
Defenses—"raging and ragging"
        control to chaos
        trial and error
Linkage to society—search for magical solutions
Goal—cover-up real issues and feelings

seeking help. They may start to get help, get frightened, or be resistant to experiencing the pain associated with acknowledging the problem and then back off from getting help. See Table 5.3.

Bargaining

The bargaining stage is usually preceded by a major crisis. The family can no longer deny or ignore the problem and cannot cover up the feelings of frustration and anger. The family is essentially saying, "We have had enough of this; it's too

---

TABLE 5.4

Bargaining, Feeling, and Acceptance Stage in Imbalanced Family Systems

Goal—"maintain the chaos of addiction"
Bargains—compromise values
        love/hate—let go/hold on
        avoid making a decision
        confused—doesn't know what is appropriate
Depression/Feelings—feelings are experienced
Acceptance
  there is a problem
  on road to recovery

---

chaotic." The family is still not ready to effect change in the system; instead, the goal is to strike some arrangement or bargain. Being held hostage by the addict, the family is willing to pay a ransom to have the addict stop bothering them with outrageous behavior. Unfortunately, the ransom often goes beyond what is reasonable or tolerable, and the family initially agrees to do almost anything to survive in this chaos. Many of the bargains are financial or object-related: "If you stop abusing alcohol/drugs, I'll buy you. . . ."

The underlying and false assumption of most bargains is that the addict can stop using. The assumption is that the addict can override the drive and allure of the alcohol/drugs for a reward. Unfortunately, the drive to use alcohol/drugs is stronger than the reward of the bargain, and willpower alone is not strong enough to overcome the drive to use alcohol/drugs.

Some of the bargains are far more subtle. Couples, families, and friends develop lives based on the bargain of maintaining addiction. See Table 5.4. Common bargains related to alcoholism and drug addiction are the following:

- *Let's ignore the addict's behavior and it might just stop.* The more you ignore the destructive behavior, the more intense and dramatic the situation becomes.
- *Let's separate or withdraw from the addict temporarily.* Unless there is strong therapeutic and personal support, the addict feeds on the partner's or family members' weaknesses. The individual usually does not have the support to break the codependent dance of addiction. (See Chapter 7.)
- *Avoid making a decision; maybe it will get better with time.* It's very rare that a spontaneous recovery occurs from alcohol/drugs. In Chapter 9 we discuss alcohol/drug intervention and "raising the addict's bottom" in an attempt to salvage and avoid further damage. Rarely do addicts decide on their own to get help. Sometimes it is so late that scary consequences are involved, such as the threat of physical harm, criminal justice and legal problems, job and financial problems, or death.

Case Study 5.3

An Alcoholic Bargain

Linda and Tom

Linda, 42, had been to a number of therapists over a 4-year period, prior to being referred to me. Married for 12 years, she had two boys, ages 5 and 8. Her husband Tom, 45, was a practicing alcoholic since they met, and his drinking was maintained throughout the years of their marriage. During one counseling session, Tom agreed that he was alcoholic but was not willing to change. When asked what it would take for him to stop drinking, he thought for a minute. Then he said, "The only thing that would stop me from drinking would be to have my liver fall apart."

This was an honest response espoused by others similarly addicted to alcohol. Linda knew that Tom had had numerous extramarital affairs throughout their marriage, and he continued to seek women in the bars and restaurants that he frequented most evenings. The tragic, innocent victims of Tom's alcoholism were his two young sons.

When asked why she put up with this behavior, Linda replied, "What can I do? I'll lose my home and my lifestyle would change."

For Linda, and many other spouses, the fear of abandonment was symbolized in the physical home. Linda had grown up in an alcoholic family, and she feared the feelings of abandonment that she would reexperience if she were to leave the relationship.

After more than three years of individual counseling and Al-Anon meetings, Linda left the relationship. Both boys are in a program for children of alcoholics. Unfortunately, Tom is still drinking and is in another bargain relationship—this time with a woman who is also an alcoholic.

At the bargaining stage, family members might seek help from experts in the field because their bargains are not working and they need advice and direction. Even when family members are fortunate in finding a counselor who knows about alcohol/drug intervention and treatment, the family members may still not follow through. The attitude at this stage is still a form of bargaining. The therapeutic bargain is to fix the identified patient (the addict) so the bargainer can avoid feeling pain. In some situations, family members may even sabotage counseling to avoid the pain of looking at their roles in the dysfunction. In a distorted sense, the failure of the trained professional validates the failure of the family member: "If the counselor can't help, then I guess we didn't do such a bad job." Many families seeking counseling soon find out that addiction is a family disease and effective treatment involves the entire family.

Feeling

At the feeling stage, family members can no longer deny, cover up with anger, or bargain their feelings away. Many feelings come to the surface and are easily accessed. Family members are crying at the slightest provocation, anxious to the point of being hypervigilant (checking things out obsessively), and in some cases feeling immobilized. These feelings are undeniable and force the family to seek help.

Acceptance

At the acceptance stage, the family has recognized that they have a problem. They are ready to do the work necessary to heal and develop healthier ways of relating. Recognizing that all the family members are suffering, they have the courage to get help. At this stage, the alcoholic/addict and the family members have begun to work on the problem. This is when treatment and recovery begin.

Summary

This chapter describes the family as a system. The alcoholic/drug addict family system is one in disequilibrium and counterbalancing denial to the depths of the problem. The term *imbalanced family system* can be used instead of *dysfunctional family* to avoid the shame implications.

Families are described as having rules, alliances, and specific patterns of communication. An imbalanced family system is described as rigid, ambiguous, overextended, or distorted. The alcoholic/addict family system is described as having survival roles, as described by Wegscheider-Cruse, to include chief enabler, family hero, family scapegoat, lost child, and family mascot.

Enabling behavior is described as a way for the family to avoid recognizing the alcohol/drug problem. Enabling is described as an unhealthy doing for others which softens the consequences for their lack of responsibility. Several kinds of enabling behavior are described, including avoiding and shielding, attempting to control, taking over responsibilities, and rationalizing and accepting.

The chapter concludes with a description of the stages of "family recovery" using the grieving model as an outline—denial, anger, bargaining, depression, and acceptance.

References

Lawson, Ann, and Gary Lawson. *Alcoholism and the Family: A Guide to Treatment and Prevention,* 2nd ed. Aspen, 1998.

MacDonald, Donald Ian. *Drugs, Drinking and Adolescents.* Chicago: Year Book Medical, 1984.

Nelson, Charles. "The Style of Enabling Behavior." In *Treating Cocaine Dependency,* ed. David E. Smith and Donald Wesson. Center City, MN: Hazelden Foundation, 1988.

Satir, Virginia. *Conjoint Family Therapy.* Palo Alto, CA: Science and Behavior Books, 1967.

———. *Peoplemaking.* Palo Alto, CA: Science and Behavior Books, 1972.

Satir, Virginia, and Michele Baldwin. *Satir—Step by Step—a Guide to Creating Change in Families.* Northvale, NJ: Aronson, Jason, 1983.

Satir, Virginia, James Stachowiak, and Harvey A. Taschman. *Helping Families to Change.* Northvale, NJ: Aronson, Jason, 1976.

Wegscheider-Cruse, Sharon. *The Family Trap.* Palo Alto, CA: Nurturing Network, 1976.

Wegscheider-Cruse, Sharon et al. *Family Reconstruction—the Living Model.* Palo Alto, CA: Science and Behavior Books, 1994.

Whitaker, Carl, and Augustus Y. Napier. *The Family Crucible.* New York: Harper & Row, 1978.

Parenting

Impact on Alcohol/Drug Use and Abuse

Chapter Objectives

1. Explain the role parent-child bonding plays in preventing problem behaviors and future alcohol/drug problems.

2. Define the key elements (diagnostic criteria) of abandonment depression.

3. Describe the child temperaments that may contribute or make the child at-risk for substance abuse.

4. Explain "quality" of parent-child relationship and its impact on substance use and abuse.

5. Define shame and describe the domains of shame and the common affect-shame binds.

6. Describe rejection sensitivity, difficulty making decisions, and poor frustration tolerance.

7. Classify behaviors that indicate parental imbalance.

8. Define and describe boundaries (including clear, enmeshed, disengaged) and boundary inadequacy.

9. Describe triangulation in the family.

10. Describe the impact of parental use or abuse of alcohol/drugs on the child's future use or abuse.

11. Describe the imbalanced life cycles of families.

Some of the parenting variables that influence a child's use and abuse of alcohol/drugs later in life are

- Parent-child bonding
- Temperament of the child
- Parenting styles and the quality of the parent-child relationship
- Parental imbalance and boundary setting
- Parents' use/abuse of alcohol or drugs
- Other family system variables

These are the factors that are the major focus of this chapter.

✂ Parent-Child Bonding

The parent-child bond is an extremely potent, primary relationship, which greatly influences be-havior. Maccoby and Martin (1983) describe the parent-child bond as unique among human rela-tionships. Nothing is as powerful as the bonding between parent and child. Extraordinary feats of strength and sacrifice have come to be identified with this strong bond. Examples of the parent-child bond include the incredible adrenaline-induced strength of a father saving a child who is pinned under an automobile and the dedication and perseverance of a mother who protects her child from the drug- and crime-infested streets of the inner city.

The child's development is often impaired as a result of a poor bond between parent and child. Self-concept, social and interpersonal relationships, achievement, and identity are negatively affected by inadequate parent-child bonding.

A positive, caring relationship is essential for healthy development. The effective parent establishes bonding experiences that develop a positive regard for the child and reinforces a positive sense of self. When

---

*The names and circumstances of case studies in this chapter have been changed to maintain anonymity.

Case Study 6.1

Early Bonding

Karen

Karen was very young—18 years old—when she had her first of two children. Over the next few years, she was extremely depressed. Perhaps it was the responsibility of two young children and being tied to the house or the constant conflicts with her husband that caused Karen to decide to leave. It was an extremely difficult decision to leave two toddlers. However, at the time, her own survival seemed more important.

Twelve years later, Karen was in counseling. She was 34 years old and struggling with the fact that her 14-year-old son, Gary, was addicted to alcohol/drugs. Over the past two years Gary had been in and out of different outpatient counseling programs and was now in his second inpatient alcohol/drug program. Karen was needing some support in setting boundaries with Gary. She first needed to talk about her guilt at abandoning him when he was 2 years old. She had left the home, had filed for divorce, and had given custody of both children to Gary's father.

As the counseling proceeded, it became clear that her own alcohol use had contributed dramatically to her problems in those early years in the marriage. It was a few years after leaving the marriage that she acknowledged her own alcoholism. Even though she had been in recovery from alcohol and drugs for several years now and extremely active in AA, she was still experiencing dramatic problems in relationships. Over several sessions, she was able to talk about her own childhood and revealed that her father had sexually violated her. Although she had talked about this several times in previous counseling sessions and during her inpatient alcohol/drug program, she was now able to see that this contributed to her own fears of abusing her own children. She slowly began to accept how her alcoholic behavior prevented her from bonding with her own children. After some time, she was able to accept that she could not recapture those lost years with her children. She could not compensate for the lack of bonding during those formative years, no matter how available she was for Gary and his younger sister today. She began to recognize that her own attempts to compensate for those early years had resulted in her enabling Gary's alcohol and drug use. It took Karen some time to grieve and accept that she missed those early developmental years. She realized that there was a permanent loss in bonding, a loss that could never be recaptured.

---

a parent loses this positive bonding with a child, the child's sense of loss and anger may never be assuaged. This loss is often found in alcoholic/addict family systems.

Often, because of certain circumstances, parents are not available. A variety of conditions may take the parents from the child—death of a parent, a parent away at war, divorce, illness, mental breakdown, criminal-justice problems, financial problems, and job relocation (e.g., military). All of these circumstances prevent bonding between child and parent and are extremely disruptive to the child's life. The child may even suffer depression as a result of times when he or she felt abandoned or rejected.

Certainly, the parent's alcoholism/drug addiction also makes the parent either unavailable or inconsistent in the quality of the parent-child relationship.

Patrick Carnes, Ph.D., author of numerous books on sexual trauma and addiction, describes the importance of developing healthy bonds with caring adults outside of the family system for children who have been sexually violated/traumatized by a family member. In an interview in *Professional Counselor Magazine,* Carnes states, "One of the things that emerges in trauma literature is why some kids, who have the same identical history of trauma, rebound from that and have resiliency. As near as I can tell from the literature and what I have seen clinically, the primary factor is the ability of children to have healthy bonds around them that are not traumatic. As an antidote to trauma bonding, you need healthy bonds" (Carnes 1995).

Two prevailing hypotheses regarding parental bonding in adolescent substance abusers are the *overinvolvement* and *functional hypotheses* (Volk et al. 1988). The overinvolvement hypothesis is that one parent (frequently the mother) is overly involved in the adolescent's life to compensate for the lack of availability by the other parent. The functional hypothesis is that the adolescent's substance abuse distracts the family from focusing on other familial problems, such as marital discord, infidelity, and parental abuse of alcohol/drugs.

Abandonment Depression

A young child needs nurturing and connection with a caring parent. James Masterson (1976), in his work with borderline personality–disordered individuals, identifies an affective (feeling) disorder that he labeled "abandonment depression." Masterson believes that a significant separation stress precipitates abandonment depression (see Table 6.1). It is also likely that this separation occurs early in life between eighteen and twenty-four months of age. The individual suffering from

---

TABLE 6.1

Childhood Experiences of Abandonment and Rejection

- Lack of physical and emotional availability of parents
- Negative blaming; verbal and nonverbal behavior or attacks
- Mixed messages (double-binds), saying one thing and meaning something else
- Unreasonably high expectations or standards; ambiguous expectations of behavior, performance, and affect
- Lack of warmth, sensitivity, security, safety, or high regard for feelings, situations, and conflicts
- Discounting of the child's sense of self or physical and psychological boundaries
- Disparaging, blaming, and generally rejecting attitude about the child's difficulty with developmental tasks
- Disregard, ridicule, blaming, teasing, or other verbal and nonverbal behavior that is either rejecting or shaming
- Threats to abandon or leave a child in a joking or real manner
- Negative and rejecting statements, actions, and comments about something that is of minor or major importance to the child

abandonment depression is metaphorically described as "a hollow eggshell with the insides removed." All the good stuff—the nutrients, the seed, the juices of life—has been removed, has rotted, or has been destroyed by a lack of nurturing.

The six key elements of abandonment depression are

1. Homicidal rage
2. Suicidal depression
3. Panic
4. Feelings of hopelessness and helplessness
5. Emptiness and void
6. Guilt

Perhaps the parent is ill, suffering from depression, or withdrawn due to a personality and/or psychiatric disorder and finds it hard to nurture his or her child. Maybe the parent didn't grow up in a family system that modeled nurturing, caring, and empathetic connection with the children. Masterson describes three elements that may produce separation stress in children:

1. Nature: Possible genetic or constitutional deficiencies such as inability to tolerate separation anxiety or to synthesize positive and negative effects as well as such conditions as attention deficit disorders and developmental disharmonies.
2. Nurture: "Maternal libidinal unavailability for the child's move toward separation-individuation or self-activation (i.e., the mother is unable or has difficulty in identifying, acknowledging, and supporting the child's emerging self-activation, experimentation, and exploration). The reasons for maternal libidinal unavailability may be many—death, divorce, physical or emotional illness, etc."
3. Fate: "Any accident of fate that impairs the child's ability to separate and/or individuate. On the separation side, events such as death or divorce can prevent the mother from being emotionally available. On the individuation side, events can impair or prevent the child from practicing his emerging individuation. For example, the child may be sickly or in a restricted environment."

Impact of Early Abandonment on Adult Interpersonal Relationships

Individuals suffering from abandonment depression express complaints having to do with intimacy. They have difficulty emotionally entering into healthy relationships and are unable to differentiate their needs from others' needs. They experience difficulty in identifying and communicating feelings or in accepting feelings and communication from others. There is either a fusing of others into self or a fission, causing them to break away emotionally from others.

Masterson described persons suffering from abandonment depression as experiencing difficulty in establishing intimacy in relationships due to a limited capacity for spontaneity, empathy, and sensitivity. These persons have difficulty in making an emotional commitment to a relationship. Such individuals experience twin fears—the fear of losing (abandonment), which leads to clinging behavior, and the fear of being engulfed (smothered), which leads to feelings of depersonalization, shutting down, distortion of reality, and desensitization (numbing, disconnecting from the body).

At first, using alcohol and drugs to facilitate feeling in interpersonal relationships may seem effective; however, as time goes on, this becomes dysfunctional and destructive. Persons feeling pain also use alcohol/drugs to alleviate the core feeling of abandonment.

Another option those suffering feelings of abandonment may choose is to enter into dysfunctional and/or alcoholic/addict relationships, or relationships with individuals emotionally and physically unavailable.

The *Diagnostic and Statistical Manual IV* (American Psychological Association, Washington, D.C. 1994) lists diagnostic criteria for borderline personality disorder, which include the following. These often result from early childhood experiences of abandonment.

1. Impulsivity or unpredictability in at least two areas that are potentially self-damaging
2. A pattern of unstable and intense interpersonal relationships
3. Inappropriate, intense anger or lack of control of anger
4. Identity disturbances manifested by uncertainty about several issues relating to identity, such as self-image, gender identity, long-term goals or career choice, friendship patterns, values, and loyalties
5. Affective instability

�轮 Child's Temperament

Each child has his or her own temperament. Temperament is described as a behavioral characteristic that researchers believe is present at birth, within the first few months of life, and during infancy (Garrison and Earls 1987; Kohnstamm, Bates, and Rothbart 1989).

There is emerging evidence that extremes in certain temperament traits, such as high activity level, emotionality, attention span, and sociability, are associated with children of alcoholics. These temperaments also cause the child to be at-risk for alcoholism/drug addiction and other problem behaviors. The parents of these children are faced with challenges beyond the average parenting techniques. Early evaluation and early intervention are essential to address the issues of children with these temperaments. Children who exhibit these genetically determined temperaments may benefit from prevention efforts, that include special educational and counseling programs. Parents also benefit from parenting skills and education in helping these children to cope better.

Aspects of temperament may predict the behavior problems and substance abuse problems that frequently arise during adolescence. There also appear to be gender differences in temperament that make children at-risk for behavior problems and substance abuse. A study by Block, Block, and Keyes (1988) found that nursery school girls who were low in ego resiliency and ego control were using marijuana at age 14, and boys' marijuana use was predicted by low ego control but not by early ego resilience. Masse and Tremblay (1997), in a study of kindergarten boys, found that high novelty seeking and low harm avoidance measured at age 6 predicted early onset of cigarette smoking, drunkenness, and other drug use in adolescence. Dobkin, Tremblay, Masse, and Vitaro (1995), in a study of 755 6-year-old boys, found that disruptive behaviors (fighting, hyperactivity, oppositional behaviors) measured at 6 years of age predicted having been drunk or using other drugs—or both—prior to age 14.

Some clusters of temperament are related to substance use/abuse, which are labeled as a "difficult temperament"—high activity level, low flexibility and task orientation, mood instability, and social withdrawal (Lerner and Vicary 1984, Ohannessian and Hesselbrook 1995). Tubman and Windle (1995) described a difficult temperament as higher activity level, lower task orientation, inflexibility, a withdrawal orientation, biological arrhythmicity, and low positive mood, as a predictor of higher levels of alcohol problems among adolescents. In a study by Martin, Kaczynski, Maisto, and Tarter (1996) a cluster of temperament traits was a predictor of the number of drugs used by adolescents. That cluster included dispositional traits characterized by heightened negative affect (depressed mood and anxiety) and behavioral undercontrol, reflecting impulsivity, aggressivity, acting out, and sensation seeking.

The research on temperament has primarily been on the traits that predict substance use and abuse and problem behaviors. There are temperament traits that may function as a protective factor, especially for high-risk groups. One such study measured the influence of cuddly, affectionate temperament style in infancy and early childhood. This longitudinal Kauai study of low socioeconomic children of alcohol-abusing parents found decreased risk for alcohol-related and other adverse outcomes in adolescence and adulthood. The explanation was that these children had resiliency as a result of more frequent and stronger social and emotional support (Werner and Smith 1982).

A *supportive* parent with a healthy relationship with his or her child is less likely to have a child who gets involved with alcohol/drugs.

Rollins and Thomas (1979) explained the differences between a supportive and controlling parent. They defined a supportive parent as possessing "parental behaviors toward the child such as praising, encouraging, and giving physical affection, which indicate to the child that she or he is accepted, approved of, and loved." In contrast, the controlling parent is defined as having "parental behavior toward the child which is intended to direct the child's behavior in a manner acceptable to the parent."

The goal of parenting is to develop a high level of parental support and a moderate level of parental control. Parents who are highly rigid, authoritarian, and controlling tend to have children who are resentful, frustrated, and angry. These children are then prone to problem behaviors, causing them to rebel or passive-aggressively get back at the rigid parent. "Children whose relationships with their parents lacked love, warmth, and closeness and exhibited signs of hostility, have children who exhibit increased levels of substance abuse, delinquency, and dysfunctional coping strategies" (Johnson and Pandina 1991).

⚔ Parenting Styles and the Quality of the Parent-Child Relationship

The children of parents who are unable to establish moderate control and effective disciplining techniques often experience problem behaviors and associate with other children who have problem behaviors.

The availability of the parent(s) is extremely important in the child's development, as is the quality of the parent-child relationship. Frequently, parents will spend a quantity of time with their children and mislead themselves into thinking they are effectively developing the relationship. The quality of the parent-child relationship is the essential ingredient. The parent needs to be fully present, listening reflectively, and exchanging ideas, while giving full attention to the child. Quality time also involves understanding, touching (hugging), playing, and sharing. Making a genuine, heart-to-heart connection is at the core of a good parent-child relationship.

Parenting Styles That Shame Children

Shame is a deep-rooted feeling, often a result of traumatic childhood experiences that are excessively shaming (e.g., sexual, physical, and emotional abuse). (See Table 6.2.) Parental imbalance and parenting dysfunction are at the core of these feelings of shame. Merle Fossum and Marilyn Mason (1986) defined shame as "the self looking in on itself and finding the self lacking or flawed." Individuals may feel exposed, vulnerable, and fearful that others know they are feeling inherently bad and inadequate. Shame is more powerful than simple embarrassment, which is a temporary situation with little long-term impact. In shame, people feel that they will never recover from the negative way others see them.

Shame is a feeling that has an integral role in the individual's development. "Shame is a basic, natural human emotion, which in moderation is adaptive, healthy, and absolutely essential for development. We could not eliminate shame even if we wanted to. It's inbred in the species" (Kaufman 1989).

Sigmund Freud used the word *guilt* to describe feelings of shame. Erik Erikson, in his description of the human life cycle, outlined two developmental

---

TABLE 6.2

Characteristics of Shameful Experiences

1. Unexpected exposure; being judged on a vulnerable aspect of oneself
2. Feeling as if there is a loss of choice
3. Feeling out of place, flawed, defective, or inadequate
4. A threat to the core of one's identity
5. Mistrust in ability to perceive things properly; unsure of self in making decisions or relating to people
6. Trust of self and others is jeopardized; boundaries are distorted; and physical, emotional, and/or sexual violations may occur.
7. Difficulty in assessing what is reality
8. Feeling helpless, powerless, and trapped, with no way out (Fossum, M. and Mason, M. Facing Shame: Families in Recovery. Norton Press, N.Y. 1986).

stages, which focused on guilt and shame: (1) autonomy versus doubt and shame and (2) initiative versus guilt.

Growing up in an alcohol/addict family system or an imbalanced family system creates a foundation of shame. Additional feelings of shame are perpetrated by peers, the school system, other institutions, and other authority figures in the child's life. These shame-based messages are internalized by children. The result is a vicious pattern of feelings and behavior, which perpetuates the feelings of shame.

Individuals from shame-based family systems often feel that (1) there is no hope for change; (2) shame is inescapable and inevitable; (3) shame is exterior-based, not an internal process; and (4) they are bad, no good, flawed, or worthless as individuals (Fossum and Mason 1986). For these individuals, feelings of shame can include verbalizations such as

No matter what I do, it's never going to be good enough, so why try?

Each time I try, I fail, anyway. The result is always negative.

I must try so much harder than others. It's so much easier for others, so I must be
    inferior and inadequate.

You have to be perfect to be O.K.

Look at _____. Now, if I could only be like them.

It's never going to get any better, no matter how hard I try.

If only others would feel good. Then I would be happy.

Shame is a fascinating topic because it affects us all in some way (see Table 6.3). Most individuals can overcome feelings of shame and grow as a result of it, getting on with their lives. However, some individuals have been shamed dramatically and frequently, especially during early developmental years, and are unable to overcome it. These individuals are at risk for alcoholism and drug dependence or developing relationships with alcoholics/addicts. Too much trauma creates shame which leads to feelings of hopelessness and helplessness.

There is almost a resignation that life is painfully unfulfilling—not worth trying to change. Expectations and aspirations are only indirectly acknowledged, for fear of reexperiencing rejection and shame. Shame-based individuals perceive themselves as trapped, inescapably destined to again experience the shame message of self-inadequacy and powerlessness. The shame-based orientation is external. The

TABLE 6.3

Shame

Definition: self looking in on self, finding the self lacking or feeling exposed—"seen"—in a public way and wanting to cover—feeling hunted

Shame-Based System	Balanced System
1. No hope—hopelessness	1. Hope—choice
2. Inescapable	2. Can make amends
3. Exterior-based	3. Internally based

Source: *Data from Fossum, M. and M. Mason. Facing Shame: Families in Recovery. Norton Press, N.Y. 1986.*

individual's sense of self is formed by others' evaluations and judgments of his or her performance and behavior. The orientation is outside (external world) in versus inside (internal self) out. Three characteristics—no hope, inescapable shame, and an exterior base—are found in shame-based systems and shame-based individuals.

In contrast, in a balanced family system, the individual has a much healthier way of approaching life and others. The individual receives feedback from the world and evaluates the feedback. The individual then chooses to make changes or adjustments in decision making, goal setting, and interpersonal communication, based on his or her evaluation of the validity of the feedback. The major focus is on *hope* and *choice.*

In a balanced-system, individuals can recognize their mistakes and not feel that they are the mistake. They can make amends to those who might have been hurt by their mistakes and can learn from their errors. The experience is valued, and there is an opportunity for self-growth. Individuals from a balanced family system have an orientation that is inside out (internal). These individuals relate well to and have empathy for others, balancing their own sense of self with the judgments and reactions of others.

The following list describes ways to avoid shame in early childhood:

1. Parents should provide unconditional love. They should let their child know that they really like him or her. Talking; touching with affection; hugging; and, most important, paying attention to the child are some of the ways in which parents express unconditional love.
2. Parents should provide safety, nurturance, security, and care.
3. Parents should communicate clearly with and support their spouse or partner.
4. Parents should resolve conflicts with their spouse or partner (invoking the Alcoholics Anonymous motto "Would you rather be right or happy?").
5. Parents should play with their infants and children.
6. Parents should be available and enjoy the growth and development of their children.
7. Parents should recognize that at times parenting is overwhelming—they need to take a break and get support.
8. Parents should protect their children from others who may hurt, violate, or shame them.
9. At times, when parents "don't like their child's behavior" or are frustrated and annoyed, parents need to minimize the impact.
10. Parents should use appropriate discipline and good judgment in parenting and learn about parenting by taking classes on parenting and child development.
11. Parents should seek help from teachers, family members, counselors, doctors, clergy, and so on when "shame-based" family issues arise. They should not isolate or deny (minimize or rationalize) these issues but take early, proactive action, which can prevent a more significant problem later on.
12. Parents should encourage children to express themselves (what they feel and think) in play, verbal and nonverbal communication, and other activities.

Parents' Shame

Parents who have not done a good job of parenting may experience feelings of shame. Gomberg (1988) describes this parental shame as falling short of expectations in being a good parent. Jessup (1983) also describes a sense of failure for mothers that is shameful. Eliason and Skinstad (1995) describe the deep sense of identity and self-esteem that many women gain from their children. "When they perceive failure at meeting the needs of their children, the sense of hopelessness that follows can be devastating. The sense of shame . . . about mothering in substance using women has been heightened by the media's attention to Fetal Alcohol Effects and 'cocaine babies' in recent years. This press is often sensationalized and contains blantant mother-blaming implications" (Eliason and Skinstad 1995).

Shame and Feelings

Shame-based messages that are internalized have a major impact on feelings. When shame is attached to normal, everyday feelings, it tends to escalate those feelings. For example, when an internalized shame-based message is attached to normal, everyday feelings of frustration or anger, it tends to escalate those feelings to rage (anger + shame = rage). The person feeling shame then directs this rage toward others, blaming and holding them responsible for feelings of anger and frustration. The rage violates others, pushes them away, and creates more of a feeling of isolation, loneliness, and hopelessness with no way out. This out-of-control emotional freight train picks up speed from all the memories of shame experienced in the family of origin. Some may think that the way to slow down this runaway emotional pain is to self-medicate with alcohol/drugs. Unfortunately, this temporary solution may even speed up the emotional turmoil or cause it to be repeated. When people do not deal with feelings of shame, this pattern continues. The next time, even less anger and shame are needed for the escalation to rage. (See Table 6.4.)

TABLE 6.4

Affect-Shame Binds

anger + shame = rage

anxiety + shame = panic

fear + shame = terror

sadness + shame = depression

depression + shame = despair

despair + shame = suicidal thoughts

suicidal thoughts + shame = suicide attempt

hurt + shame = pain

pain + shame = trauma (deep or chronic pain)

trauma + shame = phobia

phobia + shame = loss of reality

unavailability + shame = lack of trust of others

lack of trust of others + shame = paranoia

paranoia + shame = loss of reality

One of the largest domains of shame is human sexuality, as evidenced by our society's problems in establishing intimate and caring relationships. We will look at three areas in particular: adolescent sexual identity, sexual violation, and drugs and sex.

Adolescent Sexual Identity and Shame

The developmental task of exploring and defining one's sexual identity is probably the most difficult task of adolescence. Shame-based messages by parents, schools, institutions, and peers may be devastating to adolescents and delay the development of a secure sense of sexual identity. Shame-based messages include the following:

You are bad if you _____. (masturbate, are feeling sexual, are aroused, etc.)
Having sexual feelings before marriage is unnatural.
Sex is dirty.
That's all that men want. Men are bad and evil.
Women use sex to manipulate you to get what they want.
Don't watch television; it promotes sexual arousal.
In our family, we don't talk with others about sex.

Sexual Violation and Shame

Sexual violations are common in alcoholic/addict and imbalanced family systems. Children often feel responsible for sexual violation, as if they caused the violation (e.g., I must be responsible for this sexual feeling in others because I am so cute, attractive, shy, or outgoing). Usually, the violation is not talked about or is enabled by the mother or, in some cases, the father. When told of the violation, the parent often denies that it happened or that it is possible and rationalizes the action: "Your uncle is that way with everyone. Try to stay away from him." Such parents fail to adequately protect children from future violations. When the behavior is acknowledged by children, usually no one in the family seeks therapeutic help for the victim and/or the perpetrator. Families deny sexual violations for fear of exposing the inappropriate and violating behavior and to avoid familial shame. Instead of families getting help, they maintain denial and scapegoat the victims by not acknowledging the violations or their pain. They take no or limited action to prevent future violations to the victim or to someone else.

Drugs, Sex, and Shame

Cocaine, marijuana, alcohol, methaqualone, and other drugs are often described as sex drugs, or aphrodisiacs. At early stages, alcohol/drugs do reduce inhibitions. This confuses people who define them as aphrodisiacs. In reality, all drugs impair performance, especially at middle and later stages of use.

Under the influence of alcohol/drugs, individuals also experience impaired judgment and may take part in sexual activities in which they would not normally engage if they were sober. The shame of these sexual experiences can be devastating, so they use alcohol/drugs to blot out these feelings of shame. This can become a vicious, negative, addictive cycle. This cycle involves alcohol/drug use, followed by sexual activity, followed by feelings of shame. More alcohol/drug use follows

Case Study 6.2
Rejection Sensitivity
Frank

A colleague, old friend, and workshop training partner of mine tells a story of his fear of rejection. Growing up in an imbalanced, alcoholic family system, Frank learned how to defend against shame by being likable and by avoiding conflict. He figured that, if everyone liked him and he avoided conflict, he would not be subject to rejection, attack, or shame. Unfortunately, his likable quality put him in a real dilemma back in the third grade.

As Frank tells the story, his classmates really liked him and nominated him for third-grade class president. Normally, he would be just likable enough, but not too popular, because that would bring the unwanted attention he feared. That year, there were no outstanding choices for class president, and his likable, nonaggressive style became the qualities that the class wanted in its president. His classmates reacted to the nomination with genuine acceptance and encouragement. Frank felt this put him in a lose-lose position. Frank thought that, if he ran and lost, he would experience tremendous feelings of rejection and shame. If he ran and won, he would disappoint his classmates by being an inadequate class president, unable to meet the responsibilities of the office. Ultimately, this would lead to the same feelings of rejection and shame. Either way, Frank felt he would be rejected and shamed. His only choice was to reject the nomination for office. He did this rather adroitly by taking the nomination as an opportunity to lend his support to another, more popular classmate. "Thanks for the nomination," he said, "but my support goes to Larry. He would make a far more capable class president than me, and he was the one I had intended to nominate." Unfortunately, Frank missed out on the opportunity to grow from experiencing what it is like to run for office and perhaps the opportunity to be class president.

(to numb the feelings of shame), succeeded by sexual activity and more shame and feelings of loss of control.

The following are ways to help children, adolescents, and adults set boundaries:

Additional Characteristics of Shame and Abandonment
Rejection Sensitivity
Feelings of shame and abandonment can make individuals extremely sensitive to rejection, so much so that they choose not to try to grow and develop. Persons suffering from rejection sensitivity avoid situations that may be potentially shaming for fear of the situation triggering feelings of abandonment or rejection. Healthy individuals can tolerate shame, rejection, or abandonment and respond adaptively to these feelings by making the necessary adjustments and healthy choices in their lives.

Fear and Difficulty Making Decisions
Feelings of rejection, abandonment, and shame result in a variety of fears. Some of these fears are so traumatic that individuals cannot choose to change extremely

Case Study 6.3
Difficulty in Making Decisions
Norman

Norman, 29, is an adult child of an alcoholic. He grew up in an extremely abusive and physically violating dysfunctional family system. Norman described his earliest childhood memories at age two to three as the fights between his parents. On one occasion in an alcoholic rage, Norman's dad shoved his mom's head through the front window of their living room. Another time, his mom hid his dad's car keys in the garbage because his dad was drunk. They both struggled with the garbage, and she severely cut her hand on the jagged edge of a coffee can. Later, two tall police officers came to quiet them down during another domestic dispute. These were just a few of his memories.

His parents' fighting had a far-reaching impact on Norman and the other children in the family. The fear of abandonment, shame, and rejection caused Norman to act out during his childhood in many destructive ways. He did not achieve at school, despite being very bright and capable.

One day in individual counseling, Norman talked about a trip he took to Reno, Nevada. This trip was a metaphor for his fear of making a career change. After watching for some time at the roulette table with his wife and a friend, he decided to place his bet. Norman placed a two dollar bet on the red and a two dollar bet on the black. He surmised that this was a secure bet. He smiled to himself smugly as the roulette wheel spun and the ball bounded around from number to number. When it landed on a red number, the croupier just pushed his two dollars from the black spot to the red spot, and Norman collected his bet. Despite the odd looks from the croupier, and his friend's efforts to explain why this was a stupid bet, Norman continued to play two dollars on black and two dollars on red simultaneously. After several spins, he stopped betting. He felt entertained and justified that he had played roulette. I didn't hesitate to point out to Norman that the numbers zero and double zero on the roulette wheel are green. If either of those numbers had come up, he would have lost both bets.

This was analogous to what Norman was doing in his conflict about his career. He was betting on his current job for security, but not actively putting himself on the line to find a more fulfilling job. The longer he waited to take action, the more time he was wasting, and the more likely it was that zero or double zero would come up, in the form of either losing his current job due to his dissatisfaction projected to the work setting or not being able to motivate himself to find a better job because he was suffering from feelings of rejection, shame, and abandonment.

Even with this therapeutic insight, Norman waited several months to take any direct action. After a great deal of work, he eventually landed a new job in the field that he really wanted. That job didn't work out but it led to another job. After two years of struggle, Norman found himself in a career position that was consistent with his feelings of entitlement and accomplishment; his job affirmed his skills and capabilities.

uncomfortable situations. The fears of failure that may activate or trigger feelings of rejection, abandonment, and shame are so great that individuals choose to maintain self-effacing, even violating situations, instead of choosing healthy, growth-oriented paths.

The fear of success can also bring fears that, once some level of success is attained, it will fall apart and return the individual to previous feelings of failure and rejection. People then sabotage the gains in anticipation of deeper feelings of shame, rejection, and abandonment. What is missing is belief in themselves, their own self-worth, and their emerging talents, skills, and capabilities.

Poor Frustration Tolerance

When goals are blocked, even temporarily, persons who feel abandoned and rejected cannot tolerate this frustration. Such individuals believe there are no alternative choices or solutions to their blocked goals. Poor impulse control and self-destructive thinking may cause people to self-sabotage the progress they have made.

Other Reactions and Defenses

Common reactions and defenses to avoid feelings of abandonment and rejection include being overly defensive, extremely critical, or judgmental; showing rage or distorted thinking; and masking true feelings and emotions. People in pain deny the real issues and feelings by being overly defensive and critical of others. These persons view the world as being similar to the depriving, rejecting, and abandoning mothers and fathers they knew while growing up. Their distorted thinking tells them that the world will respond to them in the same way.

In her review of the literature, Carol L. Kempher (1987) identified various factors that contribute to parental imbalance. Often parents are imbalanced as caregivers; sometimes they are overwhelmed by problems of their own. (See Table 6.5.) This prevents them from providing the kind of care, support, structure, and healthy encouragement that children require to effectively develop and grow. Kempher summarized these characteristics of parental imbalance:

⚔ Parental Imbalance and Boundary Setting

1. Increased alcoholism, drug use, and nicotine dependence
2. Increased antisocial or sexually deviant behavior in parents
3. Increased mental and emotional problems, such as depression, personality disorders, or narcissism
4. Increased marital conflict
5. Increased parental absenteeism due to separation, divorce, or death

Parents who are not aware of their own emotional and psychological issues may deny the impact their anger, rage, and physical and emotional unavailability have on their children. Parents play an integral role in the development of their children.

It is natural and essential for parents to set appropriate boundaries with their children. Boundaries act as guideposts for children to bump into as they test their own independence and developmental skills. Good boundaries are a sign of good

T A B L E   6 . 5

Parental Imbalance

Chemically dependent and/or imbalanced parents often
- Lack knowledge and skill in parenting
- Have unrealistic expectations and lack information on what is developmentally appropriate behavior at various ages
- Are insensitive to the special needs of their children
- Have decreased family-management skills
- Have inappropriate disciplining techniques and maintain inconsistent, rigid, or ambiguous boundaries
- Have decreased positive responses to and reinforcement of their children
- Have decreased parental involvement and poor bonding or parent/child attachment

communication, respectful negotiation, and connection between parents and children. Poor boundaries escalate conflict and frustration, leading to disrespect and poor communication.

It is natural for children to test the limits of parental authority as they explore their own capacity for taking on more responsibility as they grow up. Poor boundary setting causes children to be exposed to situations before they have the developmental skills to handle the situations.

Boundaries are not rules for behavior of children; nor are they processes of limit setting. Boundaries exist between each member of the family, between subsystems, and between the family and society. These are the rules of interaction and the methods of functioning (Lawson and Lawson 1998).

Minuchin (1974) defined three types of boundaries; clear boundaries are essential to balanced families. Enmeshed and disengaged boundaries are characteristic of imbalanced families.

Clear boundaries allow mutual respect and concern by allowing separateness for each member yet maintaining closeness. Freedom and flexibility in these healthy relationships are developed by clear, direct, and understanding communication. Clear boundaries allow children to develop, grow, and differentiate from the family. Individuation can be accomplished only when clear boundaries are functioning within the family system.

Enmeshed boundaries are inflexible, are unyielding, and leave no room for differences. Differentness or separateness is not tolerated; individuation is not a goal of enmeshed relationships. Families with enmeshed boundaries view differentness as disloyalty and as a threat to the rules of the system. The needs of the individual are subjugated to the needs of the parents or system. Satisfying the parents' definition of unity and sameness is stressed. Individual boundaries are blurred, and the individual is often swallowed up by the system. Individuals discount their own feelings, needs, and desires; they feel smothered and numb. They often use alcohol/drugs to counteract these feelings and the underlying resentment and anger.

Disengaged boundaries are overly rigid, with little or no opportunity for communication. Individuals in families that maintain disengaged boundaries have little sense of belonging, often feeling isolated from one another. The family also isolates from community and society. The parents are emotionally unavailable to each other, to the children, and, for that matter, to anyone else.

Boundary Inadequacy

Boundary inadequacy has been defined as the inability to set consistent and appropriate boundaries in relationships. The three major forms of boundary inadequacy identified by Eli Coleman and Phillip Colgan (1986) are ambiguous, overly rigid, and invasive.

Ambiguous boundary inadequacy involves a pattern of double messages exchanged within the relationship. The double messages create an atmosphere of tension wherein the recipient of the communication can never be sure what can be believed. The inability of the communicator to send clear messages lays the groundwork for the cycle of ambiguity to begin.

Overly rigid boundary inadequacy is characterized by patterns of behavior wherein smooth and efficient functioning is a priority over being responsive and adaptable. Adherence to a preset code of behavior is maintained, regardless of intervening situational variables, wherein roles are played and rules are strictly enforced.

Invasive boundary inadequacy involves patterns of behavior wherein an imbalance of power is used to objectify people. Other people become objects for the person to use in satisfying all needs (e.g., sexual and physical abuse).

Boundary Ambiguity

Boss and Greenberg (1984) use the term *boundary ambiguity* in describing when family members' perceptions of who is in and out of the family and who is performing various family roles and tasks are confused. The alcoholic family system organizes around the alcoholic, or the family member(s) who exhibit dysfunctional behavior. In recovery, the family is challenged to reorganize as a viable system or become dysfunctional with continued boundary ambiguity (i.e., the dry-drunk family).

Ziter (1988) describes the alcoholic/imbalanced family as going through four recovery stages to overcome boundary ambiguity. These stages are very similar to the grieving stages of denial, anger, bargaining, depression, and acceptance described earlier in this chapter.

- *Stage 1—Clustering.* This is described as an early denial stage, when the family members sacrifice in order to maintain family harmony. The family task at this stage is to assure themselves that a family exists and to try to keep the alcoholic in the family system.
- *Stage 2—Conflict.* The reality of the situation is beginning to be understood at this stage. Individual differences are penetrating the denial system, and the family members are experiencing the stress and uncertainty of these ambiguous differences. It is at this stage that anger replaces denial to control family differences.

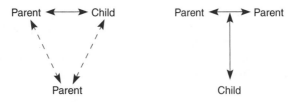

FIGURE 6.1   *Triangulation*

- *Stage 3—Individuation.* At this stage of family recovery, the family members are able to recognize the individuality of each person. The family's task is to support each other in exploring "self" while negotiating living together. Boundaries are becoming clearer.
- *Stage 4—Connection.* Family members are making connections with each other. There is a new way of relating that perhaps was not experienced before—an intimate linking. Mutuality emerges, and family members maintain boundaries through their own assertiveness and the respect of other members.

One can see how family members move from a system with imbalance and boundary ambiguity to a balanced system with connection and clarity in boundaries.

Eli Coleman (1987) underscored the importance of setting appropriate boundaries for members of imbalanced families:

> Developing skills at boundary setting is an essential ingredient in the recovery from chemical dependency or codependency. For many it is learning to say "no" to someone's request for physical, sexual, or emotional intimacy. Through saying "no," the individual learns that he or she can have a personal boundary and have it respected. This leads to a clear sense of self-wants and self-desires and it develops a sense of power and control in interpersonal relationships. After learning to say "no," the individual can learn to say "yes," and not lose a sense of individuality.

Triangulation—Another Boundary Issue

Jay Haley, a noted family therapist, defined triangulation (Figure 6.1) as at least two adults involved in an offspring's problem, where the parent-child dyad is pitted against a more peripheral parent, stepparent, or grandparent. The triangle may involve a parent's lover, an estranged parent, or another relative.

The destructive nature of the triangle is that the parent-child dyad, or alliance, is established at the expense of the peripheral parent. Often the parent-child dyad creates a marital conflict. The parent is overly enmeshed in this alliance, seeking the child's favor despite the reality of the situation.

✂ Parents' Use/Abuse of Alcohol and Drugs

Kandel and Andrews (1987) postulated that parents can influence their offspring's behavior by modeling actions and defining norms, by controlling the child's susceptibility to the influence of others, and by providing positive attachments.

The modeling of drug use and alcohol use by parents, inadequate supervision of children, and lack of physical and emotional availability are factors that may put children at-risk for substance abuse.

Case Study 6.4

Triangulation

John and Mary

John and Mary have significant marital problems. John is the head of the fire department for the county in which they reside and escapes the conflicts at home by spending much of his time with the men at the various fire stations. The couple actively attend community events and act as if their marriage were perfect. Their adopted 16-year-old daughter Michelle knows the truth. Michelle frequently argues with her mom to the point of hysteria. Mary often gives Michelle reason to be angry by giving her ambiguous, mixed messages (e.g., I want to be close to you, yet I don't trust you because you are stealing my husband, whom I can no longer hold in the marriage). Mary buys Michelle clothes and jewelry but is emotionally cold and unavailable. Mary has no insight into the way she antagonizes Michelle. Michelle is very bright but acts out her frustration with her mom by ditching classes, stealing things from her dresser, and being extremely flirtatious with boys. John and Michelle maintain an enmeshed dyadic alliance. John is frustrated with his wife's coldness, emotional and sexual unavailability, and constant arguments with Michelle and nagging of him. Michelle makes sexual overtures to young men while with her father and makes other sexually inappropriate remarks. In effect, she is flirtatious with her father; they are acting out their unconscious desires to be intimate with each other. These unconscious conflicts put more pressure on Michelle and she has begun to use alcohol/drugs excessively and to have sex with numerous young men. At this point, the family has sought counseling, a process that involves unraveling this triangulation and establishing clearer boundaries and lines of communication.

Grace M. Barnes, in her chapter "Impact of the Family on Adolescent Drinking Patterns" (1990), describes the three major family system variables necessary to prevent problem behaviors by children: **family cohesion, flexibility,** and **communication clarity.**

> ## ✂ Other Family System Variables

Cohesion is defined as the emotional bonding of family members toward each other. Family members respect one another, support each other, and have appropriate boundaries. Cohesion is not possible if family members are enmeshed or disengaged from each other. Instead, there is a balance in roles, tasks, and ability to resolve conflicts.

Flexibility is the family members' ability to alter family roles and rituals in response to situational stress.

Communication clarity is the ability of family members to develop coalitions and to understand each other.

Parental competence is described by Burton White, director of the Harvard Preschool Projects, as the ability and willingness of parents to

- Sensibly design the world of the child
- Serve as a child's personal consultant
- Set limits effectively, for the sake of the child (not the parent) (White, Kaban, and Attanucci 1979)

Case Study 6.5

Family System Variables

Jane

Jane grew up with four sisters. Dad's alcoholism was denied for most of their childhood. It was Jane's responsibility to take care of Mom emotionally. When Mom experienced chronic fatigue, Jane took care of the other, younger sisters, giving them dinner, getting them to bed, and trying to keep them quiet. Despite her efforts, Mom's physical symptoms increased in frequency. The other sisters didn't seem to be as affected by Mom's pain and Dad's alcohol use. It took Mom's "nervous breakdown" and her being hospitalized for a month in a psychiatric hospital for the other children to recognize the problem. Jane and her next younger sister were now responsible for the house. The middle sister began drinking during this time, and the youngest seemed to spend more time playing quietly by herself.

A few months after Mom returned home, Dad started attending AA meetings. Mom still experienced fatigue and physical pain, but less frequently. Jane went away to college, rarely visiting, immersing herself in studies, and marrying right out of college. The middle sister declared she was gay and went off to school 3,000 miles from home. The youngest and next to oldest stayed close to home, alternating the emotional caretaking of both Mom and Dad.

It was only in later years that the sisters started to share their memories of their painful childhood. Each had sought counseling for various relationship problems. Each had learned about being an adult child of an alcoholic. They were now beginning to heal by talking about their recovery. Mom was now actively pursuing interests outside of the home and spending time on her own. Dad was several years sober now and beginning to communicate more effectively with his daughters.

Interestingly, adolescents in single-parent and stepparent families report more alcohol use than do adolescents in traditional families (Burnside et al. 1986). A study of high school students (Barnes and Nindle 1987) reported a tendency for adolescents living with both natural parents to have fewer alcohol-related problems.

Older siblings can exert a tremendous influence of alcohol/drug use on younger children in the family. Often it is an older sibling who initiates younger brothers and sisters into the rite of alcohol and drug use. The older sibling frequently has better access to alcohol/drugs and is often a more experienced user. Sometimes it is older cousins, stepbrothers/sisters, or friends of the family who initiate alcohol/drug use. Adolescents who have close, quality relationships and good communication with their parents are less likely to be influenced negatively by older siblings or peers.

The adolescent's positive sense of self, attainment of developmental skills, and ability to individuate also minimize negative peer influence. Studies have indicated that the level of closeness and trust in the parent-child relationship determines the choice of positive peer relationships.

Children who grow up in an abstinent family system may also develop alcohol/drug dependence and addiction. People who become alienated from their abstinence backgrounds may use excessive drinking to express their frustration with early rigid familial, religious, and community teachings. Problem drinking or excessive drug use is symbolic of a rebellion or revolt against early family values that became overly rigid. Sometimes alcohol/drug problems skip a generation as well. The child growing up in an alcoholic/addict system decides to "never be like his or her alcoholic/addict dad or mom" and chooses to abstain from any alcohol/drug use as an adult. The genetic predisposition for alcoholism/drug addiction is still passed on to his or her children, who may develop problems with alcohol/drugs, even though they grew up in a household where there was no parental use of alcohol/drugs.

The size of the family may also influence alcohol and drug use by children. As the number of siblings increases, the family becomes more complex in role relationships and tasks. Some children may experience increasing levels of frustration (blocked goals). In very large families, parents may be more controlling/coercive, less available, and less supportive, resulting in problem behaviors by some of the children and perhaps overly responsible (codependent) behaviors by siblings. This is illustrated in Case Study 6.5.

Jay Haley (1971) described the following major stages in the family life cycle:

1. Relationships between families through unattached young adults
2. Joining of families through marriage
3. Family and the young child
4. Family and the adolescent
5. Launching of children
6. Later life

⚔ Imbalanced Life Cycles of Families

As a result of the imbalance in alcoholic/addict family systems, developmental and interpersonal tasks are impaired at each stage of the family life cycle.

Relationships Between Families and the Joining of Families

During the first two stages, the relationships between families are often filled with conflict and tension. Cooperation between families is difficult because the alcoholic/addict family system is trying to deny, minimize, and cover up the family secret of alcoholism/addiction. This results in the families' inability to develop trust and closeness.

Family and the Young Child

At the third stage, the family is either isolated or involved with other families that have similar problems with alcohol/drugs. The child is the innocent victim at this stage. The young child is often embarrassed by his or her parents' unpredictable behavior. As a result, the child frequently prefers playing at other children's homes and rarely invites other children to his or her home. Often, children from

Case Study 6.6

An Imbalanced Family System

Steve

At the age of eight, Steve was always with his friend Joe's family. He would have breakfast and dinner with them and spend most of his free hours playing with Joe and talking with Joe's parents. When Steve had problems, concerns, or conflicts, he would talk to Joe's parents and not discuss the issues with his own family. Steve's actions illustrate that children with imbalanced families often adopt surrogate families to survive.

alcoholic/addict homes literally adopt their friends' parents. Becoming stepchildren, they spend a great deal of time with their friends' families.

Family and the Adolescent

The fourth stage is the time of most turmoil. Tumultuous even in the balanced family system, adolescence becomes even more dramatic in an imbalanced family system. The adolescent's exploration of a healthy personal identity is incongruent with the imbalanced, unhealthy alcoholic/addict system. The conflict of holding allegiance to the family, imbalanced as it is, and exploring self through individuation and differentiation creates tremendous guilt and anxiety for adolescents. If this conflict is unresolved, adolescents can either internalize their own frustration and anger and develop an imbalanced sense of self or act out their anger in a demonstrative and destructive manner. The acting-out behavior often includes problems with alcohol/drugs, sexual promiscuity, problems in school and with authority figures, and criminal-justice problems. The internalized anger is sometimes more subtly manifested in the need for constant approval from peers, a poor self-concept, insecurity, or fears of abandonment and rejection.

Launching of Children

During the fifth stage, when the children are launched, the parents' alcohol and drug use usually intensifies. The empty-nest syndrome forces the parents to look at the dissatisfaction in their own marital system. The usual way to avoid the issues of marital imbalance is to increase the use of alcohol/drugs.

Of course, adult children of alcoholics/addicts are at risk for creating imbalanced relationships with their partners and for recapitulating the family of origin by developing imbalanced family systems as well. If there is no help, the result is the repetition of the same imbalanced system from generation to generation.

Later Life

In the sixth stage, the issues intensify in an alcoholic/addict family system. Consciously or unconsciously, the adult recognizes the imbalanced patterns of relating during childhood. Adult children of alcoholics/addicts enter treatment as they notice the imbalances in their own lives. Contacts with their parents in these later years may bring highly emotionally charged conflict to the forefront, making it difficult to have caring or effective relationships with their parents. If the parents are still using alcohol/drugs, this even further intensifies the difficulty in maintaining or developing better relationships. Working through the stages of grief and accepting the painful limitations of these imbalanced relationships are other developmental tasks for adult children. Healing may occur before the parents die. Perhaps the legacy of alcoholism/addiction will not be passed on to the next generation.

How does a counselor get resistant family members to participate in counseling? Alcoholic/addict families are among the most difficult families to get into treatment, whether the setting is inpatient, residential, or outpatient treatment. Families often abdicate responsibility for the alcoholic/addict's problems. It is too difficult for them to admit their feelings of embarrassment, shame, and personal feelings of inadequacy in trying to control family members' abuse of alcohol/drugs. P. Mason (1958) reported that, of 1,000 eligible parents of alcoholics/addicts, only 30 to 40 would appear at monthly parent-staff meetings and almost none of these attended more than three times.

Not only are family members resistant to attending sessions but also the alcoholics/addicts themselves often sabotage family involvement. Alcoholics/addicts are often self-protective of their families, not wanting them to experience more pain. Alcoholics/addicts may even feel a sense of betrayal in assisting counselors to get the rest of the family involved. This would be disloyal to the rules of the imbalanced, enmeshed family system.

For many alcoholics/addicts, having their spouses or other family members involved in treatment might blow their cover. Alcoholics/addicts may have lied or deceived counselors in giving inaccurate or distorted information about their alcohol/drug use, family interactions, or other information. There is also fear that counselors would blame, criticize, or shame other family members; then these family members would get back at the alcoholics/addicts.

⚔ Fathers of Alcoholics/ Addicts— Dealing with Resistance

The fathers of alcoholics/addicts are by far the most difficult family members to get into family sessions. A large percentage of these fathers have alcohol/drug problems themselves and don't want this brought to the attention of the counselor (the same may hold true for mothers). The father is difficult to engage in the process of family therapy because he has generally been unavailable to the drug user and other family members. The father is often angry and defensive.

I have heard many a father say, "Since nobody ever listened to me or allowed me to follow through in what I thought would work in the first place, I am angry and don't want to get involved." The truth of the matter is that most fathers are frightened by the emotional content of counseling and profess not to believe in counseling. They see therapists as invading the family systems the fathers have tried to control. Fathers are also trying to avoid their own emotional pain and issues.

In an attempt to engage fathers in treatment, K. Labate (1975) recommends a kind of romancing of the father by acknowledging the positive intentions that the father possesses, emphasizing that the father's participation in treatment is needed to make treatment successful. Labate suggests the following:

1. Reassuring the father that he is important
2. Pointing out that changes depend on his participation
3. Making the father aware that he has the power to sabotage treatment
4. Noting that the father has choices, such as transferring to another counselor, who might work with him individually
5. Placing responsibility for change squarely on the father's shoulders
6. Getting the father to consider realigning his priorities (e.g., choosing his family's happiness over acquisition of more material goods)

Labate's strategies can be used on any family member of the alcoholic/addict—the spouse, brothers, sisters, or other family members—who may have the same resistance to family treatment.

✂ Noble Ascriptions to Counteract Defensiveness

"Anyone working with addicts' families for the first time is impressed with the tremendous defensiveness that most of them show. It sometimes seems as if they are just waiting for the therapist to cast even a minor aspersion so they can protest or perhaps abort therapy prematurely" (Stanton et al. 1982). In approaching alcoholics/addicts and family members in treatment, it is essential that the counselor's style be nonpejorative, nonjudgmental, sensitive to the patient's issues of shame, and in no way blaming. Duncan Stanton suggested that the treatment be put in the context that each family member's intentions were and are noble and that there is a good reason or adaptive function for even the most destructive behavior. For example, anger, frustration, and generally attacking behavior can be relabeled as "a concern that is painful to tolerate," rather than "You are really angry for no reason" or "There he goes again, using anger to hurt and control us." Destructive enabling behavior can be nobly ascribed as "It is difficult to see your child in pain, pain that you would prefer that the child not go through."

"Simply defining problems as interactional or familial stumbling blocks serves to have them viewed as shared, rather than loading the blame entirely on one or two members—'we're all in this together'" (Stanton et al. 1982). This approach does not abandon the therapist's role in challenging the thoughts, beliefs, and behaviors that might hinder the family from becoming more functional. Instead, the counselor expresses perspectives and viewpoints in a human, caring, and nonshaming manner, facilitating trust in the therapeutic alliance. The ascribing of noble intentions or characteristics takes the shame out of the therapeutic work—shame that would inevitably cause one or more family members to sabotage treatment.

Summary

The six factors that are the major focus of this chapter, which influence a child's use/abuse of alcohol or drugs later in life, are

1. Parent-child bonding
2. Temperament of the child
3. Parenting styles and the quality of the parent-child relationship
4. Parental imbalance and boundary setting
5. Parents use/abuse of alcohol or drugs
6. Other family system variables

Poor bonding is described in the context of separation stress, leading to feelings of abandonment and rejection. The six key elements of abandonment depression in adults are feelings of homicidal rage, suicidal depression, panic, hopelessness and helplessness, emptiness and void, and guilt.

The child's temperament is described as a behavioral characteristic present at birth, or within the first few months. Certain temperaments make the individual more at-risk for substance abuse. A so-called difficult temperament makes the individual at-risk for problem behaviors, including substance abuse. A difficult temperament includes high activity level, low flexibility, task orientation, mood instability, and social withdrawal.

Shame is described as playing a major role in devastating the parent-child relationship. Shame is a deep-rooted feeling as a result of traumatic childhood experiences. Shame is defined as the self looking in on itself and finding itself lacking. When shame attaches to feelings, those feelings are usually escalated (e.g., anger + shame = rage).

The family system that has not effectively dealt with issues of loss, trauma, shame, and separation (abandonment) develops unresolved grief, feelings of melancholia, and depression. These unresolved feelings often lead to self-destructive behaviors, such as drinking and drugging.

Parental imbalance is defined as parents who lack knowledge and skills in parenting. These parents have unrealistic expectations of their children and are insensitive to the needs of their children.

Imbalanced families often have difficulty in setting appropriate boundaries. Boundary inadequacy is defined as the inability to set consistent and appropriate boundaries in relationships, as evidenced by ambiguous, overly rigid, and invasive boundaries. Triangulation is another form of boundary inadequacy, in which the parent-child affiliation is established at the expense of the peripheral parent. Frequently, these problems in boundary setting lead to physical and sexual violations and emotional and psychological abuse. This is especially true in alcoholic/addict family systems.

Parents who use/abuse alcohol or drugs model the same behavior in their offspring. Conversely, family cohesion, flexibility, and communication clarity can positively influence a child against using/abusing alcohol or drugs.

The chapter concludes with a description of the imbalanced life cycles of families and the difficulty in getting fathers of alcoholics/addicts to be involved in family counseling. Noble ascriptions are described as a way to engage fathers to get involved in family treatment.

References

Barnes, Grace M. "Impact of the Family on Adolescent Drinking Patterns." In R. Collins et al., *Alcohol and the Family* (1990): 137–62.

Barnes, G.M., and M. Nindle. "Family Factors in Adolescent Alcohol and Drug Abuse." *Pediatrician-International Journal of Child and Adolescent Health* 14 (1987): 13–18.

Block, Block & Keyes, 1988.

Boss, P., and J. Greenberg. "Family Boundary Ambiguity: A New Variable in Family Stress Theory." *Family Process* 23 (1984): 535–46.

Burnside, M.A. et al. "Alcohol Use by Adolescents in Disrupted Families." *Alcoholism: Clinical and Experimental Research* 10 (1986): 274–78.

Carnes, Patrick. "Patrick J. Carnes: Riding the Tides, Navigating Counseling's Turbulent Waters," interview by the author. *Professional Counselor Magazine,* December 1995, 47–52.

Coleman, Eli. *Chemical Dependency and Intimacy Dysfunction.* New York: Haworth Press, 1987.

Coleman, Eli, and Phillip Colgan. "Boundary Inadequacy in Drug Dependent Families." *Journal of Psychoactive Drugs* 18 (1986): 21–30.

Diagnostic and Statistical Manual IV, Amreican Psychological Association. Washington, D.C., 1994.

Dobkin, Tremblay, Masse, and Vitaro (1995) (see Windle)

Eliason, M.J., and A.H. Skinstad. "Drug/Alcohol Addictions and Mothering." *Alcoholism Treatment Quarterly* 12, no. 1 (1995): 83–95.

Garrison, W.T., and F.J. Earls. "Temperament and Child Psychopathology." *Developmental Clinical Psychology and Psychiatry* 12 (1987).

Gomberg, E.S.L. "Shame and Guilt Issues Among Women Alcoholics." *Alcoholism Treatment Quarterly* 5 (1988): 139–55.

Haley, Jay. *Changing Families: A Family Therapy Reader.* New York: Grune and Stratton, 1971.

Jessup, M. *Chemically Dependent Women in San Francisco: A Status Report.* San Francisco Community Substance Abuse Services, Department of Public Health, 1983.

Johnson, Valerie, and Robert J. Pandina. "Effects of the Family Environment on Adolescent Substance Use, Delinquency and Coping Skills." *American Journal of Drug and Alcohol Abuse* 1, no. 17 (1991): 71–88.

Kandel, D.B., and K.A. Andrews. "Processes of Adolescent Socialization by Parents and Peers." *International Journal of Addiction* 22 (1987): 319–42.

Kempher, Carol. "Special Populations: Etiology and Prevention of Vulnerability to Chemical Dependency in Children of Substance Abusers." In *Youth at High Risk for Substance Abuse,* eds. B.S. Brown and A.R. Mills. NIDA Monograph, DHHS Pub. No. (ADM) 1987, 87–153.

Kohnstamm, Bates and Rothbart, (1989) in Windle.

Labate, K. "Pathogenic Role Rigidity in Fathers: Some Observations." *Journal of Marriage and Family Counseling* 1 (1975): 69–79.

Lerner and Vicary (1984) (in Addictions)

Maccoby, E.E., and J.A. Martin. "Socialization in the Context of the Family: Parent-Child Interaction." In *Handbook of Child Psychology,* Volume IV, Socialization,

Personality, and Social Development, ed. E.M. Hetherington. New York: John Wiley & Sons, 1983.

Mason, P. "Mother of the Addict." *Psychiatric Quarterly Supplement* 32 (1958): 189–99.

Masse and Tremblay, (1997) in Addictions McCrady

Masterson, James (1976).

Minuchin, Salvador. *Families and Family Therapy.* Cambridge, MA: Harvard University Press, 1974.

Ohanessian and Hesselbrook, (1995) in Addictions.

Rollins, B.C., and D.L. Thomas. "Parental Support, Power, and Control Techniques in the Socialization of Children." In *Contemporary Theories of the Family,* vol. 1, ed. W.R. Burr, R. Hill, F. Inye, and I.L. Reiss. New York: Free Press, 1979.

Stanton, Duncan M., and Thomas C. Todd, and associates. *Family Therapy of Drug Abuse.* New York: Guilford Press, 1982.

Tubman and Windle, (1995) in Windle.

Volk, R.J. et al. "Family Systems of Adolescent Substance Abusers." *Family Relations* 38 (1988): 266–72.

Werner and Smith, (1995) in Windle.

White, B., B. Kaban, and J. Attanucci. *The Origins of Human Competence: The Final Report on the Harvard Preschool Project.* Lexington, MA: Lexington Books, D.C. Heath, 1979.

Windle, M. Alcohol Use Among Adolescents, Sage Publications, 1999.

Ziter, MaryLou Politi. "Treating Alcoholic Families: The Resolution of Boundary Ambiguity." *Alcoholism Treatment Quarterly* 5, no. 314 (1988): 221–33.

Growing Up in an Alcoholic Family System

Chapter Objectives

1. Describe the scope of the problem and awareness of adult children of alcoholics.

2. List several behavioral characteristics of adults who grew up in alcoholic homes.

3. Compare growing up in an alcoholic family system with post-traumatic stress disorder (PTSD) and describe the five major symptoms of PTSD.

4. Identify the scope of the adult-child of an alcoholic problem, including an estimate of how many people are affected.

5. Describe the behaviors and communication patterns of parents and children in an alcoholic family system.

6. Describe the kinds of denial that children in an alcoholic system maintain and some behavioral characteristics of children of alcoholics.

7. Define codependency and list the criteria of codependency.

8. Describe the family disease model.

9. Describe the impact of alcoholism on marriage.

10. Describe the thoughts, feelings, and behaviors of overseparated and overattached individuals.

11. Discuss the rationale for doing grief work with adult children of alcoholics.

12. Describe second-order change and changing interactions with family members.

13. Identify the 11 curative factors of group psychotherapy and their applications to adult children of alcoholics therapy groups.

This chapter focuses on children of alcoholics. In the 1980s, this was an emerging issue that still is significant, in that it shifted the focus away from the alcoholic/addict to the children in the alcoholic/addict family system.

Alcoholism is described as a family disease, that includes codependency, enabling behavior, and marital discord. The children in an alcoholic system, much like the nonalcoholic spouse, compensate to keep the system in homeostasis. The family is organized around the alcoholic's behavior and drinking. The alcoholism is the central organizing principle around which the family focuses.

Children growing up in an alcoholic/addict family system experience traumas, which result in specific adult behavioral characteristics and developmental disabilities. Adult children of alcoholics (ACAs) have

trouble establishing effective boundaries in relationships and are often either overseparated or overattached in partner relationships. Recovery for adult children involves dealing with unresolved feelings of childhood grief and working through feelings of shame, abandonment, and rejection.

By understanding the healing and recovery process for adult children, perhaps this pattern of imbalance can be broken for the next generation.

✖ The Adult Children of Alcoholics Movement

In the 1980s, one of the most significant alcohol/drug issues brought to the attention of the general public was the awareness of the characteristics of adult children of alcoholics. Children who grew up in alcoholic families are now adults, hence the term *adult children of alcoholics.* These adults report difficulties in establishing effective, intimate, interpersonal relationships.

The talent and dedication of people such as Timmen Cermak, Claudia Black, Stephanie Brown, Janet Woititz, Sharon Wegscheider-Cruse, Robert Ackerman, and Lori Dwinell created an awareness of the trauma of growing up in an alcoholic family system. Because of this awareness, our society has not only recognized but today is dealing with the imbalanced aspects of alcoholism on the family members.

In 1979, a *Newsweek* article about adult children of alcoholics reported the early work of Claudia Black (1982) and Stephanie Brown, who both described and labeled the characteristics of ACA. Brown (1988) described the reaction after the *Newsweek* article as "a prairie fire of interest." The proliferation of articles, materials, books, general information, workshops, and speakers on ACA issues was dramatic from 1979 to the late 1980s. Adult children of alcoholics were finally recognized as a treatment population that had generally been ignored for years. This explosion of interest was in direct proportion to the neglect and oversight that occurred as professionals focused myopically on the alcoholics, while ignoring the children who grew up in alcoholic families. W. Bosma appropriately described children of alcoholics in 1972 as *victims in a hidden tragedy.* In 1983, the National Association for Children of Alcoholics (NACOA) was formed. Timmen Cermak, one of the founders, was its first president. Numerous planning meetings established the NACOA as a central organizing force in disseminating information, providing direction, and developing resources for adult children of alcoholics. The NACOA organized national conferences to provide a forum for the dissemination of ACA treatment information for both professionals and the lay public.

In 1983, the NACOA developed some basic facts about children of alcoholics in its charter statement:

- An estimated 28 million Americans have at least one alcoholic parent.
- More than half of all alcoholics have an alcoholic parent.
- Children of alcoholics are at the highest risk of developing alcoholism themselves or marrying someone who is alcoholic.
- In up to 90 percent of child abuse cases, alcohol is a significant factor.
- Children of alcoholics are frequently victims of incest, child neglect, and other forms of violence and exploitation.

The popularity of the ACA movement also brought with it some concerns for overgeneralization and a lack of clinical foundation. Appropriately, this point is made by one of the pioneers of the movement. "Like many social movements, the sudden recognition, widespread interest, and emotional intensity have been powerful and helpful for many children and adults. However, there continues to be a lack of a solid clinical research and theoretical foundation on which to base important decisions for intervention, education, prevention, and treatment" (Brown 1988).

❧ Characteristics of Adult Children of Alcoholics

Some of the behavioral characteristics of ACA are

1. Fear of losing control
2. All-or-none, black-or-white thinking
3. Fear of experiencing feelings
4. Overdeveloped sense of responsibility or irresponsibility
5. Difficulty with intimacy and with asking for what is wanted or needed
6. Flashbacks of childhood but many memory gaps
7. Feelings of being little, or like a child, when under stress
8. Unreasonable loyalty
9. Addiction to excitement
10. Difficulty relaxing
11. Feelings of guilt, abandonment, and/or depression
12. Tendency to confuse love with self-pity
13. Backlog of shock and grief
14. Compulsive behaviors
15. Living in a world of denial
16. Guessing at what is normal
17. Tendency toward physical symptoms (e.g., headaches, gastrointestinal problems)

❧ Growing Up in an Alcoholic Home as Post-Traumatic Stress Disorder

Timmen Cermak (1984) stated that the effect of growing up in an alcoholic family system is analogous to the post-traumatic stress disorder (PTSD) of war veterans or survivors of the Holocaust because the same coping mechanisms are used. The soldier who helplessly watches as a buddy is shot and killed shuts down his own emotions to survive the trauma, which can later be reexperienced in a safe environment. This same reaction of shutting down emotionally occurs in the children of alcoholics. After these children become adults, they reexperience feelings of childhood traumas and suffer chronic symptoms of acute anxiety, depression, sleep disturbances, and nightmares, as well as an inability to work or function effectively at daily activities.

The following major symptoms of PTSD are similar to symptoms experienced by ACA:

1. Reexperiencing the trauma, as evidenced by
   a. Nightmares
   b. Recurrent obsessive thoughts
   c. Sudden reemergence of survival behavior in the face of events that resemble the original trauma
   d. Emotional overload
2. Psychic numbing, as evidenced by
   a. A sense of depersonalization
   b. A sense of not fitting into one's surroundings
   c. A feeling of emotional anesthesia

Case Study 7.1

ACA and Post-Traumatic Stress Disorder

Joe

Joe was a client who had experienced both the trauma of growing up in an alcoholic family system and post-traumatic stress as a result of military service in Vietnam. Joe was referred to me by a colleague, who was counseling Joe's 12-year-old daughter.

Joe came home drunk one evening, went to his daughter's bedroom to kiss her good night, and began crying and talking about how unhappy he was. Although there was no sexual violation, the daughter was extremely upset by her father's behavior. She was frightened and concerned about his drinking and his deep emotional sadness.

Joe was one of those patients for whom I initially had very little hope; he turned out to be a case that reinforced my belief in the inherent goodness in people. Joe was 25 minutes late for his first counseling session. Joe insisted that his lateness was due to a business appointment and wondered why I was so concerned with time. He believed that his only problem was his business. He said, "If I could only get out from under the financial pressure, everything would be back to normal." Joe agreed to come back for counseling to help with stress management although he felt that his daughter needed assistance, not him.

Gradually, I was able to establish a therapeutic bond with Joe. Once I got to know him, I soon realized that he had the heart of a puppy dog and he had suffered significant disappointments and trauma in his life.

Joe's alcoholic father, who was well-read and extremely bright, owned his own business. His dad spent most of his time drinking at the office and the local bar while discussing many topics with his customers and friends; he was wellversed in politics, philosophy, religion, physics, even psychology. Although he was a friendly and entertaining drunk with his friends, he was emotionally unpredictable at home. At times, Joe's dad was maudlin about his childhood and his father's death when he was eight. At other times, he raged around the house, screaming resentments for his need to work so hard to support his wife and children. Once Joe was so angry with his father that he took a baseball bat and was going to smash him in the face.

Sometimes Joe felt sorry for his father and put him to bed after a drinking binge; when things got to be overwhelming, Joe just ran out of the house. On those evenings, Joe frequently went down to the school and threw rocks at the classroom windows. This and similar aggressive behavior kept him in trouble throughout his childhood. Joe was extremely bright and, despite his aggressive behavior, pulled good grades in high school. Because he spent more time drinking than studying in college, in 1968 his military deferment was revoked.

In the service, Joe was put through training for military intelligence and could have avoided Vietnam if his alcoholism and aggressive anger hadn't gotten him into trouble with his top sergeant. In Vietnam, Joe's major job was to fly to battle zones after conflicts and get a body count for Vietnamese and American soldiers.

Joe felt sadness for the Vietnamese children; he described them stealing, cheating, and manipulating the GIs to survive. It reminded him of his own childhood anger and aggressive behavior. In counseling sessions, Joe initially denied the emotional trauma of his experiences in Vietnam. He insisted that he had had it good, compared with others. Joe suffered from this traumatic exposure as well as from survivor's guilt. He experienced all the traditional signs of post-traumatic stress: sleep disorders and nightmares, night sweats, inability to concentrate, hypertension, disorientation, and explosive temper. All of these symptoms were complicated by his alcoholism.

After a year and a half of individual counseling, followed by group counseling with other ACAs, Joe was able to maintain sobriety, grieve the loss of his father, and grieve his experiences in Vietnam. After some time in counseling, Joe and some other group members visited the Vietnam War Memorial in Washington, DC. This was an important event in his painful journey to recovery.

      d. Constriction of emotions, especially in situations demanding intimacy, tenderness, or sexuality

      e. Lack of feelings during times of stress

      f. Sudden experience of a wall between the self and the feelings

      g. Confusion instead of having feelings

      h. A lump in the throat instead of allowing feelings to emerge or pressure and tightness in the jaw, shoulders, or other parts of the body

      i. Feelings that emotions will be overwhelming if one gets in touch with them

3. Hypervigilance, as evidenced by

      a. Inability to relax

      b. Frequent startle responses

      c. Chronic anxiety

      d. Panic attacks

4. Survivor guilt, as evidenced by

      a. Chronic depression

      b. A sourceless sense of guilt

5. Intensification of symptoms by exposure to events that resemble the original trauma

In order to have a diagnosis of post-traumatic stress disorder, the trauma must be significant. Severe emotional or physical abuse and/or sexual violation can be so traumatizing to the child that symptoms of PTSD might occur. Unfortunately, the diagnosis of PTSD has frequently been used too loosely, without evidence of significant trauma. Just growing up in an alcoholic family does not mean one suffers from PTSD. Cermak is using PTSD as a model to understand the symptoms of ACA, not as a generalized label.

✷ Childhood in an Alcoholic Home

Children in alcoholic families learn to distrust their own observations (what they see and hear) and feelings (what they sense), and they feel powerless to change the family system. They cannot speak out and cannot trust their feelings because the rules in an alcoholic family system are don't talk, don't feel, and don't trust. Because these children distrust their own observations and feelings, they must wonder or guess at what is normal. At a time when most functional families are providing structure, discipline, and natural consequences for their children's behavior, alcoholic families provide control; rigidity; fear; irresponsibility; immaturity; and, most important, *unpredictability.* Children in alcoholic families try to control the behavior of the alcoholic parent and the codependent spouse by becoming super-responsible and trying to do everything correctly to obtain the parent's approval. They soon find out that, despite their best efforts to be perfect, the parent always finds fault with something. While desperately trying to predict or control the behavior of their parents, children do not realize that alcoholism and drug addiction is a disease that results in unpredictable behavior.

Child growing up in an alcoholic family.

Robert Ackerman (1978) described the various behavioral characteristics of children of alcoholics, including the following:

- Being superachievers or perfectionists or exhibiting efforts that go far beyond the reasonable criteria of every task
- Exhibiting an inordinate need to control their environment and therefore becoming anxious with the slightest threat to their security (e.g., a teacher who unknowingly comments on homework not done or an unusually low grade may provoke emotional upset)
- Displaying social disengagement from or excessive attention to the peer group (as an isolated loner or a class clown)
- Exhibiting signs of physical neglect (untidiness, soiled clothing, poor hygiene) and/or physical abuse (bruises, cuts, etc.)
- Being unable to concentrate and sometimes showing marked variations in academic performance, especially when parents are in a binge pattern of alcohol use or in codependent conflict

⚔ Identification of Children of Alcoholic Families

The alcoholic family swears an allegiance to the family secret of alcoholism. Family members dedicate themselves to denying that Dad and/or Mom is out of control. The children hope that perhaps their family secret will change and continually explore ways to make it change.

⚔ Denial of Feelings in an Alcoholic Family

Sometimes this becomes an almost magical quest by the children to find that special way of being or ritualistic behavior that can make Dad and/or Mom change. Children give up their own sense of self in their search for the key that will change their parents' dysfunctional behavior.

A friend tells this story illustrating how children's feelings are discounted: When the alcoholic dad falls down, drunk, and spends the night on the front lawn, still in his work clothes, does the child really believe Mom's explanation? "You know your dad loves astronomy; he came home late last night, lay down to gaze at the stars, and, since he was tired from working late, just fell asleep, gazing at the constellations."

Children must maintain the *illusion of normalcy,* the illusion that their families are normal. The child defensively maintains the belief that this is what other families go through.

Howard Clinebell (1985) reported that the following factors produce damage in the lives of children of alcoholics:

1. *Role reversal:* Children may undertake parental duties because the parent is unable to be responsible or because the parent forces responsibilities on the children. The alcoholic may be treated as a child and, in return, act helpless. In incestuous families, the daughter and mother often switch roles.
2. *Unpredictability:* An inconsistent and unpredictable relationship with the alcoholic emotionally deprives the children.
3. *Unavailability:* The nonalcoholic, inadequate parent is struggling with major problems; because this parent's own needs are unmet, he or she is unable to attend to the needs of the children.
4. *Social isolation:* The damaging factor is the social isolation of the family, as protection from further pain and suffering, due to embarrassment.

Even periods of parental sobriety have negative effects on the children in alcoholic families. This is due primarily to the inconsistency and shattered hope that this time it will be different. The alcoholic father "inspires the natural love of his offspring, who build there from an ideal father image of omnipotence and loving kindness. This disillusionment of the drunken episode is shattering to the frail superego structure of the child who is subjected to alternating experiences of exalted hopes and blighting disappointments" (Newell 1950).

❧ Perspective of the Child in an Alcoholic Family

M. Cork (1969) interviewed 115 children living in alcoholic families in an attempt to understand the child's perspective. Cork found that the children react to the alcoholic family system in a number of common ways. The interviewed children in alcoholic families

1. Would not go to a friend's house because they would not dare reciprocate and invite friends to their homes due to the unpredictability and embarrassing behaviors of their parents
2. Were angry at everybody

3. Were preoccupied at school with worry about what would happen when they returned home
4. Envied their friends who seemed to have fun with their families
5. Felt alone when they were only children
6. Felt neglected when both parents were drinking
7. Felt they had to be parentlike, especially if the mother was drinking
8. Worried about each parent's loneliness if the parents were separated; they wished for their parents to reunite, even if their home was calmer during the separation; the children seemed to feel an even deeper loss if the alcoholic parent moved out of the house
9. Were unable to separate and individuate from their parents as adolescents; it was difficult to break away from somebody with whom they had no ties; one child poignantly said, "I want to be somebody, but I feel like nobody"
10. Excused the alcoholic of his or her behavior and often condemned the nonalcoholics for being hostile and angry; children could deduce from this that love and caring would come from alcoholics; research, unfortunately, indicates that many ACA do marry alcoholics to try out their hypothesis
11. Experienced multiple separations and reunions of their parents and learned not to depend on any consistent state
12. Continued to have problems, even when the alcoholic stopped drinking; see Tables 7.1 and 7.2 for a list of these problems

---

Codependency

Timmen Cermak quotes the metaphor of Charles Alexander (1985) that codependency is "like being a lifeguard on a crowded beach, knowing that you cannot swim, and not telling anyone for fear of a panic." This is the sense of desperation that ACA feel as they guess at what is normal.

TABLE 7.1

Problems of Children in Alcoholic Families

Physical Neglect or Abuse	Acting-Out Behaviors	Emotional Reaction to Alcoholism and Chaotic Family Life	Social and Interpersonal Difficulties
Serious illness	Involvement with	Suicidal tendencies	Family relationship problems
Accidents	police and courts	Depression	Peer problems
	Aggression	Repressed emotions	Adjustment problems
	Alcohol and other	Lack of self-confidence	Feeling different from norm
	drug abuse	Lack of life direction	Embarrassment
		Fear of abandonment	Overresponsible
		Fear of future	Feeling unloved and unable to trust

From G. Lawson, James S. Peterson, and Ann Lawson, *Alcoholism and the Family: A Guide to Treatment and Prevention,* Aspen Publications, 1983. Reprinted by permission of G. Lawson.

TABLE 7.2

Problems of Alcoholic Families Affecting More Than One Person

Marital	Parental	Cross-Boundaries— Parent and Child Relationships
Marital instability	Inadequate parenting	Physical and sexual abuse of children
Prolonged separation	Lack of structure	Parentification of children (child becomes the parent)
Divorce	Inconsistencies	
Death of a spouse	Emotional neglect of children	Role reversal
Physical abuse of a spouse	Inability or unwillingness to perform parental duties	Family conflict
		Isolation of family from society
		Isolation of individual family member within the family
		Incongruent communication (mixed messages)
		Lack of trust between family members
		Family secrets

From G. Lawson, James S. Peterson, and Ann Lawson, *Alcoholism and the Family: A Guide to Treatment and Prevention*, Aspen Publications, 1983. Reprinted by permission of G. Lawson.

Cermak, himself an adult child of an alcoholic, has defined codependency in diagnostic terms in the hope that codependency would be recognized as a psychiatric disorder. These diagnostic criteria for codependent personality disorder are

1. Continual investment of self-esteem in the ability to influence or control feelings and behaviors in the self and others in the face of obvious adverse consequences
2. Assumption of responsibility for meeting others' needs to the exclusion of acknowledging one's own needs
3. Anxiety and boundary distortions in situations of intimacy and separation
4. Enmeshment in relationships with personality-disordered, drug-dependent, and impulse-disordered individuals
5. Maintenance of a primary relationship with an active substance abuser for at least two years without seeking outside support and/or exhibiting three or more of the following characteristics:
   a. Constriction of emotions with or without dramatic outbursts
   b. Depression
   c. Hypervigilance
   d. Compulsions
   e. Anxiety
   f. Excessive reliance on denial
   g. Substance abuse
   h. Recurrent physical or sexual abuse
   i. Stress-related medical illnesses

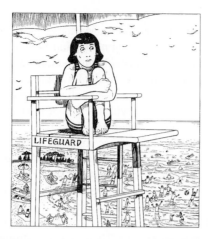

Codependency is "like being a lifeguard on a crowded beach, knowing that you cannot swim, and not telling anyone for fear of a panic."

An individual who has all five criteria of codependency would then be diagnosed as having a codependent personality disorder. A personality disorder affects all aspects of one's life because pervasive personality traits become inflexible and maladaptive. The results are significant subjective distress and social and occupational impairment. Treatment for codependent personality disorder often involves extensive education, counseling, therapeutic interventions, and sometimes medication to deal with major anxiety and depression.

If you find yourself identifying with some of the diagnostic criteria for codependent personality disorder but not all of them, you probably would be described as having some codependent traits, not a full-blown disorder. If these codependent traits result in significant difficulties in establishing effective, caring, and intimate relationships, they probably need to be investigated.

✄ Family Disease Model

Just as alcoholism is classified as a disease (i.e., it has a known etiology, progressive nature, and known outcome), the alcoholic family is often described in the context of a "family disease." The family members are described as suffering from alcoholism, codependency, and enabling behavior, perpetuating both the alcoholism- and alcohol-related problems. The family is organized around the alcoholic's drinking and the consequences of that drinking. The central organizing principle of the family is focused around the alcoholic's behavior (e.g., Is she drinking? Will she drink? How much will she drink? When and with whom will she drink? Will she get drunk?). The family responds to the alcoholic in a codependent (giving up of self) fashion or enables both alcoholic behavior and drinking. The family disease model describes the family as trying to maintain homeostasis, compensating for the disequilibrium of the alcoholic's behavior and drinking. This results in family members' disconnecting from their own feelings, distorting their perceptions, and invoking the "no-talk, no-feel, no-trust" rule.

⚔ Alcoholism/ Drug Addiction— Impact on Marriage

Marriages are at-risk when there is a substance abuse problem. Feelings of betrayal, continuous conflict, chaos, loss, resentments, and pain are constant parts of the marital cycle when one partner is alcoholic/drug-addicted. Ironically, some studies indicate that, if spouses drink together and with approximately equal patterns and amounts of use, it may not initially create a problem. However, problems will arise when one partner goes out to drink with friends, or a partner cuts back his or her drinking, enters into treatment, or voluntarily seeks sobriety.

Sexual problems related to substance abuse are very common, confounded by problems of intimacy. John Gottman, author of *Why Marriages Fail,* describes the four horsemen of the apocalypse of marriages—criticism, contempt (nonverbal), defensiveness, and withdrawal. The codependent dance of couples where there is an alcohol or drug problem frequently involves an "in the marriage," "out of the marriage," and "on the fence" attitude toward the marriage and each other. Frequently, all four horsemen are present. There is also a strong ambivalence that the wife of an alcoholic has toward her husband. There is a vacillation between being supportive and understanding and feeling hopeless and withdrawn.

Certainly, recovery not only involves treatment for alcoholics/addicts or problem users but also involves treatment for the spouse "Behavioral marital therapy focuses on teaching partners how to communicate with each other, solve problems together and resolve their conflicts. Husbands and wives look directly for ways to break the cycle of criticism, denial and blame that characterizes a chemically dependent family and develop new roles and new ways of interacting that will support recovery" (*Springbrook Northwest Newsletter,* pages 1–4, 1999).

⚔ Overattachment and Overseparation

In their work on chemical dependency and intimacy dysfunction, Eli Coleman and Philip Colgan (1987) focused on overattachment and overseparation in men who grew up in alcoholic families. They identified thoughts, feelings, and behaviors common to both the overseparated and overattached individuals. Table 7.3 lists these thoughts, feelings, and behaviors.

The thoughts of the overattached and overseparated sound like common lyrics to country-western songs. These codependent lyrics include "You should be grateful," "I want so little," "You don't care," "What am I doing wrong?" and "I'm nobody without you." Many people identify strongly with either the overseparated or the overattached column in Table 7.3; others cross over, having both overattached and overseparated characteristics. Overseparated individuals tend to develop relationships with overattached individuals and vice versa. Frequently, ACA duplicate the kind of relationship their codependent parents had. Not only does the disease of alcoholism and drug addiction but also the patterns of inadequate boundary setting and codependent relationships progress from generation to generation.

The most traditional codependent dance is between alcoholics/addicts and their codependent partners. Alcoholics/addicts and their partners are both codependent; alcoholics/addicts need partners who enable them to continue to use alcohol/drugs and not suffer the full impact of their addiction. Their partners need alcoholics/addicts to avoid their own fears of abandonment and depression. Both of them fear feelings of loneliness, isolation, anxiety, and depression.

TABLE 7.3

Overseparation and Overattachment

Overseparation	Overattachment
Thoughts	
You're not good enough.	I'm not good enough.
They want so much.	I want so little.
They give so little.	I give so much.
I'm ambivalent.	You don't care.
If only they would	What am I doing wrong?
I am a rock.	I'm nobody without you.
You should be grateful.	I'm so unappreciated.
Feelings	
Fear, smothering	Fear, abandonment
Self-controlled	Out of control
Indifferent	Needy, burdened
Unsafe with others	Unsafe alone
Trapped	Shut-out
Numb	Desperate
Behaviors	
Is self-protective	Is self-sacrificing
Controls others	Pleases others
Acts to guard feelings	Acts contrary to feelings
Denies	Explains
Is compulsively independent	Is compulsively dependent

From Eli Coleman and Philip Colgan, "Chemical dependency and intimacy dysfunction" in *Journal of Chemical Dependency*, Vol. 1 (1), 1987. Copyright © 1987 by the Haworth Press, Inc. For copies of the complete work, contact Marianne Arnold at The Haworth Document Delivery Service (Telephone 1-800-3-HAWORTH; 10 Alice Street, Binghampton, NY 13904). For other questions concerning rights and permissions contact Wando Latour at the above address.

The fear of abandonment and rejection is so strong for ACA that they choose not to develop an individual sense of self. This neglect of oneself while preoccupied or obsessed with changing the partner is codependency. The codependent dances these couples perform have some common features: (1) shame-based styles of communicating and interacting; (2) a denial by at least one partner of dysfunctional and/or codependent behavior; (3) a relationship of bargaining, not an intimate partnership; and (4) shame-based litany of the past. Each partner holds on to unresolved conflicts and continues to use them to shame the other.

⚔ Grief Work

As previously described, children who grow up in alcoholic families experience loss, violation, and trauma growing up in imbalanced alcoholic family systems. Frequently, there is not an opportunity to mourn the loss. Mourning is a process of allowing feelings of loss to come to the surface, to be felt, and to be grieved.

An analogy is the improper healing of a cut. In the child's case, an emotionally damaging cut or violation of self has occurred. The cut has healed over but was not cleaned out first; the dirt (leftover unresolved issues and feelings) was not removed. The result is a numbing pain, which is tolerated and denied for years and is thought to be quite normal. Grief work involves going back and cleaning out this wound by gently and sensitively removing the dirt. By avoiding the feelings and pain accompanying proper healing of this infected wound, individuals are unable to function to a fuller potential. Once their wounds are cleaned, true healing allows ACA to make more effective choices.

Grief work requires the help of a professional therapist trained and experienced in ACA recovery. The counselor/therapist must be sensitive to the patient's ego-strength, general level of functioning, underlying psychiatric issues, and support system. Attempting to do ACA grief work without an experienced professional may cause unnecessary emotional harm by going too deep, too quickly into traumatic issues of the past. A professional trained and experienced in ACA recovery recognizes the pace and depth of the work to be done and shows appropriate judgment in helping patients through this work.

⚔ Choice Making

Changing old imbalanced patterns is possible only if individuals feel they have choices. Discouraging voices of doom and gloom need to be quieted for recovery efforts to be implemented. Self-pity, victim roles, and the poor-me syndrome prevent ACA from even entertaining a choice to change. The old familial belief system whispers in the ACA's ear: "Change is not possible, so why even try? You'll just waste time and energy and fail, anyway, just as you always have in the past."

Changes involve integration and congruency with feelings and choosing not to respond in dysfunctional, codependent ways. There is the acknowledgment that change is difficult, takes time, may involve pain, and requires support. Sometimes small changes and positive choices can establish the foundation for more significant growth-related choices later. As the Rolling Stones' lyric goes, "You can't always get what you want, but, if you try sometimes, you get what you need."

A variety of therapeutic issues must be explored before ACA can improve interpersonal relationships. Some of the cognitive and affective therapeutic themes are

- Family of origin issues (beliefs, roles, rules, and thoughts about relationships)
- Sense of self, or self-concept, and interpersonal interaction, choosing relationships, and maintaining dysfunctional imbalanced relationships
- Boundary setting and decision making in interpersonal situations
- Self-sabotage or destructive behavior, poor impulse control, poor anger and frustration tolerance, and an inability to set and maintain healthy long-range goals.

⚔ Second-Order Change

Second-order change is a cognitive-behavioral technique to change the way one traditionally responds to situations and interpersonal interactions. Many interactions are mechanical, automatic, even rhetorical. These are first-order interactions. Individuals can choose to respond differently to the first-order cues in communication and interaction. This new response or new order of interaction is second-order change. The following examples illustrate a very common first-order interaction and one possible second-order change. The meta-message, or the underlying true feeling message, is in parentheses.

First-Order—Phone Call from Mom

Mom: Why haven't you called? (Shame on you for not caring about your mom. You probably don't like me. I know I'm just a bother now that I am old.)

Adult child: Well, Mom, I have been very busy with my new job and everything. (Please give me a break, Mom. I'm not in the mood for shame right now. I feel overwhelmed, considering the new job, and other adjustments I am going through. I don't need this right now.)

Mom: Well, I guess your job is more important than your mother. (Double shame on you for not making your mother number one in your life.)

Adult child: Mom, it's not that my job is more important than you. I just didn't get around to calling because I've been so busy at work. (Let me explain. Please, please, understand.)

Mom: You haven't asked me how my back is. (More shame—I don't care about your silly job. I want you to be more concerned with my ailments.)

Adult child: Now, Mom, that isn't fair. You didn't even give me a chance to ask you how you were. (I'm beginning to get angry and lose patience with you. Here we go again. I can't even talk with you without getting angry—self-shame.)

Mom: Now, don't get so upset, dear. (Watch it. This is your powerful supermom, able to abandon and hurt you with the slightest provocation.)

Adult child: [Change in tone] How are you feeling, Mom? I have been worried about you. (I don't want to fight or be abandoned. I'll just give her what she wants. I'm feeling like a helpless child again.)

Mom: Well, you know those doctors want me to come in for some more tests. But I don't think they know what they are talking about. I just don't have any way to get into the hospital, with my back hurting the way it does. (I am helpless. I want you to come home and be with me and take care of me. If you don't, I'll just punish you by suffering.)

Adult child: Mom, can't you get Aunt Joanie to take you in for the tests? (I am worried. I can't come. Maybe I can fix it for you by getting you some help.)

Mom: Oh dear, don't worry about me; I'll be all right. (Worry about me. Shame on you for not coming right away. You ungrateful daughter, I'll just suffer alone.)

This dialogue need not be carried out in this first-order manner. The anger, resentments, and shame do not have to be responded to in this traditional codependent dance. The following second-order change occurs after the adult child has done some therapeutic work on the underlying issue of her mother's not wanting to let go of her, for fear of having to work on her (mom's) own issues of loneliness and abandonment.

Second-Order—Change

Mom: Why haven't you called? (Shame on you for not caring about your mom.)

Adult child: Mom, boy, I've been wondering about you. How are you doing? (I'm not going to respond to the shaming question. I'll change the focus to you and your reason for calling.)

Mom: Well, I'm surprised that you asked. Most of the time you're too busy with your job to even call me. (I'll try some more shaming to see if I can get you angry, because I am angry that your job comes before your dear old mom.)

Adult child: Mom, it's unfortunate that I had to move out of town for this job promotion. I know it's hard on you. By the way, how is Aunt Joanie? (I had to take care of myself. I recognize that you feel abandoned and would prefer that I stay at home, but we all have to let go sometime. Why can't you understand like Aunt Joanie?)

Mom: She's fine. But you know my back has been killing me. The doctors want me to go to the hospital for some more tests, but I hurt too much, and I don't know how I can get there. (Poor me, won't you please come home and help me?)

Adult child: I know your back has been a problem for quite some time now. It would be nice to find out what the problem is. (I'd like to see you get in for the tests, but I can't help you get to the hospital. If you want some results, you'll have to figure out transportation.)

Mom: So would I. But I need someone to help me, and Aunt Joanie doesn't drive. (Please, won't you come back home and help?)

Adult child: Well, there are other ways for you to get a ride to the hospital. I hope you can figure out a way. (I'm not coming, just for this. There are other solutions to the problem and you are capable of figuring it out.)

Mom: Well, I just don't know if I can do it myself. (Poor me. Shame on you for not helping your poor old mom.)

Adult child: Well, Mom, I'm sure you'll be able to figure it out. You were always pretty resourceful when we were growing up. I love you. I'll talk to you soon. (You must take care of this yourself. You were very capable raising three children practically on your own, considering Dad's alcoholism. I'm not jumping in to help. I still love and admire you. I am ending this conversation and not giving you an opportunity to feel sorry for yourself.)

You can see the difference in the second-order change. The adult child avoided the shame-based messages and did not get emotionally hooked by displaying anger, rage, or lack of emotional control. Instead, in the second-order model, she focused on the real issues and stayed balanced and in emotional control while maintaining appropriate boundaries.

Robert Ackerman (1978), a noted author, speaker, and counselor specializing in ACA work, tells a story that illustrates the difficulty in changing interactions with family: after working with Ackerman for a few months, one of his patients felt she had made enough progress to share her new therapeutic awareness with her family. She was going home for Christmas (an emotional time for most families, especially alcoholic families) and wanted to talk to her parents about her new insights. Ackerman suggested that she think about what her goal was in sharing her insights. Essentially ignoring his advice, on returning home she told her parents all about her childhood pain resulting from growing up in an alcoholic family and described how this had affected her relationships with men. Initially, her parents were actively listening and seemed to understand. However, the next few days the family returned to the traditional dysfunctional arguments, escalated emotions, and shame-based communications of the past. The daughter had to spend the next few days at a friend's home to survive the rest of the holiday.

⚹ **Changes in Interactions with Family**

At her next therapy appointment, the patient expressed surprise that her parents could engage her in the old dysfunctional dances. She asked, "Why were they still able to push all of my buttons?" Dr. Ackerman, in the wisdom of his years of experience, matter-of-factly said, "They installed the buttons."

The same struggle goes on for most ACA who interact with their families. Some of these families have members still actively using alcohol/drugs or maintaining dysfunctional behavior. It might be necessary for ACA to let their parents know how they feel about their continued use of alcohol/drugs. In some situations, with the help of their therapists, patients have decided to send a letter to their parents who are still using alcohol/drugs. The goal of the letter is to assist ACA in healing and accepting their parents' disease. It is a way for ACA to get in touch with their feelings about their parents' continued use of alcohol/drugs. Patients decide for themselves whether the letter is appropriate for the goal they have in mind, and whether they want to send the letter.

Many ACA must ultimately let go and accept that their parents may never choose to stop using alcohol/drugs. Each patient continues to struggle with personal recovery issues in an ongoing process of self-discovery, supported by others in recovery. At times, it is a process of two steps forward, one step backward, but the process and progress continue.

Group psychotherapy is the next step once ACA have worked through some of the previously described core issues. Group psychotherapy is a dynamic process in which each group member gets feedback from other group members. Members share their perceptions, feelings, and insights into each other's behavior.

⚹ **Group Psychotherapy**

Irvin D. Yalom (1975) describes the following 11 curative factors that make group psychotherapy such an effective process.

1. *Instilling hope.* ACA group members see firsthand the growth of other group members. Continued contact with other group members who have improved while doing their work in the group gives ACA hope for their own recovery and confidence in the group process.

2. *Sharing universality.* ACA realize that they are not alone and that others share common problems. Group therapy reveals that ACA characteristics are universal to those who grew up in alcoholic/addict family systems, as well as imbalanced family systems. ACA no longer suffer in social or interpersonal isolation. There is the opportunity for affirmation by other group members, who understand them and identify with the issues they have in common.

3. *Imparting information.* Group therapy provides information, education, and training on ACA issues, including family systems, alcoholism/addiction, codependency, and boundary setting in relationships. Both the therapist and other group members offer suggestions, advice, and direct guidance about life problems.

4. *Fostering altruism.* Altruism is the act of giving to others and caring about others' life situations. The group is a place for support, reassurance, encouragement, insight, and sharing, all of which help both the giver and the receiver to grow.

5. *Recapitulating the primary family group.* Recapitulation offers an opportunity for the group to act as a functional family with positive corrective capabilities. Early familial conflicts can be acted out. With the help of the group, ACA can resolve these conflicts in a functional manner, rather than the previously dysfunctional and rigid manner of the family of origin.

6. *Developing socializing techniques.* Socializing is an obvious curative factor of group therapy. ACA can explore maladaptive social behavior through honest and caring feedback from group members. Alternative social choices and techniques can be developed with the feedback of the group. ACA are particularly vulnerable to choosing dysfunctional relationships and maintaining codependent interactions in relationships. The group can alert ACA who try to return to codependent ways of interaction and dysfunctional choice making.

7. *Imitating behavior.* By seeing the reactions and behaviors of others, ACA have numerous new models of behavior.

8. *Sharing interpersonal learning.* The group is a social microcosm of the real world. ACA tend to duplicate the way they approach the real interpersonal world in their therapy group. Insights into adult children's interpersonal behavior and corrective emotional strategies can be explored in the safe environment of the group setting.

9. *Developing group cohesiveness.* The bonding that occurs in therapy groups results in a cohesive understanding, which makes the group a safe place to go with stressful problems, interpersonal conflicts, difficult decisions, and other issues. The group develops a functional interpersonal cohesiveness, allowing members to pull for and struggle with the difficult issues in their lives.

10.   *Sharing catharsis.* The group is a place where ACA feel safe in expressing feelings not safely expressed in other settings. Fears, insecurities, destructive thoughts, suicidal ideation, rage, shame, and other emotions are safe to express in the group.

11.   *Exploring existential factors.* The group helps its members explore meaning in their lives. Issues of attachment in relationships, congruency in work efforts, and spirituality are all safe for each group member to explore and develop. In other words, the functional therapy group explores the human condition.

In summary, group therapy is a dynamic process that has a tremendous potential for ACA recovery, especially after ACA have spent time exploring their issues in individual counseling.

Summary

In the 1980s, a significant issue brought to the attention of the public was the awareness of the impact of alcoholism on children. The focus had expanded to include the children of alcoholics, not just the alcoholic and spouse. As a result, several feeling and behavioral characteristics were identified for these adults who were children in alcoholic systems (adult children of alcoholics). Growing up in an alcoholic family system was described in the context of PTSD.

Children of alcoholics tend to distrust their own feelings and to deny reality.

Codependency is defined in this chapter as continual investment of self-esteem in the ability to influence or control feelings and behaviors in the self and others in the face of obvious adverse consequences.

Alcoholism is described as a family disease, where the family is centrally organized around the alcoholic's behavior and/or drinking. Codependency and enabling behavior, plus denial, end up perpetuating both the alcoholism and the alcohol-related problems. The marriage is also at-risk, with sexual and intimacy problems.

One of the results of growing up in an alcoholic system is that interpersonal relationships are often imbalanced in the form of overattachment, overseparation, and codependent dances.

Grief is described as a feature of recovery from growing up in an alcoholic system, in order to grieve the feelings. Second-order change is described as one technique to change family interaction, and the 11 curative factors of group therapy are outlined as a way for adult children of alcoholics to pursue recovery.

References

Ackerman, Robert J. *Children of Alcoholics: A Guidebook for Educators, Therapists, and Parents.* Holmes Beach, FL: Learning Public, 1978.

Black, Claudia. *It Will Never Happen to Me.* Denver, CO: M.A.C., 1982.

Brown, Stephanie. *Treating Adult Children of Alcoholics, a Developmental Perspective.* New York: John Wiley & Sons, 1988.

Cermak, Timmen. "Children of Alcoholics and the Case for a New Diagnostic Category of Co-dependency. *Alcohol, Health and Research World* 8 (1984): 38–42.

Clinebell, Howard J., Jr. *Understanding and Counseling the Alcoholic Through Religion and Psychology.* Nashville, TN: Abingdon Press, 1985.

Coleman, Eli, and Philip Colgan. "Chemical Dependency and Intimacy Dysfunction." *Journal of Chemical Dependency Treatment* 1 (1987): 75–91.

Cork, M. *The Forgotten Children.* Toronto: Addiction Research Foundation, 1969.

Newell, Nancy. "Alcoholism and the Father Image." *Quarterly Journal of Studies on Alcoholism* 11 (1950): 92–95.

Springbrook Northwest Newsletter, "After Drug Treatment . . . What Happens to the Marriage," Summer 1999.

Yalom, Irvin D. *The Theory and Practice of Group Psychotherapy.* New York: Basic Books, 1975.

Prevention, Intervention, and Treatment

Prevention of Substance Abuse Problems

Chapter Objectives

1. Describe the ineffectiveness of early prevention approaches, including scare tactics, converting programs, and drug-specific information.

2. Define and list "alternative activities" as a prevention approach and the qualities of a successful alternative activity.

3. List some of the skills emphasized in the 1980s prevention programs.

4. Define primary, secondary, and tertiary prevention.

5. List the competencies and coping skills emphasized in school-based prevention programs.

6. Identify key components of a prevention program in the 1990s.

7. Describe the Rhodes and Jason social stress model of substance abuse (i.e., the coping and abuse tracts).

8. Classify the risk factors for substance abuse and intervention strategies as identified by Hawkins et al.

9. Define resiliency and survivor's pride as it relates to the Wolins challenge model of prevention.

10. Identify the key elements of emotional intelligence and their application to prevention.

11. Describe the factors associated with healthy behaviors and those associated with risk behaviors.

12. Classify the developmental assets emphasized in the Search Institute model of prevention.

13. Identify the school-based prevention programs and community models in the new millennium.

14. Describe the special needs for prevention programs for people of color, elders, and college students.

Alcohol/drug prevention has often been a misunderstood and neglected aspect in addressing the American drug problem. This chapter provides a foundation so that you can apply prevention efforts at home, in school systems, and in the community. Prevention efforts have shifted from scare tactics (dangers and evils of drugs) to emphases on the worth of people and the coping skills needed to avoid a destructive pattern of alcohol/drug dependence. Specific prevention skills outlined in this chapter include goal setting, decision making, and conflict resolution. The goal of prevention, outlined in this chapter, is to develop active, involved, empowered, and capable young people.

� Early Prevention Approaches

For years, society has searched for easy ways to prevent drug dependence and addiction. Initially,

frightening movies and horror stories of drug abuse failed to make young people too scared to use drugs. Early prevention efforts to deter potential drug use focused primarily on providing

- Information on the dangers of specific drugs
- Warnings of physical, social, and psychological harm
- Punishments for sale, use, and possession

Scare tactics proved to be an ineffective prevention strategy. Much of the information was invalid, exaggerated, and overgeneralized, causing young people to question the credibility of the program.

Similar programs were developed and labeled by drug educator Walter M. Mathews (1975) as **converting programs.** These programs attempted to dissuade young people from using drugs by

1. Directing: Teacher tells students what they must believe, value, and do.
2. Preaching: This was similar to directing, with an added appeal to the students' duty to a vague external authority.
3. Convincing: Teachers appealed to logic where lecturing was the method used.
4. Scaring: Teachers emphasized the dangers of drug use.

Additional converting approaches emphasized admonishment, indoctrination, persuasion, distortion, and fear.

Adolescence is a time of questioning and self-exploration. The information provided in these approaches was not geared to the sensitivity of young people; it insulted their individuality and ability to make decisions. Adults in authority told them what to do, rather than talking with them. These propaganda approaches did not emphasize communication and open discussion.

The failure of these approaches led to a new prevention strategy of providing factual information about drugs, or **drug-specific approaches.** These approaches emphasized each drug and its pharmacological properties and assumed young people would make responsible decisions about drug use if they knew the negative effects. Inadvertently, these drug-specific approaches heightened curiosity and caused the opposite, alleviating fears of drugs. Many students acquired the knowledge to better attain desired levels of intoxication.

As a result of the failure of scare tactics and drug-specific approaches, the government's Special Action Office on Drug Abuse Prevention (SAODAP) declared a six-month moratorium in 1973 on all prevention materials development, prevention program implementation, and prevention activities. The moratorium allowed further review of research and determined that, because scare tactics and drug-specific information did not significantly deter drug use, they were ineffective. In 1974, Robert DuPont, then the director of the National Institute on Drug Abuse (NIDA), surveyed drug education programs and concluded that the educators and students believed that the majority of school-based drug education programs were ineffective and should be abolished. In a review of research on school-based drug education programs, Michael Goodstadt (1975) concluded that "there is an almost total lack of evidence indicating beneficial effects of drug education, very few educational programs have been evaluated and almost none have shown any significant improvement in anything other than levels of knowledge; attitudes and drug use have generally remained the same."

In 1974, the prevention branch of the National Institute of Drug Abuse initiated a nationwide, 14-month planning process to develop a national strategy for primary prevention. This planning process involved over 400 prevention specialists in a series of nine planning conferences. In 1975, the institute published the resulting recommendations in *Toward a National Strategy for Primary Drug Abuse Prevention.* The report defined primary drug abuse prevention as "a constructive process designed to promote personal and social growth of the individual to full human potential and thereby inhibit or reduce physical, mental, emotional, or social impairment which results in or from the abuse of chemical substances."

The report established three basic themes for primary prevention: (1) primary prevention must be understood as the development and reinforcement of positive behaviors; (2) primary prevention programs must be responsive in both design and operation to the needs of those they are intended to serve or support; and (3) primary prevention should, wherever possible, use collaborative efforts to utilize the already available capacities and resources of existing human service institutions.

The result of SAODAP's moratorium and prevention planning meetings was a major shift in focus from drugs to the young people and from pharmacological effects to healthy children.

In 1977, NIDA and other agencies developed an interagency report entitled *Recommendations for Future Federal Activities in Drug Abuse Prevention.* The three major goals for prevention activities outlined in that report were

1. Reducing the percentage of frequent use of the three gateway drugs (tobacco, alcohol, and marijuana) by 15 percent among 8- to 20-year-olds.
2. Reducing the destructive behavior associated with alcohol and other drug abuse by 20 percent among 14- to 20-year-olds, as evidenced by a reduction in overdose deaths, emergency room visits, drug arrests, and other alcohol/drug–related incidents.
3. Retraining attitudes concerning the use of psychoactive substances, especially the gateway drugs, by maintaining current levels of awareness regarding the addictive nature of heroin and alcohol and raising awareness of the addictive nature of tobacco by 50 percent.

✖ Alternative Activities as a Prevention Approach

In Chapter 1, we examined the primary function of alcohol/drugs as serving our natural innate drive to alter our sense of consciousness. Ronald Siegal, in his book *Intoxication,* describes altering one's consciousness as the fourth drive, after hunger, thirst, and sex. The primary goal of alternative activities is to teach people that they are capable of altering their consciousness in a meaningful, longer-lasting, life-enhancing, and satisfying way that is incompatible with alcohol/drug use.

The late 1970s saw a strong movement toward alternative activity programs for young people. The programs usually involved wilderness activities, requiring teamwork, challenge, and risk that developed feelings of competence, skill, and self-worth. Today, many adolescent and adult inpatient and residential chemical dependency treatment programs are including alternative activity program elements as a natural part of the clients' recovery program. This can include rope courses, climbing structures, even what one program calls "equine therapy" (i.e., working with horses).

Alan Cohen (1972), a strong advocate of alternative activities, defines alternatives as pursuits that are valued and truly preferred by individuals and seen as incompatible with drugs. Cohen emphasizes that alternatives are not just a substitution for drugs; they are an integrated and valued part of the person's life.

Alternatives Are Actively Pursued by the Individual

Cohen felt that, for an alternative to be successful, the process of searching for the alternative should be a potent alternative in itself. Individuals are encouraged to find other activities they can develop, persevere through to mastery, and enjoy. The process of being able to choose ways to get high naturally through one's own interests is truly empowering. It follows that alternatives are more effective if they call for activity, assertion of will or will power, and effort and commitment. Alternatives are less successful if individuals are passive recipients of the activity. This is consistent with the function of drug dependence and alcoholism as a rather passive activity. All alcoholics/addicts have to do is sit back and passively wait for the alcohol/drug to take effect.

Cohen illustrates this in the example of listening to music: "Passively listening to music is not necessarily a promising alternative to drugs, since one could be passively stoned at the time. Training in active listening and deep study of music is more likely to be frustrating to drug use since the clarity of one's senses and cognition become important in successful completion of the task." (1972)

Alternatives Are Acceptable, Attractive, and Attainable

Alternatives must be acceptable and attractive. Any alternative offered must be realistic, attainable, and meaningful. Alternatives must also assist people in finding self-understanding

Hang gliding is an alternative activity.

and improve self-image and personal awareness. Dohner (1972) outlined the following characteristics of positive alternatives:

1.   They must contribute to the individual's identity and independence.
2.   They must offer active participation and involvement.
3.   They must offer a chance for commitment.
4.   They must provide a feeling of identification with a larger body of experience.
5.   Some of the alternatives must be in the realm of the noncognitive and the intuitive.

Alternatives Have Mentors and Role Models

Another essential feature of alternatives is a successful role model or mentor—someone who can guide, facilitate, and encourage the successful attainment of the alternative skill. This person could be a positive parent model, a coach, a teacher, a peer, or anyone else who understands and respects the boundaries in the development of the alternative skill.

Alternatives Integrate Self-Concepts

Alternative activities are effective as preventive tools if they enhance the development of skills associated with improving one's sense of self. Table 8.1 lists Allan Cohen's categories for various alternative activities based on personal attributes and attraction.

Use the alternatives worksheet as shown in Table 8.2 to list your motives and preferred alternatives to alcohol/drug use. Also identify the steps and resources necessary to implement each alternative.

TABLE 8.1

Motives for and Alternatives to the Use of Drugs

Level of Experience	Corresponding Motives	Alternatives to Drugs
Physical	Desire for physical satisfaction, physical relaxation, relief from sickness, more energy, maintenance of physical dependency	Athletics, dance, exercise, hiking, diet, health training, carpentry, or outdoor work
Sensory	Desire to stimulate sight, sound, touch, taste; need for sensual-sexual stimulation; desire to magnify the brain's sensoriums	Sensory awareness training, sky diving, experiencing sensory beauty of nature (lovemaking, swimming, running, mountaineering), *skiing, surfing, massage
Emotional	Relief from psychological pain, attempt to solve personal perplexities, relief from bad mood, escape from anxiety, desire for emotional insight, liberation of feeling, emotional relaxation	Competent individual counseling, well-run group therapy, instruction in psychology of personal development (sensitivity training), *self-help meetings, *emotional support system
Interpersonal	To gain peer acceptance; to break through interpersonal barriers; to communicate, especially nonverbally; defiance of authority figures; cement two-person relationships; relaxation of interpersonal inhibition; solve interpersonal hangups	Expertly managed sensitivity and encounter groups, well-run group therapy, instruction in social customs, confidence training, social-interpersonal counseling, emphasis on assisting others in distress via education, marriage, *participation in organizations and community activities within personal interests
Social (including sociocultural and environmental)	To promote social change; to find identifiable subcultures to tune out intolerable environmental conditions	Social service; community action in positive social change; helping the poor, aged, infirm, young; tutoring handicapped; improving the environment; *Peace Corps work with the homeless, hungry, impoverished, and oppressed
Political	To promote political change; identify with antiestablishment subgroup to change drug legislation out of desperation with the sociopolitical order; to gain wealth or affluence of power	Political service; political action; nonpartisan projects such as ecological lobbying; fieldwork with politicians, and public officials

* The author's additions are indicated by asterisks.

TABLE 8.1 (CONTINUED)

Motives for and Alternatives to the Use of Drugs

Level of Experience	Corresponding Motives	Alternatives to Drugs
Intellectual	To escape mental boredom; out of intellectual curiosity to solve cognitive problems; to gain new understanding in the world of ideas; to study better; to research one's own awareness for science	Intellectual excitement through reading, discussion; creative games and puzzles; self-hypnosis; training in concentration; synectics training in intellectual breakthroughs; memory training; *seminars, workshops, and conferences; study or discussion groups; work with computers; writing a book or article
Creative-aesthetic	To improve creativity in the arts, to enhance enjoyment of art already produced, to enjoy imaginative mental productions	Nongraded instruction in producing and/or appreciating art, music, drama, crafts, handiwork, cooking, sewing, gardening, writing, singing
Philosophical	To discover meaningful values, to grasp the nature of the universe, to find meaning in life, to help establish personal identity, to organize a belief structure	Discussions, seminars, courses in the meaning of life; study of ethics, morality, the nature of reality; relevant philosophical literature; guided exploration of value systems
Spiritual, mystical	To transcend orthodox religion, to develop spiritual insights, to reach higher levels of consciousness, to have divine visions, to communicate with God, to augment yogic practices, to get a spiritual shortcut, to attain enlightenment, to attain spiritual powers	Exposure to nonchemical methods of spiritual development; study of world religions, introduction to applied mysticism, meditation, yogic techniques; *attending churches with recovery orientation; all activities that enhance spiritual awareness (nature, human connectedness, and activities that deal with existential despair)
Miscellaneous	Adventure, risk, drama, kicks, unexpressed motives, prodrug general attitudes	Outward Bound survival training; combinations of preceding alternatives; pronaturalness attitudes; brainwave training; meaningful employment

From Allan Y. Cohen, "The Journey Beyond Trips: Alternative to Drugs" in David E. Smith and Dr. George R. Gay, Eds., *It's So Good, Don't Even Try It Once, Heroin in Perspective.* Copyright © 1972 Prentice Hall, Inc., Englewood Cliffs, NJ.

TABLE 8.2

Alternatives Worksheet

Level of Experience	Corresponding Motives	Steps and Resources to Implement Alternatives to Alcohol/Drugs
Physical	_____	_____
	_____	_____
Sensory	_____	_____
	_____	_____
Emotional	_____	_____
	_____	_____
Interpersonal	_____	_____
	_____	_____
Social	_____	_____
	_____	_____
Political	_____	_____
	_____	_____
Intellectual	_____	_____
	_____	_____
Creative-aesthetic	_____	_____
	_____	_____
Philosophical	_____	_____
	_____	_____
Spiritual, mystical	_____	_____
	_____	_____
Miscellaneous	_____	_____

✄ Prevention Approaches of the 1980s

In the 1980s, the new preventive strategy shifted from drugs to people, emphasizing

- Educational information
- Coping skills
- Personal competence
- Decision making
- Refusal skills
- Alternative activities

The goal of these programs was to develop capable young people able to make responsible decisions about alcohol/drugs. The focus changed to understanding the impact of drugs on individuals, rather than understanding the pharmacological properties of alcohol/drugs. The affective aspect focused on the individual's needs, feelings, and emotions about alcohol/drugs.

These new prevention programs develop the following skills:

- Clarifying personal values and ethics
- Improving self-concept
- Learning effective decision making
- Understanding and listening to each other's viewpoints
- Communicating about alcohol/drugs with peers, parents, and others
- Being involved in social and interpersonal activities
- Dealing effectively with feelings of anger, depression, and anxiety
- Having the ability to relax, play, and enjoy daily activities
- Developing and exploring ways to alter one's sense of consciousness through alternative activities

Agencies originally focused on prevention in secondary schools for adolescents 12 to 17 years of age. It became apparent quickly that in many cases it was already too late to provide preventive education to adolescents. This group required more intervention, skill building, and treatment-related approaches.

As a result, alcohol and drug curricula and primary prevention activities shifted to kindergarten through the sixth grade. Agencies also developed secondary and tertiary prevention approaches for grades 7 to 12.

A definition of prevention covers three basic categories:

1. **Primary prevention** assumes that the individual has never tried drugs or alcohol and enforces a no-use norm by building positive self-esteem, developing good coping and refusal skills, and providing information on alcohol and drugs.
2. **Secondary prevention** assumes that the individual is in the early stages of use but does not regularly use drugs. Secondary prevention/intervention strategies try to stop drug use by providing drug information, developing decision-making and refusal skills, and improving family communication; it may also include individual counseling.
3. **Tertiary prevention** assumes that the individual is regularly using drugs but has not become a habitual user. Tertiary prevention/intervention includes counseling, drug education, and family therapy. There is a very fine line between the tertiary level of prevention and intervention and treatment services.

In 1983, "Drug Abuse Prevention Research," a U.S. Department of Health and Human Services monograph, outlined four dimensions of prevention:

1. Course content centers on mental health, drug information, human development, nutrition, ethics, and chemical safety; these courses usually fit into regular social studies, language arts, science, and other subject area curricula

⚔ School-Based Prevention Curricula— Examples

2. Courses on values clarification, problem-solving and decision-making skills, communication skills such as reflection and confrontation, alternative means for meeting needs, group process skills, role-playing, and dramatization
3. Courses that include competencies in human development, interpersonal relationships, personal autonomy, self-esteem, identity, decision-making skills, personal accountability, and accurate attributions of causality
4. Courses that also include general knowledge, conceptual frameworks, implicit assumptions and perspectives that define and describe the way each individual perceives the meaning of self, the nature of the world external to self, and the interrelatedness of things

The following examples of school-based prevention programs reveal typical competencies and coping skills emphasized in such programs. Prevention programs are not limited to alcohol/drug prevention; many health issues are included in school-based prevention programs.

Here's Looking at You—Kindergarten Through Senior High School

One of the most widely used school-based curricula, *Here's Looking at You,* was originally published in 1975. With significant revisions in 1978, 1982, and 1985, it is one of the most highly tested and developmentally sound curricula in the prevention field.

Program goals for students include developing

- Self-concepts to realize they are unique and special persons who are continually growing and changing and who are capable of directing their growth
- Decision-making skills for making responsible choices
- Coping skills so they can cope responsibly with stressful situations

Counseling Leadership Against Smoking Pressure (CLASP)

One of the major efforts of prevention has been the reduction and elimination of cigarette smoking by young people. A variety of successful programs have been developed; one of the most successful is CLASP. The key element of this project is the use of peers as leaders. Peer leaders promote and develop group strategies for coping with peer pressure.

Other antismoking program methods focus on dealing with social pressure, the use of personalized role models and peer opinion leaders, and group commitment to nonsmoking. All of these programs are implemented by the seventh grade.

Cognitive-Behavioral Skills Training

Schinke and Gilchrist (1983), who have done extensive research in the area of pregnancy prevention, developed a cognitive-behavioral model that systematically teaches the skills necessary to enjoy positive lives and to avoid unnecessary risks. Their junior and senior high school model emphasizes

- Social coping skills necessary to handle current problems
- Anticipation and prevention of future problems and conflicts
- Skills in mental health awareness
- Issues of health, social, economic, and physical well-being
- Strategies to enhance skills such as decision making, problem solving, and interpersonal communication in a variety of social situations

Cognitive Interpersonal Skills Training

Spivak and Shuve (1979) developed a program similar to Schinke and Gilchrist's for kindergarten and first grade. The method uses games designed to increase cognitive skills, followed by training in alternative responses to interpersonal problem solving. The concepts taught in this model are the following:

- Creating alternative solutions to problems
- Developing sensitivity to interpersonal problems
- Understanding means-ends relationships

Life Skills Training

The methods used in the *Life Skills Program* are instruction, modeling, rehearsal, and role-playing. Botvins' (1985) program has five major skill areas:

- Enhancing self-esteem by developing goal-setting skills, behavioral change techniques, and positive self-statements
- Resisting persuasive appeals by first identifying persuasive appeals and formulating counterarguments
- Coping with anxiety through relaxation training and mental rehearsal
- Developing verbal and nonverbal communication skills
- Developing a variety of other social skills, such as initiation of social interactions, social communication skills, complimenting, and assertiveness skills

Law-Related Education

Developed by the Center for Action Research, *Law-Related Education* deals with the criminal-justice system. Its goal is to deter the antisocial behavior of young people by increasing their conceptual and practical understanding of the law and legal processes. The program's target populations are kindergarten through sixth grade, and sixth to twelfth grade. The goals of the program are

- To improve citizenship skills
- To enhance the ability to work with the legal system
- To promote favorable attitudes toward law enforcement and the justice system

Skills for Adolescence

As part of the program, students set goals for healthy living. The students also develop projects offering their service to others in the community. This program for grades 6 through 8 focuses on

- Entering the teen years
- Building self-confidence
- Learning about emotions
- Improving peer relationships
- Strengthening family relationships
- Developing critical thinking skills

Skills for Living

A high school program, *Skills for Living* emphasizes self-discipline, responsibility, good judgment, and the ability to interact with others. The curriculum focuses on

- Building self-concept
- Dealing with emotions
- Building constructive relationships
- Preparing for family life
- Building trust and commitment
- Parenting successfully
- Understanding financial management
- Goal setting and life planning
- Developing a personal perspective

Prevention Skills in Decision Making

Many prevention lessons focus on effective decision making. An important aspect of decision making is to help young people identify how they feel about a decision, rather than ignoring feelings that signal a potentially destructive decision. The decision-making model teaches individuals to

1. Explore personal values, feelings, and goals related to a decision
2. Gather information on the subject of the decision (e.g., factual written resources: consumer reports, opinions of others in the field or of those who have made similar decisions successfully, opinions of others who are valued and supportive)
3. Review alternatives and consequences
4. Evaluate resources, responsibilities, and support as necessary
5. Make a decision
6. Reevaluate the decision and explore feelings about the decision
7. Make necessary adjustments

Empowerment

A term often used in prevention programs is *empowerment*. Many prevention programs emphasize the empowering of the individual. The basic goal of prevention is to empower individuals and prevent the destructive passive choice of alcohol/drug dependence and addiction. Empowerment is a feeling that is developed by being able to

- Say "no" when that is what one feels and wants

- Establish the core aspects of a sense of self
- Be aware of what one feels and integrate and communicate those feelings to others in establishing goals and making decisions
- Establish and set boundaries, especially in interpersonal and intimate relationships
- Establish integrity in relationships and a healthy, nondestructive, nonsabotaging approach to life

These prevention programs are usually targeted at the general school population, rather than the high-risk students who have already exhibited problem behaviors in and outside of school.

Goal Setting

A model lesson for goal setting would include lessons on (1) setting goals, (2) ranking priorities, (3) making decisions in relation to the goals, (4) persevering in the face of difficult situations, and (5) maintaining effort (motivation) until goals are attained or modified.

Capability Development

Other prevention lessons involve developing capabilities. I had the good fortune many years ago to work with Stephen Glenn at the National Drug Abuse Center in Washington, DC. Today, Glenn lectures throughout the United States on the family prevention theme of developing capable people. His model for developing capable children includes

1. Identification with viable role models
2. Identification with and responsibility for family process
3. Faith in personal resources to solve problems
4. Adequate development of intrapersonal skills (responsibility)
5. Adequate development of interpersonal skills (communication)
6. Well-developed situation skills (demand skills)
7. Adequately developed judgment skills (application)

Another skill-building concept is the ability to be "capable." A capable person has the 10 *C*s, which include the ability to

⚔ The 10 *C*s of Capability

- Resolve conflict
- Make effective choices
- Deal effectively with criticism
- Persevere through times of crisis
- Communicate effectively—understand and be understood
- Deal with competition (rivalry) and competence
- Establish credibility and integrity in an approach to people and life in general
- Express concern and empathy for others
- Be creative

⚔ Key Components of a Prevention Program in the 1990s

Address Community Needs

Alcohol/drug prevention should address itself to the needs of the community and interface with community leaders, agencies, and the people. Edward M. Brecher knew community was important when he wrote in *Licit and Illicit Drugs* (1972) "Stop viewing the drug problem as primarily a national problem to be solved on a national scale. In fact, as workers in the drug scene confirm, the drug problem is a collection of local problems. The predominant drugs differ from place to place and from time to time. Effective solutions to problems also vary; a plan that works now for New York City may not be applicable to upstate New York and vice versa. With respect to education, . . . the need for local wisdom and local control is particularly pressing. Warning children against drugs readily available to them is a risky business at best, requiring careful, truthful, unsensational approaches."

Include Youth in Prevention Planning

A prevention program must take into account the consumer of that program. To develop prevention programs in a vacuum, or from a strictly theoretical base, does not take into account the most important variable, the needs of youth.

Promote Proactivity

A core theme in prevention is to teach young people to move from being passive to being active, or proactive. Being proactive involves taking initiative, anticipating potential problems, and integrating your feelings. Too many young people spend excessive time in passive activities (e.g., watching television, playing computer games).

Parents can teach and model active behaviors and encourage activities that help young people develop a capable, positive sense of self. Proactive choices help develop the child's coping skills and ability to overcome setbacks.

Develop a Long-Term Perspective

Prevention is a long-term strategy. Longitudinal studies over 5 to 10 years are necessary to determine the effects of prevention. Unfortunately, most prevention programs have short-term funding, which limits the evaluation of their true effectiveness. Currently, we focus on the short-range perspective of drug enforcement and interdiction without the balance of a comprehensive prevention strategy to deal with the demand side of alcohol/drugs with youth. Our true hope is the prevention and family approaches used with 3- to 10-year-olds—the next generation—may break this cycle of problems with dependence and addiction to alcohol/drugs.

In summary, an effective substance abuse prevention strategy should

Emphasize cognitive and affective skills that help young people accept responsibility and motivate them to make wise decisions about alcohol and drugs.

Focus on people, not pharmacology, emphasizing educational information, coping skills, personal competence, decision making, refusal skills, and alternative activities.

Develop prevention programs that provide information plus communication,
establish credibility, and meet community needs.

Take into account the needs of youth and develop prevention approaches
cooperatively with young people in the community.

Develop primary efforts (those who have never used alcohol/drugs), secondary
efforts (those in early stages of alcohol/drug use), and tertiary prevention
efforts (those in regular stages of alcohol/drug use).

Develop longitudinal commitment to long-term prevention efforts.

Jean Rhodes and Leonard Jason (1988) developed a model that emphasizes the development of **attachments, competence,** and **coping skills** as preventing risk for substance abuse. The more stress the child experiences, without appropriate and strong bonding to parents, attachment to drug-free role models, access to models with a strong sense of self, plus poor coping skills and resources, the higher the risk of substance abuse.

    Based on Albee's social stress model, Rhodes and Jason illustrate two potential tracts, or pathways, that drug use may take: the abuse tract or the coping tract.

⚔ Social Stress Model

Abuse Tract

If attachments, coping skills, and resources are not available early, initiation to alcohol/drug use can allay stress during early childhood. If functional coping mechanisms, attachments, and resources are still not available during adolescence, alcohol/drug use may proceed to heavy use. When this pattern continues into adulthood, alcohol/drug abuse occurs. See Figure 8.1.

Coping Tract

Low stress, combined with good attachments, coping skills, and resources, leads to abstinence during childhood, abstinence or limited experimentation during adolescence, and reduced risk of problems with alcohol/drugs in adulthood.

Clinicians and researchers have identified a variety of factors as predictive of later substance abuse by young people. Antisocial behaviors and aggressiveness can predict, as early as the first grade, early alcohol/drug initiation and later substance

⚔ Programs Aimed at At-Risk Youth

FIGURE 8.1

From Rhodes, Jean E. and Leonard A. Jason *Preventing Substance Abuse Among Children,* 1992, Allyn & Bacon.

abuse. Family imbalance, parental problems with alcohol/drugs, and parental dysfunction are also predictive of children having problems with alcohol/drugs.

At-risk youth require a more intensive and modified prevention program than
students with no real social and interpersonal problems, who are supported by fairly
functional family systems.

Often, teachers and parents cooperatively identify at-risk youth appropriate
for the program. Sometimes, key school personnel—teachers, coaches, dean of students, school-nurse, counselor, psychologist—develop a team approach with parents in identifying students at-risk for alcohol/drug problems.

The number of young people who are high risk for developing substance
abuse problems is astounding. (See Table 8.3.)

High-risk youngsters are hard to reach because they resist traditional authority, often have a low literacy level, and may be on the streets instead of in school or
in structured community settings.

Their self-efficacy makes them less likely to respond to appeals based on caring about self, such as "take care of your health" or "don't take unnecessary risks
that may hurt you." Also, these youth are already drinking and, in some cases,

TABLE 8.3

American Youth—High Risk for Alcohol Use and Other Problems

1. More than 20 percent (nearly 12.5 million) of all U.S. children (43 percent of Black and 40 percent of
   Hispanic/Latino children) live at or below the poverty level. Children living in extreme poverty and deprivation
   are more likely to become enmeshed in delinquent and drug-using behavior, particularly persistent (as opposed to
   occasional) drug use and delinquent activity.
2. There are 6.6 million children under the age of 18 living in a home with an alcoholic parent.
3. About 85 percent of child abuse cases in 1984 involved a parent-child relationship. In sexual abuse of children,
   66 percent of offenders were parents and another 19 percent were other relatives.
4. More than 1 million young people run away from home or are homeless each year, and runaways are at a greater
   risk for alcohol and other drug problems.
5. One million students drop out of high school each year. One of every four ninth graders will not graduate—the
   dropout rate reaches 50 percent in some urban areas—and those who drop out are more at risk for developing
   alcohol and other drug problems.
6. One of eight 17-year-olds in the United States is functionally illiterate. At-risk adolescents with low skills who
   drop out of school are three times more likely than their more successful peers to become unwed parents. Those
   youth headed for college are less likely to abuse drugs.
7. More than 1 million adolescents become pregnant annually; half of these young mothers will never complete
   high school.
8. Nearly 1,900 teens took their own lives in 1984, making suicide the third leading cause of death for young people
   ages 15–24. Up to 80 percent of all adolescent suicides have been reported to be children of alcoholics.
9. In 1985, more than 1.7 million young people ages 14–17 were arrested for crimes, not including traffic violations.
10. Epidemiological studies show that one in four American children ages 10 to 17 are at high risk of multiple
    problem behaviors and negative long-term consequences because of their current behavior involving alcohol and
    other drug use, failure in school, early sexual activity and risk of pregnancy, and delinquency.

Source: Office for Substance Abuse Prevention, 1988.

using multiple drugs at early ages. It is too late for refusal skills (saying "no"). Other obstacles include the following:

- Rejection of help because of fear and lack of trust or perhaps bravado
- Feelings of ambivalence and confusion about alcohol as a result of the many conflicting messages about alcohol use in U.S. society
- Fear by children and youth of being rejected again
- Hopelessness by young people in inner cities about the possibility of ever having a worthwhile future with a decent job and a chance of achieving the "American dream"
- The presence in some inner-city neighborhoods of an open, accessible drug culture without apparent social sanctions and of large sums of money for youth who deal in drugs (Office for Substance Abuse Prevention 1988)

Often, the special relationship with a parent, a family member, a teacher, a minister, a coach, or others is what keeps some children on the road to a sober and successful life. Strong religious training is an example of a family ritual that also may save many young people from the streets.

One example of a school-based program for at-risk youth is *Interpersonal Problem Solving.* The program's major focus is on effective problem solving and effective interpersonal skills. Program topics include

- Dealing with authority figures
- Developing empathy
- Standing up for one's rights
- Resisting peer pressure
- Improving behavior in school
- Getting along better with family members

In the early years of alcohol/drug prevention, efforts were primarily focused on generic prevention programs. The thinking was "this is a good thing to promote; maybe it will prevent substance abuse" (e.g., good health habits). These programs were global and aimed at the entire school population. Prevention in the new millennium is targeted at specific at-risk populations, communities of high risk, while focusing on specific risk factors.

J. David Hawkins, Richard E. Catalono, and Janet Y. Miller, in their extensive study "Risk and Protective Factors for Alcohol and Other Drug Problems in Adolescence and Early Adulthood: Implications for Substance Abuse Prevention," outline 5 risk factors for substance abuse and accompanying interventions (see Table 8.4). These interventions and risk factors allow prevention efforts to be focused and targeted. Table 8.5 presents factors associated with risk behaviors. Table 8.6 presents factors associated with healthy behaviors.

⚔ Risk Factors for Substance Abuse

Steven Wolin, M.D., a professor at George Washington University, and his wife, Sybil Wolin, Ph.D., a developmental psychologist, are co-authors of *The Resilient Self: How Survivors of Troubled Families Rise Above Adversity* (1994) and developers of Project Resilience, Washington, DC.

⚔ Resiliency

TABLE 8.4

Risk Factors for Adolescent Substance Abuse with Corresponding Prevention Findings

	Risk			Intervention	
Risk Factor	**Etiological Study**	**Evidence (Findings)**	**Implications**	**Study**	**Effects on Risk Factor or Use/Abuse (Findings)**
1. Laws and norms (a) Taxation	Levy and Sheflin 1985	1% increase in tax on alcohol led to 1/2% decreases in consumption.	Raise taxes on alcohol.	Levy and Sheflin 1985; Cook and Tauchen 1982; Saffer and Grossman 1987	Higher alcohol taxes were related to decreases in consumption and accompanying effects.
	Cook and Tauchen 1982	Increase in alcohol tax led to sharp decrease in consumption and cirrhosis mortality.			
	Saffer and Grossman 1987	Higher taxes associated with lower teen drinking and fatalities. Higher tax more salient than drinking age.			
(b) Laws regulating to whom liquor is sold	Saffer and Grossman 1987; Krieg 1982; Cook and Tauchen 1982; Joksch 1988	Higher drinking age associated with fewer teenage traffic fatalities, driving while intoxicated citations.	Increase and enforce age restrictions on purchase of alcohol.	Decker et al. 1988; Krieg 1982; Saffer and Grossman 1987; Cook and Tauchen 1982; Joksch 1988	Increasing age restrictions on alcohol purchases can reduce alcohol-related traffic fatalities.
(c) Laws regulating how liquor is sold	Holder and Blose 1987; Blose and Holder 1987	Liquor-by-the-drink sales increased consumption of distilled spirits but not proportion of drinkers in the population.	Discourage liquor-by-the-drink sales.		
(d) Criminal laws making drugs illegal	Polich et al. 1984	Neither doubling of interdiction nor increased arrests of drug dealers would affect retail prices or availability of illegal drugs.	Deemphasize interdiction and criminal sanctions.		

Risk Factors for Adolescent Substance Abuse with Corresponding Prevention Findings

Risk		Intervention		
Risk Factor	**Etiological Study**	**Evidence (Findings)**	**Implications**	**Study**	**Effects on Risk Factor or Use/Abuse (Findings)**

Risk Factor	Etiological Study	Evidence (Findings)	Implications	Study	Effects on Risk Factor or Use/Abuse (Findings)
(e) Cultural norms	Watts and Rabow 1983; Flasher and Maisto 1984; Robins 1984; Vaillant 1983	Alcohol consumption and other alcohol-related effects are associated with sociodemographic factors, ethnic and other group norms.	Foster social norms opposing drug use.	Johnson and Solis 1983; Perry et al. 1988	Community health promotion associated with cessation or reduction of smoking.
	Atkin et al. 1984	More exposure to ads promoting alcohol among teens reporting higher drinking levels.		Black 1989	Saturation advertising accompanied increases in negative attitudes toward drugs, drug users; talking about drugs with parents, teachers, siblings among college students, children but less for 13- to 17-year-olds.
				Pentz, Brannon et al. 1989; Moskowitz and Jones 1988	Comprehensive school policies emphasizing prevention; restrictions on opportunities for use may reduce smoking.
				Hansen et al. 1988; Perry 1986; Pentz Dwyer et al. 1989; Botvin 1986; Klepp et al. 1986	Some social influence resistance programs include normative-change components (e.g., depicting drug use as socially unacceptable, use of peer leaders to teach curriculum).
				Robins 1984; Johnston 1991	Norms antithetical to use are associated with reductions in prevalence of frequent marijuana, other illicit drug use.

TABLE 8.4 (CONTINUED)

Risk Factors for Adolescent Substance Abuse with Corresponding Prevention Findings

Risk Factor	Risk		Intervention		
	Etiological Study	Evidence (Findings)	Implications	Study	Effects on Risk Factor or Use/Abuse (Findings)
2. Availability	Gorsuch and Butler 1976	Increased alcohol availability led to increases in drinking prevalence, amount of alcohol consumed, heavy use of alcohol.	Enforce drug and alcohol laws; resistance skills training.		(Risk factors 1b and 2 are related, all involving social influences to use.)
	Maddahian et al. 1988; Dembo et al. 1979; Gottfredson 1988	Availability affected use of alcohol and illegal drugs.			
3. Extreme economic deprivation	Bursik and Webb 1982; Farrington et al. 1985; Bachman et al. 1981; Zucker and Harford, 1983; Murray et al. 1987	Poverty associated with childhood conduct problems, delinquency, chronic offenses. Parental education and occupation positively correlated with teen alcohol and marijuana use.	Target intervention to economically disadvantaged children.	Lazar et al. 1982; Ramey et al. 1988; Seitz et al. 1985	Interventions with low-income families, including day care, preschool, parenting, home visitors, health care, show promising effects on antisocial behavior in adolescence, aggression, special education placements, criminal involvement.
	Robins and Ratcliff 1979	Extreme poverty one of three factors increasing risk of adult alcohol and drug abuse in adults who were antisocial as children.		Swift 1988; Olds et al. 1986; Bronson et al. 1984; Pierson et al. 1983; Seitz et al. 1985	Early family support interventions have shown positive effects on child abuse, early school performance and attendance, family size, maternal employment.
				Berrueta-Clement et al. 1984	Follow-up of low-income 5- to 6-year-olds form Perry Preschool Program at age 19 reveals less mental retardation, school dropouts, crime, and welfare reliance and greater literacy, employment, college/vocational school for participants.

TABLE 8.4 (CONTINUED)

Risk Factors for Adolescent Substance Abuse with Corresponding Prevention Findings

Risk			Intervention		Effects on Risk Factor or Use/Abuse (Findings)
Risk Factor	**Etiological Study**	**Evidence (Findings)**	**Implications**	**Study**	
4. Neighborhood disorganization	Murray 1983; Herting and Guest 1985; Wilson and Herrnstein 1985; Fagan 1988; Simcha-Fagan and Schwartz 1986; Sampson et al. 1981; Sampson 1986; Cloninger et al. 1988	Characteristics of neighborhoods such as population density, mobility, physical deterioration, low attachment, high crime are related to juvenile crime and drug trafficking.	Target families in high-risk neighborhoods.	(See studies under Risk Factor 3, economic deprivation.)	
		Low socioeconomic status in childhood related to greater drug use in adolescence. Brook et al. 1990			
5. Physiological factors (a) Biochemical	Zuckerman 1987; von Knorring et al. 1987; Tabakoff and Hoffman 1988; Suwaki and Ohara, 1985; Schuckit 1987	Sensation seeking and low harm avoidance predict early-onset alcoholism. Sensation-seeking, early-onset alcoholism linked to platelet monoamine oxidase activity. Aldehyde dehydrogenase differences found in Asians with lower rates of alcoholism than controls.	Target youngsters with certain central nervous system disorders or biochemical levels and with low socioeconomic status and central nervous system disorders.		
(b) Genetic factors	Blum et al. 1990	Genetic susceptibility to at least one form of alcoholism suggested by polymorphic pattern of dopamine D2 receptor gene.	Target interventions to children of alcoholics, especially boys.		

TABLE 8.4 (CONTINUED)

Risk Factors for Adolescent Substance Abuse with Corresponding Prevention Findings

Risk			Intervention	
Risk Factor	Etiological Study	Evidence (Findings)	Implications	Study	Effects on Risk Factor or Use/Abuse (Findings)
	Pollock et al. 1983	More slow-wave electroencephalogram activity in children of alcoholics than nonalcoholics.			
	Schuckit et al. 1983; Schuckit 1980; Schuckit and Rayes, 1979; Schuckit 1987	Differences between children of alcoholics and nonalcoholics in serum prolactin response, muscle response, and levels of acetaldehyde after administration of alcohol.			
	Kaij 1960; Hrubec and Omenn 1981	Monozygotic twins were more than twice as likely as dizygotic twins to be concordant for alcoholism (all males).			

From J. David Hawkins, R. Catalono, and J. Miller. "Risk and Protective Factors for Alcohol and Other Drug Problems in Adolescence and Early Adulthood: Implications for Substance Abuse Prevention." *Psychological Bulletin* 112 (1): (1992) 64–105.

TABLE 8.5

Factors Associated with Risk Behaviors

Demographic

Less education
Low income
Unemployment

Psychosocial

High level of stressful life events
Poor social support[a]
Poor ethnic identity[b]

Ecological

Exposure to community and interpersonal violence[c]
Poor interactions with health care workers[d]

Individual

Psychological status (e.g., alienation,[e] powerlessness, depression,[f] or post-traumatic stress disorder)
Perceptions of levels of stress
Experiences of racism

[a]Neighbors and Jackson, 1984; Gombeski et al. 1982.
[b]Bullough 1967; Abrams, Allen, and Gray 1993; Carter 1991; Munford, 1994.
[c]Sanders-Phillips 1994a, 1994b, 1996a; Cohen et al. 1991.
[d]Freimuth and Mettzger 1990; Harrison and Harrison 1971; James et al. 1984; Perez-Stable 1987; Webb 1984; Makuc, Fried, and Kleinman 1989; Sanders-Phillips 1996a; Balsheim 1991; Farris and Glenn 1976.
[e]Bullough 1972; Cohen et al. 1982; Hibbard 1985; Morris, Hatch, and Chipman, 1966; Seeman and Evans 1962; Seeman and Seeman 1983.
[f]Cohen et al. 1991; Leftwich and Collins 1994.

The Wolins define resiliency as an internal protective factor and the ability to bounce back. In their research on adult children of alcoholics, they found that some children of alcoholics grow up free of drinking because they

- Build on their own strengths
- Develop their own lifestyle and values, which are an improvement over their parents
- Establish healthy "rituals" in their own family

Applying this knowledge, the Wolins worked with adolescents and young adults from the inner city who grew up in dysfunctional and abusive, alcoholic/addict family systems. They applied their "challenge" model of resiliency, helping these young people realize their own resiliency in attaining healthy growth. They called this "survivor's pride"—a sense that you have been tested and that you have prevailed.

Resiliency is described by the Wolins as not getting stuck in the "damage model" but, instead, challenging yourself and celebrating your survival and growth. Resiliency work is about reframing the damage, uncovering strength in a damage/

TABLE 8.6

Factors Associated with Healthy Behaviors

Demographic

High education level
High income
Employment
Positive marital status[a]

Psychosocial

High level of social support[b]
  Emotional support
  Information sharing
  Provision of tangible goods and services
Church participation

Individual

Internal locus of control
Greater self-efficacy regarding the prevention of disease
Positive perceptions of health status
Greater knowledge and positive attitudes about health-promoting behaviors

[a]Cohen et al. 1991; Gottlieb and Green 1984; Rakowski 1988.
[b]Gottlieb and Green 1984; Neighbors and Jackson 1984; Shumaker and Hill 1991.
Source: Glantz, Meyer D., and Christine R. Hartel. Drug Abuse: Origins and Interventions, 1999.

deficit–oriented story. In the damage model, the individual is seen as helpless, fragile, passive, and trapped. The Wolins emphasize that you need to help the individual understand the damage, express the anger, grieve the past, and move to resiliency.

Resiliency involves deliberation (making a plan). In many abusive family situations, it is a "getaway plan," creating distance from unhealthy situations. Resiliency skills also involve eventually choosing a spouse who is healthy and is developing healthy rituals.

They also describe how, too frequently, therapists perpetuate the victim's trap by

- Maintaining the myth that family problems will inevitably be perpetuated from one generation to the next
- Having the patients deplete themselves by continually blaming their parents for hurting them

Instead, they describe a more positive therapeutic goal of helping patients get revenge by seeking resiliency: by living healthy, productive lives rather than blaming and finding fault.

They describe seven resilient factors as follows:

1. Insight—the habit of asking tough questions which pierce the denial and confusion in troubled families

2. Independence—emotional and physical distancing from a troubled family, which keeps survivors out of harm's way
3. Relationships—fulfilling ties to others that provide the stability, nurturing, and love that troubled families do not give
4. Initiative—a push for mastery that combats the feelings of helplessness troubled families produce in their offspring
5. Creativity—representing one's inner pain and hurtful experiences in art forms; "building a new world on the ruins of the old"
6. Humor—the ability to minimize pain and troubles by laughing at oneself
7. Morality—an informed conscience, which imbues the survivor surrounded by "badness" with a sense of his or her own "goodness" (From Steven Wolin and Sybil Wolin, *The Resilient Self: How Survivors of Troubled Families Rise above Adversity,* Villard Books, Random House, 1994)

⚔ Emotional Intelligence

In 1995, Daniel Goleman, in his book *Emotional Intelligence,* made a case for a new kind of intelligence, or IQ—an IQ that goes beyond the traditional verbal and performance scales of most IQ tests and redefines what skills make up a successful person. Goleman labels this new IQ as emotional intelligence and defines it as abilities such as

- Being able to motivate oneself and persist in the face of frustration
- Being able to control impulse and delay gratification
- Being able to regulate one's mood and keep distress from swamping the ability to think
- Being able to empathize and hope

The characteristics of emotional intelligence make one more successful at work, at relationships, at parenting, at coupleship, and at life in general. As we see increases in domestic violence, abuse, physical violence, and alcohol/drug abuse in homes, schools, community, our nation, and throughout the world, we see the importance of emotional intelligence. Managing anger and other moods (depression, fear, worry, and anxiety) is one of the key components of emotional intelligence.

"Of all the moods . . . anger is the mood people are worst at controlling . . . . Anger is the most seductive of the negative emotions, the self-righteous inner monologue that propels along filling the mind with the most convincing arguments to vent rage" (Goleman 1995).

The goals of the emotionally intelligent individual are optimism, motivation, perseverance, and self-efficacy.

⚔ Domains of Prevention

Schools, religious and voluntary organizations, the media, the private sector, law enforcement, and health care are the secondary line of defense against drug and alcohol abuse by young people (see Figure 8.2). Families can make a real difference. Secondary approaches have little effect if the home and family environment are not involved and supportive of prevention efforts.

In conducting alcohol/drug educational and skill activities for parents over the past twenty years, I have found that the parents who don't need the information

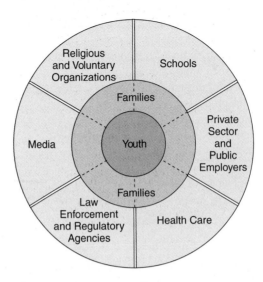

FIGURE 8.2 *A Conceptual Model for Preventive Approaches to Alcohol and Drug Abuse*

From Attorney General John Van De Kamp's Commission of Drug and Alcohol Abuse, 1986, Sacramento, CA
Reprinted by permission of California Attorney General's Office.

and are already effective parents are the ones that come to every event. The parents who need help are either in denial, too embarrassed or shamed, or too out of control to attend. Until we develop programs that can get these parents to participate, we are fighting an uphill battle.

✗ Prevention Programs and Prevention Emphasis in the New Millennium

Developmental Assets Model

The Search Institute of Minneapolis has developed a research-based framework of developmental assets, or factors that are critical for young people's successful growth and development. The institute's Healthy Communities—Healthy Youth programs are part of a national initiative to "motivate and equip individuals, organizations, and their leaders to join together in nurturing competent, caring, and responsible children and adolescents." The institute has identified and measured 40 developmental assets (see Table 8.7). These assets are the foundation that children and adolescents from many cultural backgrounds need to be responsible, successful, and caring human beings.

"These assets are more than just nice ideas. Research on youth in hundreds of communities finds that these assets are powerful influences on behavior [see Figure 8.3]. Yet, the average 6th- to 12th-grade student experiences only 18 of the 40 assets" (Search Institute 1999). The application of education and skill development of these developmental assets takes place in the schools, with parents and other adults, with young people, with youth serving organizations, in neighborhoods, in communities, in business and industry, in local government, in congregations, in the juvenile justice system, in community care systems, and in community organizations.

TABLE 8.7

Forty Developmental Assets

Type	Asset Name and Definition
Support	1. **Family support**—Family life provides high levels of love and support.
	2. **Positive family communication**—Young person and his or her parent(s) communicate positively, and young person is willing to seek parent(s') advice and counsel.
	3. **Other adult relationships**—Young person receives support from three or more nonparent adults.
	4. **Caring neighborhood**—Young person experiences caring neighbors.
	5. **Caring school climate**—School provides a caring, encouraging environment.
	6. **Parent involvement in schooling**—Parent(s) are actively involved in helping young person succeed in school.
Empowerment	7. **Community values youth**—Young person perceives that adults in the community value youth.
	8. **Youth as resources**—Young people are given useful roles in the community.
	9. **Service to others**—Young person serves in the community one hour or more per week.
	10. **Safety**—Young person feels safe at home, at school, and in the neighborhood.
Boundaries and Expectations	11. **Family boundaries**—Family has clear rules and consequences, and they monitor the young person's whereabouts.
	12. **School boundaries**—School provides clear rules and consequences.
	13. **Neighborhood boundaries**—Neighbors take responsibility for monitoring young people's behavior.
	14. **Adult role models**—Parent(s) and other adults model positive, responsible behavior.
	15. **Positive peer influence**—Young person's best friends model responsible behavior.
	16. **High expectations**—Both parent(s) and teachers encourage the young person to do well.
Constructive Use of Time	17. **Creative activities**—Young person spends three or more hours per week in lessons or practice in music, theater, or other arts.
	18. **Youth programs**—Young person spends three or more hours per week in sports, clubs, or organizations at school and/or in community organizations.
	19. **Religious community**—Young person spends one or more hours per week in activities in a religious institution.
	20. **Time at home**—Young person is out with friends, "with nothing special to do," two or fewer nights per week.
Commitment to Learning	21. **Achievement motivation**—Young person is motivated to do well in school.
	22. **School engagement**—Young person is actively engaged in learning.
	23. **Homework**—Young person reports doing at least one hour of homework every schoolday.
	24. **Bonding to school**—Young person cares about his or her school.
	25. **Reading for pleasure**—Young person reads for pleasure three or more hours per week.

TABLE 8.7 (CONTINUED)

Forty Developmental Assets

Type	Asset Name and Definition
Positive Values	26. **Caring**—Young person places high value on helping other people.
	27. **Equality and social justice**—Young person places high value on promoting equality and reducing hunger and poverty.
	28. **Integrity**—Young person acts on convictions and stands up for his or her beliefs.
	29. **Honesty**—Young person tells the truth, even when it is not easy.
	30. **Responsibility**—Young person accepts and takes personal responsibility.
	31. **Restraint**—Young person believes it is important not to be sexually active or to use alcohol or other drugs.
Social Competencies	32. **Planning and decision making**—Young person knows how to plan ahead and make choices.
	33. **Interpersonal competence**—Young person has empathy, sensitivity, and friendship skills.
	34. **Cultural competence**—Young person has knowledge of and comfort with people of different cultural/racial/ethnic backgrounds.
	35. **Resistance skills**—Young person can resist negative peer pressure and dangerous situations.
	36. **Peaceful conflict resolution**—Young person seeks to resolve conflict nonviolently.
Positive Identity	37. **Personal power**—Young person feels he or she has control over "things that happen to me."
	38. **Self-esteem**—Young person reports having a high self-esteem.
	39. **Sense of purpose**—Young person reports that "my life has a purpose."
	40. **Positive view of personal future**—Young person is optimistic about his or her personal future.

School-Based Programs
The Personal Growth Class—a School-Based Prevention Program (Thompson et al. 1997)
Target: Adolescents At-Risk for School Dropout

This school-based program helps adolescents

1. Reduce their involvement in substance use behaviors
2. Improve school performance
3. Improve mood management (e.g., decrease depression, increase anger-management skills)

The two major components of the program are social support and life skills training. The life skills training addresses self-esteem enhancement, decision-making skills, personal control, and interpersonal communication.

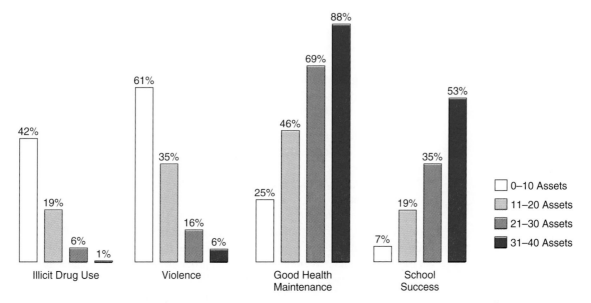

FIGURE 8.3 *The Power of Developmental Assets* The more assets young people experience, the less likely they are to engage in a wide range of risky behaviors, and the more likely they are to engage in positive behaviors.

Based on Search Institute's study of almost 100,000 youth in 312 towns and cities across the United States during the 1996–1997 school year.

Jump Start (Harrington and Donohew 1997)

Target: African American adolescents, economically disadvantaged, those high on sensation seeking

Curriculum includes aspects of social-influence model, social skills training and alternatives-based programs.

The Iowa Strengthening Families Program (ISFP: Spoth and Redmond 1996)

Target: A Family-based Prevention Program Adapted from the Strengthening Families Program (Kumpfer 1996), a Target Intervention for High-risk Families

The primary goal of Project Family is to enhance family functioning in rural families by teaching parenting skills and other relevant skills to prevent adolescent substance use and other problem behaviors.

Comprehensive Community Prevention Programs

Target: Focus on Both the Demand and Supply Aspects of Adolescent Substance Use

---

The Resolving Conflict Creatively Program (RCCP) is a comprehensive, school-based program in conflict resolution and intergroup relations that provides a model for preventing violence and creating caring and peaceable communities of learning.

RCCP serves 6,000 teachers and 175,000 young people in 375 schools nationwide, including the New York City schools and 12 other diverse school systems.

⋈ **Resolving Conflict Creatively Program (RCCP)**

Schools can play a critical role in encouraging young people to actively contribute to the well-being of others if they provide meaningful opportunities to reconnect students with their communities. To this end, the Resolving Conflict Creatively Program offers schools and communities a model for creating democratic and caring learning communities by developing young people's skills in dealing with emotions, resolving conflict, and honoring differences.

The goals of the RCCP National Center are to use the RCCP model to

- Prepare educators to provide high-quality instruction and effective school programs in conflict resolution and intercultural understanding in a variety of educational settings
- Reduce violence and increase intercultural understanding in school districts across the country
- Transform the culture of participating schools so they model the values and principles of creative, nonviolent conflict resolution and respect for diversity
- Inform school systems, educational leaders, and the general public about the efficacy of social and emotional learning programs and the ingredients that constitute successful implementation
- Provide technical assistance to school systems about long-range, comprehensive program design and implementation

✖ Community Partnership Program (1990–1996)

The Prevention Works Through Community project was evaluated by the Center for Substance Abuse Prevention (CSAP). There were 48 communities in the study, and the best evaluations were models in diverse communities—Springfield, Missouri; Lala County, Illinois; El Paso, Texas; South Central Los Angeles; and Knox, Laurel, and Whitley Counties, Kentucky.

The common features of these successful community models were

- A comprehensive vision, covering all requirements and all aspects of community life
- A wide sharing of this vision, agreed upon by groups and citizens across the community
- A strong core of committed partners at the outset
- An inclusive and broad-based membership, welcoming all segments of the community
- Avoidance of resolution of severe conflict that might reflect misunderstandings about a partnership's basic purpose
- Decentralized units, encouraging participation and action at small-area or neighborhood levels
- Nondisruptive staff turnover of a reasonable rate
- Extensive prevention activities and support for local prevention policies

✖ Healthy People 2010

This project has the support of such people as former president Jimmy Carter and other leaders. The goal is to promote healthy living through prevention interventions and proven clinical services.

People of Color and Other Minorities

A variety of factors make people of color and other minorities at-risk for substance abuse problems. Minorities as a group have more unemployment, have less prestigious occupations, and live in poverty and lower socioeconomic conditions. Thus, they experience more feelings of frustration, anger, resentment, and powerlessness. Inadequate education, housing, income, and other factors create additional stress and pressure, which may lead to problems with alcohol/drugs.

For people of color, prevention must go beyond the approaches previously described. One of the biggest problems facing people of color is the crack epidemic in the inner cities, the increase in young cocaine and heroin addicts' giving birth to cocaine- and heroin-addicted babies, and the rise in methamphetamine use.

Prevention for people of color and other minorities must be community based. Residents must conceptualize the problem and jointly develop appropriate strategies.

Community-based prevention programs also must emphasize a systemic strategy to uproot the factors in the system that oppress people of color, such as prejudice and racism, and to implement training in diversity and methods of accessing the system.

Elders and Prevention

Our elders make up another arena of prevention that is often forgotten or ignored. The lack of any true role experienced by some elders leads to feelings of loneliness, boredom, frustration, rejection, abandonment, anxiety, fear, and depression. When elders complain about these feelings, sometimes the response is to prescribe medication.

Prevention efforts with elders frequently involve training and educational projects to assist them to keep accurate records of their medications or to develop methods to have someone monitor their medication. Elders need to be approached with individuality and dignity. They need to be empowered to develop their own advocacy. Pharmacists, physicians, and other health providers must act in cooperation and be sensitive to each individual case. Drug dosages and regimens must meet individual needs and be sensitive to the elders' ability to maintain their treatment plans.

Stewart and Cluff (1972) found that the rate of elder noncompliance with medication directions ranges from 20 to 80 percent. Doyle and Hamm (1976) found that 72 percent of the elders in Florida reported that they did not discuss medications given by one doctor while being treated by another physician.

Monitoring and educating the elder population are necessary prevention strategies. Advocacy for alternatives to medication are also essential, as well as the expansion of senior services. The more active and involved the lifestyles of elders, the healthier are the later years of their lives.

Prevention with elders also involves proactive approaches to healthy activities that promote physical movement (health permitting), interpersonal interaction, and a sense of value and worth. In the years to come, a majority of the population will be elders. Prevention programs and services need to be further developed now to meet the needs of this ever-expanding population.

⚹ **Prevention and Special Populations**

College Students At-Risk

During their first year of college, most students dramatically increase alcohol/drug use. The MTV spring break party illustrates the pervasive "let loose and get loaded" attitude of young college students.

Alcohol/drug use and abuse is a glamorized way of escape from the pressures of school. The newly acquired freedom of being away at college allows students more opportunities to use alcohol/drugs. The anxiety of adjusting to college and living away from home can result in escalated alcohol/drug use. The functions of alcohol/drugs on college campuses are many—to party, to stay up late and study, to explore a personal sense of self and identity, to facilitate social and interpersonal relationships, and so forth.

Prevention and the Family

Unfortunately, prevention activities take place almost exclusively in school systems. We expect the school systems to prevent this epidemic of alcohol/drug use. The reality is that the families are the real first line of defense against alcohol/drug use by young people.

Summary

The early prevention approaches focused primarily on supplying information on the dangers of specific drugs; on warnings of physical, social, and psychological harm; and on punishment for sale, use, and possession. These scare tactics were ineffective, as were other converting programs, which tried to direct, preach, or convince young people not to use drugs. The information in these early prevention approaches was often invalid, exaggerated, and overgeneralized, causing young people to question the credibility of the prevention efforts.

The next prevention efforts focused on drug-specific information in the hope that young people would make wise decisions about drugs. Unfortunately, these approaches heightened curiosity and alleviated fears, leading to an increase in drug experimentation, rather than the intended decrease.

The ineffectiveness of scare tactics and drug-specific approaches led to a moratorium on prevention efforts by the government and a review of those features of a prevention program that were effective.

In the 1980s, the thrust of these new prevention strategies shifted from drugs to people, emphasizing educational information, coping skills, personal competence, decision making, refusal skills, and alternative activities.

Alternative activities are successful if they are acceptable, attractive, and attainable.

Examples of effective school-based curricula give readers a better understanding of the content and skills emphasized in effective programs. These curricula develop skills such as

1. Goal setting, problem solving, conflict resolution
2. Development of capabilities and dealing with authority figures
3. Development of proactive versus passive involvement and empowerment

Today credibility is a basic premise for the effectiveness of any alcohol/drug prevention program. Effective prevention must include youth, be sensitive and include community needs, promote proactivity, and make a longitudinal commitment to long-term prevention efforts. Special programs are also necessary for prevention efforts for at-risk students, people of color, college students, and elders.

Current prevention programs should be aimed at at-risk youth and people of color, and other minorities and should be community-based.

The chapter includes the 5 at-risk factors for substance abuse and accompanying interventions—laws and norms, availability of alcohol and drugs, extreme economic deprivation, neighborhood organizations, physiological factors (biochemical, genetic), family drug behavior, family management practices, family conflict, low bonding to family, early and persistent problem behavior, academic failure (intelligence, school failure), low commitment to school, peer rejection in elementary grades, association with drug-using peers, alienation and rebelliousness, attitude favorable to drug use, and early onset of drug use.

The resiliency work of Steven Wolin and Sybil Wolin is described in their challenge model, and the concept of emotional intelligence is introduced by Daniel Goleman. The domains of prevention are outlined as primary and secondary defenses. The developmental assets model is outlined, describing 40 developmental assets in the areas of support, empowerment, boundaries and expectations, constructive use of time, commitment to learning, positive values, social competence, and positive identity. School- and community-based programs are described for the new millennium. The chapter concludes with an emphasis on the prevention needs of special populations-people of color and other minorities, elders, and college students.

References

Brecher, Edward M. *Licit and Illicit Drugs.* Boston: Little, Brown, 1972.

Cohen, A.Y. "Alternatives to Drug Abuse: Steps Toward Prevention." Rockville, MD: National Institute on Drug Abuse, 1972.

Doyle, J.P., and B.M. Hamm. *Medication Use and Misuse Study Among Older Persons.* Jacksonville, FL: The Cathedral Foundation of Jacksonville, 1976.

"Drug Abuse Prevention Research," Monograph No. 33. Washington, DC: Department of Health and Human Services, 1983.

Fields, Richard. Book review "Repairing the Damage—the Resilient Self: How Survivors of Troubled Families Rise Above Adversity." *Professional Counselor Magazine,* February, 1996, vol. 1, p. 62.

Glantz, Meyer D., and Christine R. Hartel, *Drug Abuse: Origin and Interventions,* Washington, DC 1999.

Goleman, Daniel. *Emotional Intelligence: Why It Can Matter More Than IQ.* New York: Bantam Books, 1995.

Goodstadt, Michael. "Evaluating Drug Prevention Programs." In *Balancing Head and Heart: Sensible Ideas for the Prevention of Drug and Alcohol Abuse,* ed. E. Schaps, A.Y. Cohen, H.S. Resnick, et al. Lafayette, CA: Prevention Materials Institute Press, 1975.

Mathews, Walter M. "A Critique of Traditional Drug Education Programs." *Journal of Drug Education* 5, no. 1 (1975): 57–64.

National Institute on Drug Abuse. *Toward a National Strategy for Primary Drug Abuse Prevention,* Final Report, Delphi II, 1975.

Office for Substance Abuse Prevention—Monograph 5—*Communicating About Alcohol and Other Drugs: Strategies for Reading Populations At-Risk,* Rockville, MD, 1988, 88–93, 100–01.

Rhodes, Jean E., and Leonard A. Jason. *Preventing Substance Abuse Among Children and Adolescents.* New York: Pergamon Press, 1988.

Schinke, S.P., and L.D. Gilchrist. "Primary Prevention of Tobacco Smoking." *Journal of School Health* 53 (1983): 416–19.

Search Institute. *Ideas for Asset Building Poster,* Search Institute 700 South Third Street, Suite 210, Minneapolis, MN 55415, 1999.

Spivak, G., and M. Shuve. *The Social Adjustment of Young Children.* San Francisco: Jossey-Bass, 1979.

Stewart, R.B., and L.E. Cluff. "A Review of Medication Errors and Compliance in Ambulatory Patients." *Clinical Pharmacology and Therapeutics* 13 (1972): 463–68.

Wolin, Steven, and Sybil Wolin. *The Resilient Self: How Survivors of Troubled Families Rise Above Adversity.* New York: Villard Books, 1994.

Motivation and Intervention for Substance Abuse Problems

Chapter Objectives

1. Describe the dimensions of motivational interviewing.

2. Define the six stages of change in motivational interviewing (precontemplative, contemplative, determination, action, maintenance, relapse).

3. Describe effective motivational strategies and the ingredients of effective brief counseling.

4. Describe the eight (8) common defense components of resistance to change

5. Describe interventions at each stage of alcohol/drug use.

6. In intervening, describe the do's and don'ts of
   - Your emotional reaction
   - Communication
   - Trust in actions, not words
   - Avoidance of distractions

7. Describe some obstacles to reaching families and parents of alcoholics/addicts.

8. Outline and describe the four basic stages of a formal intervention.

9. Describe the kind of information to be elicited at the assessment stage of a formal intervention.

10. Describe the need for and importance of the development of caring, behavior-specific communication during the intervention, as well as for the avoidance of generalized and blaming statements.

11. Outline the script format and the tasks of the preintervention phase of the intervention.

12. Describe the key elements in the actual intervention.

13. Explain the bottom-line script in the intervention.

14. Explain why there is the need for a postintervention session for a family.

❧ Motivational Interviewing

Overview

William Miller and Stephen Rollnick (1991) developed a form of intervention known as motivational interviewing. They recognized that formal and informal interventions are effective for many individuals who are in denial of having a problem with alcohol or drugs, but for some individuals the traditional form of intervention doesn't work. De-

spite the intervention, the individual is not motivated to seek abstinence or recovery from alcohol/drugs.

The same holds true for many individuals who, once in alcohol/drug treatment, either terminated treatment early against medical advice (AMA) or didn't respond when confronted by counselors about their denial. Miller and Rollnick espouse a different approach with individuals who are resistant to traditional intervention methods. Some individuals respond negatively to interventions.

Motivational interviewing draws its strategies from a number of disciplines, including client-centered counseling, cognitive therapy, systems theory, and the social psychology of persuasion. The work comes from Miller and Rollnick's contention that there is no one kind of alcoholic or addict or, for that matter, an addictive personality. "This idea of a common alcoholic or addictive personality is supported neither in the original writings of Alcoholics Anonymous, nor by five decades of psychological research" (Miller and Rollnick 1991). It therefore makes sense that alcoholics/addicts need a variety of approaches to engage them into recovery. Perhaps a different approach might reach those alcoholics/addicts who resist traditional confrontive interventions. Motivational interviewing was therefore designed to help clients build commitment and reach a decision to change.

Miller and Rollnick described motivation as a state of readiness or eagerness to change, and they recognized that motivation may fluctuate over time, situation, and circumstance. They described the basic stages of change and the influences a therapist can make in influencing motivation to change. (See Table 9.1.)

TABLE 9.1

Stages of Change and Therapist Tasks

Client Stage	Therapist's Motivational Tasks
Precontemplative	Raise doubt—increase the client's perception of risks and problems with current behavior. Decrease desirability to status quo, build rapport so you can later provide information about the negative consequences or risks of maintaining the status quo, get to know the client well enough to find out what's important to him or her (what he or she values most). Find something the client did well (maybe it was only being open-minded enough to listen to the counselor's views) and affirm that. Make sure client comes back in the future.
Contemplative	Tip the balance—evoke reasons to change, risks of not changing. Strengthen the client's self-efficacy for change of current behavior. Raise awareness of ambivalence by eliciting and reflecting both sides of the client's ambivalence: the pros and cons of animating the status quo (or the pros and cons of changing, if client prefers to discuss that). Then explore which of these pros and cons mean the most to the client. Try to point out how that status quo is in conflict with the client's deeply held values and how changing might bring the client more in line with those important values.
Determination	Help the client determine the best source of action to take in seeking change.
Action	Help the client take steps toward change. Focus on the plan, what the client is going to do. What is the client willing to do, not willing to do, and ambivalent about doing? People in action still suffer from ambivalence and fear of the unknown, and that ambivalence must be dealt with as you go along. Emphasis on action is on removing barriers to change and problem solving each of these barriers.
Maintenance	Help the client identify and use strategies to prevent relapse.
Relapse	Help the client renew the processes of contemplation, determination, and action without becoming stuck or demoralized because of relapse.

Their approach uses brief, individual counseling, which helps the clients explore and resolve their "ambivalence" about change. Ambivalence is defined as feeling two ways about something, being in conflict between the pros and cons of the status quo (or the pros and cons of changing). Ambivalence is a good description for the conflict many people have about changing, whether it is recovery from alcohol/drugs, unhealthy and self-destructive behaviors (e.g., smoking, overeating), a dysfunctional relationship, a bad work situation, or illegal activities. At the precontemplative stage of change, they are not considering change and may not see or admit problems with the self-destructive behavior (addiction). In the contemplative stage, they are considering change but are ambivalent about it. These are the individuals who waver from day to day and seem easily influenced to go in either direction. When it comes to alcohol/drug abuse and addiction, the alcoholic/addict wants to continue to use alcohol/drugs yet may recognize the risks and negative consequences of use. At the determination stage the individual decides to do something. The action stage is when there has been a recent change or an implemented plan of change. The maintenance stage involves a commitment to a long-term change, where the change has become habit, or part of the person's lifestyle. The relapse prevention stage explores strategies to not return to earlier stages.

Client-Centered Motivational Interviewing

Motivational interviewing is "client centered," which means "that the counselor's top priority—always—is to elicit and understand the client's view. In contrast, more forceful interventions emphasize the views of the significant others staging the intervention" (Dunn 1996).

The motivational interviewing technique is quite different from the intervention model. It is controversial because the active alcoholic/addict wants to continue to drink and will often delay taking action despite significant negative consequences. Many counselors believe that not confronting denial, and giving control back to the alcoholic/addict, will only result in continued destructive, maybe even life-threatening patterns of alcohol consumption. However, the motivational interviewing approach has the perspective that people follow through better and are more committed to recovery if they voluntarily make the decision to choose treatment for themselves. Another controversial aspect of motivational interviewing is the counselor eliciting the client's doubts about recovery, as well as the positive aspects. This helps the counselor reflect back to the client the positive and negative aspects of the decision.

Effective Motivational Strategies

There are eight general motivational strategies.

1. Giving *advice.* Well-timed and tempered advice to change can make a difference. Advice should (a) clearly identify the problem or risk area, (b) explain why change is important, and (c) advocate specific change.
2. Removing *barriers.* Address blocks to change, such as resistance to go to AA meetings.

Case Study 9.1

Contemplative and Action Stages

Don

Don knew he had a problem with alcohol/drugs. He took some action by attending AA meetings, yet he still didn't want to stop drinking. He would maintain abstinence for limited periods of time (30–100 days) but then would lapse into drinking. Despite negative consequences at home and at work, and having gone through two inpatient programs, he still was not committed to recovery. He tried to convince himself that he wasn't really an alcoholic, yet he soon found himself in alcoholic binges. Each time he relapsed, he seemed motivated to get sober and work at a program of recovery, yet, despite attending AA, attending outpatient counseling, even working with a sponsor, he was ambivalent about recovery. At the suggestion of his sponsor, he attended several different AA meetings. After attending an AA meeting at a local mission for the homeless, he wondered if he had to "hit bottom" by losing his job, family, and home to stop drinking. The very next day, he talked to an old-timer at another AA meeting who told him, "Maybe things have to get really bad before you get better." He was then convinced that he had to continue to drink until things got worse, before he would stop. In his ambivalence, he called his sponsor with this new idea and was told, "You'll come up with any excuse to continue drinking." His resolve to seek recovery was so ambivalent and such a struggle that he could easily be influenced to go either way—recovery or self-destruction.

Don talked to his outpatient counselor about this conflict during a one-on-one session, and the counselor effectively used motivational interviewing techniques to help Don resolve this ambivalence, so he could move closer to action. The counselor focused more on Don's ambivalence about committing to AA, rather than the global issue of ambivalence about recovery in general.

Counselor:	It's good to see you again, Don. Tell me how have you been doing for the past few weeks, so I can get caught up? [open question]
Don:	Not great, if you really want to know. I haven't drunk or used in over four weeks now. In fact, I'll be 30 days sober tomorrow. But, big deal, I'm more screwed up than ever. I don't mean to sound sorry for myself, but I just feel lousy. And I know I've got to do something, but I don't know which end is up.
Counselor:	Congratulations on making it to one month! You've been working hard and it hasn't been a picnic for you. [affirmation acknowledging client's progress and empathic statement]
Don:	[silent]
Counselor:	But things are tough, and you aren't getting the rewards of feeling better yet. [accurate reflection] Tell me what you mean when you say you're more screwed up now than ever? [open question]
Don:	I was talking with my sponsor yesterday, and he told me he's worried about me. He thinks I'm gonna go out and drink again. He says I'm subconsciously planning a relapse.
Counselor:	What do you think he means? [open question]

Case Study 9.1 (continued)

Contemplative and Action Stages

Don

Don:	He says I'm looking for an excuse to go back out and drink. He said he wasn't sure I had enough willingness to get active in AA like he wants me to. And he told me I'm just setting myself up for a drink.
Counselor:	And this is all making you feel screwed up?
Don:	Yup. Really bad.
Counselor:	There were three things that you just mentioned: your sponsor, your degree of involvement in AA, and your chances of drinking again. Does any one of those three stand out for you? [summary and open question]
Don:	I don't know what you mean.
Counselor:	Well, first you said you feel really screwed up right now, and then I was hearing you mention three things: your sponsor, AA, and a possible relapse. Which one do you think has got you the most screwed up?
Don:	Oh, I don't know. I know my sponsor's right. If I keep finding excuses to stay away from AA, and not get involved, I know I'll relapse, like I did that last time. I know what I gotta do, but I can't make myself get into it.
Counselor:	So you agree with your sponsor and you share his worry about relapse? [reflection]
Don:	Yeah, I know he's right. [Don stares at the floor.]
Counselor:	And you said you know what you need to do, but you can't get going. [reflection]
Don:	Yeah.
Counselor:	You've already thought this over and figured out what it is you need to do. [affirmation]
Don:	[silent]
Counselor:	That's a pretty good start for somebody who feels more screwed up than ever.
Don:	Big deal. It's not helping me any if I don't *do* anything. [Counselor decides to further explore Don's ambivalence about AA by asking about the pros and cons of AA, as Don sees it. The counselor begins with a summary reflection.]
Counselor:	You were telling me that you're afraid of relapsing if you don't take certain actions, yet you can't seem to get yourself to take those actions. And being stuck that way is making you miserable.
Don:	Right.
Counselor:	Will you let me in on what those certain actions are? [open question acknowledging Don's power to talk or not talk about it]
Don:	It's the same old stuff. I gotta get a home group that I go to all the time and get involved in service.
Counselor:	And you feel two ways about choosing a home group. First of all, what are some of your objections to getting one?
Don:	I don't like joining groups because it's corny or something.
Counselor:	Okay. What else?

Case Study 9.1 (continued)

Contemplative and Action Stages

Don

Don:	I don't want to have to go to the same group every week because I get tired of the people there.
Counselor:	Okay, some groups seem corny to you and you get tired of some people. What else?
Don:	I don't know; that's all I guess.
Counselor:	O.K., what about the other side of the coin? What are the most positive things you might get from choosing a home group?
Don:	Well, it might help me stay sober.
Counselor:	How?
Don:	Just by staying close to a group. They get to know you and, if you start to drop off meetings, somebody might ask you if you're okay.
Counselor:	So people get to know you and care enough to say something to you to help you get back on track, and you might not mind hearing it because you know them, right?
Don:	Yes.
Counselor:	So people can help you stay on track. What else might be positive for you if you decided to get a home group?
Don:	Well, they say people get to know your story and you get to know everybody there pretty good, because you hear their stories as well.
Counselor:	So if you spend more time with your home group you could get to know them better than the people in other groups if you just "shop around" from group to group.
Don:	Right.
Counselor:	Almost as if each person in your home group were a separate TV show that you tune into each week to see how things are going with them. Kind of entertaining.
Don:	Yeah, I never thought of it that way before.
Counselor:	[summarizing] On one hand, you're not much of a joiner and you might get tired of seeing some people every week. But, on the other hand, you could get to know those people better and actually get some support, even enjoyment from being around them each week. Maybe even get so you look forward to going each week?
Don:	I suppose so, although I don't think I'd ever feel really comfortable there. The way it is now, I just go to whatever meeting I feel like. But I never look forward to meetings, because I know I'm just gonna bolt right after it is over.
Counselor:	[reflecting, then trying to tip the balance in favor of change] Sounds a little lonesome. As you look at the balance, pros and cons of getting a home group, Don, do any of those pros or cons stand out as more important to you?
Don:	[arguing for change] Yeah, making friends. It might be nice to get to know some people who don't drink. I never got that far last time I quit drinking. I stayed away from my old drinking buddies, but I also stayed away from people in AA.

Case Study 9.1 (continued)

Contemplative and Action Stages

Don

Counselor: People are a big deal to you. And you think you might find some that you like if you were to hang around one meeting long enough. Well, Don, the decision is totally in your hands. It's understandable that you haven't acted yet, considering that you basically feel two ways about getting a home group. But being stuck where you're at doesn't sound comfortable either. Based on what you've told me, it sounds like getting people in your life that you like and may even begin to trust might make your sobriety nicer. But what do you think?

Summary—Counselor tried to move client from contemplation into preparation and action, regarding the specific behavioral issue of getting a home AA group.

[Counselor turns over the responsibility for the decision to Don and then asks if he's ready for action—i.e., getting a home group. If the answer is no, the counselor affirms the work that Don did in acknowledging both sides of the painful issue and lets the issue rest for now, closing the topic on good terms, to be returned to later. If the answer is yes, they proceed with discussing an action plan for getting a home group and removing barriers to doing so.]

---

3. Providing *choice*. Few people like to be told what to do. Intrinsic motivation is enhanced by the perception that one has freely chosen.
4. Decreasing *desirability*. Weigh the benefits and costs of change against the merits of continuing as before.
5. Practicing *empathy*. This kind of empathy is not an ability to identify with a person's experiences. Rather, it is a specifiable and learnable skill for understanding another's meaning through the use of reflective listening, whether or not you have had a similar experience yourself.
6. Providing *feedback*.
7. Clarifying *goals*. Help the client to restate the goal in realistic or attainable terms.
8. Helping *active*. Express actively and affirmatively your interest in your client's change process.

Active Ingredients of Effective Brief Counseling

Miller and Rollnick (1991) have developed the mnemonic of FRAMES to remind counselors of the effective ingredients for motivational interviewing and brief counseling: FRAMES—feedback, responsibility, advice, menu (i.e., a list of choices), empathy, self-efficacy (i.e., you can do it). (See Figure 9.1.)

TABLE 9.2

The "Nondirective" Part of Motivational Interviewing (MI): OARS (Tools for Rowing Along with Your Clients)

"OARS" symbolizes the way motivational interviewing therapists act during a session.

Open-Ended Questions

Can't be answered with "yes" or "no"
Keep resistance down
Build trust rapidly
Encourage client to talk about what's important to him or her
Reveal what's "delicious" to clients
Help therapist find the "carrot" for change

Affirmations

Very hard to use genuinely; requires much practice
Build self-esteem
Show respect
Reduce treatment dropout rates
Get a "winning streak" going for clients (clients who succeed come back for more success)

Reflecting

Takes practice; sounds phony at first
Is like throwing "empathy darts" while client holds up the target
Client will always let you know if you're accurate or not.
Very satisfying for both to be accurate
More than just paraphrasing the client's message content; also reflects underlying feelings
Happens after every few sentences spoken by clients
About three of every four statements by MI therapist is a reflection (how do you get anything done?)

Summarizing

Gathers together what client said, so it can be heard again (especially the positive change talk)
Shows client what's been accomplished during the session
Can help therapist close one topic and move on to another
Can help end sessions on good terms

Whenever you are stuck, you can fall back on this style of being with your client, until you figure out what your directive strategy is going to be. Without adding the directive motivational interviewing techniques, OARS will only help you row about in circles (but at least you're not sinking. . .).

The general principles of motivational interviewing (see table 9.2) are the following:

1. Express empathy. Acceptance facilitates change; skillful reflective listening is fundamental; ambivalence is normal.
2. Develop discrepancy. Awareness of consequences is important; a discrepancy between present behavior and important goals will motivate change; the client should present the arguments for change.
3. Avoid argumentation. Arguments are counterproductive; defending breeds defensiveness; resistance is a signal to change strategies; labeling is unnecessary.

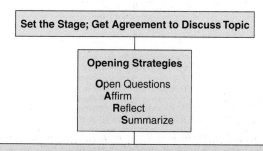

Set the Stage; Get Agreement to Discuss Topic

Opening Strategies

Open Questions
Affirm
Reflect
Summarize

Assess Readiness for Your Agenda

Not Ready	**Unsure**	**Ready for Action**
Goal: Raise Doubt	Goal: Tip the Balance	Goal: Commit to a Plan
Use F R A M E S	Use F R A M E S	Use F R A M E S
Close on Good Terms	Close on Good Terms	Close on Good Terms

F R A M E S

Feedback: Ask to Give It; Make It "Customized" for That Person
Responsibility: Stress Whose Responsibility It Is to Change
Advice: Ask to Give It; Be Neutral About It
Menu: Offer More Than One Choice
Empathy: Make Accurate Empathy Statements, Not "Sympathy"
Self-Efficacy: (a) You Can Do It, and (b) It Will Benefit You to Do It

FIGURE 9.1   *One of Many Ways to Do a Brief Intervention*

Source: Miller and Rollnick, Motivational Interviewing, 1991.

4.   Roll with resistance. Momentum can be used to good advantage; perceptions can be shifted; new perspectives are invited but not imposed; the client is a valuable resource in finding solutions to problems.

5.   Support self-efficacy. Belief in the possibility of change is an important motivator: the client is responsible for choosing and carrying out personal change; there is hope in the range of alternative approaches available.

Everything one does to create awareness of an alcohol/drug problem is an intervention. The slightest suggestion to a friend, colleague, or family member that he or she may be drinking/drugging too much is an intervention. Everyone is different. Those who are at early stages of substance abuse without a family history of alcoholism/addiction may very well pay attention to your observations. If enough people are bringing the drink/drug problem to the person's attention, he or she might decide to do something about it. On the other hand, there are individuals who, if they were hit over the head with a two-by-four, wouldn't recognize their sustance abuse problem.

Resistance is a natural part of the change cycle. Whether it is an adolescent who resists cleaning up his or her room or an adult who delays paying his or her taxes, resistance is embedded in our nature. For some, it is laziness, and procrastination, probably related to family-of-origin issues. But most people resist doing something that may bring discomfort or dysphoria or that is just downright uninteresting.

✄
Intervention

Resistance comes out in the various defense mechanisms used by people to avoid taking action on a problem behavior (e.g., substance abuse).

Common Defense Components of Resistance to Change

1. Denial—most common
    Counselor tip: look for the usefulness of the defense to person, what he or she is avoiding and why wait to point out denial, premature disclosure can "turn off" the client (i.e., you are judging them)
2. Minimization—used to maintain self-esteem (e.g., "My drinking/drugging never had an impact on my children, since I drank outside of the house")
    Counselor tip: suggest client get feedback from valued and reliable other sources, rather than getting into a tireless debate with client
3. Projection—has important protective function, may cover deeper disturbance
    Counselor tip: be sensitive to self-blame and guilt, and the client feeling shamed by any suggestion of criticism preface feedback with "some people might think"
4. Rationalization—clever answers used to avoid responsiblity and maintain frozen feelings
    Counselor tip: avoid your own frustration and anger in trying to get through to a highly intellectualizing client
5. Compliance—hidden form of resistance, may cover up magical expectations
    Counselor tip: recognize the potential of provoking rebellion at some point
6. Conflict avoidance—problems handling feelings of anger and disappointment, need to be liked and approved
    Counselor tip: provoking client to deal with conflict too much may be a hazard
7. Obsessive focusing—all-or-none thinking, may be overly self-critical or, overly critical of others, may be perfectionistic
    Counselor tip: understand the person's situation while suggesting that he or she "lighten up"
8. Acting out—lacks awareness of feelings, impulses communicated by behavior, most provocative of defenses
    Counselor tip: direct to needed change, stay out of harm's way (i.e., be careful not to put self in jeopardy)
    (Adapted from lecture by Choppel, M.D., Honing Our Clinical Skills with Resistant Patients)

Interventions at Various Stages of the Alcohol/Drug Use Continuum

Alcohol/drug intervention is any action taken by someone to interrupt the progression of problems with alcohol/drugs. This definition can be expanded to any attempt to help someone from further developing problems with alcohol/drugs. At each stage of alcohol/drug use (i.e., initial contact, experimentation, integrated use, excessive use, addiction), intervention attempts may prevent progression to the next, more damaging stage of alcohol/drug use. This may take the form of an employer expressing concern about an employee's job performance or a teacher talking with parents and letting them know their child is tired and falling asleep in class. There have been a variety of intervention programs in the school system.

One such program helps teachers develop core teams (usually involving the school nurse, an administrator, a coach, a dean, etc.), which identify students with behaviors, attitudes, and problems that may indicate alcohol/drug problems. All of these approaches are interventions. Whether it is a conversation expressing concern about alcohol/drug use or a formal intervention, the common goal is to let the individual know that we are concerned about him or her.

In Chapter 4, the various stages of alcohol/drug use are described—nonuse, initial contact, experimentation (situational and circumstantial), integrated use, excessive use (periodic and continuous), and addiction. At each of these stages, there are opportunities for intervention. If one can effectively intervene at earlier stages and interrupt the progression to later stages of alcohol/drug use, the negative consequences may be avoided. Obviously, the later stages of alcohol/drug abuse require more concerted efforts, such as a formal intervention.

The following suggestions illustrate various interventions for children at each stage of the alcohol/drug use continuum.

Stage 1—Nonuse Interventions

- Parental, peer, and other support to maintain nonuse
- Emotional support during difficult times, conflicts, developmental tasks, and emotionally charged events that may make the individual at-risk try alcohol/drugs
- Affirmation and support in activities that promote a good sense of self and alternative activities to alcohol/drug use
- Focus on refusal skills and dealing with peer pressure
- Education and implementation of effective parenting, communication skills, and other alcohol/drug prevention skills

Stage 2—Initial Contact Interventions

Two common problems at this stage are overreaction and underreaction. As a parent, you don't want to be an alarmist and overact in rigid, shaming, and blaming ways to a child's initial contact with alcohol/drugs. You also don't want to ignore the use, disregard the significance, and minimize the impact on the child. As a result,

- Become more aware of the child's behavior and signs of alcohol/drug use.
- Talk with other parents about the child's behavior in their homes.
- Once aware of initial contact, talk with child (i.e., break the no-talk rule); don't ignore the fact that your child used or avoided the opportunity to discuss his or her use of alcohol/drugs.
- If your child has used, let him or her describe the situation, without being judgmental, blaming, or negative.
- Express concerns about safety (e.g., Was your child with friends that he or she could trust? Was it a safe place if problems occurred? Was your child in physical or psychological danger?).
- Without being negative and an alarmist, or lecturing, let the child describe his or her own perception of safety.
- Discuss at-risk factors of alcohol/drug dependence and addiction (especially if there is a family history of alcoholism and/or drug dependence).

- This may be an opportunity to reevaluate other aspects of the child's life (e.g., school, friends, activities).
- This may be an opportune time to explore other family problems and seek an assessment from a counselor who specializes in alcohol/drug recovery and family systems.

Stage 3—Experimentation Interventions

- Focusing on communication and exploration of values, attitudes, and feelings about alcohol/drugs
- Teaching and modeling skills in decision making, conflict resolution, goal setting, and so on
- Teaching and modeling skills in coping with conflicts, dealing with authority figures, and controlling destructive impulses
- Providing information about chemical dependency and addiction
- Providing information about at-risk factors if there is a family history of chemical dependency (e.g., if one parent has or had problems with alcohol/drugs, the child has a four times higher risk of developing problems with alcohol/drugs; if both parents have or had a problem, there is an eight times higher risk for the child to develop problems with alcohol/drugs)
- Identifying, assessing, and perhaps counseling for problems in the family, at school, and so on
- Educating about alcohol/drug prevention and family systems

Stage 4—Interventions at the Integrated Stage

- Identification and communication of concerns and negative consequences as a result of integrated alcohol/drug use
- Expression of concern—in a caring, nonjudgmental way—regarding the well-being of the individual using alcohol/drugs
- Point out the individual's denial of an alcohol/drug problem
- Assessment by a trained chemical dependency family counselor to assess alcohol/drug use and family dynamics
- If problems are identified, work on these issues in counseling (i.e., family members attend Alanon; take educational classes on chemical dependency, parenting, and family systems; and attend regular counseling)

Stages 5 and 6—Interventions at the Excessive Use and Addiction Stages

All of the previous strategies are appropriate at both the excessive and addictive stages. However, the longer and more pervasive the problems with alcohol/drugs, the more difficult and intense the level of intervention.

- Alcohol/drug assessment, including regular urinanalysis for drugs and blood alcohol tests
- Intensive outpatient counseling for chemical dependency and family issues
- Strong boundary setting and consequences for violation of family rules and alcohol/drug use

- Formal alcohol/drug intervention
- Inpatient/residential treatment for chemical dependency
- Involvement in AA and other self-help meetings, including active involvement in 12-step work with a sponsor

Table 9.3 describes the do's and don'ts of dealing with someone who has an alcohol/drug problem.

TABLE 9.3

Do's and Don'ts of Dealing with Someone Who Has an Alcohol/Drug Problem

1. Deal with your emotions.

If possible, try to be calm, balanced, and caring. This may be difficult; however, remember that, if you lose control, you lose.

Do Not

Try to talk with someone while he or she is under the influence of alcohol/drugs; if your child or spouse comes home late at night under the influence of alcohol/drugs, wait until the morning to discuss it.

Threaten to make ultimatums unless you have had time to think them through (e.g., Is it realistic? Can you follow through? What is the impact of the ultimatum on other family members?). Threats said in anger can be unrealistic, inflexible, and abusive. Idle threats or constant threats that are not followed through are meaningless in changing behavior. Threats only set up a lack of consistency, poor trust, and lack of credibility.

Lose your temper, rant and rave, or lose control. It might temporarily make you feel good to let out your frustration and anger, but it does not help the child or adult in addressing the alcohol/drug problem.

Do

Express a willingness to get help and resolve the problem. This is usually in the form of counseling.

Communicate your concern and feelings (e.g., fear, worry, love) without trying to control or lecture the alcohol/drug user.

Set boundaries that are reasonable (to promote appropriate behavior and consistent family rules).

Follow through with consequences for boundaries that were violated.

2. Communicate with behavior-specific examples, rather than generalizations and secondhand or speculative information.

Do Not

Ask why the person is using alcohol/drugs. "Why" questions are often blaming questions, as if asking, "How could you do this to your mother and me?"

Use words such as *drunk, loaded, wasted.* Instead, describe specific behaviors you observe (e.g., slurred speech, staggered gait, etc.).

Generalize about alcohol/drug use. Be specific about alcohol/drug use, if possible (e.g., "I saw you drink five glasses of wine and snort two lines of cocaine").

Use sarcasm, ridicule, and other behaviors that may shame or embarrass the alcohol/drug user. This only perpetuates resentments and often results in later passive-aggressive behavior.

Do

Seek professional counseling to help with family communication about alcohol/drug problems. Seek out a counselor experienced in alcohol/drug treatment and family systems.

TABLE 9.3 (CONTINUED)

Do's and Don'ts of Dealing with Someone Who Has an Alcohol/Drug Problem

3. Trust what you see (behaviors), not what the addict/alcoholic or problem user says.

Do Not

Expect that things will get better on their own. Often, the problem alcohol/drug user will decrease his or her use when he or she suspects that you may do something. Alcoholism and drug addiction are progressive diseases that only get worse over time unless the individual is motivated to change.

Expect that the problem alcohol/drug user will recognize his or her use as a problem. Denial is often the case.

Assume that the alcoholic/addict will be rational and logical. Instead, he or she may exhibit self-deception and delay getting help.

4. Avoid being distracted from the real issue—the individual's abuse of alcohol/drugs.

Do Not

Spend time or physical and emotional energy on distracting wild goose chases (e.g., finding out who gave the person alcohol/drugs or blaming the school system or other parents). These are all secondary issues. The primary issue is that your child or family member may have an alcohol/drug problem.

Compare the alcohol/drug problems of others that are more involved in alcohol/drug use. This is a form of rationalizing away the problem. Expressions such as "kids will be kids," "he or she will outgrow this," and "most people drink/drug this way" tend to discount the real dimensions of alcohol/drug dependence.

Get distracted by excuses for alcohol/drug abuse (e.g., "I'm experiencing a great deal of pressure right now" or "It's because my girlfriend just broke up with me"). The fact is the person has a problem with alcohol/drugs and is vulnerable to relapse when normal, stressful events happen again.

Take responsibility for the total problem. Avoid self-blaming statements (e.g., "I'm an awful parent" or "I should have _____; then he or she wouldn't have an alcohol/drug problem"). Self-blame serves only to distract from the issue at hand—the fact that your child or family member has an alcohol/drug problem and needs help. You cannot go back and change the past; you can only work on the future.

Obstacles to Interventions

There are many obstacles that prevent families from getting help for alcohol/drug problems. Getting the family member with the alcohol/drug problem into treatment may not be realistic unless these obstacles are first addressed. Some common obstacles to families getting help are listed in Table 9.4.

The Olympic Story

On an extremely hot summer day in 1984, I attended the Olympic Games in Los Angeles. Like most spectators that day, I tried to find a shady area on the lawn outside the stadium while awaiting the afternoon field events. While we watched Carl Lewis qualify for the long jump, a quiet, unsettling nervousness ran through the crowd in anticipation of the finish of the first women's marathon in Olympic history. The wide screen monitor at one end of the stadium broke the boredom and heat by showing Joan Benoit with a significant lead in the marathon. The men's 800-meter qualifying race drew our interest, distracting us from the heat of the afternoon.

TABLE 9.3 (CONTINUED)

Do's and Don'ts of Dealing with Someone Who Has an Alcohol/Drug Problem

4. Avoid being distracted from the real issue—the individual's abuse of alcohol/drugs. (continued)

Do

Seek treatment for the addicted person and the entire family. The sooner you do this, the better is the prognosis.

5. Seek professional help for alcohol/drug assessment, education, prevention, intervention, and treatment.

Do Not

Isolate from others and hide the family alcohol/drug problem. The longer you hide the problem from others to avoid feelings of shame and embarrassment, the more damage occurs to your family system.

Get advice from people who may have an alcohol/drug problem themselves or individuals who deny the problem. This only reinforces denial.

Attempt to counsel the family member who has the alcohol/drug problem yourself. This will inadvertently end up being another form of enabling behavior.

Do

Attend Alanon, Codependency Anonymous, and other self-help meetings and develop a relationship with a sponsor. This will help you develop a support system necessary to make changes.

Attend educational presentations, classes, and conferences that focus on parenting, family systems, prevention, alcohol/drug recovery, intervention, codependency, and other personal growth issues.

Find a counselor who specializes in alcohol/drug treatment, family systems, and codependency. For more information on choosing a counselor, see Chapter 11.

Take care of yourself and continue with your own recovery, regardless of whether the family member who has the alcohol/drug problem gets help.

The slow, methodical repertoire of the shot-putters was in full progress when the wide video screen came alive with Joan Benoit maintaining a significant lead. The crowd began to buzz with excitement. The shot-putters were caught by surprise as the more than 40,000 people in the coliseum began to applaud Benoit. The ensuing 30 to 40 minutes were like a New Year's Eve party as the crowd counted down the minutes until Benoit entered the stadium for the final two laps of her 26-mile ordeal. We were all standing, watching both the video screen and the western entrance to the coliseum. Finally, the moment came: the crowd exploded in cheers as Benoit entered and began her last two laps around the track. As she circled the track, each section of the stadium stood, cheering and waving little American flags. It was truly a wave of human emotion and pride affirming her accomplishment: the first women's Olympic marathon winner was an American. This was the crowd's hope and, for some, their only reason for attending the Olympics that day.

A few minutes later, I became aware of another struggle. A Swedish runner was approximately the sixth runner to enter the stadium. Benoit had already finished the race, and the crowd was still alive with energy. Its focus soon shifted to the Swedish runner, who, on entering the track, was staggering. She took two steps forward, then two steps sideways, then another step forward. Clearly, she had hit the wall and was suffering from oxygen deprivation. As she advanced on the track,

TABLE 9.4

Obstacles to Reaching Parents and Families

- Denial of family dysfunction/imbalance and alcohol/drug problems
- Skepticism about alcohol/drug messages that don't fit parents' own experience
- Assumption by parents that children's alcohol/drug use will be O.K.
- Distorted, depressed view of life by dysfunctional families
- Fear of being stigmatized or labeled as dysfunctional
- Fear of loss of confidentiality
- Narcissism of parents
- Lack of insurance resources for parenting/counseling services
- Lack of energy/time by parents
- Distrust of the system
- Lack of credible message sources for cultural/racial minority groups
- Lack of concern/respect for experts' opinions about alcohol/drugs
- Lack of awareness of community resources, discomfort with middle-class settings
- Overwhelming need for services for basic survival
- Cultural mores

Source: Office for Substance Abuse Prevention, 1990.

each section of the crowd rose and cheered her on. The human wave was in slow but full motion as the section where I was sitting stood up and cheered her on. As she began her second and last lap around the track, a medical team, dressed in their whites, ran alongside her. The thought struck me: what if we were all cheering and encouraging her to her death? The woman was clearly suffering, yet we applauded her to continue on despite the possibility of bodily harm. Fortunately, she did finish the race without any permanent physical damage. A physician in attendance told me that within a few hours her vital signs and physical functioning were back to normal. However, what if she had not been that fortunate?

This raises some important questions. Should there have been a medical intervention to assess her condition? In the heat of the race, do runners have a proper frame of physical and mental reference to decide if they are capable of continuing? Do we have a responsibility to intervene when someone is in danger of harming himself or herself?

This brief scenario from the 1984 Olympics illustrates one situation in which we might intervene. Other sports, on recreational to professional levels, also illustrate situations when there may be a need for intervention. Boxing, football, weight lifting, even team sports such as soccer, basketball, and baseball may require interventions to safeguard players. The use of protective equipment, rules that lower the risk of serious and/or permanent injury, and other advances minimize unnecessary harm to athletes, yet some athletes choose to disregard their own health to enhance performance. As pointed out in Chapter 3, they use steroids, painkillers, stimulants, and other drugs to attain a competitive edge. Advances in sports medicine are being applied as an intervention and preventive approach to injuries, in an attempt to stop serious long-term damage. Another situation where we might intervene is when individuals have alcohol/drug problems and may harm themselves or others.

Intervention Services

The concept of alcohol/drug intervention began in the 1960s, when Vernon Johnson—at that time, a pastor—felt frustrated when he was unable to help spouses of alcoholics. Deciding to abandon the traditional approach of waiting until the alcoholic/addict hit bottom, he tried a strategy that he later called intervention (Johnson 1986).

Intervene is defined by *Webster's Tenth New Collegiate Dictionary* as "to occur, fall, or come between points of time or events."* Alcohol/drug intervention is a process that prevents, alters, or interrupts the progression of the disease. The intervention is a process of getting involved or stepping into a situation in an attempt to interrupt the disease and to get the individual into alcohol/drug treatment. Persons who intervene choose to talk about the issue of alcohol/drug dependence that is destructive to the individuals, their families, and friends. Due to the alcoholic/addict's strong denial system, a trained interventionist with an expertise in chemical dependency treatment must lead or facilitate the intervention.

Intervention services are offered by most chemical dependency inpatient and residential treatment centers. Trained chemical dependency counselors also specialize in conducting interventions. The choice of the interventionist is a critical element in determining the success of an intervention. Local, state, and national alcohol/drug help lines are excellent referral sources for finding trained and experienced interventionists.

Intervention Approaches

There are a variety of approaches to the alcohol/drug intervention, including formal and informal chemical dependency interventions, in which each interventionist has his or her own style of conducting the intervention. The principles described in this chapter form a basic framework within which most interventionists work.

Professional Intervention Assistance

Whatever the format or style, conducting an intervention without professional guidance is often doomed to failure, no matter how powerful the individual. Untrained, grandstanding individuals who coerce someone into chemical dependency treatment often cause further resistance by the individual needing help. Do not use this information to try to conduct an intervention on your own; consult a professional interventionist for help.

Intervention as a Caring Response

The most important aspect of an intervention is that it is a caring effort designed to interrupt the disease of alcoholism and drug addiction. Individuals involved in an intervention can be effective only if they maintain a caring, behavior-specific approach and support each other within the basic guidelines of their intervention group.

---

*By permission. From Merriam-Webster's Collegiate® Dictionary, Tenth Edition © 1993 by Merriam-Webster, Inc., publisher of the Merriam-Webster® dictionaries.

Goals of Intervention

The primary goal in developing an intervention is to get the addicted person to recognize that he or she has an alcohol/drug problem and to get that person into appropriate chemical dependency treatment. Treatment is usually a minimum 21- to 28-day inpatient or residential program.

Secondary goals of the intervention are to

1. Provide an opportunity for those who care about the alcoholic/addict to express concern about the impact the alcoholic/addict's dysfunctional behavior has had on them
2. Provide information on alcohol/drug addiction and family patterns of interaction, such as enabling behavior, to the significant others (parents, spouses, family members, employers, and peers)
3. Promote the development of a healthy family system and provide resource information for family members to continue working on their issues

Family Interventions

Interventions are 100 percent effective in that, regardless of whether the alcoholic/addict decides to get help and go to treatment, family members go on with their recovery. The family has begun a process of change. The growth that the family members experience in developing an intervention can empower them to continue to be true to their feelings and to their own individual recovery, whether or not the alcoholic/addict decides to seek treatment. Via the intervention process, the family members learn about the disease of alcohol/drug addiction. They recognize their own enabling behavior and the role they play in the dynamics of the disease. The intervention may be the first time in a long time that the family members have interacted by functionally discussing their feelings. It may be the first time they have candidly discussed the impact the alcoholic/addict's alcohol or drug use has had on each of them.

Candidates for Intervention

Using a formal intervention process on adolescents, or young adults who are developmentally still at the adolescent stage, is usually ineffective. Adolescents often feel violated by the process of intervention. Because they are still exploring their own issues of identity and boundaries, they feel that it is unfair for family members to be planning an intervention without their knowledge. Adolescents fail to recognize or acknowledge that all previous direct efforts have not been effective in getting them to listen and understand the true dimensions of their problems.

Interventions are far more effective in getting individuals into treatment, when addicts recognize that their behavior has been a problem. The addict who still values and respects members of the intervention group is the best candidate. In some situations, addicts have alienated so many people that only job-related people are left. This relationship with an employer or business associates might be the integral element that makes some addicts good candidates for intervention.

Stages of Formal Intervention

The four basic stages of a formal intervention are assessment, preintervention, intervention, and postintervention. The rest of this chapter describes these stages with many examples and a case study.

Assessment

Families consider an alcohol/drug intervention because a family member recognizes that the family needs to do something about the person with the alcohol/drug problem. Likely, people have approached the addict about getting help on numerous occasions. Despite their efforts, the addict still chooses not to recognize the problem or get help. The alcoholic/addict's goal is to continue drinking or drugging.

A family member begins the intervention process by contacting a professional who conducts interventions. The interventionist schedules an appointment with family members to assess the alcohol/drug problem and to determine if an intervention is appropriate.

An experienced interventionist is trained to assess alcohol/drug problems. In the initial assessment sessions, several family members, friends, colleagues, and even the employer describe what they know about the alcohol/drug use of the person being assessed for the intervention. Individuals seeking to intervene on a family member with an alcohol/drug problem are often at a late stage of frustration with the alcoholic/addict's dysfunctional and destructive behavior. Many look at the intervention as a last-ditch alternative. Despite the family's urgency to conduct an intervention, the interventionist conducts a proper assessment to determine if the person really does have an alcohol/drug problem.

The key element of the assessment is eliciting *behavior-specific information* and avoiding hearsay and generalized information. The interventionist needs specific times, dates, and firsthand knowledge of the actual level of consumption of alcohol and drugs. Some assessment questions are "What makes you think the individual has a problem with alcohol/drugs?" "What have been the consequences of this individual's alcohol/drug use?" The interventionist asks family members to explain or clarify the

Frequency of use, amounts used (dose and routes of administration), and set and setting of use

Patterns of use—binges, periods of nonuse, and cycle of use

History of negative consequences—overdoses, medical complications, and physical and emotional harm

Periods of abstinence, if any, and methods used

Any medical conditions that affects alcohol/drug use

Use of coffee, cigarettes, and medications and other addictions

Difficulties with the criminal-justice system

Financial problems and interpersonal problems

Family members at the assessment sessions are asked to describe specifically what they know about the addict's use of alcohol and drugs and resulting dysfunctional and destructive behavior. The assessment clarifies the dimensions

Case Study 9.2

Intervention Without Proper Assessment

J.R.

J.R., an aspiring vice-president in a developing company, contacted an interventionist and requested an intervention for another vice-president in the same company. The family members of the person with the supposed alcohol problem believed that Roger had been drinking regularly but were not sure that he had an alcohol problem. Insisting that his coworker's drinking was a problem, J. R. was unable to come up with any behavior-specific examples of increased alcohol use. Despite the limited information and secondhand generalizations, the interventionist decided to go ahead with the intervention. The result was disastrous. Roger did not have an alcohol problem and quickly identified sabotage by his colleague, who desired his sales territory. Needless to say, Roger was justified in proceeding with litigation against the interventionist for not conducting a proper assessment.

This story illustrates the pivotal importance of making an accurate assessment of the alcohol/drug problem before proceeding with the intervention. This is a very rare situation. In most situations, it is very clear that there is an alcohol/drug problem and that an intervention is justified.

---

of the problem with alcohol/drugs. The family, and others present, usually recognize, confirm, and validate their own worst fears—the individual has an alcohol/drug problem.

Another extremely important aspect of the assessment is to determine whether the person you are going to intervene on is able to listen and understand. Someone who is going to physically attack, verbally explode, or rage at others at the intervention is not appropriate for an intervention. During the assessment stage, interventionists often ask the family members and others present, "How does the person you are planning to intervene on deal with anger?" "What do you think his or her reaction is going to be to the intervention?" These questions should elicit responses that determine if the individual is violent and if there have been some physical violations in the past. Sometimes individuals can be paranoid and/or delusional, especially if they have been using cocaine, crack, or free base. Obviously, you do not want to do an intervention if there is a high risk that the individual will be violent or unable to listen and understand. One alternative is to videotape the intervention and give it to the addict.

Some people have a negative reaction to the concept of an alcohol/drug intervention. They believe that it is an invasion, or a violation, of the individual and his or her right to use alcohol/drugs. For the intervention to be effective, it must be planned without the knowledge of the person being intervened on. Some individuals have difficulty with this behind-the-scenes aspect. Once the interventionist has assessed that an intervention is warranted, members of the intervention group must decide whether they are comfortable proceeding with the intervention.

Preintervention

The preintervention stage consists of all the sessions necessary to prepare for the actual intervention to take place. The ingredients essential for a successful intervention include (1) the commitment and participation of meaningful and significant others (family members, friends, relatives, peers, and children); (2) a proper assessment by the interventionist; and (3) specific, nonjudgmental information about the individual's alcohol and drug behavior.

In preparation for the intervention, preintervention sessions develop a cohesive group of significant others—a group that has the goal of getting the alcoholic/addict into appropriate treatment.

The interventionist begins developing this group by educating the members, giving them information about the dynamics of chemical dependency. The education emphasizes the progressive nature of the disease of alcoholism/drug addiction, which affects the entire family.

The group members then develop their scripts and role-play the intervention. Role-playing allows the group to anticipate the reactions of the person they are going to intervene on. The group members can then redevelop their intervention to make it more effective.

The alcoholic/addict is a master in distracting the intervention group from the goals of the intervention. When each family member communicates generalizations and judgments, the alcoholic/addict picks at their statements and distracts the group, thus weakening their ability to get the alcoholic/addict to commit to treatment. Therefore, the members of the intervention group must develop and communicate behavior-specific examples of the alcoholic/addict's dysfunctional and self-destructive behavior.

The following examples illustrate generalized statements, followed by the alcoholic/addict's distracting statements. The appropriate behavior-specific statement follows each set of generalized and distracting responses.

Example 1

Generalized and blaming statements: "Boy, you were really wasted at the party picnic and got violent. You were drunk and loaded on cocaine."

Alcoholic/addict distracting statements: "What do you mean wasted? You were drinking just as much as I was. Weren't you? Boy are you hypocritical. You use cocaine."

Behavior-specific statements: "John, I'm here because I care about you. On Saturday, July 4, 1991, at the company picnic, I saw you drink five beers from 1 to 3 P.M., then snort six lines of cocaine, which was followed by two more beers. You sat down in the outfield during the softball game and fell asleep. When I went over to wake you up, you threw a punch at me, right in front of the head of our company. You left the field. I found you a half hour later, with a six-pack in the back of your car. Two of the cans of beer were already empty. I am worried about you. I'm afraid you are going to lose your job. You've been like a brother to me. I pray that you will get help. I know it's the alcohol and drugs."

Example 2

Generalized and blaming statements: "You are an awful husband and father. You are always using drugs and drinking too much. Last night you were drinking and snorting cocaine all night. You scared the kids to death that night by yelling so loud at them, like a madman."

Alcoholic/addict distracting statements: "You think you are such a great mother? I remember the time you. . . ."

Behavior-specific statements: "John, I'm your wife and I'm here because I care about you. On Friday night, November 3, I went to the church meeting. When I came home at 10:15 P.M., I smelled alcohol on your breath and clothes. There was an empty gram bottle of cocaine on the kitchen table and three lines of cocaine still on the mirror. There were 12 empty beer cans on the living room floor and the kids were hiding in their closet upstairs. When I went into their room, they ran to me, shaking and out of control. That night I had to sleep with them because they were so frightened. The next day, they told me you threw beer cans at them and told them you would kill them if they didn't stop bothering you. I love you, John; I know it's the alcohol and drugs. I would like all of us to get help."

Each person involved in the intervention uses the following script format to avoid generalized, blaming statements:

"I'm here because I care about you. You are my _____. I *care* about you."
"I saw _____" (describe the behavior-specific incidents that occurred)
"I feel _____" (embarrassed, hurt, frightened, worried, ashamed, etc.)
"I know it's the drugs." (or the alcohol or cocaine)
"I want you [us] to get help."

Script Example

"John, I'm here because *I care* about you. We've been friends a very long time. During Christmas, *I saw* you snort half a gram of cocaine. In the next hour, you drank four beers. *I felt embarrassed* when you were trying to kiss your niece. *I felt ashamed. I saw* the hurt on your wife's face. *I know it's the cocaine. I know it's the alcohol. I want you to get help.*"

Some interventionists prefer the words "I want you to get help." Others prefer "I want us to get help" because everyone in the family is going to get help to stop enabling the alcoholic/addict's use of alcohol/drugs.

During the preintervention, the intervention group members determine

1. When the intervention will take place
2. Where the intervention will take place—usually a neutral setting such as the interventionist's office is best
3. Who will bring the person to the intervention
4. Their scripts, role-play the intervention, and determine the most effective way of communicating their message
5. In which order each member will talk during the intervention
6. Who is going to ask for a commitment to listen from the person being intervened on

7. That arrangements have been made with the alcohol/drug treatment program; insurance and other details have been completed; and a bed is reserved at the treatment center starting on the day of the intervention
8. All contingencies, so that the individual can go directly to the treatment program; bags have been packed and are in the car; and a family member drives the addict directly to the treatment program.

Every detail is planned, even the seating arrangement. The actual intervention session will start and flow as planned. The family members will be prepared to continue their own recovery, regardless of the addict's decision. The session will not escalate into an uncontrollable situation. The family will approach the intervention as a process, rather than a static event. Bear in mind that, if the preintervention sessions have gone well, the interventionist is available to help the family members during the intervention, but most often he or she plays a minimal, facilitating role.

Intervention

Each intervention is unique. However, they all have the same common ingredients for success, such as a nonjudgmental tone and behavior-specific caring responses by family and friends. The following is an example of an intervention.

Audrey is an attractive, energetic 33-year-old. She owns a very successful travel agency. She is the single parent of two children: Andy is 12 years old and Bridget is 7 years old. Audrey is dynamic, aggressive, and—the most critical feature—an alcoholic.

Audrey's sister Mary, 39, is concerned enough to seek intervention for her sister. Both sisters grew up in an alcoholic family system. Their father died of alcoholism when Mary was 16 and Audrey was 9 years old. Those involved with the intervention are the following:

Mary—Audrey's older sister
Ann—a very successful businesswoman, Audrey and Mary's mother
Roger—Mary's son, Audrey's nephew, a 20-year-old student at the University of
    Washington
Andy—Audrey's 12-year-old son

Mary has taken Audrey to the interventionist's office under the pretense that they have been having some family counseling sessions for her son Roger. She said they wanted Audrey to participate in one session. All the family members are present at the office, waiting for Audrey and Mary to arrive.

Mary:	Audrey, this is Dr. Fields. [Shakes hands.] Just sit right here. Audrey, we are all here because we care about you. We are concerned about you and the children. We would like to be able to talk to you about our concerns. We would each like to say some things. We need your commitment to listen to us and not to respond until we are finished. You will have an opportunity to respond then. Will you promise to first listen to us and not talk until we are finished?
Audrey:	But, I thought we were here for Roger.
Mary:	We are here for you, Roger, and all the family members.

Audrey: Yeah, but you didn't let me know what this was about.

Mary: Audrey, we wanted you to come. Will you just hear us out? Then you can have your chance.

Audrey: I, I . . . don't . . . yeah, I guess so. O.K., I'll listen to what you have to say.

[Establishing ground rules allows each family member to talk without being distracted by the addict's ambiguous arguments. Having the addict agree to listen and not talk back is an essential ingredient for the intervention to be successful. Even though Audrey has been deceived in getting her to the intervention, she knows or suspects what the meeting is about. She is curious and is even challenging the group to try to affect her.]

Roger: Thank you. You've been like a big sister to me, even though you are my aunt. You have provided a lot of opportunities to me. You've taken me on vacations and introduced me to all sorts of people, activities, and even jobs that I never would have had access to. I care about you a great deal. You've been a tremendous influence and I am very proud of you. I am here because I love you.

Lately, however, I find that I'm not so proud of you anymore. I'm worried about you. I'm worried about Andy. I'm worried about Bridget. At your birthday party on January 7, you came home smelling of alcohol. You had three margaritas within an hour. I saw you in the kitchen, downing two doubles, as if they were water. You stumbled out of the kitchen and fell and cut your lip.

Audrey: That was my birthday party. Don't you understand?

Roger: You promised you would listen. After you cut yourself, when Andy, Bridget, and I came into the kitchen to help, you screamed and yelled at us to get away. Andy was so frightened he hid in his room and Bridget couldn't stop crying. They said they were so frightened that you were going to hit them again.

This isn't the first time this has happened. The same thing happened when we went down to Mexico. You had four drinks at the airport bar and four drinks on the flight. I was so embarrassed when you were flirting with the man next to you. The kids were embarrassed when you were kissing him and when you yelled at me for interfering. When we got to our hotel, the first thing you did was to order more booze.

In February, I was at the travel agency and you went into the bathroom. You invited me in and you had some lines of cocaine that you offered me. I saw you do 10 lines of cocaine and then come out and act as if everything was O.K. You made six trips to the bathroom in the hour that I was there.

Audrey: I didn't do that much. As if you are so innocent!

Roger: You promised that you would listen and not interrupt. I was with you the night you got arrested for driving under the influence of alcohol. The kids were frightened sitting in the back seat. Despite my arguing with you, you insisted on driving. I was so frightened that we all would be killed. I went along because I felt guilty that you would kill yourself and the kids. I tried to take the keys away from you, but you wouldn't let me. I was so angry with your boyfriend, Al, for insisting that you were O.K., when you couldn't even walk straight. I was so angry with you when the police arrested you in front of your children. But I was more upset with myself for allowing myself to get drawn into the whole situation.

Audrey, despite all of this I love you and the children and I want you to get help.

Audrey: What kind of help?

Roger: [No response, head tilted down to ground, feeling emotionally spent.]

Ann: Audrey, you were a beautiful child; I gave birth to you. I love you a great deal. You were always so fun loving, energetic, and interested in so many things. We went shopping the other day, last Wednesday, and you had four beers at lunch, after you said you would cut back. You told me that you were just wired. You were agitated, nervous, jittery. Audrey, I'm frightened for you. When we came home from the travel agency last Friday, you smelled of alcohol. You were driving erratically. I was afraid we would get pulled over and you'd be arrested again. When I told you that you were in no condition to drive, you yelled at me to stop nagging.

Audrey: You, you're always telling me what to do. You're always bothering me. You're always involved in my life, telling me how to parent my kids.

Ann: That day, I saw you drink three beers before we left the agency.

Audrey: You guys are in this together. I don't even know why I'm here.

Roger: You said you'd listen.

Audrey: How can I listen to you if you keep on getting together? How could you guys get together behind my back to do this?

Ann: We're here because we care about you. We love you. I know it's the drugs. I know it's the alcohol. I want us to get some help.

Mary: We've grown up together. We've always been close. I love you. I care about you. Last week, we went out to Morgan's restaurant. You drank five margaritas within an hour and a half. You were snorting cocaine in the bathroom. You left the restaurant with two men whom you didn't know. I am really frightened for you. The next day you called me and told me you had a problem with alcohol and wanted help. Two days later, on Sunday, when I asked you about getting help, you said that you were doing much better and were getting your act together.

It was only a week later, that Friday night, when you were back at Morgan's. I saw you drink three doubles in an hour. You insisted that I stay. It was too hard to stay and watch you order another drink. I'm afraid that you are hurting yourself. I worry about you. I want my younger sister back. I want you to get help.

Andy: [Tears rolling from his eyes] Mommy, I am afraid when you drink and use drugs that you will hurt me. I am afraid that you will hurt Bridget. I want you to go get help. Will you?

Audrey: [Hugs Andy] Yes, I'll get help. I love you and don't want you to be frightened.

Mary: We have reserved a bed at the treatment center and Roger will drive you there.

Audrey: You mean you want me to go right now?

Mary: Yes.

Audrey: But what about the appointments at the agency?

Mary: I've arranged for Natalie to come in and manage the agency while you are gone.

Audrey: But what about the meeting with the accountant on Thursday?

Ann/Mom: I can cover the meeting, since I know all about the new bookkeeping system.

Audrey: What about clothes?

Mary: I packed some of your things in a suitcase. Anything else you want I can get to you tomorrow.

Audrey: Can the children come and visit?

Mary: After the first week, there are regular family visits and a family counseling program. We chose this program because it specializes in providing counseling for young children.

Audrey: I guess you thought of everything.
              [In reality, the family did think of everything. Any potential form of denial was anticipated, so that Audrey and her family could get the help they needed.]

In the event that Audrey did not agree to go into treatment, the family had prepared another bottom-line script. The purpose of the bottom-line script is to let the addict know that, if she refuses to go into treatment, the family is not going to continue to enable her alcohol/drug use, as they have in the past. In implementing the bottom-line script, family members have to be willing to follow through with their bottom lines. Otherwise, there is no point in stating them. For example, if Audrey had refused to go into treatment, the bottom-line stage of the intervention would have followed:

Roger: Audrey, I care about you. You've been a person that I greatly admire. I love you a great deal. I'm frightened about the alcohol and drugs. I'm fearful that you'll hurt yourself or the kids. If you don't go into treatment, I can no longer come over to the house. I won't see you until you get help. It's too difficult for me to see you killing yourself.

Ann/Mom: Audrey, I love you. You are a wonderful, caring mother. I see you teaching the kids to read and doing wonderful, creative things with them. You'll always be my daughter. If you don't get help I'm going to have my lawyer start the process of declaring you unfit. It hurts me to do this, but I can't allow the children to be abused the way they are. I know it's the alcohol and drugs, and I want us to get help. [Ann cries.]

Mary:	We've been more than sisters. We've been best friends. If you don't get help, I'll help Mom get the children in a safe environment and away from the alcohol and drugs. I'm afraid for the children and their future. Please get help.

The bottom-line script is implemented only if the individual refuses to get treatment. If the individual still refuses treatment after the bottom line, the intervention is over, and the family members implement the bottom line.

Postintervention

The trauma and emotion of the intervention affects all of the family members and friends involved in the intervention. Immediately after a successful intervention, families are often relieved and hopeful. However, the road to family recovery has just begun. The family should get together with the interventionist within a month, prior to the end of the 30-day inpatient program attended by the person who was intervened on. This gives the family members an opportunity both to reflect on their original commitment to the intervention and on their own enabling behavior and to reiterate their commitment to recovery.

Summary

Any attempt to create awareness in others that they might have an alcohol/drug problem is an intervention. Intervention is defined as an action taken by someone to interrupt the progression of problems with alcohol/drugs.

Some defense components of resistance to change are denial, minimization, projection, rationalization, compliance, obsessive focusing, and acting out.

An intervention model explored in this chapter is motivational interviewing. Motivational interviewing is a client-centered approach that uses cognitive therapy, systems theory, and social psychology to aid the patient in taking action toward beneficial change, as well as maintaining change and avoiding relapses once change is implemented. The stages of motivational interviewing are precontemplative, contemplative, determination, action, maintenance, and relapse prevention. The "OARS" of motivational interviewing are open-ended questions, affirmations, reflecting, and summarizing. The FRAMES of motivational interviewing are feedback, responsibility, advice, menu, empathy, and self-efficacy.

A formal intervention is a caring, nonjudgmental, behavior-specific effort by the family to get an alcoholic/addict into treatment. Intervention is of benefit to the family because it creates an awareness of the actual dimensions and progressive nature of alcoholism/drug addiction. Interventions empower family members to change their codependent, enabling behavior. An intervention is a key approach to starting the process of recovery, not only for the alcoholic/addict but also for the family members.

References

Johnson, Vernon E. *Intervention: How to Help Someone Who Doesn't Want Help.* Minneapolis, MN: Johnson Institute Books, 1986.

Miller, William, and Stephen Rollnick. *Motivational Interviewing: Preparing People to Change Addictive Behavior.* New York: Guilford Press, 1991.

Co-occurring Disorders with Substance Abuse

Chapter Objectives

1. Define the terms *dual disorder, comorbid disorder,* and *co-occurring disorder,* and cite some prevalence rates.

2. Describe the vegetative signs of depression (affective disorders).

3. Describe the differences among major depression, dysthymia, atypical depression, bipolar disorder, and cyclothymic disorder.

4. Identify some common problems, based on the chapter case studies, in treating a depression co-occurring with chemical dependency.

5. Define and describe some common features of personality disorders, especially antisocial and borderline personality disorder.

6. Identify some common problems, based on the chapter case studies and chapter content, in treating the co-occurring disorder of antisocial personality disorder.

7. Identify some common problems, based on the chapter case studies and chapter content, in treating the co-occurring disorder of borderline personality disorder.

⚔ Definition of a Co-occurring Disorder

The terms *dual disorders, comorbid disorders,* and *co-occurring disorders* have been used interchangeably to describe the condition of having both a psychiatric diagnosis and a chemical dependency diagnosis. The symptoms produced by psychiatric disorders and chemical dependency can overlap. The concept reminds us of this overlap in symptoms and highlights the need to make an accurate diagnosis, so that appropriate treatment can be provided.

Until recently, counselors in the mental health and chemical dependency fields took a somewhat provincial outlook. Each has accused the other of minimizing the importance of his or her own perspective. In many ways, the situation has become like the story of the blind men asked to describe an elephant. Each described it according to the body part he could touch but without regard to the remaining, unseen portions of the beast. Recent

years have witnessed the emergence of a greater understanding and acceptance of the dual disorders or co-occurring disorder concept. Increasingly, members of both fields are educating themselves about each other's areas of specialty.

Clinically, we think of patients as existing on a continuum between purely psychiatric disorders at one end and purely chemical dependency problems on the other. Most patients lie somewhere between the extremes. An evaluation would take into account the relative position on the continuum. Today, it is rare to find a patient who has purely one condition, either psychiatric or chemical dependency. Many psychiatric patients are affected by alcohol/drugs, and many patients with alcohol/drug problems have psychiatric symptoms.

It is common to see prevalence rates of substance abuse ranging between 40 and 60 percent of any psychiatric population. A report of a commis-

---

Some material in this chapter has been adapted from Field and Vanderbelt 1992a, 1992b.

sion of mental health providers in New York State estimated that, of the 75,000 individuals hospitalized in New York each year for psychiatric conditions, close to 40,000 admissions "involve persons with dual disabilities or a serious psychiatric illness and an alcohol and/or drug abuse condition" (Bauer 1987).

A more recent, community-based survey of 20,291 people found that 53 percent of the surveyed drug abusers and 39 percent of the alcohol abusers had at least one mental illness, and 29 percent of the mentally ill in the survey abused either alcohol or drugs (Regier et al. 1990). Kenneth Minkoff, M.D., associate professor of psychiatry at Harvard and a proponent of the integrated model of disorders, believes that co-occurring disorders are an expectation, not an exception.

The evolution of the co-occurring disorders concept has paralleled our expanded understanding of the biological nature of both alcoholism and certain mental disorders. The 1990s was labeled the "decade of the brain," as we learned more about brain functions and their relation to affect. Research suggests that the causes of mental illness such as schizophrenia, depression, anxiety disorders, and affective disorders are substantially, if not primarily, biological. Genetic research of families with a history of alcoholism has supported the biological nature of alcoholism. There is a higher rate of alcoholism and other drug abuse in the families of patients with affect and mood disorders and vice versa. Quite possibly the genetic traits that predispose one to depression or other mental illness may be the same or similar genetic traits for chemical dependency.

The two major co-occurring disorders covered in this chapter are (1) affective (feeling) disorders and chemical dependency and (2) personality disorders and chemical dependency.

The Difference Between a Depressive Mood and a Depression Disorder

It is common to feel down, sad, or even depressed after experiencing disappointment, frustration (blocked goal), setback, or trauma. Feelings of sadness, melancholia, grief, and loss are normal aspects of life. Working through the grief or loss is an essential feature of growth. However, when these depressive feelings persist beyond the common period of time to work through them, an affective disorder may be developing.

It is also normal to feel bad or low in early recovery from abusing alcohol and other drugs. Some of this is due to withdrawal from the chemicals but, even after withdrawal, problems in mood may persist. Chemical dependency causes financial, civil, criminal, interpersonal and family problems in the lives of many alcoholics/addicts—all of which can cause lasting pain. However, what is going on if the depression continues beyond normal alcohol/drug recovery?

Everyone experiences symptoms of depression from time to time. When symptoms become severe and persistent, however, diagnosis of an affective (feeling) disorder could be warranted. As researchers and clinicians have used various systems of classifying depression over the years, they have increasingly recognized the different types and subtypes of depression. What differentiates various types from one another is their **severity, frequency, duration,** and **precipitating factors.**

✗ **Affective (Feeling) Disorders and Substance Use Disorders**

Affective disorders are different from the normal emotions of feeling down or sad. The following questions may help distinguish common depressive feelings from an affective disorder:

Severity: How deep is your depression? How low do you feel? Are you suicidal or self-destructive?

Frequency: How often do you feel depressed?

Duration: How long does the depression last? Are there periods when you are not depressed?

Precipitating factors: What triggers your depression? Do you know what is causing your depression?

Regardless of what causes depression initially, once it has been present for long enough it locks in and takes on a life of its own. This is another way of saying that the brain changes physiologically in response to internal or external events that have persisted for a sufficient time. After the physiological changes have taken place, a number of biological, or physical, signs of depression emerge. These *vegetative signs* include disturbances in the basic biological functions that the brain regulates. Vegetative signs of depression include the following:

- Disrupted sleep patterns
- Difficulty with appetite and weight regulation
- Decreased cognitive functioning (including problems with concentration, memory, and problem solving)
- Decreased libido, or sex drive
- Lack of motivation, decreased energy (anergia)
- Difficulty experiencing pleasure (anhedonia)

Denial and Depression

The psychological aspects of depression bring with it feelings of shame, as outlined in Chapter 6. Many individuals are extremely frightened to be labeled depressed, labeled manic-depressive (with bipolar disorder), or labeled with other affective and mood-cycling disorders. The denial of these feeling disorders is often self-medicated with the use of alcohol/drugs in an attempt to avoid the shame. Despite the fact that a vast majority (99 percent) of individuals suffering from affective disorders can be helped, only one in three depressed individuals seeks help. It is estimated that over 10 million people suffer from depressive illness, and 2 million people suffer from bipolar disorder. Serious depressions are "whole body" disorders affecting body, feelings, thoughts, and behaviors (U.S. Department of Health and Human Services 1987). Most people view themselves as weak and inferior in not having the will power to overcome depressive illness. This is much like the denial of the disease of alcoholism and drug addiction. In fact, depressive disorder is a disease much like alcohol/drug addiction in that it has a known etiology, gets progressively worse over time, and has significant negative consequences if untreated.

Categories of Mood Disorders

Some common affective disorders are

- Major depression
- Dysthymic disorder (a low-grade depression)

Case Study 10.1

Major Depression and Addiction

Elaine

Elaine is a 53-year-old divorced woman with two previous psychiatric hospitalizations for severe depression. These were treated successfully with antidepressant medication. She returned to her psychiatrist after a 10-year absence due to progressively worsening depression for two months. Further questioning revealed that she had experienced anxiety symptoms last year and her gynecologist had prescribed diazepam (Valium). She took the medication in low doses as prescribed until sustaining a neck injury in an automobile accident five months ago. At that time, the doctor prescribed narcotic pain medication. Initially, she took the pain medication as prescribed but later took the medication in increasing doses. She found that her pain and anxiety symptoms were manageable with the higher doses and she simultaneously increased her daily dose of Valium, taking a moderate to heavy dose at night to help her overcome her physical discomfort and to improve sleep. Her escalating use of the medication surprises her since, she had never used similar drugs in the past and had avoided alcohol and street drugs because of religious beliefs. She is troubled by a growing preoccupation with suicide and fears that she may commit suicide, as her mother and maternal grandmother did. A physical exam by her internist later in the day revealed slightly elevated blood pressure, sweaty palms, and slightly dilated pupils.

Elaine is a patient with a history of major depression episodes and a superimposed addiction to prescription drugs. Similar to many patients, anxiety symptoms predated the onset of depression symptoms. These had been fairly well controlled with a low dose of diazepam until she sustained an injury and developed chronic pain. Increase in use of pain medication and diazepam then followed, and she rapidly developed a high tolerance to the medication. She is now experiencing mild withdrawal symptoms (sweaty palms, elevated blood pressure and dilated pupils) and is in the midst of a depression. She needs to be withdrawn from the narcotic and benzodiazepine medication. This might be accomplished as an outpatient, but her thoughts of suicide complicate the picture. It would be more prudent to hospitalize her for detoxification. Many patients experience irritability and agitation during withdrawal; these symptoms might make her more likely to act on her suicidal thoughts. Given her strong family history of depression (suicide by mother and grandmother) and her previous personal history of depression, it is likely that she will need treatment with an antidepressant. It might be best to wait for a few days until her physical symptoms of withdrawal subside before adding another medication to her system. She will benefit from an outpatient chemical dependency treatment program following inpatient detoxification.

- Atypical depression (depression related to sudden loss)
- Organic depression
- Bipolar disorder, formerly referred to as manic-depressive illness (severe mood swings)
- Cyclothymic disorder (a less severe form of mood swings)

Case studies in this section give you an understanding of the dynamics of the affective disorder and chemical dependency. In some case studies, chemical dependency is the primary diagnosis. Other case studies demonstrate that, even after sobriety, the underlying affective disorder still persists and requires treatment.

Major Depression

This depressive syndrome may occur as a single episode or as repeated episodes over the years. This diagnosis generally connotes a severe depressive episode with fairly clear onset and accompanying vegetative signs. Individuals suffering from major depression exhibit difficulty in the most basic of tasks (e.g., getting out of bed, brushing their teeth).

Episodes of major depression typically last from 6 to 12 months and then clear sometimes even without treatment. However, an episode can last significantly longer. Episodes of depression that are longer in duration require adequate and careful attentiveness and sensitivity to potential suicide attempts. (See Table 10.1.)

TABLE 10.1

Diagnostic Criteria of Major Depressive Disorder

A. At least five of the following symptoms have been present during the same two-week period and represent a change from previous functioning; at least one of the symptoms is either (1) depressed mood or (2) loss of interest or pleasure. (Do not include symptoms that are clearly due to a physical condition, mood-incongruent delusions or hallucinations, incoherence, or marked loosening of associations.)
   1. Depressed mood (or can be irritable mood in children and adolescents) most of the day, nearly every day, as indicated either by subjective account or observation by others
   2. Markedly diminished interest or pleasure in all, or almost all, activities most of the day, nearly every day (as indicated either by subjective account or observation by others of apathy most of the time)
   3. Significant weight loss or weight gain when not dieting (e.g., more than 5% of body weight in a month), or decrease or increase in appetite nearly every day (in children, consider failure to make expected weight gains)
   4. Insomnia or hypersomnia nearly every day
   5. Psychomotor agitation or retardation nearly every day (observable by others, not merely subjective feelings of restlessness or being slowed down)
   6. Fatigue or loss of energy nearly every day
   7. Feelings of worthlessness or excessive or inappropriate guilt (which may be delusional) nearly every day (not merely self-reproach or guilt about being sick)
   8. Diminished ability to think or concentrate, or indecisiveness, nearly every day (either by subjective account or as observed by others)
   9. Recurrent thoughts of death (not just fear of dying), recurrent suicidal ideation without a specific plan, or a suicide attempt or a specific plan for committing suicide
B. 1. It cannot be established that an organic factor initiated and maintained the disturbance.
   2. The disturbance is not a normal reaction to the death of a loved one (uncomplicated bereavement).
      Note: Morbid preoccupation with worthlessness, suicidal ideation, marked functional impairment or psychomotor retardation, or prolonged duration suggest bereavement complicated by major depression.
C. At no time during the disturbance have there been delusions or hallucinations for as long as two weeks in the absence of prominent mood symptoms (i.e., before the mood symptoms developed or after they have remitted).
D. Not superimposed on schizophrenia, schizophreniform disorder, delusional disorder, or psychotic disorder.

From American Psychiatric Association: *Diagnostic and Statistical Manual of Mental Disorders*, Fourth Edition, Revised, Washington, D.C., American Psychiatric Association, 1994.

Dysthymic Disorder

Dysthymic disorder is a mood disorder of longer term than major depression but is a lower-grade depression. Patients with dysthymic disorder frequently comment that they have never felt completely happy or that, if they do achieve a period of feeling well, it is relatively short-lived. Anxiety symptoms, headaches, and muscle tension are frequent, in addition to symptoms of depression. (See Table 10.2.) Patients with dysthymic disorder come to assume that their own baseline mood is normal; they are frequently surprised that they actually do experience improvement with treatment. Only 25 percent of patients with major depression receive adequate diagnosis and treatment; it is very likely that the percentage is even lower for dysthymic disorder, given the less intense and less notable degree of symptoms.

Atypical Depression

Atypical depression is not a common condition, as the symptoms and duration of symptoms are different from those of major depression or dysthymic disorder.

Atypical depression is frequently the diagnosis for many adult children of alcoholics. Usually, a patient with atypical depression experiences intense and sudden depressions in response to interpersonal loss or threatened interpersonal loss.

TABLE 10.2

Diagnostic Criteria for Dysthymic Disorder

A. Depressed mood (or can be irritable mood in children and adolescents) most of the day, more days than not, as indicated either by subjective account or observation by others, for at least two years (one year for children and adolescents)

B. Presence, while depressed, of at least two of the following:
    1. Poor appetite or overeating
    2. Insomnia or hypersomnia
    3. Low energy or fatigue
    4. Low self-esteem
    5. Poor concentration or difficulty making decisions
    6. Feelings of hopelessness

C. During a two-year period (one year for children and adolescents) of the disturbance, never without the symptoms in A for more than two months at a time

D. No evidence of an unequivocal major depressive episode during the first two years (one year for children and adolescents) of the disturbance. *Note:* There may have been a previous major depressive episode, provided there was a full remission (no significant signs or symptoms for six months) before development of the dysthymia. In addition, after these two years (one year in children or adolescents) of dysthymia, there may be superimposed episodes of major depression, in which case both diagnoses are given.

E. Has never had a manic episode or an unequivocal hypomanic episode

F. Not superimposed on a chronic psychotic disorder, such as schizophrenia or delusional disorder

G. It cannot be established that an organic factor initiated and maintained the disturbance—e.g., prolonged administration of an antihypertensive medication.

From American Psychiatric Association: *Diagnostic and Statistical Manual of Mental Disorders,* Third Edition, Revised, Washington, D.C., American Psychiatric Association, 1987.

Case Study 10.2

Eeyore Syndrome

The donkey, Eeyore, in the children's story *Winnie-the-Pooh,* could be clinically described as suffering from major depression or dysthymic disorder.

When Eeyore is asked by Pooh and other characters in the story, "Would you like to go swimming today?" Eeyore answers, in his low, depressed voice in a number of negative statements, "No, I'm so tired today and it's too far to walk to the swimming hole," or "I might get sun burned on a sunny day like today," or "It's too hot and I might get overheated."

Eeyore worries about everything. Instead of enjoying being with his friends, he isolates. Instead of enjoying the activity (swimming) and a beautiful summer day, he can't see anything positive. He is constantly in the black cloud of depression, even though it is a bright, sunny day.

Case Study 10.3

Dysthymic Disorder

Duane

Duane is a 39-year-old married male who completed inpatient treatment for alcoholism and cocaine dependence nearly three years ago. Since then, he has maintained sobriety, while regularly attending his aftercare counseling sessions and cocaine and alcoholics anonymous meetings. He has also been involved in individual and group counseling to deal with the effects of growing up in an alcoholic and emotionally abusive family system. Despite these efforts, he continues to experience symptoms of low energy, periods of irritability, and an inability to have fun without a great deal of effort. His therapist has referred him for a psychiatric evaluation.

Most notable in Duane's history is that earlier he was abstinent from alcohol and drugs for approximately four to five months. During that time, he experienced the same depressive symptoms. Besides alcoholism, his family history includes several relatives with depression. A recent physical exam was unremarkable.

Duane is a patient with a dysthymic disorder underlying his chemical dependency. His symptoms do not clear up after substantial periods of abstinence from alcohol/drugs. Although many patients with dysthymic disorder do respond to psychotherapy techniques, many would benefit from trying antidepressant medication. Typically, such medication can be expected to improve Duane's baseline mood with simultaneous improvement in energy level, mood stability, and ability to experience pleasure.

Case Study 10.4

Atypical Depression

Gail

Gail is a 28-year-old single accountant. She is extremely shy and often feels uncomfortable in social situations. She is 7 years sober and attends AA meetings regularly. Gail cries easily whenever she is involved in conflict. She suffered a number of losses in her childhood, including the loss of her father, who was reported missing in action in the Vietnam War. Around the same time, Gail's maternal grandmother, to whom Gail was extremely close, died while sleeping in the same bed with Gail. Gail has also had to deal with the issue of having been sexually abused at 12 years of age.

After Gail began counseling, her self-confidence improved. But she still felt sad, so she got an evaluation from a psychiatrist experienced in alcohol and drug recovery. The psychiatrist recommended an antidepressant. After two weeks, Gail felt tremendous relief and realized that she had been struggling with depression for quite some time.

Gail is still active in AA. She continues to work with her 12-step sponsor, attend group counseling, and take her antidepressant. She recently applied for a promotion, and, although she didn't get it, she took the rejection extremely well. She also began graduate school.

We may, in fact, be talking about a condition similar to that described by James Masterson (1976) as abandonment depression.

This condition is common in patients who may also have severe personality disturbances, such as borderline personality disorder. Psychodynamically, a sudden severe depression in response to feelings of loss, rejection, and/or abandonment may be related to a childhood loss so traumatic that it triggers this depression when feelings of loss are activated in present-day situations.

Atypical depression is also different because these patients may not report a loss of appetite and insomnia but, instead, experience an increase in appetite and sleep. Perhaps this is also indicative of the frequent problems in body image, binge patterns of eating, and other eating disorders that these clients exhibit. Patients with atypical depression may increase alcohol/drug use in a similar manner.

Organic Depression

Depression may also occur as a result of organic factors, such as brain tumors, head injuries, nutritional deficiencies, physical illness, or alcohol/drug use. Many chemically dependent patients have nutritional deficiencies as a result of decreased intake, malabsorption, and poor eating habits. Alcohol is especially high in calories with poor nutritional value. Other drugs disrupt the appetite (e.g., cocaine reduces appetite) and create problems in nutrition. After initial recovery from alcohol/drug use, depression may continue for a while due to nutritional causes. However, once a

Case Study 10.5

Bipolar Disorder

Gustav

Gustav is a 45-year-old salesman with a history of binge drinking and erratic job perfor-mance. He goes on two- to three-week binges every spring and uses alcohol only socially at other times. He feels remorseful about these binges. In the weeks preceding a binge, he typi-cally is quite productive, energetic, and successful in making sales. Gustav comments that his springtime burst in earnings helps compensate for his lackluster winter performance, when he typically feels lethargic and moody. In the past, he has used cocaine intermittently during the winter months to help brighten his mood. His finances have not allowed him to do cocaine in recent years. His occupational history is notable for multiple sales jobs across the country. He has made a number of impulsive springtime moves to pursue hot job possibili-ties. He does not find this unusual because his father, uncle, and brother all have similar his-tories. Closer questioning reveals that, during the springtime bursts of increased sales activ-ity, he has less need for sleep, a feeling of euphoria, and an increased philosophical preoccupation. Coworkers have commented on his high energy level and rapid speech. He has no history of previous psychiatric treatment.

Gustav's history reveals a patient with a bipolar disorder who binge drinks when he is high. There is a seasonal component to his mood swings, as he experiences manic symptoms in the springtime and symptoms of depression in the winter. Notably, he has a family history of similar mood swings and a personal history of minimal alcohol or drug use when he is not high. He is a good candidate for treatment with a mood-cycling agent, such as lithium, and would benefit from counseling on how to manage his impulses to drink. He should use avail-able resources for support, such as AA.

From the *Diagnostic and Statistical Manual of Mental Disorders*, Fourth Edition. Copyright 1994 American Psychiatric Association.

normal diet and vitamin therapy have been reimplemented, organic (nutritional) de-pression should improve.

Head injuries are fairly common, especially in end stage alcoholics, and may contribute to cognitive deficits as well as mood disturbances. Pancreatic cancer is also more common in the alcoholic population and can look identical to major de-pression clinically.

Prolonged use of opiates, benzodiazepines, alcohol, sedative hypnotics, and especially stimulant drugs can produce depression. Users of cocaine and amphet-amines typically experience a crash at the end of a binge pattern of cocaine use. This occurs because of the depletion of the neurotransmitter that the stimulant drug causes to be released in greater than normal quantities.

Bipolar Disorder

The first bipolar disorder described and understood was the classic manic-depressive illness. Manic-depressive illness consists of repeated depressive episodes over the years; these episodes are typically briefer than those in a major depression. In addition, a manic-depressive has less frequent but equally intense highs, or manic episodes. Characteristics of the manic phase of the disorder include the following:

- Euphoria
- Irritability
- Racing thoughts
- Decreased need for sleep
- Excessive spending
- Grandiosity
- Pressured speech
- An increased preoccupation with sexuality, religious, and/or philosophical themes

A manic episode may also include delusional beliefs and disorganization of thinking. Highs may not always involve euphoria; many patients simply become much more irritable, bizarre, and erratic in their behavior.

A variety of bipolar disorders have somewhat different patterns. Some patients experience recurrent depressive episodes with smaller and less intense manic episodes (hypomania) in between. During a hypomanic episode, a patient might typically experience all of the preceding symptoms except for the psychotic symptoms, such as disorganization of thinking, delusional material, and bizarre behavior.

Patients with bipolar disorder are typically plagued by mood instability; they may experience mood swings as frequently as daily. Patients who have significant mood swings, more than four times per year, are said to have a rapid cycling bipolar disorder. A growing accumulation of evidence suggests that some of these rapid cycling bipolar disorders may actually be a variation of epilepsy. Some of these patients may respond favorably to the medication that had previously been used only for epilepsy.

Mood-Cycling Disorder

The frequency of the cycling and the amplitude of the highs and lows are aggravated by alcohol/drug use. A relatively low-grade mood-cycling pattern may become much more aggravated with the use of alcohol/drugs, and the symptoms may become more clinically apparent.

Patients who otherwise have no psychotic symptoms, such as delusions, hallucinations, or disorganization of thinking, and have a mood-cycling disorder may develop psychotic symptoms, given the extra push from alcohol/drug use. (This is especially apparent with cocaine, amphetamines, hallucinogens, and even marijuana use.) Again, this stresses the importance of taking a thorough alcohol/drug history with each patient.

Personality Traits vs. a Personality Disorder

In describing people's personalities, we may think of traits that describe the way people behave, experience life, and interact in relationships. Personality is an important dimension that defines who we are. "Each of us is known not only by his or her physical features, occupation, and family background, but especially by what is called personality" (Nace 1990).

✎ **Personality Disorders and Substance Use Disorders**

Case Study 10.6

Depression and Withdrawal Symptoms

Evan

Evan is a 27-year-old male who is receiving inpatient treatment for his cocaine dependency. He was referred for a psychiatric evaluation because of his current severe depression symptoms. He had been freebasing cocaine for two to three months prior to admission to the treatment unit three days ago. Now he is feeling severely depressed and experiencing cocaine cravings.

Evan has no history of depression and no family history of psychiatric disorders. During childhood, he experienced hyperactivity and had mild learning disabilities. He notes that, since beginning drug use in his mid-teens, he has preferred stimulant drugs because they "calm me down." He has received inpatient treatment for cocaine dependence once previously and had two years of complete abstinence before relapsing several months ago. During his clean time, he experienced no mood difficulties but continued to feel somewhat hyper.

Evan is a patient who experiences severe depression as part of cocaine withdrawal. There is no reason to suspect an underlying problem with depression, given his personal and family history. He would benefit from a short course of treatment with desipramine, an antidepressant that is particularly effective for treating acute depression and cocaine cravings during cocaine withdrawal. Such treatment typically lasts for two to four weeks.

His history suggests a childhood hyperactivity disorder (attention-deficit hyperactivity disorder, ADHD), which has extended into early adulthood. Many patients with this type of history do gravitate toward stimulant drugs that produce a paradoxical calming effect, much like Ritalin, which is commonly used for treating ADHD.

Evan could also benefit from individual and group counseling on relapse prevention strategies. Perhaps his relapse could have been avoided if he had established better support from self-help participation, a sponsor, and a program that kept him from relapse situations. At 27 years of age, Evan could also benefit from the support of counseling to assist him in assessing his developmental skills, such as career, self-concept, and interpersonal relationships, which may have been jeopardized by his cocaine use.

The American Psychiatric Association defines personality as "the ingrained pattern of behavior that each person evolves, both consciously and unconsciously, as the style of life or way of being in adapting to the environment" (American Psychiatric Association 1984).

Most personality traits have both adaptive and maladaptive qualities or features. For example, being logical and organized are valuable traits in a computer programmer. But always being ruled by logic and being compulsively organized can also be maladaptive, since these traits may limit one's capacity to be emotionally expressive. On the other hand, a creative and artistic person might not be as suited to a situation or an occupation that requires logical, politically correct, and decisive action. We all have a mix of personality traits, which define us as individuals. *When personality traits are persistently maladaptive and lead to chronic dif-*

Case Study 10.7

Alcoholism

Charlie

Charlie is a 53-year-old married engineer at a local aerospace company. He has a long-standing, but progressively worsening, history of irritability, nervousness, and difficulty sleeping. Charlie is under the care of Dr. Greenhorn, a physician just out of his internal medicine residency. Dr. Greenhorn assumed the practice of Charlie's previous physician and golfing buddy, Dr. Barleycorn.

Dr. Greenhorn reviews the previous medical record and notes difficulties with stomach irritation and ulcers, elevated triglyceride and cholesterol levels, and persistent complaints of decreased libido, or sex drive. Charlie requests some of the sleeping pills that Dr. Barleycorn had prescribed. Further questioning reveals a history of regular heavy drinking, which began when Charlie and Dr. Barleycorn were fraternity brothers. This heavy drinking behavior persisted over the years. Charlie typically drinks three or four mixed drinks or glasses of beer per weeknight and six or seven drinks per night on the weekends. He can recall going two to three days without alcohol during a church retreat several years ago. At that time, he felt very shaky and irritable. Physical examination reveals a moderately enlarged liver, and laboratory studies reveal elevated liver enzyme levels and mild anemia.

Charlie is a classic example of a patient whose primary diagnosis is chemical dependency (alcoholism). The irritability and insomnia are a direct result of the alcohol and repeated episodes of the beginning phases of alcohol withdrawal. Maintenance drinkers can avoid withdrawal symptoms by frequent, repeated administration of the drug in question or a cross-tolerant drug, such as sedative-hypnotic sleeping pills.

Like many other patients with similar backgrounds, Charlie's problems with alcohol have long been overlooked or ignored. His relationship with Dr. Barleycorn is unique and points to the difficulty physicians may have in assessing their patients adequately because of their personal relationships with the patients and their own drinking habits.

Treatment for Charlie should include abstinence from alcohol and cross-tolerant medications. Given his long-standing history of alcohol use, he will likely be referred to an alcohol treatment program. He will need help to gain better insight into how his drinking has affected his life.

Realistically, sleep disturbances and irritability may persist for even a few months and could be treated symptomatically with a nonaddicting sleeping agent, or even with a low-dose antidepressant.

---

ficulty in interpersonal, occupational, and social functioning, there is a personality disorder.

The *Psychiatric Diagnostic and Statistical Manual IV* (American Psychiatric Association 1994) recognizes 11 personality disorders and divides them into three clusters, or groups (see Table 10.3):

Cluster A is a group characterized by odd and eccentric traits and may lead to psychiatric conditions, such as delusional disorder or schizophrenia.

TABLE 10.3

Personality Disorders

To qualify for a personality disorder diagnosis, an individual's traits and behaviors must be long-standing and must cause significant impairment in social or occupational functioning or subjective distress. The following are the 11 DSM III-R personality disorders.

Cluster A	Cluster B	Cluster C
Paranoid	Antisocial	Avoidant
Schizoid	Borderline	Dependent
Schizotypal	Histrionic	Obsessive-Compulsive
	Narcissistic	Passive-Aggressive

From American Psychiatric Association: *Diagnostic and Statistical Manual of Mental Disorders,* Third Edition, Revised, Washington, D.C., American Psychiatric Association, 1987.

Cluster B is a group characterized by behavior that is erratic, emotional, or dramatic. This cluster has the strongest association with substance abuse, particularly antisocial and borderline personality disorder.

Cluster C is a group characterized by feelings of fear and anxiety. Substance abuse occurs in this group, but not as frequently as in Cluster B.

Personality Disorder vs. Chemical Dependency Disorder

The difficulties in differentiating between a personality disorder and an alcohol/drug disorder are often confounded by a common overlap in behaviors associated with each disorder. "Some behaviors that are symptomatic of particular Axis II disorders (manipulativeness, exploitativeness, dishonesty) may be integral or sometimes even adaptive aspects of addicted behavior, particularly among individuals who use illicit drugs" (Weiss 1996).

Personality-disordered individuals may be attracted to alcohol/drugs to self-medicate feelings of discomfort, anxiety, depression, anger, grief, and even shyness. V.M. Hesselbrook and associates (1983) reported that 52 percent of a sample of male alcoholics had a current or lifetime diagnosis of antisocial personality disorder.

Kleinman and colleagues (1990) found that, of 76 lower-social-class cocaine abusers, 71 percent had at least one personality disorder and 40 percent had two or more. The four most common personality disorders identified were

- Antisocial personality disorder—21 percent
- Passive-aggressive personality disorder—21 percent
- Borderline personality disorder—18 percent
- Self-defeating personality disorder—18 percent

Weiss and Mirin (1986), in their study of an upper-middle-class addict population, found borderline personality disorder and narcissistic personality disorder to be the most common diagnoses.

Craig (1988) used the very sensitive Millon Clinical Multiaxial Inventory and found that, of 121 opiate addicts from the Chicago area, all of them (100 percent) had at least one personality disorder and 27 percent had more than one. The most common diagnoses were

- Antisocial personality disorder—22 percent
- Narcissistic personality disorder—18 percent
- Borderline personality disorder—16 percent
- Dependent personality disorder—16 percent.

This surprising result brings up the question of to whether drug abuse and addiction lead to behaviors that are characteristic of personality disorders. Edward Kaufman, author of *Psychotherapy of Addicted Persons* (1995), points out that the characteristic inherent in substance abusers—such as unstable and intense interpersonal relationships; inappropriate, intense, out-of-control anger; affective instability; and physically self-damaging acts—can all meet the diagnostic criteria for borderline personality disorder and other personality disorders. Widiger et al. (1986) state that there is good evidence that many substance abusers who are diagnosed as having borderline personality disorder are really "pseudoborderline."

It is clear from the research that personality traits and personality disorders play a major role in substance abuse. The extent and depth of the role personality plays in substance abuse is confounded by the old "chicken or egg" question. Did the personality disorder cause substance abuse, or did substance abuse lead to behaviors that resemble the criteria for a diagnosis of a personality disorder?

Antisocial Personality Disorder
Antisocial Personality Disorder and Chemical Dependency
Antisocial personality disorder (ASPD) is estimated to be found in 2 to 3 percent of the male population. Of all the personality disorders, the strongest relationship with substance abuse is with antisocial personality disorder. ASPD has been found in 15 percent of alcoholic men, as compared were a 4 percent lifetime prevalence in nonalcoholic men (Helzer and Pryzbeck 1988). Hesselbrook, Meyer, and Kenner (1985) found ASPD to be the most common additional diagnosis in a hospitalized sample of more than 200 male alcoholics—49 percent met the diagnostic criteria for ASPD. The diagnosis is predominately attributed to men, whereas borderline personality disorder is primarily found in women. The ratio of men to women with antisocial personality is approximately 8 to 1. In contrast, the ratio of women to men is 8 to 1 for borderline personality disorder.

Childhood Precursors of Antisocial Personality Disorder
Conduct disorders and attention-deficit hyperactive disorder (ADHD) in children are precursors of both substance abuse and antisocial personality disorder. Early assessment, intervention, and counseling with these young people and their families are recommended to address current problems and to prevent future problems.

Denial, Alcohol/Drugs, and Antisocial Personality Disorder
The shame attached to identifying one's personality traits as causing problems in life and in relationships often results in denial. It is easier to blame others for conflicts, problems, and personality issues than to take responsibility. A major feature of a

personality disorder is that the individual may not consider the personality trait that is causing conflict as undesirable. The individual might attribute others' complaints about them as the fault of others—"The hell with them if they can't take a joke."

The traditional denial defense mechanisms of rationalization and minimization are used to deny the true dimensions of a personality disorder. Integrity, honesty, and responsibility are discounted in the self-centered behavior of the ASPD.

Difficulty *regulating behaviors* (poor impulse control, recklessness, and a failure to anticipate consequences) and *affect intolerance* (the inability to recognize, regulate, and tolerate emotions) lead to substance abuse (Khantzian 1981).

Nace and associates (1983) described alcohol/drugs as providing immediate gratification followed by regressive behaviors. These regressive behaviors include the following:

- *Impulsivity*—cannot delay gratification; has stimulus-bound decreased frustration tolerance; is impatient; overreacts to situations; is inconsistent
- *Self-centeredness*—is stubborn and defiant; lacks empathy; exhibits grandiosity; either overvalues or undervalues self; sees things in either/or, rather than shades of gray; can't compromise; exhibits perfectionism, sees self as unique
- *Passivity*—is withdrawn; is isolated; feels helpless; is "mentally lazy"; avoids self-revelation
- *Affect intolerance*—has difficulty in recognizing feelings; fears feelings; has decreased ability to endure or regulate painful emotional states

Some questions that may identify antisocial personality traits are the following:

- Do you exaggerate your achievements and talents?
- Are you preoccupied with thoughts of great success, power, brilliance, beauty, achievement, or idealized love?
- Do you often want a great deal of attention and admiration?
- Do you have a tendency to dominate conversations and activities (perhaps "showing off")?
- Do you expect special favors but feel you don't have to return them?
- Do you sometimes feel surprised and angry that people do not do what you want them to?
- Do you ever take advantage of others so that you can get what you want?
- Do you sometimes disregard the rights or personal boundaries of others?
- Do you alternate between thinking too much and too little of a person?
- Do you sometimes feel you don't care enough about other people's pain and feelings?
- Do you change jobs frequently? Have you changed jobs three or more times in the past five years, but not because of the kind of job or because of economic or seasonal fluctuations?
- Have you been unemployed for six months or more during a period of five years, when you might have been able to work?
- Have you walked off jobs at various times without having another job already lined up?
- If you have children, do you feel you adequately provide food, safety, and shelter for them?

Case Study 10.8

Antisocial Personality Traits

Tony

Tony is a 24-year-old construction worker. He says he began working after leaving high school at the age of 15. As a child, he was hyperactive, and his behavior problems caused him to perform poorly in school. Thus, school was frustrating for Tony and his teachers.

Tony told lies, stole, and fought with other children. His family took him to a counselor (a behavioral specialist) after Tony repeatedly set fires. During one school year, Tony was treated with Ritalin, a medication that helps children calm down and stay focused, and he did better in school. But during summer vacation he stopped taking the medication and refused to resume taking it the next fall.

Since dropping out of high school, Tony has held a number of jobs. Usually, he gets fired because he fights with his coworkers or doesn't show up for work; this irritates Tony, who feels victimized. Although his employment—or lack of it—has caused financial problems, Tony admits that he has lied and not paid his bills. He tells friends, creditors, and bill collectors, "The check is in the mail," or "I'll send the payment as soon as. . . ." Although he has a relationship with a woman, he has also had several one-night stands with other women he has met at bars. He has snorted and smoked cocaine, often squandering his money while partying with friends and women he picks up. His parents have bailed him out financially several times. Tony's attitude was "They have the money, so they should be able to help me out."

After two DUIs, Tony was referred to a chemical dependency program as part of a deferred prosecution. He is now slowly working on both his chemical dependency and his personality problems.

- Have you spent money on drugs, alcohol, or personal items that probably should have been spent on *necessities?*
- Have you committed repeated thefts or engaged in illegal occupations (fencing, selling drugs, prostitution, pimping, etc.)?
- Have you had multiple arrests or been convicted of a felony?

Extreme difficulties in relationships with your spouse or partner could also indicate antisocial personality traits. The following are some further questions to consider.

- Have you been separated (whether legally married or not) or divorced several times?
- Have you had 10 or more sexual partners in one year?
- Do you sometimes feel that you are overly irritable and aggressive?
- Have you frequently been involved in physical fights or assaults?
- Have you ever physically abused your spouse or children?
- Have you failed to plan ahead for the future or have you been extremely impulsive?

TABLE 10.4

Diagnostic Criteria for Antisocial Personality Disorder

A.   There is a pervasive pattern of disregard for and violation of the rights of others occurring since age 15, as indicated by three (or more) of the following:

1. Failure to conform to social norms with respect to lawful behaviors as indicated by repeatedly performing acts that are grounds for arrest
2. Deceitfulness, as indicated by repeated lying, use of aliases, or conning others for personal profit or pleasure
3. Impulsivity or failure to plan ahead
4. Irritability and aggressiveness, as indicated by repeated physical fights or assaults
5. Reckless disregard for safety of self or others
6. Consistent irresponsibility, as indicated by repeated failure to sustain consistent work behavior or honor financial obligations
7. Lack of remorse, as indicated by being indifferent to or rationalizing having hurt, mistreated, or stolen from another

B.   The individual is at least 18 years.

C.   There is evidence of conduct disorder with onset before age 15 years.

D.   The occurrence of antisocial behavior is not exclusively during the course of schizophrenia or a manic episode.

From American *Psychiatric Association, Psychiatric Diagnostic & Statistical Manual IV,* (1994) Washington D.C.

- Have you lied repeatedly, used aliases, or "conned" others to get what you wanted?
- Have you frequently driven while drunk?

The diagnostic criteria for antisocial personality disorder are identified in the *DSM-IV* (see Table 10.4).

Borderline Personality Disorder and Chemical Dependency

The second most common personality disorder that has a high incidence of substance abuse is borderline personality disorder. A number of studies have reported co-occurring substance abuse and borderline personality disorder—43 percent (Koenigsberg et al. 1985), 28 percent (Johnson and Connelly 1981), and 13 percent (Nace, Saxon, and Shore 1983).

In Chapter 6, abandonment depression is described as the common factor in borderline personality disorder. As previously mentioned, the term *abandonment depression* was coined by James Masterson to describe a personality disorder that has six key elements: (1) feelings of emptiness and void; (2) hopelessness and helplessness; (3) panic; (4) guilt; (5) suicidal depression; and (6) homicidal rage.

Someone suffering from abandonment depression probably had a highly stressful separation from parent(s) or a primary caregiver early in life (18 months to two years of age). The separation could have been caused by natural events (death, separation, divorce, health, etc.), or the parent(s) might not have been emotionally available.

Some common questions that may help identify abandonment follow. Did you have parents or guardians who

- Were not open or available to you physically and emotionally?
- Attacked you verbally or physically or blamed you for many of their problems?
- Gave mixed messages, called *double binds,* saying one thing but meaning something else?
- Had unreasonably high expectations or standards for you or had ambiguous expectations of how you should behave, what you should do, and how you should feel?
- Did not show you warmth or sensitivity, did not make you feel secure or safe, or did not pay much attention to your feelings, concerns, and conflicts?
- Discounted your sense of self or violated your physical and psychological boundaries, such as by committing physical, emotional, or sexual violations?
- Disparaged, blamed, or rejected you if you had any difficulty with developmental tasks?
- Disregarded, ridiculed, blamed, or teased you?
- Jokingly or seriously threatened to abandon or leave you?
- Made you feel that your fears were unwarranted or inappropriate?
- Did not understand you or were insensitive to your needs and desires?

Patients with borderline personality disorder have a marked instability of mood and often form intense interpersonal attachments. They typically feel abandoned and rejected during instances of real or perceived interpersonal loss. Many borderline patients engage in repeated self-destructive or suicidal acts during episodes of intense depression and despair. Theoretical explanations of the origin of this personality disorder range from developmental to biochemical explanations. In all probability, the condition is a result of both nature and nurture (i.e., inadequate bonding and parenting during early years and a genetic predisposition). Most clinicians agree that borderline patients have a great deal of difficulty regulating their degree of attachment to others. They want the closeness and trust that intimacy brings but fear the dependency, vulnerability, and possible rejection that may occur. Not surprisingly, these patients have a high incidence of chemical dependency as they attempt to blunt the intensity of their emotions by using alcohol/drugs. They are especially prone to becoming dependent on addicting prescription drugs, such as benzodiazepines. Their impulsivity, frequent thoughts of suicide, and substance abuse make them especially at risk when prescribed psychiatric medication. Many psychiatric medications are lethal when taken in amounts only 5 to 10 times the usual dosage, especially if the individual is already toxic with alcohol or drugs.

Abstinence from alcohol/drugs is essential in treating borderline patients, as their already fragile mood stability is quite sensitive to alcohol/drugs. Such patients generally need psychotherapy. When medication management is indicated, doctors commonly prescribe antidepressant or mood-cycling agents. Which medication the patient receives depends on the clinical symptoms that are most troublesome (more on treatment of dual disorders appears in Chapter 11).

Do you have a pattern of unstable and intense personal relationships? For instance, does your attitude about your relationships keep changing? Do you

Case Study 10.9

Borderline Personality Disorder

Francine

Francine is 26 years old and single. Her alcoholic parents divorced when she was 3 years old. She lived with her mother, who drank heavily and had a series of live-in boyfriends. Her mother was physically and emotionally unavailable and spent a great deal of time at bars. Her mother's boyfriends physically and sexually abused Francine. To try to cope, Francine began using alcohol in mid-adolescence. She was also sexually promiscuous. She was involved in shoplifting and occasionally went on eating binges. Today, she acknowledges that she drinks to blunt emotional pain.

As an adult, she has had intense relationships with men. When a relationship breaks up, her rage and anger have been equally intense. Francine cannot cope with rejection in relationships and says she feels "empty inside" when she thinks she has been abandoned. Her sudden shifts in mood and her occasional threats of suicide have alienated boyfriends and other friends.

Although she drinks alcohol to lessen the intensity of her feelings, it ultimately causes deeper depression and leads to impulsive, self-destructive behavior. Several times, when her relationships have broken up, Francine has taken overdoses and cut her wrists.

Francine ended a previous therapy after three or four sessions—she said the therapist was getting "too close" and she felt too vulnerable. But she is once again in counseling and is making progress in dealing with her addiction and the personality traits that have caused problems.

Francine's story dramatically illustrates the dual disorder of a borderline personality disorder and addiction. She will improve if she can maintain abstinence from alcohol and drugs, continue counseling to explore the grief of her past trauma and abuse, and examine her current boundary and self-sabotaging problems.

---

idealize or romanticize your friends? Do you put them down, manipulate them, or often use them to meet your own needs? Do you find yourself treating some friends very well and some very poorly? Do you have intense anger that is not really justified? Or do you lack control of your anger? Are you concerned about your self-image, your gender identity, your long-term goals or career choice, your friendship patterns, your values, or your loyalties? (If you are concerned, you might have thoughts like these: *"Who am I?"* or *"I feel just like my sister when I'm good."*) Do you have deep mood swings? Are you depressed when alone? Do you try very hard to avoid being alone? Do you feel empty or bored most of the time?

The diagnostic criteria for borderline personality disorder are identified in the *DSM-IV* (see Table 10.5).

TABLE 10.5

Diagnostic Criteria for Borderline Personality Disorder

A pervasive pattern of instability of interpersonal relationships, self-image and affects, and marked impulsivity beginning by early adulthood and present in a variety of contexts, as indicated by five (or more) of the following:

1. Frantic efforts to avoid real or imagined abandonment
2. A pattern of unstable and intense interpersonal relationships characterized by alternating between extremes of idealization and devaluation
3. Identity disturbance: marked and persistently unstable self-image or sense of self
4. Impulsivity in at least two areas that are potentially self-damaging (e.g., spending, sex, substance abuse, reckless driving, binge eating)
5. Recurrent suicidal behavior, gestures, or threats or self-mutilating behavior
6. Affective instability due to a marked reactivity of mood (e.g., intense episodic dysphoria, irritability, or anxiety usually lasting a few hours and only rarely more than a few days)
7. Chronic feelings of emptiness
8. Inappropriate, intense anger or difficulty controlling anger (e.g., frequent displays of temper, constant anger, recurrent physical fights)
9. Transient, stress-related paranoid ideation or severe dissociative symptoms

Pyschiatric Diagnostic and Statistical Manual, IV, American Psychiatric Association, Washington D.C., 1994.

One can clearly understand why depressive disorders may lead to suicidal ideation and suicide. The combination of depression and alcohol/drug use places patients at an even higher risk for suicide. Self-destructive acts that otherwise might be contemplated and dismissed are frequently acted on impulsively by those who are intoxicated and disinhibited. In earlier chapters, we discussed alcoholism and drug addiction as a kind of death wish. Disaster might also occur when a depressed, forgetful patient is drinking and inadvertently takes an overdose of antidepressant medication. The antidepressants, especially the tricyclic antidepressants, are lethal when mixed with alcohol.

✄ Affective Disorders and Suicide

The vicious psychological pattern of affect (feelings) plus shame can also contribute to suicidal ideation and actions—for example,

depressive feelings + shame = feelings of despair

Shame is exemplified as "I shouldn't feel depressed; I'm weak to have these feelings. I feel unable to control my feelings and there must be something inferior about me."

This cycle continues to the next stage of

feelings of despair + shame = suicidal ideation

The shame takes the form of thoughts such as "I'm not worthy. There is no hope; things won't change; I don't have any choices. Things are so painful and never change; they only get worse. There is nothing to get any pleasure or joy from life."

The next and often fatal stage is

$$\text{suicidal ideation} + \text{shame} = \text{suicide}$$

It is no wonder that initial or normal feelings of sadness, or melancholia from unresolved trauma from childhood, is avoided and not grieved. The individual suffering from depressive illness is fearful that any negative experience will start this cycle in motion of depression to self-destruction. As a result, feelings of sadness and emotional pain are often self-medicated with alcohol/drugs. One can see the importance of supportive counseling for depressed patients in addition to the appropriate use of antidepressant medication.

Summary

The Epidemiologic Catchment Area (ECA) study by Regier et al. (1990) found that over 53 percent of drug abusers and 39 percent of alcohol abusers have at least one mental illness.

The term co-occurring disorder refers to the condition of having both a psychiatric diagnosis and a chemical dependency diagnosis.

This chapter describes the problems related to mood disorders and chemical dependency, with specific emphasis on major depression, dysthymia, atypical depression, bipolar disorder, and cyclothymic disorder. What differentiates these various types of affective (feeling) disorders are their severity, duration, frequency, and precipitating factors. Common vegetative signs of a mood disorder are

- Disrupted sleep
- Difficulty with appetite and weight regulation
- Decreased cognitive functioning (including problems with concentration, memory, and problem solving)
- Decreased libido, or sex drive
- Lack of motivation, decreased energy (anergia)
- Difficulty experiencing pleasure (anhedonia)

This chapter also explores the co-occurring disorder of personality disorders and chemical dependency. Most personality traits have both adaptive and maladaptive qualities or features. When personality traits are persistently maladaptive and lead to chronic difficulty in interpersonal, occupational, and social functioning, there is a personality disorder. The two major personality disorders most frequently associated with chemical dependency are antisocial personality disorder and borderline personality disorder.

Case studies throughout the chapter describe the special features of co-occurring-disordered clients and their specific treatment needs.

References

American Psychiatric Association. *Diagnostic Criteria from DSM-IV.* Washington, DC: Author, 1994.

American Psychiatric Association. *Psychiatric Glossary.* Washington, DC: American
     Psychiatric Press, 1984.

Bauer, Anne. "Dual Diagnosis Patients: The State of the Problem." *The Information
     Exchange (TIEUNES),* a quarterly bulletin. Published by the Information Exchange on
     Young Adult Chronic Patients, Inc. 9, no. 3 (July 1987): 1–4, 8.

Craig, R.J. "A Psychometric Study of the Prevalence of DSM-III Personality Disorders
     Among Treated Opiate Addicts." *International Journal of the Addictions* 23, no. 2,
     (1988): 115–24.

Fields, Richard, and Russell Vandenbelt. *Understanding Mood Disorders and Addiction.*
     Pamphlet published by Hazelden Educational Materials, Center City, MN, 1992a.

Fields, Richard, and Russell Vandenbelt. *Understanding Personality Problems and
     Addiction.* Pamphlet published by Hazelden Educational Materials, Center City, MN,
     1992b.

Helzer, J.E., and T.R. Pryzbeck. "The Co-occurrence of Alcoholism with Other Psychiatric
     Disorders in the General Population and Its Impact on Treatment." *Journal Studies on
     Alcohol* 49 (1988): 219–24.

Hesselbrook, M.N., R.E. Meyer, and J.J. Kenner. "Psychopathology in Hospitalized
     Alcoholics." *Archives of General Psychiatry* 42 (1985): 1050–55.

Hesselbrook, V.M., E.G. Shaskan, and R.E. Meyer. "Summary of Bio/Genetic Factors in
     Alcoholism." *NIAAA Research Monograph Series 9* (1983): 159–66.

Johnson, R.P., and J.C. Connelly. "Addicted Physicians Take a Closer Look." *Journal of
     American Medical Association* 245 (1981): 253–57.

Kaufman, Edward. *Psychotherapy of Addicted Persons.* New York: Guilford Press, 1995.

Khantzian, E.J. "Some Treatment Implications of the Ego and Self-Disturbance in
     Alcoholism." In *Dynamic Approaches to the Understanding and Treatment of
     Alcoholism,* ed. M.H. Bean and N.E. Zinberg. New York: Free Press, 1981.

Kleinman, P.H., A.B. Miller, and R.B. Millman. "Psychopathology Among Cocaine Abusers
     Entering Treatment." *Journal of Nervous and Mental Disease* 178 (1990): 442–47.

Koenigsberg, H.W. et al. "The Relationship Between Syndrome and Personality Disorder in
     DSM-III: Experience with 2,462 Patients." *American Journal of Psychiatry* 142, no. 2
     (1985): 207–12.

Masterson, James. *Psychotherapy of the Borderline Adult—a Developmental Approach.* New
     York: Brunner/Mazel, 1976.

Nace, E.P., J.J. Saxon, and N.A. Shore. "A Comparison of Borderline and Non-Borderline
     Alcoholic Patients. *Archives of General Psychiatry* 40 (1983): 54–56.

Nace, E.P. "Substance Abuse and Personality Disorder." In *Journal of Chemical
     Dependency Treatment*—special issue on Managing the Dually Diagnosed Patient:
     Current Issues and Clinical Approaches, ed. David F. O'Connell, 3, no. 2 (1990):
     183–98.

Regier, Darrel A. et al. "Commorbidity of Mental Disorders with Alcohol and Other Drug
     Abuse: Results from the Epidemiologic Catchment Area (ECA) Study." *Journal of the
     American Medical Association* 19, no. 264 (November 1990): 2511–18.

U.S. Department of Health and Human Services. "Helpful Facts About Depressive
     Illnesses." Pamphlet by DART (Depression Awareness, Recognition, and Treatment),
     NIMH, Rockville, MD, 1987.

Weiss, R.D., and S.M. Mirin. "Subtypes of Cocaine Abusers." *Psychiatric Clinics of North
     America* 9 (no. 3) (1986): 491–501.

Weiss, Roger. "Personality Parallels." *Professional Counselor Magazine* (January/February
     1996): 15–16, 40–41.

CHAPTER **11**

Alcohol/Drug Treatment and Relapse Prevention

Chapter Objectives

1. Identify the key elements of Alcoholics Anonymous (AA) and its advantages in alcohol/drug recovery. Also identify some resistance people have with self-help meetings.

2. List some other self-help meetings in addition to AA.

3. Describe the principles of rational recovery.

4. Describe the four basic alcohol/drug treatment modalities of the 1970s.

5. Describe the development of the insurance-reimbursed inpatient alcohol/drug treatment program.

6. Clarify the impact the cocaine epidemic has had on chemical dependency treatment.

7. Identify behavioral, cognitive, emotional, and relational symptoms in each stage of recovery using Rawson's model.

8. Identify the problems and methods in engaging the alcoholic/addict into treatment.

9. Describe appropriate counseling/treatment for early, middle, and later stages of chemical dependency recovery.

10. Explain the importance of relapse prevention as part of the alcohol/drug recovery cycle.

11. Clarify the differences between a relapse-prone and recovery-prone orientation by the recovering alcoholic/addict.

12. Identify the three stages of changing a habit, according to Marlatt.

13. Identify and explain the factors that make the recovering alcoholic/addict prone to relapse.

14. Define cravings and identify relapse-prevention approach to cravings.

15. Give some examples of triggers that cause craving for alcohol/drugs.

16. Describe how alcohol can induce a drug relapse.

17. Explain the key elements to deal with in relapse prevention.

18. Identify the advantages and drawbacks of structure in alcohol/drug recovery.

19. Discuss the problems and issues involved in controlled drinking as a treatment goal.

20. Explain harm-reduction approaches, citing examples (e.g., needle exchange).

21. Identify the key elements in an effective chemical dependency treatment strategy.

22. Describe the troublesome treatment behavior patterns of co-occurring-disorder patients.

23. Describe methods to break through the denial of co-occurring-disorder patients and their families.

24. Describe cognitive-behavioral approaches, solution-focused, and short-term treatment models with alcohol/drug treatment and co-occurring-disorder clients and their families.

25. Describe the dimensions of suicide with alcohol/drug use.

The final chapter gives a balanced overview of alcohol/drug treatment while placing major emphasis on relapse prevention. Sobriety and abstinence from alcohol/drugs is an ongoing process. Recovery is a life-long process involving not only alcoholics/addicts but also their entire family systems.

The chapter highlights specific alcohol/drug treatment and co-occurring-disorders treatment issues and approaches. You are encouraged to explore referenced material, take counseling courses specific to alcohol/drugs, and pursue supervised internships for more in-depth counseling skill development.

It's appropriate to start this chapter on treatment with the most widely used approach for recovery from alcoholism and drug addiction—self-help groups.

⚔ Self-Help Meetings

Alcoholics Anonymous

Alcoholics Anonymous (AA) was founded in the early 1930s by Bill W., a stockbroker, and Bob S., a surgeon. Both of these men found that willpower alone was not enough to keep them from using alcohol. After admitting to each other their common disease and shared frustration with alcohol recovery, they discovered that they could help one another remain sober through mutual support. They soon discovered that others had the same experiences in struggling with recovery from alcoholism, and the movement was begun. Small groups of alcoholics met on a regular basis to share their experience, strength, hope, and support for one another. In 1938, the basic principles of AA were first outlined as the now famous Twelve Steps. (See Table 11.1.)

Alcoholics Anonymous has been the most successful program of recovery to date. There are AA meetings every day in almost every city and town in the United

---

TABLE 11.1

The Twelve Steps

1. We admitted we were powerless over alcohol—that our lives had become unmanageable.
2. Came to believe that a Power greater than ourselves could restore us to sanity.
3. Made a decision to turn our will and our lives over to the care of God as we understood Him.
4. Made a searching and fearless moral inventory of ourselves.
5. Admitted to God, to ourselves, and to another human being the exact nature of our wrongs.
6. Were entirely ready to have God remove all these defects of character.
7. Humbly asked Him to remove our shortcomings.
8. Made a list of all persons we had harmed and became willing to make amends to them.
9. Made direct amends to such people wherever possible, except when to do so would injure them or others.
10. Continued to take personal inventory and, when we were wrong, promptly admitted to it.
11. Sought through prayer and meditation to improve our conscious contact with God as we understand Him, praying only for knowledge of His will for us and the power to carry that out.
12. Having had a spiritual awakening as the result of these steps, we tried to carry this message to alcoholics and practice these principles in all our affairs.

The Twelve Steps are reprinted with permission of Alcoholics Anonymous World Services, Inc. Permission to reprint the Twelve Steps does not mean that AA agrees with the views expressed herein.
AA is a program of recovery from alcoholism—use of the Twelve Steps in connection with programs and activities that are patterned after AA but that address other problems does not imply otherwise.

States. Throughout other parts of the world, more than 90 countries have AA meetings. The fellowship crosses all religious and racial barriers; the only requirement for membership is a desire to stop drinking.

"There are no dues or fees for AA membership; they are self-supporting through their own contributions. AA is not allied with any sect, denomination, politics, organization, or institution; does not wish to engage in any controversy; neither endorses nor opposes any causes. Our primary purpose is to stay sober and help other alcoholics to achieve sobriety" (Alcoholics Anonymous 1978).

Advantages of AA as a Recovery Model

Lawson, Peterson, and Lawson (1983) identified the following key factors that contribute to the success of AA as a recovery model:

1. Mutual sharing by members, which provides solutions to alcohol-related problems and helps alleviate guilt by showing members that others have acted irrationally also
2. Provision of a regular support group of individuals working toward the goal of abstinence
3. Frequent and regular meetings to help members structure their time
4. Availability of AA as an adjunct to other treatments, such as counseling and psychotherapy
5. Absence of membership fees and nondiscrimination by race, sex, or socioeconomic status
6. Establishment of comprehensive goals covering the emotional, behavioral, and spiritual life of the members

A number of studies have found favorable treatment outcomes from participation in AA (e.g., Armor, Polich, and Stambul 1978; Bateman and Peterson 1971; Browne-Mayers, Seeley, and Brown 1973; Kish and Herman 1971). In 1965, a study by Robson, Paulus, and Clark found that 71 percent of regular AA attendees improved and 57 percent improved from attending no more than 10 meetings.

Despite these figures, treatment programs that are exclusively AA-oriented without the incorporation of other treatment methods and modalities have been less effective. Costello and associates (1976) found that the effectiveness of intermediate care was doubled (18 to 36 percent) when the unit converted from an exclusively AA-oriented model to a program with many treatment methods, AA being one of them.

Resistance to Attending AA and Other Self-Help Groups

For a variety of reasons, individuals in early alcohol/drug recovery often resist attending self-help meetings. Some of the reasons they give are the following:

1. Difficulty with the concept of a higher power, or references to God
2. Lack of tolerance by self-help members, at times, to
   a. Use medication for affective or feeling disorders and other psychological conditions
   b. Help understand that there are different types of alcoholism
   c. Reject treatment (therapy and other treatment modalities)

3. People are uncomfortable in group settings and are concerned with the group's maintaining strict confidentiality
4. The disruptive influence of people (especially court-referred) who don't have a true desire to be sober

Despite these drawbacks, which can be overcome, AA and other self-help meetings have been a positive and extremely beneficial source of inspiration and hope for millions of recovering alcoholics/addicts.

Application of Self-Help to Other Problems

Other standard self-help meetings that have adapted the AA 12-step model for a variety of problems, include the following:

NA—Narcotics Anonymous
CA—Cocaine Anonymous
MA—Marijuana Anonymous
Al-Anon—for family members of alcoholics
Narcanon—for family members of drug addicts
Alateen and Alatot—for teenagers and youngsters of alcoholics
ACA—for Adult Children of Alcoholics
FA—Families Anonymous
OA—Overeaters Anonymous
CODA—Co-Dependents Anonymous

There are self-help meetings for survivors of incest and sexual abuse; meetings for those addicted to gambling or compulsive sexuality; and meetings to help those having problems with spending and those grieving the loss of a child. There are even self-help groups for people suffering from similar physical, psychological, and emotional conditions. In California, while working in a community mental health center, I ran across a group for people suffering from bipolar disorders. The group appropriately called itself the "Ups and Downs Group." Whatever the condition, the self-help model is being applied as a successful treatment modality, especially when it is integrated with a variety of other treatment modalities. Alcohol/drug self-help meetings are the most widely used modality for recovery from alcoholism and drug addiction. Table 11.2 lists a directory for several self-help groups.

Rational Recovery

Rational Recovery (RR) was started by Jack Trimpey in 1986 as an alternative to Alcoholics Anonymous and other self-help meetings. The principles of RR are based on the rational-emotive approach developed by Albert Ellis, Ph.D. The major focus of rational recovery is on changing the way people think and feel about themselves and their use of alcohol/drugs. "In RR, we learn to take control of our emotions so that we are not compelled to reach for an anesthetic when we are feeling bad" (Trimpey 1991). Trimpey, a clinical social worker in California, wrote *The Small Book* (1985), which attacked the principles of the AA *Big Book*. Unfortunately Trimpey's book is too intent on bashing AA, rather than outlining another alternative for people who have problems with AA meetings or principles.

TABLE 11.2

The Recovery Directory (National Telephone Numbers Included Where Available)

Adult Children of Alcoholics	Overeaters Anonymous
Adult Survivors of Child Abuse	Partners of Survivors of Incest Anonymous
Al-Anon/Alateen (800) 344-2666	Phobics Anonymous (619) 322-COPE
Alcoholics Anonymous	Prostitutes Anonymous (818) 905-2188
Chemically Dependent Anonymous	Racism and Bigotry Anonymous
Chronic Fatigue Immune Disease Syndrome Anonymous	Recovering Couples Anonymous (314) 830-2600
Cocaine Anonymous	Self-Help Group Information (800) 222-5465
Co-Dependents Anonymous (602) 277-7991	Self-Mutilators Anonymous
Debtors Anonymous	Sexaholics Anonymous
Emotions Anonymous (612) 647-9712	Sex and Love Addiction Anonymous
Emphysema Anonymous (813) 391-9977	Sexual Addiction Hotline (800) 321-2066
Gamblers Anonymous (213) 386-8789	Shame Anonymous
Incest Survivors Anonymous (213) 428-5599	Shoplifters Anonymous (800) 848-9595
Marijuana Anonymous (800) 766-6779	Smokers Anonymous
Nar-Anon Family Group (213) 547-5800	Survivors of Incest Anonymous
Narcotics Anonymous	Survivors Reaching Out (916) 967-0424
Nicotine Anonymous	Workaholics Anonymous

From Joan Ellen Zweben, Ph.D., in *Psychotherapy and Substance Abuse: A Practitioner's Handbook,* Arnold M. Washton, Ph.D., editor, Guilford Press, N.Y., 1995.

In 1990, Trimpey set up a for-profit organization, Rational Recovery Systems, Inc. Many people had problems with the incongruity of a self-help meeting that had a for-profit motive. In 1993, a new organization, RRSN (Rational Recovery Self-Help Network), was developed as a nonprofit organization, with new by-laws and elected officers. Trimpey also developed Addictive Voice Recognition Training (AVRT) in 1993–1994. Many psychologists who were involved in the original Rational Recovery groups developed a new organization, called SMART Recovery. SMART Recovery is based on rational-emotive behavioral therapy and cognitive-behavioral approaches.

F. Michler Bishop's article "Rational-Emotive Behavior Therapy and Two Self-Help Alternatives to the 12-Step Model" (1995) outlines in more detail the history and dimensions of these approaches. The article describes some of the common tenets of these approaches as the following:

1. People are largely responsible for their behaviors, including addictive behaviors.
2. A person can recover; that is, a person can gain control over his or her addictive behaviors.
3. Lifetime membership is not required; many people can recover in a year or two.
4. Labeling of all kinds is discouraged; a person does not have to call himself or herself an alcoholic to begin to recover.
5. Alcoholism may or may not be a disease; however, a person has to find a way to cope and take responsibility for his or her life in any case.
6. The value of a person is not linked to his or her behavior, addictive or otherwise. A person will not be a better person if he or she gives up alcohol

or some other addictive behavior; he or she may be a happier person, a person who has better relationships and can keep a job, but behavioral change does not affect the "goodness" of the self.

7. A person is not necessarily, ipso facto, "in denial" if he or she does not accept the basic AA tenets.

8. A person is not doomed to a life of alcoholism if he or she does not accept help from AA, a rehabilitation clinic, a hospital, and so on. People can recover on their own with or without the help of professionals and/or self-help groups. (From F. Michler Bishop in *Psychotherapy and Substance Abuse: A Practitioner's Handbook,* edited by Arnold M. Washton, Ph.D., editor, Guilford Press, N.Y. 1995.)

Regardless of your own viewpoint about Alcoholics Anonymous, the Rational Recovery movement poses another alternative that may help a specific population. However, the approach may also cause others to continue to deny their alcoholism and drug addiction and continue to suffer the negative consequences of their alcohol/drug use.

Drug Addiction Treatment, 1960–1980

⚔ **History of Alcohol/Drug Treatment**

The four basic kinds of treatment that had federal, state, and local government support in the 1960s were

1. Therapeutic communities
2. Outpatient methadone clinics
3. Outpatient drug-free programs
4. University-affiliated clinical research centers

Therapeutic Communities

In 1958, Synanon was established as a model for most therapeutic communities, and the approach was expanded to other programs, including Day Top Village, Phoenix House, and Odyssey House in New York, and Delancey Street and The Family in California.

By 1978, a national organization, Therapeutic Communities of America, was organizing and unifying the goals of more than 300 therapeutic communities.

These communities were essentially residential programs, where alcoholics/addicts lived together in a family atmosphere, which promoted

- Addicts helping addicts to recovery in a structured lifestyle
- Confrontational and group therapies
- Adherence to the principles of AA and the 12 steps
- Honesty, drug abstinence, self-reliance, and personal responsibility through example

Methadone Treatment

The monumental methadone treatment work of Dole and Nyswander (1965) became a treatment model that spread throughout the United States. In 1980, 48 out of 50 states had methadone treatment programs.

Dole and Nyswander believed that heroin addiction is a metabolic disease and that a single administration of a narcotic can change a person's metabolism. Therefore, multiple administrations of the narcotic has even more potency in changing the person's nervous system. Dole and Nyswander searched for a medication to replace the metabolic need and craving for opiates (heroin). They found methadone, a long-acting, orally administered drug that eliminates the craving for heroin and other opioids. By successfully reducing the need for heroin, methadone reduces the antisocial, crime-related behavior of many addicts.

Methadone treatment involves detoxification and maintenance. *Detoxification* helps patients gradually reduce their dependence on opiates by giving them decreasing doses of methadone over 21 days. After detoxification, the individual is then drug free.

Maintenance essentially helps addicts develop a productive nondrug-using lifestyle. In effect, methadone replaces the devastating addiction to heroin and other opiates. Methadone does not affect the pleasure centers as do opiates, and addicts do not experience highs. The craving for heroin is stopped with the rather benign dependence on methadone. There is still some controversy with methadone maintenance because addicts are still dependent on another drug—methadone.

The treatment methods in both methadone detoxification and methadone maintenance include individual and group education, counseling sessions, self-help 12-step recovery, and rehabilitative services.

Outpatient Programs

A variety of outpatient treatment clinics existed in the 1970s and 1980s, including medically supervised programs and storefront centers. Medically supervised programs provided crisis-oriented medical services for alcohol/drug detoxification and overdose. At storefront drop-in/crisis counseling centers, treatment was unstructured, often focusing on crisis intervention, legal and criminal-justice counseling, medical care and/or health-related services, welfare and social services, employment, and couseling for family and interpersonal problems. The outpatient clinics served as a community-based entry point into the health care system for drug users in low-income communities.

University Research Centers

The drug revolution of the 1960s saw some significant changes. Drug use was no longer confined to inner-city, lower socioeconomic groups. When drugs began affecting the campus population, government spending increased for alcohol/drug research and treatment. During the same period, the government foresaw that large numbers of soldiers returning from Vietnam would need treatment for heroin addiction.

As a result, university-based research treatment centers opened, and many affiliated with the Veterans Administration. These centers tested new pharmacological aids. They evaluated medications, such as naltrexone, propoxyphene, levo-alpha-acetylmethadol (LAAM), and clonidine, for treatment of opiate craving and addiction.

Alcohol Treatment, 1970–1980

Private commercial, inpatient, and residential 28- to 30-day treatment programs rapidly expanded during the 1970s. Their tremendous financial success caused these programs to become a major standard of alcohol treatment. The 28- to 30-day length of stay was developed as a standard, not as a result of empirical study but, instead, as the negotiated arrangement between the hospital-based inpatient providers and the insurance companies. These inpatient programs were also successful because they were modeled after AA 12-step principles and integrated AA self-help meetings as part of the program.

When former first lady, Betty Ford, entered an alcohol treatment facility, public disclosure of her alcoholism did much to bring this kind of treatment into public view and acceptance (Ford 1987). "Her forthright discussion of her alcoholism and addiction and subsequent sponsorship of the Betty Ford Treatment Center provided a turning point in the alcoholism field" (Rawson 1991).

Disinterest in Alcohol/Drug Treatment, 1970s and 1980s

In the late 1970s, public interest in therapeutic communities, methadone treatment, outpatient programs, and university research centers seemed to wane. A variety of factors caused this loss of interest. First, the anticipated epidemic of heroin addicts returning from Vietnam was not realized. Many returning soldiers withdrew from heroin on the long boat and plane ride back home. For many of these young men, heroin use was inconsistent with their lifestyles back home. Others did not have the connections at home to maintain their addiction to heroin. Most discontinued opiate use without significant involvement in the treatment system.

Second, a dramatic reduction took place in the use of hallucinogens, sedative-hypnotics, and amphetamines. The primary nonopiate drugs used by the white population shifted primarily to marijuana and cocaine. At the time, the treatment community and general public thought marijuana and cocaine had a low risk for dependency. Most experts were still referring to marijuana and cocaine as psychologically dependency-producing rather than addicting. That mistake caused one of the major drug problems of the 1980s.

Third, the confrontive strategies of some therapeutic communities got out of control. Many therapeutic communities were exposed as dysfunctional systems much like the alcoholics/addicts' dysfunctional families of origin. Fourth, there was also opposition and public disenchantment with methadone maintenance on the principle that, rather than recovering, heroin addicts were addicted to a new drug—methadone.

Fifth, the efficacy and success of drop-in counseling centers was questioned. The criminal-justice system was often in conflict with these centers because clients were protected from criminal prosecution. Funding misappropriation and failure to adequately document client charts created tremendous conflict between centers and various government funding sources.

Due to these developments, public interest in drug addiction problems had decreased by the late 1970s. Although a treatment network had been established and some promising new treatments were in development, there appeared to be a societal loss of interest in drug addiction treatment. The one drug problem that obviously was going to persist was heroin. However, heroin was predominately a lower-income, inner-city, minority problem. Since middle-class Americans did not appear to be significantly at-risk from heroin problems, there was to be a loss of commitment to continued funding for new treatments. Funding levels in many of the programs dropped, resulting in a reduction in treatment slots and a reduction in ancillary services for the remaining slots. Research funding decreased, and many of the clinical strategies developed during the 1970s were put on the back burner. As the 1980s began, the drug treatment system appeared to have lost momentum (Rawson 1991).

Changes in the 1980s
Cocaine Epidemic

The explosive emergence of cocaine addiction in the 1980s challenged the alcohol/ drug treatment system to develop new treatment strategies. In 1984, Mark Gold and Arnold Herman described cocaine as a major public health concern. What experts thought was a rather benign, psychologically dependency-producing drug became known as the most addicting drug to date.

Animal studies, human studies, and clinical human reports all validate co-caine as the most highly addicting drug. Thus, warnings not to try it even once are not scare tactics but frightening reality. Sidney Cohen, the most prolific writer in the drug field, predicted in the early 1980s that "if cocaine were readily available and inexpensive, this would create the biggest drug epidemic we had ever known." His prediction has come true with crack cocaine.

In the early 1980s, there were no treatment programs for cocaine addiction. This new addict population, however, soon found treatment at inpatient alcohol treatment facilities. Facility directors responded to the need by developing cocaine treatment programs. Financial reward motivated these inpatient facilities, which saw a tremendous treatment population developing. Their television commercials added taglines stating, "We treat cocaine addiction, too." The constant flow of sports figures, celebrities, and other public figures further created an attractive no-toriety for these treatment programs.

The cocaine epidemic was even further catapulted into the public conscious-ness with the development of freebase cocaine. In the mid-1980s, crack cocaine use made cocaine available to all socioeconomic levels. Crack cocaine was marketed to new populations: those who could not afford cocaine in the inner city and young people. "Smokable cocaine, preprocessed in ready-to-smoke dosage units flooded major American cities from 1985 to today. Use of the drug in this form produced ad-diction very rapidly, and the availability of the drug in lower-cost dosage units made cocaine available to lower-income users. This combination produced a fire storm of addiction among lower income, minority, inner-city residents" (Rawson 1991).

Risk of AIDS

Exacerbating our crack cocaine epidemic is the AIDS crisis. The fact that the AIDS virus can be spread by high-risk sexual practices and the sharing of needles used to inject drugs has identified intravenous drug users as being at high risk for the spread of the HIV virus.

Treatment Trends

Some research has indicated that intensive outpatient alcohol/drug treatment is as effective as inpatient treatment. Ritson (1968) found no significant difference in effectiveness between inpatient and outpatient alcoholism treatment programs and questioned the routine hospitalization of alcoholics.

Due to the high cost of inpatient treatment, the trend in the 1990s was to refer more patients to outpatient treatment. Instead of the expensive, traditional, hospital-based 28-day inpatient chemical dependency treatment program, the alternative is intensive outpatient programs for 30 to 180 days. This is a more appropriate recovery period because it allows support during the time when the recovering alcoholic/addict is most vulnerable to relapse. It also minimizes the costly aspects of inpatient hospitalization.

Managed care is the trend today. Inpatient treatment programs are becoming part of a managed care network in order to survive. Approximately 40 percent of inpatient alcohol/drug treatment programs have gone out of business or have been consumed by managed care operations. Certainly, the preferred trend for managed care of alcohol/drug problems is outpatient counseling to minimize cost. As a result, the entire fields of alcohol/drug recovery, mental health, and co-occurring–disorders treatment have been affected by managed care. In his workshops "Brief Targeted Strategic Therapy for Relapse Prevention," Terence T. Gorski (1996) emphasizes treatment that is brief (up to 20 sessions), targeted (What is the problem?), strategic (What am I going to do about it? Step by step plan), and outcome-focused.

In the 1990s, there was a major focus on cognitive-behavioral therapies, solution-focused therapy, motivational interviewing, and other techniques that allow for brief, targeted therapies.

Arnold Washton, in his book *Psychotherapy and Substance Abuse* (1995), comments on solution-focused, brief therapy: "along the way we have discovered that regardless of what the problems are, the solutions to them seem to be so similar and yet so mundane; to do what will be good for clients and their families, such as talking to each other, being open and honest with each other, doing kind deeds, working hard, developing healthy habits, and looking for ways to change tomorrow by creating a vision of what they want."

Richard Rawson and associates (1988) outlined five basic stages of cocaine recovery, which also apply to alcohol/drug recovery. The time periods for each stage vary from individual to individual and based on the kinds of drugs used. The stages are

�ક Stages of Alcohol/Drug Recovery

0–15 days—withdrawal
16–45 days—honeymoon
46–120 days—the wall
121–180 days—adjustment
181+ 365 days—resolution
1 year—after resolution and beyond

Withdrawal Stage

Most of the physical aspects of withdrawal clear up after 3 to 7 days. Emotional feelings of anxiety, fatigue, pain, and depression persist throughout the first 15 days. Patients require education and direction during the withdrawal phase. Once patients go through the initial physical withdrawal, they want to leave treatment to avoid the emotional issues. (See Table 11.3.)

TABLE 11.3

Withdrawal Stage (0–15 Days)

Behavioral Symptoms	Cognitive Symptoms	Emotional Symptoms	Relationships
Increased need for sleep	Difficulty concentrating	Depression	Hostility
Behavioral inconsistency	Cravings for alcohol/drugs	Anxiety	Confusion
Impulsive, erratic behavior	Short-term	Self-doubt	Maladaptive coping
Anergia (lack of energy)	memory disruption	Shame	responses (inappropriate
			actions and behavior)
			Fear

From Richard Rawson et al., "Neurobiological treatment for cocaine dependency," in *Journal of Psychoactive Drugs* 22 (2), 159–71. Haight-Ashbury Publications, San Francisco, CA. Reprinted by permission.

TABLE 11.4

Honeymoon Stage (16–45 Days)

Behavioral Symptoms	Cognitive Symptoms	Emotional Symptoms	Relationships
High energy (perhaps manic)	Inability to prioritize	Optimism	Denial of addiction disorder
Poorly directed behavior	Abbreviated tension span	Overconfidence	Desire for things to
Excessive work and/or play	Inability to recognize	Feelings of being cured	return to normal
Return to alcohol, marijuana,	relapse potential		Conflict between spouse
or other drug use			or partner, family,
			and treatment

From Richard Rawson, et al., "Neurobiological treatment for cocaine dependency," in *Journal of Psychoactive Drugs* 22 (2), 159–71. Haight-Ashbury Publications, San Francisco, Calif. Reprinted by permission.

Honeymoon Stage

The honeymoon stage is the opposite of the withdrawal stage. (See Table 11.4.) The neophyte to recovery has gone through the difficult withdrawal stage and now feels energetic, confident, and optimistic. Cravings for alcohol/drugs are usually reduced and moods improve. This may lead clients to believe that recovery is easier than they thought it would be. Unwittingly, they begin to stray from the elements of their recovery program that helped them stay sober. Their behavior becomes more unstructured, inconsistent, and at times frenetic. They may go through a manic cycle, doing many things and overextending themselves. These behaviors then disrupt their recovery. This is the time when patients are most at-risk to return to alcohol use, marijuana use, or other drug use. They may convince themselves that they had a problem with a particular drug, not that they are at-risk with all alcohol/drugs.

The Wall Stage

After 45 days of sobriety, the largest percentage of relapses to alcohol/drugs occur, as shown in Table 11.5. Personal and interpersonal issues are emotionally experi-

TABLE 11.5

The Wall Stage (46–120 Days)

Behavioral Symptoms	Cognitive Symptoms	Emotional Symptoms	Relationships
Sluggishness, anergia (lack of energy)	Cognitive rehearsal of relapse, thinking, planning, or playing over the idea of relapse	Depression	Mutual blaming
Sexual disinterest/dysfunction	Euphoric recall, remembering the feelings and good times of drug/alcohol use	Anxiety	Irritability
Insomnia		Fatigue	Devaluation of progress
Discontinuation of treatment, recreational, exercise, diet, and/or occupationally appropriate behaviors	Increased frequency of drug/alcohol thoughts, dreams, and cravings	Boredom	Threatened separation or expulsion from home
Resumption of alcohol, marijuana, and/or other drug use	Denial or rationalization of emotional feelings and reactions	Anhedonia (inability to feel pleasure with things that normally give pleasure)	
	Difficulty concentrating	Irritability	

From Richard Rawson, et al., "Neurobiological treatment for cocaine dependency," in *Journal of Psychoactive Drugs* 22 (2), 159–71. Haight-Ashbury Publications, San Francisco, Calif. Reprinted by permission.

enced more fully during this stage. Relapse vulnerability increases as patients start feeling these emotional issues and begin to further sort out some of the problems in their lives and in their relationships. Patients often get discouraged and may verbalize that they "feel this will go on indefinitely." Patients may lose hope, strength, and motivation to continue in their process of recovery. This is a time when the supportive elements of their recovery program need to be strengthened, even though patients may attempt to alienate those who can help. Group counseling can be especially helpful at this stage. Others in the group who have gone through this difficult stage can share their struggle and ultimate success and lend support.

Adjustment Stage

The achievement of working through the intense feelings of the wall stage gives patients new hope and energy for recovery. Patients begin to accept that this is a life-long struggle. The achievement of being sober for 120 or more days affirms the addicts' ability to be sober for a long time. This is the longest time that most patients have ever been sober. (See Table 11.6.)

Resolution Stage

Completion of an intensive six-month program signals a shift from learning new skills to monitoring for relapse signs, maintaining a balanced lifestyle, and developing new areas of interest. Some clients may need individual psychotherapy or relationship work. (See Table 11.7.)

TABLE 11.6

Adjustment Stage (121–180 Days)

Behavioral Symptoms	Cognitive Symptoms	Emotional Symptoms	Relationships
Return to activities that may have been inappropriate and had relapse potential in early stages Return to normal behavior	Reduced frequency of drug/alcohol thoughts, dreams, and cravings	Reduced depression, anxiety, irritability Continued boredom Loneliness	Emergence of long-term relationship problems Resistance to assistance with relationship problems

From Richard Rawson, et al., "Neurobiological treatment for cocaine dependency," in *Journal of Psychoactive Drugs* 22 (2), 159–71. Haight-Ashbury Publications, San Francisco, Calif. Reprinted by permission.

TABLE 11.7

Resolution Stage (181+ Days)

Behavioral Symptoms	Cognitive Symptoms	Emotional Symptoms	Relationships
Emergence of other excessive behavior patterns: gambling, sex, work, eating, alcohol use	Questioning of the need for long-term monitoring and support	Emergence of psychodynamic material Boredom with abstinence	Conflict between recovery principles and relationship needs

From Richard Rawson, et al., "Neurobehavioral treatment for cocaine dependency," in *Journal of Psychoactive Drugs* 22 (2), 159–71. Haight-Ashbury Publications, San Francisco, Calif. Reprinted by permission.

Period After the Resolution Stage

After the resolution stage, the individual may need to do more in-depth counseling on family of origin and family systems issues. Issues of underlying affective disorders and other psychiatric disorders may also be more fully explored during this stage.

The factor most predictive of alcohol/drug treatment success is the counselor's attitude about treatment. When counselors truly believe that they can help patients, and have the necessary insight and training, treatment tends to be more successful. The same holds true for treatment programs.

"Since the addictive alcoholic patient is fundamentally hostile, his behavior is unconsciously designed to arouse negative feelings and to invite retaliation. Hostility and retaliation must be constantly guarded against by all treatment personnel" (Chafetz, Blane, and Hill 1970). Many mental health counselors are uncomfortable working with alcoholics/addicts because of the hostility and resistance of these patients in complying with treatment. The alcoholic/addict's grandiosity and denial of reality causes him or her to always be just one step away from terminating treatment and to rationalize away the need for change. "The pervasive hopelessness that some clients feel regarding themselves and their lives is apt to be projected into the treatment process and the counseling relationship, so that the client feels, 'This is useless; it isn't going to get me anywhere'" (Marks, Daroff, and Granick 1987).

Breaking through denial and the evasive tactics of alcoholics/addicts and their families requires a special kind of counselor. M. Duncan Stanton described that counselor as needing to be energetic to engage clients/patients and their families into treatment.

Addicts and alcoholics are constantly testing counselors' competency by pushing boundaries and testing to see if counselors know what they are talking about. Denial is the defense mechanism of addiction; alcoholics/addicts wonder if counselors are strong enough to break through their denial system.

"Basically, what I hear you saying, Mr. Smith, is 'Help!' "

Due to shameful feelings about self, alcoholics/addicts naturally seek or provoke rejection, hostility, anger, frustration, and even rage. Alcoholics/addicts test the counselor, as they do everyone in their own family systems. If counselors become provoked, alcoholics/addicts can play familiar "bad child at odds with authority" roles.

To effectively engage alcoholics/addicts and their families in treatment, counselors must exhibit a combination of both patience and boundary setting. Counselors need to be powerful yet sensitive, while recognizing both the need for limit setting and the inner vulnerability and sensitivities of the patients. Counselors must establish control of the therapeutic process, while being flexible to the patients' weak ego-strength and sensitivity to shame.

Group counseling is an effective treatment modality because alcoholics/addicts can be confronted in a caring way by other alcoholics/addicts. Each person in the group observes other group members struggling with similar issues and modeling growth and success in that struggle to maintain abstinence and sobriety.

Early Phases: Safety and Stabilization

In the early phases of counseling with substance abusers, the therapist must be concerned with *safety* and *stabilization.*

Safety and stabilization focus on a variety of factors that help the recovering alcoholic/addict maintain sobriety and a basic sense of balance in his or her life. Mistakenly, in their zealousness to uncover traumatic content, therapists may open up wounds without first determining if the individual has the emotional strength, resources, and support network to help him or her heal these wounds. Opening up these wounds may exacerbate already fragile relationships with family members and the spouse or partner. The result inevitably is a relapse to alcohol/drug use.

⚔ **Counseling and Chemical Dependency**

Not long ago, psychoanalytically trained therapists maintained that they could cure alcoholics/addicts. Psychoanalysts tended to approach alcohol/drug users with the fixed, often rigid perception that all addicts have personality and/or affective disorders, such as narcissism, depression, bipolar disorder, and borderline personality disorder. The psychoanalysts then tried to treat alcoholics/addicts by personality reorganization and lumped all of the disorders together. The psychoanalysts attempted to show the addicts that the etiology of their drinking/drugging was due to personality disorders. "Analysts had unreal expectations of their patients, such as that they could give up their drug use immediately while in therapy, come in at fixed times, fit into the fifty-minute sessions, and adhere to the requirements of therapy" (Brill 1981).

Probing into feelings so early in recovery often caused alcoholics/addicts to reexperience traumatic emotional issues that they were not emotionally ready or able to deal with. As a result, alcoholics/addicts did what they had done before when feeling emotionally vulnerable—go back to using alcohol/drugs.

Unfortunately, this treatment still continues today, as professionals try to validate their theoretical models, without insight into when and how it is appropriate to deal with underlying issues and feelings. These psychoanalytical issues are best dealt with when alcoholics/addicts have maintained a significant period of sobriety (usually one to five years), have a strong support system, have the ego-strength to tolerate the feelings, and have the insight and motivation to work on these issues. This happens during Stage 3 of alcohol/drug treatment, as Table 11.8 shows. The first phase of counseling, therefore, focuses on strengthening both the alcoholic/addict's alcohol/drug recovery support system and the therapeutic alliance.

In the early stages of counseling with alcoholics/addicts the therapist needs to be extremely active, focusing on relapse prevention, helping the client overcome fears of and resistance to AA or other self-help programs, facilitating the development of a sponsor relationship, focusing on stress and anger management, and using other factors that will meet safety and stabilization needs. The need for interventions to stop the drinking and drugging and a solid period of sobriety are prerequisites for successful counseling/psychotherapy (Fox 1958, Tiebout 1962).

TABLE 11.8

Stages of Drug Alcohol Treatment

Stage of Treatment	Patient Status	Treatment
1	"I can't drink." (need for external control)	Alcohol detoxification, directive psychotherapy, AA, Al-Anon, family therapy, Antabuse
2	"I won't drink." (internalized control)	Directive psychotherapy, supportive psychotherapy, AA, consider discontinuing Antabase
3	"I don't have to drink." (conflict resolution)	Psychoanalytically oriented psychotherapy

From S. Zimburg, "Principles of Alcoholism Psychotherapy" in *Practical Approaches to Alcoholism Psychotherapy*, 2d ed, edited by S. Zimberg, J. Wallace, and S.B. Blume, Human Science Press, 1985.

Affect (Feeling), Recognition, and Modulation

Once stabilization and safety needs are addressed, the next stage of counseling may focus on affect, recognition, and modulation. The therapist slowly works with the client in labeling and tolerating feelings. The counseling can then take many forms, exploring a variety of issues relevant to the chemical dependency. Throughout this process, regular review of relapse dynamics and support for a stable and secure recovery from alcohol/drugs are maintained.

Counseling approaches explore both the conscious and the unconscious levels of feelings. The Johari window in Table 11.9 is a training model that describes the domain of counseling. Counseling focuses on all four of these areas of self. These areas cover the following:

1. Public self: The public self includes all the aspects about the individual that are known by the individual and others close to the individual (e.g., age, marital status, hobbies, job, interests, basic personality type).
2. Private self: The private self involves information that the individual is aware of but others don't know (e.g., sexual practices, mistakes in the past or present, private feelings or thoughts, family of origin issues).
3. Blind self: The blind self includes things the individual is not consciously aware of that others are aware of about the individual (e.g., personality characteristics; denial about others' behavior or own behavior; lack of awareness of interpersonal, occupational, social, and marital issues).
4. Discovery self: Discovery self is the category of the future. These things are not in the conscious awareness of the individual or of others and will be discovered in the future (e.g., the natural changes that occur in life's unexpected journey).

By placing a major emphasis in counseling on Category 2, the private self, and Category 3, the blind self, individuals can see changes in Category 1, the public self, and Category 4, the discovery self. When individuals are defensive or unwilling to deal with their feelings about their private selves and blind selves, there are limitations to progress and personal change. Clients would do well to follow Louise Hay's (1984) advice: "If you think of the hardest thing for you to do and how much you resist it, then you're looking at your greatest lesson at the moment. Surrendering, giving

---

TABLE 11.9

Johari Window

Others	Self	
	Things You Know About Self	**Things You Don't Know About Self**
Things They Know About You	1. Public	3. Blind
Things They Do Not Know About You	2. Private	4. Discovery

Adapted from *Group Processes: An Introduction to Group Dynamics* by Joseph Luft. Mayfield Publishing Company, Copyright © 1984, 1970, and 1963 by Joseph Luft. Reprinted by permission.

up the resistance, and allowing yourself to learn what you need to learn, will make the next step easier."

Other techniques that are often included as part of the counseling approach to chemical dependency recovery include relaxation training (e.g., biofeedback), stress reduction, anger management, problem-solving/coping skills, communication skills, exercise, nutrition, life management (i.e., balance in activities), relationships, and work.

The common goals of all counseling approaches are education; the provision of information and resources; catharsis (patients' release of emotion and feelings); connectedness and trust, which facilitates disclosure of feelings and concerns; support for positive growth; awareness and insight; and personality change (reorganization).

Family Treatment

Peter Steinglass (1979) outlined five major family modalities for alcohol/drug treatment:

1. Pure family therapy is based on a family systems mode, in which all family members are present at the same time in therapy sessions.
2. Individual or group treatment approaches fulfill specific criteria suggested by a family therapy theory of alcoholism, such as the concept of homeostasis.
3. Therapies involving concurrent therapeutic work with both the alcoholic and family members rely on a more traditional, individual, psychodynamic theoretical base.
4. Specific therapies designed for the spouses or partners of alcoholics
5. Supportive treatments assist nonalcoholic family members in dealing with common problems related to having an alcoholic family member.

Some of the goals of the family treatment modality are to

1. Develop family commitment for recovery
2. Identify enabling behaviors and counter them
3. Encourage leveling or open communication
4. Validate members' reality and feelings regarding the chemical abusing member and the negative consequences of chemical abuse
5. Educate the family to the family disease concept
6. Elaborate on concrete rules and consequences
7. Plan and define family leisure activities
8. Solidify the parental coalition
9. Specify attitudinal and behavioral changes for each member
10. Prepare relapse prevention guidelines and family response

According to Steinglass (1979), the advantages of a family systems approach are the following:

1. It bridges the disparity between psychodynamic and stress-reduction explanations of drinking.
2. It explains diversity in alcoholic families by redirecting the focus from common etiological characteristics in alcoholic families to the common function of alcohol to maintain imbalanced family systems.
3. It gives therapists an understanding of alcoholism as a total system's behavior.

Group Therapy

Therapy groups have the same guidelines as individual counseling. Members adhere to strict confidentiality and do not socialize outside of the group. The group's purpose is to provide a safe environment to explore individual and interpersonal issues.

Most therapy groups are led by professional counselors trained in group therapy and experienced in the dynamics of chemical dependency recovery, family systems, and related areas of expertise. Some therapy groups have co-therapists, usually male-female counseling teams that co-lead and clarify issues in the group.

Therapy groups can take many forms. I have found more success leading all-male recovery groups, and female therapists have seen a benefit to all-female therapy groups. This avoids some of the sexual and gender-specific issues that may distract from the focus on alcohol/drug recovery. Most groups have from four to eight members to allow adequate opportunity for interaction by all group members.

As discussed in Chapter 7, the 11 curative factors of group psychotherapy outlined by Yalom are

1. Instilling hope
2. Sharing universality
3. Imparting information
4. Fostering altruism
5. Recapitulating the primary family group
6. Developing socializing techniques
7. Imitating behavior
8. Sharing interpersonal learning
9. Developing group cohesiveness
10. Sharing catharsis
11. Exploring existential factors

Intensive Treatment

Intensive treatment modalities include intensive outpatient treatment, inpatient detoxification, and residential and inpatient treatment. These programs use a variety of treatment methods too lengthy to describe here.

An integral component of counseling alcoholics/addicts is relapse prevention. The traditional inpatient, residential alcohol/drug treatment program has people leave the program after 28 days. They leave because this is the usual time period that insurance companies have established as reimbursable. Unfortunately, from 30 to 120 days is the time when alcoholics/addicts are most at risk for relapse. The initial glow of the alcoholics' first 30 days of recovery is soon replaced with awareness of the reality of struggling to stay sober in the real world. After the first 30 days, the alcoholic/addict faces the first pivotal relapse point, or the wall. In the next 90 days, there are repeated situations that threaten the addicts' sobriety. "About two-thirds of relapses occur within the first 90 days following treatment" (i.e., between 30 and 120 days of sobriety) (Marlatt and Gordon 1985).

❈ Relapse Prevention

Recognition of the Signs of Relapse

One must be trained to recognize the signs and problems that may cause relapse. (See Table 11.10.) The defense mechanisms of denial (rationalization and minimization) may be invoked to avoid looking at the potential for relapse. Many alcoholics/addicts tend to discount the stressful situations and distressful lifestyles and behaviors that contribute to relapse. The alcoholic/addict trained in relapse prevention can recognize these problem areas and avoid being blindsided by high-risk relapse situations. (See Table 11.11.)

Habit

Alan Marlatt and Judith Gordon (1985) described the following stages in changing a habit:

1. Preparation for change, involving commitment, desire, and motivation to change
2. Implementation of the specific behavioral change (such as to eat healthy, balanced meals or to stop using alcohol/drugs)
3. Maintenance of change in long-term goals

Marlatt and Gordon quote Mark Twain, who said, "Quitting smoking is easy; I've done it hundreds of times." Deciding to change a habit is easy. However, implementing the change is a bit more difficult, and maintaining change is the most difficult stage because it's an ongoing, long-term goal.

For alcoholics/addicts, the beginning step is admitting that they are powerless over alcohol/drugs and have the desire to stop using. Quitting is just the beginning of the journey; implementing the change by working a program of recovery is the next difficult step. Maintaining that program despite stressful situations and life events is the most difficult, day-at-a-time struggle for recovering alcoholics/addicts.

TABLE 11.10

Relapse-Prone vs. Recovery-Prone

Denial and Evasion	Recognition and Problem Solving
Relapse-Prone	*Recovery-Prone*
Evade or deny the sticking point	Recognize a problem exists
Stress	Accept that it is O.K. to have problems
Compulsive behavior	Detach to gain perspective
Avoid others	Ask for help
Problems	Respond with action when prepared
Evade/deny new problems	

© Terence T. Gorski, The Cenaps Corporation, Homewood, IL., 708-799-5000. Published by Herald House Press, Independence, MO., 1-800-767-8181.

Caution: relapse ahead.

Drawing by Ed Arno; © 1980 The New Yorker Magazine, Inc. Reprinted with permission.

TABLE 11.11

Analysis of Situations for Relapse

Situations	Example	Sample Number	Percentage
Frustration/anger	Patient tried to call his wife (they were separated); she hung up on him; he became angry and took a drink.	14	29%
Social pressure	Patient went with friends to a bar after work. They put pressure on him to join the crowd, and he was unable to resist.	11	23
Intrapersonal temptation	Patient walked by a bar and just unconsciously walked in for no real reason; could not resist the temptation to take a drink.	10	21
Negative emotional state	Patient living alone, no job, complained of feeling bored and useless; could see no reason he should not take a drink.	5	10
Miscellaneous other situations	Patient reported that everything was going so well for him that he wanted to celebrate by having a drink.	5	10
No situation given or unable to remember		3	7

Source: Data from Alan Marlatt and Judith Gordon, *Relapse Prevention*, Guilford Press, New York, 1985.

The first 120 days of chemical dependency recovery are the most difficult because it is a significant period of time to establish a period of maintenance. Even after this primary period of maintenance, there is still no guarantee. Stressful situations, places, times, and interpersonal interactions may still cause a relapse. Even after one year of maintenance, there are pressures, as evidenced by the many alcoholics/addicts who have problems at their one-year anniversary of sobriety. After two to five years of sobriety, alcohol/drug use is not a choice for most, even during stressful periods.

Causes of Relapse

A study by Marlatt and Gordon (1985) identified three major categories that cause recovering alcoholics to be vulnerable to relapse:

1. *Negative emotional states* cause 35 percent of all relapses. In these situations, individuals experience negative emotional states, moods, or feelings, such as frustration, anger, anxiety, depression, or boredom. (See Table 11.12.)
2. *Interpersonal conflict* causes 16 percent of all relapses. These situations involve an ongoing or a relatively recent conflict associated with any interpersonal relationship, such as marriage, friendship, relationships with family members, employer-employee relations. Arguments and interpersonal confrontation occur frequently in this category. (See Table 11.13.)
3. *Social pressure* causes 20 percent of all relapses. In these situations, individuals respond to the influence of another person or group of people exerting pressure on them to engage in the taboo behavior. (See Table 11.14.)

TABLE 11.12

Negative Emotional States

Difficulty Managing Negative Emotional States	Difficulty Managing Stress Effectively	Difficulty Dealing with Feelings from Family of Origin	Difficulty with Blocked Goal-Directed Activities	Physical States That Contribute to Negative Emotional States
Feelings of depression, anxiety, rage, and distress exacerbated by feelings of shame and a poor sense of self	Feelings of confusion and overreaction to problems and conflicts	Feelings of emotional pain, loss, grief, separation, abandonment, violation, rejection, and isolation	Feelings of aggressiveness and rage Feelings of being hassled by normal daily living Feelings of boredom loneliness, isolation, uselessness, helplessness, or hopelessness; lack of purpose in life	Physical health problems, pain, illness, injury, fatigue, specific physical disorders (e.g., chronic or recurrent pain caused by headaches, menstrual cramps, back pain) Physical states associated with prior substance abuse

Sometimes recovering alcoholics/addicts do not develop or maintain all aspects of their recovery program. Table 11.15 lists some of the reasons certain persons are more prone to relapse. These factors may lead people to make impulsive decisions to test their recovery by using alcohol/drugs. In effect, this testing of their willpower to go back to controlled alcohol/drug use frequently leads to relapse.

Cravings and Urges

Thoughts, desires, even dreams about using alcohol/drugs are very common in chemical dependency recovery. A variety of things can trigger this craving for alcohol/drugs, and cravings acted on can lead to relapse. The most effective way of coping with cravings and urges is to detach from the craving. "Instead of identifying with the urge (e.g., I really want a cigarette right now) the client can be trained to

TABLE 11.13

Interpersonal Conflicts

Conflicts with Partner/Spouse	Conflicts with Family	Other Stressful Interpersonal Conflicts
Once sober, the recovering person begins to see dysfunctional aspects of the relationship. Different stages of recovery: one person is working on her recovery program and the other is not actively working on his issues New adjustment in relationship due to recovery Fear that the relationship will not be maintained or improve	Recognition of family dysfunction may lead to unresolved feelings of loss, abandonment, violation, and rejection; then these issues are stuffed and not worked out. Family system does not change or adapt to alcoholic/addict's recovery but maintains some dysfunctional patterns of communication and interaction.	Separation; divorce; or continued physical, sexual, or emotional violations Conflicts with employer, employees, friends, and other social situations Pattern of excessive fighting, arguments, and conflicts that go unresolved and are a repetitive cycle Pleasing people, avoiding conflicts, not telling others how one feels, acquiescing, and avoiding anger and other feelings associated with conflict

TABLE 11.14

Social Pressure

Peer Group	Isolating
Return to old alcohol/drug–using peer group Hang out with alcohol/drug users	Withdrawing from friends who support recovery; nonattendance or passive involvement with support group, such as AA or NA Not maintaining contact with sponsor, counselor, or aftercare program Emotionally shutting down, not sharing feelings with others who are trusted and supportive of recovery; AA's motto is "Silence is the enemy of recovery"

T A B L E   1 1 . 1 5

Other At-Risk Factors for Relapse

Miscellaneous Factors

High-stress personality type

Mood swings, temper, rage

Shutting down, withdrawing emotionally

Overseparation and overattachment

Difficulty establishing intimacy and maintaining appropriate boundaries in relationships

Personality disorders: narcissism, bipolar disorder, borderline personality, codependent personality, depression (affective disorder), anxiety disorders, obsessive-compulsive disorders, and others

High-risk lifestyle: constant changes, high-stress job (i.e., always wheeling and dealing), financial and employment roller coaster, partner/spouse relationship changes and/or conflicts, always around others who use alcohol/drugs (entertainment industry, business-related drinking, bars, nightclubs, etc.)

Financial: problems in managing finances, inability to control spending, making inappropriate financial commitments and taking on inappropriate financial obligations

Problems in employment, career change with poor planning

Trouble with back taxes and the Internal Revenue Service or other previous debt

Thinking and Perceptual Factors

Self-defeating or self-sabotaging thoughts

Painful memories and/or euphoric recall of alcohol/drug use

Return of denial and inability to consciously recognize loss of control over alcohol/drugs

Poor judgment and negative or grandiose thinking, which leads to impulsive self-destructive decisions

Overreacting, crisis building, and creating problems when things are beginning to go better

Spiritual Factors

Feeling at a loss, not feeling that life has meaning

Difficulty maintaining sobriety or having a reason for staying sober

Existential despair: not seeing a function of or reason for living

---

monitor the urge or desire from the point of view of a detached observer (I am now experiencing the craving/urge to smoke). By externalizing and labeling the craving/urge and watching it come and go through the eyes of the observer, there will be a decreased tendency to identify with the urge and feel overwhelmed by its power" (Marlatt and Gordon 1985).

Recovering alcoholics/addicts can identify triggers leading to cravings for alcohol/drugs and develop an awareness as to why cravings occur. Then the alcoholics/addicts can structure their lives either to avoid these triggers or to desensitize themselves to the trigger.

A trigger is "a stimulus which has been repeatedly associated with the preparation for, anticipation of, or the actual use of alcohol/drugs. These stimuli include people, places, things, times of day, emotional states, and alcohol/drugs" (Rawson 1989). The following lists of time, place, thing, and people triggers show how diverse triggers are:

Time

- Periods of idle or leisure time
- Periods of extended stress
- Payday, holidays, Fridays, and Saturdays
- Birthdays and anniversaries
- Specific times of the day or evening
- Vacation
- Periods of unemployment

Place

- Drug dealers' home, bars, and parties
- Neighborhoods where drugs are dealt
- Clubs, concerts, and social events
- Places where alcohol/drugs have been used before

Things

- Drug dealers' car, telephone number, or name
- Large amounts of cash, $100 bills, and bank machines
- Paraphernalia: pipes, syringe, and rolling papers
- Movies, films, and television shows about alcohol/drugs and alcohol/drug lifestyle
- Particular music
- Alcohol and tobacco advertisements
- Conferences or seminars on alcohol/drugs
- Sexually explicit movies or magazines

People

- Alcohol/drug using friends
- Drug dealers and bartenders
- Partner/spouse, relatives, and family members who use alcohol/drugs
- Sexual encounters
- Groups of people talking about or using alcohol/drugs

Drug Relapse Induced by Alcohol Use

Some individuals in recovery test their recovery by using alcohol instead of drugs. They rationalize that they were addicted to drugs but never had a problem with alcohol. This rationalization is unfounded. Once addicted to drugs, people have an addiction potential to all drugs, including alcohol. It is only a matter of time before individuals build tolerance and become addicted to alcohol or alcohol use impairs judgment and they return to drugs.

TABLE 11.16

Percentage Return to Regular Cocaine Use, Matrix Study, 1988

Did return to alcohol use	50%
Did not return to alcohol use	6
Sierra Tucson, 1988	
Did return to alcohol use	61%
Did not return to alcohol use	8

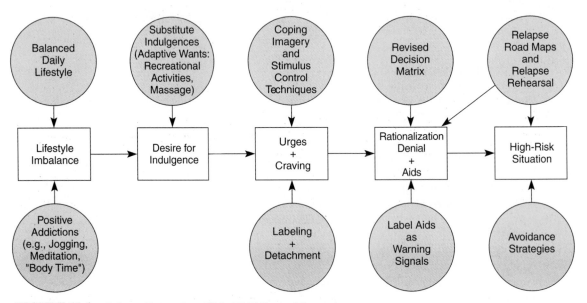

FIGURE 11.1   *Relapse Prevention: Global Self-Control Strategies*

Richard Rawson (1988) has established that a return to alcohol use by cocaine addicts increases their cocaine relapse vulnerability by an astounding 800 percent. (See Table 11.16.)

✗ Relapse-Prevention Strategies

Once recovering alcoholics/addicts understand which factors contribute to relapse, they can try to prevent relapses. Also, all chemical dependency treatment programs have the responsibility to conduct relapse prevention to help maintain the client/patient's chemical dependency recovery. Alan Marlatt and Judith Gordon have developed a very organized model of global self-control strategies in relapse prevention (see Figure 11.1).

Lifestyle Imbalance

You may recall that homeostasis is an organism's natural tendency to seek a balanced state. If a life is imbalanced, the individual experiences too much or too little

Case Study 11.1

Alcohol-Induced Relapse

Mary

Mary, 42 years old, married with three children, was hospitalized for severe depression, panic reactions, and post-traumatic stress. She was also assessed as having an addiction to pain medication and tranquilizers. As part of her treatment plan, Mary worked with the co-occurring team (alcohol/drug and psychiatric problems) on her addiction to pills. Gradually, she was physically withdrawn from the tranquilizers and pain medication, while she received individual and group counseling on alcoholism and drug addiction. Mary also attended AA meetings and educational classes on various aspects of the disease model of alcoholism and drug addiction.

Approximately six weeks after her discharge from the hospital, Mary's aftercare nurse asked if it was appropriate for Mary to be drinking wine with dinner each evening. Despite in-service training on alcoholism and drug addiction with the hospital staff, Mary's psychiatrist had approved her use of wine with dinner. When asked about his counsel, the psychiatrist felt that Mary had no history of alcoholism and her problem was with drugs (medication).

Despite interventions by the treatment team, the psychiatrist insisted that Mary's use of alcohol with dinner was appropriate. Mary was only able to maintain this use of wine with dinner for a short time. Two weeks later, under the influence of alcohol, Mary tripped and broke her leg. She then lapsed back to using pain medication and alcohol. Six weeks later, she was readmitted to the hospital.

Unfortunately, there are many Marys who continue on this revolving door cycle with treatment facilities.

---

stress; eventually, that results in a compensation in some area of life, or a breakdown. The imbalance can be evidenced by

- Too much work (workaholism) or overresponsibility, resulting in a neglect of self
- Difficulty relaxing; lack of spontaneity; and an inability to have fun, enjoy others, and feel emotions (shut down or emotionally unavailable to self or others, especially spouse and family)—"too many shoulds, too many wants"
- Too much play or irresponsibility, resulting in procrastination, laziness, avoidance of conflicts and pain, and avoidance of life-maintaining activities (passively forgetting or avoiding responsibilities)—"too many wants, not paying attention to needs"

Both workaholic and playaholic behavior have common root issues: the avoidance of taking up painful issues of self-concept interpersonal and life situation displeasure and the avoidance of recognizing and integrating true feelings. Usually, some deeper family of origin issues that have not been worked through are recapitulated (duplicated) in present-day life situations.

The alcoholic/addict has lived a life structured around alcohol/drugs. Removing the alcohol/drugs is a challenge to the individual and family's systemic organization. Triggers for alcohol/drug cravings, and potential relapse, are frequently related to the lack of organization and structure in the lives of the newly sober alcoholic/addict and the family. Structure promotes a variety of important recovery functions. First, structure redirects idle time through time scheduling, goal setting, and planning of activities. This includes work, play, vacation, recreation, and leisure time. Structured time maintains a focus on activities and is based on an integration of feelings. Second, structure teaches balance in daily activities, balance between work and play, balance in responsibility, and balance in establishing effective boundaries in relationships. Third, structure promotes self-concept by placing emphasis on moving from passive dependence to proactive involvement in life. Structure reduces fears and anxieties, and it promotes self-reliance and preparedness. *Freedom* is a word often misused to represent lack of responsibility. Freedom is choosing your own version of responsibility to self and others and the structure necessary to achieve such freedom.

The following pitfalls of structure are adapted from Richard Rawson (1989):

- A rigid dysfunctional approach, overdoing, scheduling unrealistically
- Burnout from workaholism and overextending of self
- Neglecting recreation and leisure activity
- Being perfectionistic and/or overly zealous about recovery
- Talking a program, rather than working a program of recovery
- Alienating others by preaching your program of recovery
- External control—structure that is not self-imposed; pleasing the counselor, sponsor, spouse, parent, instead of working a program for self; blind adherence without self-involvement in program
- Failure to maintain spontaneously to others, and life in general

Areas of structure for the recovering alcoholic/addict include the following social, health, and cognitive facets of life.

Interpersonal and Social Recovery Support System

- Drug-free friends who understand and support recovery from alcohol/drugs
- Self-help groups, such as Alcoholics Anonymous, Narcotics Anonymous, Adult Children of Alcoholics, and Co-Dependents Anonymous
- Spouse/partner and family members who understand recovery and are involved in their own recovery and counseling
- Support of an AA or NA sponsor; someone who has strong personal recovery is available and active in pointing out relapse vulnerability
- Support from an aftercare program, group, or individual and family counseling on a regular basis

Health and Physical Well-Being

- A regular program of exercise: athletic activities, slow long-distance walking, or jogging/running, minimum three to five times per week
- Balanced, nutritionally sound, and structured diet
- Adequate sleep, functional stress level, appropriate balance between work and play and activity and rest

Cognitive, Emotional, and Spiritual Self

- Good sense of self, as a person (1) who is unique and worthwhile with emerging talents and skills; (2) who can accomplish things, has good

decision-making and problem-solving skills—no self-sabotaging; (3) who can trust and be trusted while setting appropriate boundaries in relationships; and (4) who has the ability to resolve conflict and communicate feelings
- Ability to be aware of feelings and thoughts and to integrate feelings and thoughts in taking appropriate action
- Ability to adapt to life changes and stresses and to choose to grow emotionally, intellectually, occupationally, and interpersonally
- Ability to achieve at work, at school, at home, and in the community
- Spiritual orientation and growth with others and to spiritual life in general

Desire for Self-Indulgence

Frustration and anger are feelings that result from not attaining personal long-range goals. After losing hope and motivation, the recovering alcoholic/addict decides to take the short-range, immediate relief by using alcohol/drugs.

The immediate gratification of drugs needs to be countered with the understanding that things change, feelings can be felt, and time changes the way one views things. The entire chemical dependency recovery program is designed to get the person back on track by using new recovery skills to instill feelings of hope. Those in recovery should follow the AA saying "Take it one day at a time."

> Waiting is not mere empty hoping. It has the inner certainty of reaching a goal. Such certainty alone gives that light which leads to success. This leads to the perseverance that leads to good fortune and bestows power to cross the great water.
>
> One is faced with a danger that must be overcome. Weakness and impatience can do nothing. Only a strong man can stand up to his fate, for his inner security enables him to endure to the end. This strength shows itself in uncompromising truthfulness (with himself). It is only when we have the courage to face things exactly as they are, without any sort of self-deception or illusion, that a light will develop out of events, by which the path to success may be recognized. This recognition must be followed by resolute and persevering action. For only the man who goes to meet his fate resolutely is equipped to deal with it adequately. Then he will be able to cross the great water—that is to say, he will be capable of making the necessary decision and of surmounting the danger. (*I Ching,* Hexagram 5)

AA Serenity Prayer as a Relapse-Prevention Technique

The serenity prayer of AA is an extremely valuable relapse-prevention technique that is easily invoked:

> God grant me the serenity
> To accept the things I cannot change,
> Courage to change the things I can,
> And wisdom to know the difference.

Accepting the things I cannot change means accepting what can't be controlled. Those in recovery need the skills to let go, to not control others or project their wishes on others. As a result, recovering alcoholics/addicts avoid the negative emotional feelings of anger, rage, anxiety, depression, and intolerable frustration.

Courage to change the things I can means controlling what can be controlled. Those in recovery need the skills to focus on today, to take action, and to work on themselves. As a result, recovering alcoholics/addicts develop positive affirmations, progress toward long-term goals, and develop a stronger sense of self.

Wisdom to know the difference means learning to discriminate between the impossible and the possible. Those in recovery need the skills to talk about feelings, accept limits, and ask "Can I change this?" As a result, recovering alcoholics/addicts can achieve a balanced lifestyle, can develop the ability to deal with urges and cravings, and can learn to avoid impulsive, destructive decisions and interactions.

> Recovery is facilitated by the individual's ability to adapt to change and integrate feelings related to change. Striving for progress rather than perfection is a healthy goal.

�ખ Controlled Drinking Controversy

Widespread controversy has arisen over the issue of the controlled drinking of alcohol. Controlled drinking has been defined as those experiencing problems with alcohol being taught to self-monitor their drinking and not return to problem drinking. "With the trend has come a maelstrom of controversy. Many traditional figures in the alcoholism field have bitterly attacked the concept of controlled drinking, maintaining that a disease model and total abstinence represents the only true hope for alcoholics" (Miller 1980).

Ruth Fox (1963) has asserted that, "among my own approximately 3,000 patients, not one has been able to achieve moderate drinking, although almost every one of them has tried to."

Once someone has been diagnosed as being addicted to alcohol/drugs, experts predominantly agree that a return to controlled alcohol or drug use is extremely difficult and could lead to a tragic outcome if pursued.

Proponents of controlled drinking agree with this position that controlled drinking is not a viable option for alcoholics, especially alcoholics already in successful abstinence recovery. They stress that controlled drinking is a viable treatment approach only for some problem drinkers. Controlled drinking is considered only when individuals have a stable marital and occupational background and do not have a family history of alcoholism.

William Miller and G.R. Caddy (1977) identified controlled drinking as an appropriate treatment approach in situations involving resistant clients who view abstinence as unachievable or undesirable. The major criteria are (1) their refusal to consider abstinence as a goal; (2) their strong external demands to drink or lack of social support for abstinence; (3) an early-stage drinking problem without a history of physiological addiction; and (4) prior failure of competent abstinence-oriented treatment.

The problem with these criteria is that denial may be ignored. Almost every alcoholic/addict would like to continue using alcohol/drugs in a controlled fashion. Refusal to consider abstinence, failure in abstinence-oriented treatment, and preference for controlled drinking may all be part of the alcoholic/addict's denial system.

Miller (1980) identified additional criteria that would favor choosing the abstinence model instead of moderation:

1. Evidence of progressive liver disease or other medical problems
2. Psychological problems of sufficient magnitude to render even moderate drinking harmful

3. Personal commitment to abstinence or strong external demands for abstinence
4. Pathological intoxication
5. History of physiological addiction and severe withdrawal symptoms
6. Use of medication considered dangerous when combined with alcohol
7. Current successful abstinence following severe problem drinking
8. Prior failure of competent moderation-oriented treatment

Additional at-risk factors for controlled drinking include a current addiction, a family history of addiction, high-stress individual, high-stress lifestyle, inability to cope effectively with stress, and other relapse dynamics present, such as poor health, negative emotional states, or psychiatric problems.

Vernon Fox (1976) and others agree that abstinence remains the viable and conservative recommendation for alcohol/drug recovery while research and guidelines establish accurate means for identifying clients appropriate for controlled drinking as an optimal treatment modality. The primary goal of recovery is complete abstinence from alcohol/drugs.

Controlled drinking is just one example of a harm-reduction approach. The harm-reduction approach has its roots in The Netherlands public health, or sociomedical, perspective. In 1984, the Dutch were concerned with "reducing the harm" of drug use, abuse, and dependence and implemented the first needle exchange program to reduce the harm of hepatitis due to injecting drugs. They saw the greater risk of hepatitis and had public support. This is very different from the moral and political perspective, in the United States, that needle exchange programs are not addressing the substance dependence problem.

The harm-reduction approach takes a more realistic perspective—that people are going to use drugs, so why not reduce the risk of other diseases? The success of the needle exchange program in The Netherlands is due to the support of the government and the Dutch people. In the United States, the limited needle exchange programs lacked that support. It is believed that the epidemic levels of HIV/AIDS in Europe never reached those levels in The Netherlands due to the needle exchange program. Other countries have successfully implemented needle exchange programs to prevent hepatitis and HIV/AIDS—England, Switzerland, and Australia.

The United States has maintained "supply reduction" as the dominant approach to the drug problem. Recent efforts to expand the methadone treatment programs is another effort at harm reduction. Methadone treatment is being expanded to primary care physicians, rather than being limited to the methadone treatment center. LAAM, a longer acting methadone, is being used as well.

Harm reduction includes a wide range of programs and policies, including the following:

1. *Advocacy for changes in drug policies*—legalization, decriminalization, ending the drug prohibition, changes in drug paraphernalia laws, reduction of penalties for drug-related crimes, and treatment alternatives to incarceration
2. *HIV/AIDS–related interventions*—needle/syringe exchange programs, HIV prevention/intervention programs, bleach distribution, referrals for HIV

⚔ Harm-Reduction Approach

testing and HIV medical care, and referrals for HIV/AIDS–related psychosocial care and case management

3. *Broader drug treatment options*—methadone maintenance by primary care physicians, changes in methadone regulations, heroin substitution programs, and new experimental treatments

4. *Drug abuse management for those who wish to continue using drugs*— counseling and clinical case-management programs that promote safer and more responsible drug use

5. *Ancillary interventions*—housing and other entitlements, healing centers, and support and advocacy groups (Inciardi & Harrison, 2000)

⚔ An Effective Alcohol/Drug Recovery Strategy

The following steps can help those in recovery achieve their goal:

1. *Break the bonds of denial.* Recovery is an ongoing process often facilitated by the support of others—friends, others in recovery from alcohol/drugs, family, or a counselor. All of these people can help alcoholics/addicts work through their denial and maintain sobriety.

2. *Actively work and apply the 12 steps and other AA principles in recovery.* This provides guidelines, structure, and support for recovery efforts. Developing a relationship with an AA or NA sponsor is a key element in effectively helping the newly recovering person understand and implement the principles of AA.

3. *Seek nonchemical altered states of consciousness.* The innate human drive to alter one's sense of consciousness can be attained through healthy and balanced activities, not the use of alcohol/drugs. These activities enhance the individual's sense of self and well-being.

4. *Work through negative emotional states and control destructive impulses.* Negative life experiences commonly result in emotions that get out of control and cause additional problems. The individual in recovery can learn new coping skills and gain support in working through impulses that may lead to destructive decisions and interactions.

5. *Move from passive to active decision making in all aspects of life.* Most addictive behaviors are passive, automatic, ritualistic, and habitual. This includes workaholism, gambling, eating disorders, and many other behaviors that fit our behavioral definition of addiction. Recovering individuals need to be involved and active in their recovery. Most learning comes from doing.

6. *Resist social or peer pressure.* When it endangers welfare or inhibits growth, peer pressure can cause those in recovery to make the wrong choices. Recovery is maintained by being and talking with others in recovery, rather than isolating. Associating with people who don't understand or, more important, don't respect the individual's recovery could require changing relationships. Recovering alcoholics/addicts should develop and maintain relationships that support a healthy alcohol/drug-free lifestyle.

7. *Improve and continue to work on the sense of self.* Those in recovery need to be involved in activities and relationships that promote a positive sense of self. To develop a sense of self, they must believe they are unique,

worthwhile individuals with emerging talents and skills; individuals who can accomplish things; individuals who can trust and be trusted while setting appropriate boundaries in relationships and avoiding codependency and dysfunctionality.

8. *Deal more effectively with stress.* Recovering addicts/alcoholics must develop awareness in recognizing stressful situations and the need for support (attachments), coping skills, and resources to deal with or adapt to the stress.

9. *Maintain the structure of the recovery program.* Recovering alcoholics and addicts should consistently attend self-help meetings, aftercare, counseling sessions, and other elements of the recovery program.

10. *Have patience and direction.* Those in recovery must have a road map, while maintaining a day-at-a-time perspective in recovery.

11. *Learn how to enjoy life and others.* By developing the capacity to relax, enjoy, and have fun with others, recovering persons can establish leisure activities, hobbies, and personal interests.

12. *Maintain a sense of humor.* Those in recovery very much need to keep things in perspective, and remember, "I'm not O.K. You're not O.K. But that's O.K."

13. *Take responsibility for self.* No matter what the event is, those in recovery have the freedom to choose their response to it. Taking responsibility for self leads to awareness, which in turn helps the individual make effective choices.

14. *Maintain physical, emotional, and spiritual well-being.* Recovering alcoholics/addicts need regular exercise, balanced nutrition, and adequate sleep and rest. Recovery also involves effective communication in relationships, especially intimate relationships. One must work on spiritual values in life and strive to experience the joy and creativity of life, while exploring one's own sense of spirituality.

15. *Avoid shame.* Mistakes may occur, but alcoholics/addicts can return to recovery without a burden of shame. Shame generated by others or themselves inhibits personal recovery and growth from situations that may be painful.

16. *Work on relapse-prevention strategies.* Those in recovery need to deal with urges and cravings to use alcohol/drugs, imbalanced lifestyles, negative emotional states, social pressures, high-risk situations, and other factors that may make them vulnerable to relapse.

17. *Adapt to changes in life.* Alcoholics/addicts can remind themselves that they are human and subject to human feelings and emotions. Life is not perfect and always involves change. Recovery is facilitated by the individual's ability to adapt to change and integrate feelings related to change. Striving for progress rather than perfection is a healthy goal.

As outlined in Chapter 10, *co-occurring disorders* describes a client who is chemically dependent and has a psychiatric disorder. The psychiatric disorders of affective (feeling) or mood disorders and personality disorders were the major focus in Chapter 10. However, any psychiatric disorder classified in the *Psychiatric Diagnostic and Statistical Manual (DSM-IV)* combined with a chemical dependency is considered a co-occurring disorder.

✂ Treatment of Co-occurring Disorders

Traditionally, co-occurring-disorders patients are viewed as difficult, distracting, and disorganized in treatment. Many co-occurring-disorder patients are multiple users of psychiatric, medical, and chemical dependency treatment facilities and are often described as "revolving door" treatment users, moving from agency to agency. Co-occurring-disorders patients are reported to be difficult, noncompliant, and resistant to treatment. They tend to become crisis users of the emergency room and of inpatient and medical detoxification services" (Hellerstein and Meehan 1987).

Boundaries with Co-occurring-Disorders Patients

Groves (1978) identified some of the troublesome behavior patterns in describing four categories of patients who arouse negative feelings in the counselor.

1. Dependent Clingers
   - Need a great deal of "attention"
   - Perceive the therapist as "inexhaustible"
   - Express gratitude to therapist, causing feelings of specialness and power in therapist (set up to continue giving to client)
   Guidelines for counselor:
   - Establish boundaries (limits of time, knowledge, skill, and stamina)
   - Avoid promises that can't be kept
   - Avoid supporting illusions that will be shattered
2. Demanders
   - Intimidate, devalue, and try to instill guilt in the counselor
   - Are unaware of their deep dependency needs and terror of abandonment
   Guidelines for counselor:
   - Resist the temptation to make a devastating response
   - Support entitlement but direct it to needed treatment ("You are entitled to the best help we can give you, but we can't give good treatment unless you help")
   - Avoid tireless debates
   - Repeat theme or acceptance that they deserve good treatment
3. Manipulative Help-Rejectors
   - Try your recommendations but nothing works
   - Seek an undivorcible marriage with an inexhaustible caregiver who will maintain the relationship as long as symptoms/problems exist
   - Intense dependency needs but fear closeness
   Guidelines for counselor:
   - You are putting out "fires"—band-aid treatment
   - Use gentle, simple reasoning rather than complicated explanations
   - Establish clear boundaries
   - Agree that progress is slow
4. Self-Destructive Deniers
   - Continue drinking/drugging, despite significant negative consequences
   - Have given up hope to have needs met
   - Seem to enjoy defeating recovery attempts

Guidelines for counselor:
- Fight the impulse to abandon these clients
- Recognize your own limitations, get help through consultation
- Intervene to try to "raise their bottom"

Many co-occurring-disorders clients present these kinds of troublesome behaviors, which make treatment difficult. However, the counselor skilled in setting appropriate boundaries and having clear expectations for these clients can be more effective.

Counseling for Co-occurring Disorders
Breaking Denial—Educating and Empowering Patients

The denial of co-occurring-disorders patients is often difficult to break through. The client may focus on one co-occurring disorder as the primary cause for his or her problems while ignoring the impact of the other disorder. The family may also focus on one cause of the problem (i.e., his or her drinking/drugging or manic-depressive behavior) to avoid recognizing the painful dimensions of the co-occurring disorder.

Education and intervention are needed to help the client and family members recognize that they are dealing with not one but two interrelated disorders. The counselor can establish rapport by educating co-occurring-disorders clients and by helping them recognize the dimensions and impact of their disorder. The primary treater is the patient. Once educated, patients become experts on their diagnosis. They are then empowered to take personal responsibility for their recovery.

Developing Skills for Co-occurring-Disorders Patients

Feelings and Emotional Buildup   Like most counseling approaches with individuals who have an alcohol/drug problem, co-occurring-disorders counseling involves helping the client identify feelings, especially feelings of anger, guilt, and shame. It is important to help these clients also identify how these feelings may build up and eventually result in psychiatric relapse.

Methods to reduce stress and deal with these feelings are an integral aspect of the counseling (e.g., redirection to recreational activities, exercise and relaxation, stress-reduction techniques).

Cognitive-Behavioral Approaches   Cognitive-behavioral techniques help in the recovery from co-occurring disorders. One major focus is to instill hope and to change depressive thinking.

The way a person thinks plays a major role in feelings of depression, mood disturbances, and personality problems. The individual's perception of events in life colors his or her emotional reaction dramatically. This can be described as depressive thinking. Although one should not ignore one's feelings, overreacting to situations may develop into a pattern or habit of depressive thinking, or thinking the worst. If the individual is already depressed, it may significantly deepen his or her depression.

Some of these negative and depressive ways of thinking may have their roots in childhood. Parents may have modeled depressive thinking and depressive patterns of behavior. Parents who shame their children with negative statements (e.g., "You are stupid") teach them to internalize these depressive messages, which are then carried into adulthood. Cognitive-behavioral approaches can teach the individual to change these unhealthy ways of thinking and of reacting to life situations by countering these negative thoughts.

Alcoholics Anonymous has a number of slogans that trigger cognitive-behavioral change from depressive thinking:

Shame statement: "No matter what I do, it's never good enough."
AA slogan: "Progress not perfection" reminds us that we don't have to see ourselves as either successes or failures, or be perfect all the time.
Shame statement: "I am aggressively argumentative, and always have to be right. I feel especially bad when I behave this way with those close to me."
AA slogan: "Would you rather be right or happy?" reminds us that always having to be right or prove another wrong is often alienating, and isolating, behavior. Some examples of common depressive thinking patterns are

- Black-and-white or right-wrong thinking: "If you're recovering, you can't take any medication, because all medications are drugs."
- "Awfulizing," or making things seem worse than they really are: "I'm probably going to get fired because I missed that deadline."
- Overgeneralizing: "Boy, I'm really stupid because I made that mistake."
- Catastrophizing: "What if they tell me I've got cancer?"
- Disqualifying the positive: "Oh, anybody could've done it."
- Jumping to conclusions: "He looked upset when I walked past his office. He probably saw me come in late."
- Feeling that temporary situations are permanent: "I'm never going to find a job."
- Shaming ourselves with "should" and "why" statements: "Why didn't I study harder?" or "I should have known the answer to that."
- Negative labeling: "I'm stupid." "I'm hopeless." "I'm a failure."
- Personalizing, or taking responsibility for things we're not responsible for: "We probably lost the account because I wasn't aggressive enough."

Since depression feeds on inactivity and depressive thinking, clients can interrupt the depressive inactivity and depressive thinking by taking action. Physical activity is the remedy prescribed most often for mood disorders. I will joke with my patients by telling them to use "LSD"—*l*ong, *s*low, *d*istance, walking for clients recovering from alcohol/drugs and/or depression. The first step is to make *taking action* as easy as possible by eliminating the obstacles. For example, to be successful, an exercise program needs to be realistic and allow little room for procrastination.

Taking action can also mean eating in a healthy manner, taking a class, working on relationships at work and home, taking a vacation, playing with friends, and so forth. All of these things help clients recover from the co-occurring disorders of chemical dependency and mood disorder.

Both chemical dependency and affective disorders are diseases that grow with isolation and withdrawal. The metaphor of the dragon in the corner, eating its own tail, describes their crippling effects. The AA proverb "Silence is the enemy of recovery" applies here. Clients must develop relationships with others in recovery. They can find friends and support by being active in Twelve-Step recovery programs, educational groups, counseling (both individual and group), and community and church groups.

Treatment Compliance—Medications

Frequently, antidepressant medication is an integral part of the recovery from co-occurring disorders. The selective serotonin reuptake inhibitors (SSRIs) category of antidepressants are most frequently used with co-occurring-disorders patients. As their name implies, they work in the brain by blocking the reuptake of serotonin into nonactive storage areas, thus increasing its availability, which has an antidepressant effect. (See Table 11.17.)

Interestingly, in double-blind studies, with nondepressed alcoholics who were given an SSRI antidepressant, approximately 20 percent reported a decrease in alcohol craving and were therefore aided in maintaining abstinence (Jancin 1994).

Unfortunately, many co-occurring-disorders patients do not comply with the directions given by their psychiatrist regarding medication. The counselor who may have more ongoing contact can help monitor medication compliance.

The common noncompliance behaviors include stopping medications abruptly, reducing dosage, and stopping and starting or forgetting to take medication

---

TABLE 11.17

Generic and Proprietary Names of Psychiatric Medications

Antidepressants

Imipramine (Tofranil, Presamine)
Doxepin (Sinequan, Apapin, Sinequan)
Desipramine (Norpramin, Pertrofrone)
Amitriptyline (Elavil)
Nortriptyline (Pamelor, Aventyl)
Protriptyline (Vivactil)
Chlomipramine (Anafranil)
Fluoxetine (Prozac)
Trazodone (Desyrel)
Maprotiline (Ludiomil)
Amoxapine (Asendin)
Bupropion (Wellbutrin)
Tranylcypromine (Parnate)
Phenelzine (Nardil)

Antianxiety

Diazepam (Valium)
Chlordiazepoxide (Librium)
Chorazepate dipotassium (Tranxene)

Lorazepam (Ativan)
Oxazepam (Serax)
Alprazolam (Xanax)
Clonazepam (Clonopin)
Buspirone (BuSpar)
Hydroxyzine (Vistaril, Atarax)

Antipsychotic

Haloperidol (Haldol)
Chlorpromazine (Thorazine)
Fluphenazine hydrochloride (Prolixin)
Trifluoperazine (Stelazine)
Perphenazine (Trilafon)
Thioridazine (Mellaril)
Thiothixene (Navane)

Mood Cycling

Lithium
Carbamazepine (Tegretol)
Valproic acid (Depakote)
Clonazepam (Clonopin)

Not all medications in each group are listed.

on schedule. Some patients will discontinue medication before they have given the medication time to begin working (usually two or more weeks). Working closely with the psychiatrist prescribing medication can assure the proper dosage, and the type of medication can be adjusted to best serve the co-occurring-disorders patient.

The Family of the Co-occurring-Disorders Client

The behavior (e.g., suicide attempts, psychotic episodes, grossly disturbed behavior, feeling disorders) of the co-occurring-disorders family member may expose other family members to tremendous stress and trauma. The severity and length of the problem may emotionally, physically, financially, and spiritually exhaust family members. Some family members (e.g., brothers, sisters) may have felt that their needs were not being met. Family members can benefit from supportive counseling.

Often, family members have unique perceptions of the co-occurring-disorders family member. This causes tremendous conflict and tension between parents and other family members.

Frequently, the mother sees her son as ill and needing acceptance and understanding (e.g., "If only we could get him the right help he will be O.K."). The father, on the other hand, sees the son as lazy and irresponsible and that the problem stems mainly from the son's drinking/drugging too much (e.g., "If he only would stop using alcohol/drugs, things would get better."). Unfortunately, they are both wrong—the problem involves both alcohol/drugs and psychological problems, and both need to be addressed.

Educating the family and engaging them in treatment early often positively effects treatment outcome. Families are more likely to cooperate if approached in a supportive manner by clinicians. Clinicians can be viewed as people who understand their experience and don't blame them. The counselors' ability to demonstrate their expertise regarding co-occurring disorders (both the psychiatric and alcohol/ drug aspects of recovery) can help in establishing trust and rapport with the family.

The goals of family treatment are

1. Acquiring knowledge about co-occurring disorders
2. Increasing self-awareness, especially each family member's role in the family
3. Helping individual members make changes in the family system
4. Maintaining family members' involvement in ongoing recovery efforts (e.g., Alanon, individual and family counseling, groups)

⚔ Suicide and Alcohol/Drugs

It is estimated that 29,000 Americans commit suicide each year. Suicide is the eighth leading cause of death in the general population and the third among adolescents. Less than 1 percent of the general population commits suicide, yet studies reveal that between 7 and 27 percent of all deaths of alcoholics are by suicide. A percentage of these suicides by alcoholics are probably due to other underlying or comorbid psychiatric disorders (e.g., primary affective disorders, antisocial personality disorder, borderline personality disorder). The San Diego Suicide Study (SDSS) of 283 consecutive suicides in San Diego County (1981–1983), found that

58 percent of the suicides had diagnoses of drug addiction, and psychiatric diagnoses frequently overlapped with the addiction diagnoses.

Frequently, alcohol or drugs impair judgment and influence suicidal ideation and behavior. The right combination of trauma, stress, loss, depression, isolation, health problems, interpersonal/spouse conflict, financial/occupational problems, and alcohol/drug use may lead to feelings of hopelessness, helplessness, and shame, making the individual vulnerable to suicide.

The following facts have been drawn from the research literature to help you understand and possibly help someone thinking of suicide.*

- Most people who commit suicide give some clue or warning of their intent; therefore, suicidal threats, gestures, or attempts should always be treated seriously.
- Suicide tends to "run in families," due, most likely, to genetic vulnerabilities to depression or other forms of mental or emotional illness.
- Having fallen out of love with life, most suicidal people remain ambivalent about dying. Thus, most can be talked back into living.
- Some depressed people appear to be "suddenly" happy after they decide to "resolve" all their problems at the same time.
- Alcohol/drug abuse greatly enhances the short- and long-term risk of suicide—even in people who are not alcoholic.
- If the person in a suicide crisis receives the proper assistance and support, he or she will probably never be suicidal again. Only about 10 percent of suicide attempters go on to complete a suicide.
- Asking someone directly about suicidal intent does not increase the risk of suicide. Rather, the question lowers anxiety, opens up communication about the problems worth dying for, and lowers the risk of an impulsive act.
- The majority of suicidal people will visit a physician within three months of an attempt to kill themselves. Too often, their thoughts of suicide are neither expressed to the doctor, nor asked for.
- Twenty to 40 percent of patients with affective disorder (depression) exhibit nonfatal suicidal behavior, including thoughts of suicide.
- Fifteen percent of patients with severe depression for at least one month eventually commit suicide.
- Sudden unemployment is associated with increased risk of suicide.
- Suicide occurs more often in midweek.
- Suicide rates decline during major holidays, such as Thanksgiving and Christmas.
- Drinking alcoholics have a lifetime suicide rate much higher than the general population and are 60 to 120 times more likely to die by suicide.
- In America, suicide rates are higher on the East and West coasts.
- Suicide increases with age, reaching a peak among older white males. Older people are at greater risk for suicide than teenagers.

---

*This section was developed by and permission granted by Paul Quinnett, Ph.D., Spokane, Wash. Dr. Quinnett is the author of *Suicide: The Forever Decision* and *Suicide: Intervention and Therapy.*

- Most suicidal people plan their self-destruction in advance and leave clues indicating they have become suicidal.
- Of those who die by their own hand, men outnumber women 3 to 1.
- Women make gestures or attempts on their lives three times as often as men.
- As age increases, so does the risk that a first attempt at suicide will end in death.
- Contrary to popular myth, those who talk about suicide often *do* make an attempt on their own lives.
- The most common emotional states of the suicidal person are ambivalence and hopelessness.
- People are not acutely suicidal forever; rather, the actual crisis during which the person may act typically lasts only a few minutes or a few hours.

Clues to Suicide

People thinking of suicide often give clues to their thoughts and feelings and plans to deal with their growing sense of hopelessness. One clue may or may not mean a great deal, but *any* clue is worth asking about. (See Table 11.18.)

TABLE 11.18

Suicidal Clues

Direct Verbal Clues*

- "I've decided to kill myself."
- "I wish I were dead."
- "I'm going to commit suicide."
- "I'm going to end it all."
- "If [such and such] doesn't happen, I'll kill myself."

Indirect or Coded Verbal Clues*

- "I'm tired of life."
- "What's the point of going on?"
- "My family would be better off without me."
- "Who cares if I'm dead, anyway?"
- "I can't go on anymore."
- "I just want out."
- "I'm so tired of it all."
- "You would be better off without me."
- "I'm not the person I used to be."
- "I'm calling it quits—living is useless."
- "Soon I won't be around."
- "You shouldn't have to take care of me any longer."
- "Soon you won't have to worry about me anymore."
- "Goodbye. I won't be here when you return."
- "It was good at times, but we must all say goodbye."
- "You're going to regret how you've treated me."

There are many motivations for suicide and suicidal behavior. Some of them include the following:

- Wanting to end psychological pain
- Wanting to escape an unacceptable situation
- Wanting to join a deceased loved one

TABLE 11.18 (CONTINUED)

Suicidal Clues

Indirect or Coded Verbal Clues* (continued)

- "You know, son, I'm going home soon."
- "Here, take this [cherished possession]; I won't be needing it."
- "Nobody needs me anymore."
- "How do they preserve your kidneys for transplantation if you die suddenly?"

Behavioral Clues

- Donating body to a medical school
- Purchasing a gun
- Stockpiling pills
- Putting personal and business affairs in order
- Making or changing a will
- Taking out insurance or changing beneficiaries
- Making funeral plans
- Giving away money and/or possessions
- Making changes in behavior, especially episodes of screaming, hitting, or throwing things or failure to get along with family, friends, or peers
- Acting suspiciously, such as going out at odd times of the day or night and waving or kissing goodbye (if not characteristic)
- Showing sudden interest or disinterest in church or religion
- Scheduling appointments with a doctor for no apparent physical causes or very shortly after the last routine visit
- Losing of physical skills; general confusion; or losing of understanding, judgment, or memory
- Relapsing into drug or alcohol use after a period of recovery

Situational Clues

- Sudden rejection by a loved one, (e.g., girlfriend or boyfriend) or an unwanted separation or divorce
- Recent move—especially if unwanted
- Death of a spouse, child, friend (especially if by suicide or accident)
- Diagnosis of terminal illness
- Flare up with friend or relative for no apparent reason
- Sudden, unexpected loss of freedom (e.g., about to be arrested)
- Anticipated loss of financial security
- Loss of cherished counselor or therapist

*Many of the following statements were made by people who subsequently went on to kill themselves.
Sources: Marv Miller, *Suicide After Sixty,* Springer, New York, 1979; Edwin Schneidman and Norman Farberow, *Clues to Suicide,* McGraw-Hill, New York, 1957; David Spain, *Post-Mortem,* Doubleday, New York, 1974; Louis Wekstein, *Handbook of Suicidology,* Brunner/Mazel, New York, 1979.

- Wanting to gain attention
- Wanting to control others
- Wanting to avoid punishment for a crime
- Wanting to control when death occurs
- Wanting to become a martyr
- Wanting to punish the survivors
- Wanting to avoid loss of face
- Wanting to avoid becoming a burden to others
- Wanting to take revenge
- Wanting to avoid social ridicule
- Wanting to please a cult leader

It is good to remember that the risk of acting on a suicidal thought or feeling shifts over time and that, although persons who have been considering death believe they are no longer at-risk, something terrible or unexpected can hit them from "out of the blue." Whatever this new source of stress is, it is essential that suicidal persons know there is someone whom they can call, someone who will listen, someone who will care enough to help. If you happen to be that person, Table 11.19 lists some things you can do.

TABLE 11.19

Do's and Don'ts with Suicidal People

Do's

- Get involved. If in doubt, ask questions. Don't wait for a call from someone in trouble; make the call yourself. Examples of how to ask the question: Are your problems so big you are thinking of harming yourself? Do you wish you could end it all? Have you been thinking of suicide?
- Be accepting and nonjudgmental. Don't offer simple solutions (they sound like brush-offs). Be realistic about the problems, but offer reassurance (hope).
- Be confident and bold. As a solution, suicide can wait. What needs fixing may take a little time, but, at least for today, suicide can wait. Buy time—any way you can.
- Remove the means of suicide. Get rid of guns, pills, razors, whatever. Suicidal people are running red lights without a seat belt; buckle them up.
- Always take a positive, hopeful approach. Suicidal people feel hopeless. Fortunately, hope is infectious, so assure them things will get better because, in fact, they usually do.

Don'ts

- Don't act shocked, dismayed, or frightened. Suicide is drastic, but it's only a solution to a problem. What's the problem worth dying for? Try to understand this and you can save a life.
- Don't ignore the person's threats. Even if he or she doesn't really intend to die, can either of you afford to ignore this cry for help?
- Don't point out the shock, embarrassment, or suffering the family or loved one will endure if the person dies, unless you are sure that isn't exactly what the person wants.
- Don't get into a debate on the merits of living or dying. You might lose the argument.
- Never put yourself at risk of injury (taking a gun or knife away) unless you are highly trained in this area.

Remember, if you feel any persons you know may be thinking about suicide, go ahead and ask. If they weren't thinking of suicide, the worst they can do is be a little offended that you would think them capable of such an act; however, if they were thinking of suicide, they may be forever grateful.

Resources

Every community has many resources to help prevent death by suicide. The mental health center, the crisis hot line, the hospital emergency room, the police or sheriff's department, firefighters, clergy, school counselors and teachers, doctors, nurses, social workers, psychologists, and psychiatrists all should and will respond to a request for help.

At the start of this textbook, we saw that there are no simple solutions to the problems of alcohol/drug dependence and addiction. Remember the wisdom of philosopher H.L. Mencken, who said, "The solution to big problems that are simple, are usually wrong."

⊀ **Conclusion**

There will always be some level of alcohol/drug problem in the United States. Despite our best efforts, many people will still choose not to get help. This is not a war on drugs but, instead, a crusade—a crusade to help people who need and want alcohol and drug treatment; a crusade to prevent the next generation from developing alcohol/drug problems; and a crusade to help those who care to intervene, when appropriate, on those who may benefit from alcohol/drug treatment.

Clinicians' efforts can help many people with alcohol/drug problems and prevent others from suffering the same devastating life of addiction. Most important, they can work on the current problems that make the next generation at-risk for chemical dependency.

Summary

Self-help meetings are the most widely used and successful approach to alcohol and drug recovery. In this chapter, the advantages of AA and other self-help meetings are outlined, as well as the resistance people may have to attending AA meetings. The history and principles of Rational Recovery are outlined to give you an understanding of an alternative to traditional Alcoholics Anonymous and Narcotics Anonymous meetings.

Government-supported chemical dependency treatment programs from 1970 to 1980 consisted primarily of therapeutic communities, outpatient methadone clinics, outpatient drug-free programs, and university-affiliated research centers. The cocaine epidemic of the 1980s changed the course of chemical dependency treatment, as did managed care in the 1990s.

Richard Rawson's model describes the five stages of alcohol/drug recovery:

0–15 days—withdrawal
16–45 days—honeymoon
46–120 days—the wall

121–180 days—adjustment
181+ days—resolution

Each of these stages has its own behavioral, cognitive, emotional, and relational symptoms.

Early phases of alcohol/drug recovery focus on issues of stabilization and safety. As recovery progresses, the individual focuses more on affect (feeling), recognition, and modulation. The advantages of family treatment and family system work are outlined in this chapter, as are the beneficial curative factors of group psychotherapy.

There is a tremendously high relapse rate following alcohol/drug treatment. Training patients in relapse prevention is an integral component of the recovery program; it was often neglected in early chemical dependency treatment approaches.

Recognizing that specific times, places, things, and people can trigger alcohol/drug cravings is an important component of chemical dependency relapse training. It has also been demonstrated that drug relapse is induced by a return to alcohol use.

Two key points made in this chapter are, first, that alcohol/drug recovery is an ongoing process and no one is cured due to the ongoing nature of the disease of alcoholism/drug addiction and, second, that chemical dependency treatment is often as good as the counselor or treatment program itself, assuming that the patient is motivated to achieve recovery.

Other relapse factors are the importance of structure and pitfalls to too much structure, health and physical well-being, and cognitive, emotional, and spiritual well-being.

The chapter also includes information on the controversy of controlled drinking and a description of other harm-reduction approaches.

There is also an outline of common troublesome behaviors attributed to many co-occurring-disorders patients and the boundaries the counselor needs to establish with these clients. Four categories of these patients are outlined—the dependent clingers, the demanders, the manipulative help-rejecters, and the self-destructive deniers. Special considerations for co-occurring-disorders patients range from education, cognitive-behavioral approaches, and medication compliance to family involvement.

The chapter closes with material on suicide and chemical dependencies.

References

Armor, D.J., J.M. Polich, and H.B. Stambul. *Alcohol and Treatment.* New York: John Wiley & Sons, 1978.

Bateman, N.I., and D.M. Peterson. "Variables Related to Outcome of Treatment for Hospitalized Alcoholics." *International Journal of Addictions* (1971): 215–24.

Bishop, F. Michler. "Rational-Emotive Behavior Therapy and Two Self-Help Alternatives to the 12-Step Model." In *Psychotherapy and Substance Abuse,* ed. Arnold Washton. New York: Guilford Press, 1995.

Brill, Leon. *The Clinical Treatment of Substance Abusers.* New York: Free Press, 1981.

Browne-Mayers, A.N., E.E. Seeley, and D.E. Brown. "Reorganized Alcoholism Services: Two Years After." *Journal of American Medical Association* (1973): 233–35.

Chafetz, Morris E., Howard T. Blane, and Marjorie Hill. *Frontiers of Alcoholism.* New York: Science House, 1970.

Costello, R.M., M.B. Giffen, S.L. Schneider, P.W. Edgington, and K.R. Maders. "Comprehensive Alcohol Treatment Planning, Implementation, and Evaluation." *International Journal of the Addictions* 11, no. 4 (1976): 553–71.

Dole, V.P., and M.E. Nyswander. "A Medical Treatment of Diacetylmorphine (Heroin) Addiction." *Journal of American Medical Association* 193 (1965): 646–50.

Ford, B., with Chris Chase. *A Glad Awakening.* Garden City, NY: Doubleday, 1987.

Fox, R. "Antabuse as an Adjunct to Psychotherapy in Alcoholism." *New York State Journal of Medicine* 58 (1958): 1540–44.

———. "Normal Drinking in Recovered Alcohol Addicts: Comment on the Article by D.L. Davies." *Quarterly Journal of Studies on Alcohol* 23 (1963): 117.

Fox, V. "The Controlled Drinking Controversy." *Journal of American Medical Association* 236 (1976): 893.

Gorski, Terence T. Presentation "Brief Targeted Strategic Therapy for Relapse Prevention" at the Third Annual Florida Dual Disorder Conference, March 16, 1996.

Groves. "Troublesome Behavior Patterns." *New England Journal of Medicine* 4 (1978).

Hay, Louise L. *You Can Heal Your Life.* Santa Monica, CA: Hay House, 1984.

Hellerstein, D., and B. Meehan. "Outpatient Group Therapy for Schizophrenic Substance Abusers." *American Journal of Psychiatry* 144 (1987): 1337–39.

Inciardi, James A., and Lana D. Harrison, eds. Harm Reduction: National and International Perspective, Sage Publications, 2000.

Jancin, Bruce. "SSRI's Help Drinkers Reduce, but Not Eliminate, Alcohol Consumption." *Clinical Psychiatry News* (April 1994).

Kish, G.B., and H.T. Herman. "The Fort Meade Alcoholism Treatment Program: A Follow Up Study." *Quarterly Journal of Studies on Alcohol* 32 (1971): 628–35.

Lawson, Gary, James S. Peterson, and Ann Lawson. *Alcoholism and the Family: A Guide to Treatment and Prevention.* Rockville, MD: Aspen Publications, 1983.

Marks, S.J., L. Daroff, and S. Granick. "Basic Counseling for Drug Abusers." In *Treatment Services for Adolescent Substance Abusers.* Washington, DC: U.S. Department of Health and Human Services, 1987.

Marlatt, Alan, and Judith Gordon. *Relapse Prevention.* New York: Guilford Press, 1985.

Miller, W.R. *Addictive Behaviors—Treatment of Alcoholism, Drug Abuse, Smoking and Obesity.* New York: Pergamon Press, 1980.

Miller, W.R., and G.R. Caddy. "Abstinence and Controlled Drinking in the Treatment of Problem Drinkers." *Journal of Studies of Alcohol* 38 (1977): 986–1003.

Rawson, R., J. Obert, M. McCann, and David Smith. *Treatment of Cocaine Dependence: A Neurobehavioral Approach.* Beverly Hills, CA: Matrix Institute on Addictions, 1988.

Rawson, Richard. "Chemical Dependency Treatment: The Integration of the Alcoholism and Drug Addiction Systems." *International Journal of Addictions* (1991).

———. *Cocaine Recovery Issues: The Neurobehavioral Model.* Beverly Hills, CA: Matrix Institute on Addictions, 1989.

Ritson, E.B. "The Prognosis of Alcohol Addicts Treated by a Specialized Unit." *British Journal of Psychiatry* 114 (1968): 1019–29.

Robson, R.A., H.I. Paulus, and G.G. Clark. "An Evaluation of the Effect of a Clinic Treatment Program on the Rehabilitation of Alcoholic Patients." *Quarterly Journal of Studies on Alcohol* 26 (1965): 264–78.

Steinglass, Peter. "An Experimental Treatment Program for Alcoholic Couples." *Journal of Studies on Alcohol* 40 (1979): 159–82.

Tiebout, H.M. "Intervention in Psychotherapy." *American Journal of Psychoanalysis* 33 (1962): 1–6.

Trimpey, Jack. *Rational Recovery: The Small Book.* Lotus Press, 1991.

Washton, Arnold M., ed. *Psychotherapy and Substance Abuse.* New York: Guilford Press, 1995.

PHOTO CREDITS

Chapter 1

Page 3: © Jack Spratt/The Image works; p. 25: © Universal Studios. Photo courtesy of the Academy of Motion Pictures Arts and Sciences

Chapter 2

Page 36: © Richard Hutching/Photo Researchers

Chapter 3

Page 64(all): DEA/Department of Justice; p.68: © Michael Siluk; p.82: DEA/Department of Justice; p.83(top): The Bettmann Archive/Corbis; p.83(bottom): Courtesy of Wiener Press Bilbbienst; p.88: © Michael Gadomski/Photo Researchers; p.89(all), 91: DEA/Department of Justice; p.103: The Bettmann Archive/Corbis

Chapter 4

Page 115,118: AP/Wide World Photos

Chapter 7

Page 195: © Michael Siluk

Chapter 8

Page 213: © Photodisc

Index